Management Accounting
for Non-Specialists

D1335710

CATHERINE GOWTHORPE

Management Accounting for Non-Specialists

Second edition

THOMSON

Australia • Canada • Mexico • Singapore • Spain • United Kingdom • United States

THOMSON

Management Accounting for Non-Specialists, 2nd Edition
Catherine Gowthorpe

Publishing Director John Yates	**Publisher** Patrick Bond	**Development Manager** Anna Carter
Production Editor Stuart Giblin	**Manufacturing Manager** Helen Mason	**Development Editor** Laura Priest
Typesetter Photoprint, Torquay	**Production Controller** Maeve Healy	**Marketing Manager** Katie Thorn
Cover Design David Brent	**Text Design** Design Deluxe, Bath, UK	**Printer** Canale, Italy

British Library Cataloguing-in-Publication Data
A catalogue record for this book is available from the British Library

Brief Contents

Contents

What is management accounting?

There are two distinct strands to accounting in organisations: management accounting and financial accounting. Management accounting produces the accounting information that managers in a business organisation use for internal decision making and control. Financial accounting, by contrast, is geared towards producing information that is useful to people outside the business. This book is concerned principally with management accounting.

Who is this book aimed at?

The aim of this book is to provide an introduction to management accounting for students who are specialising in some other business discipline, or in a discipline for which some knowledge of management accounting is useful. The book is suitable for students of:

- general business qualifications, for example: undergraduate and higher national diploma courses in business and finance;
- specific business disciplines such as marketing and human resource management where some fundamental knowledge of management accounting is helpful;
- disciplines which lie outside the traditional business area. Students of, for example, engineering, fashion, fine and applied arts may all benefit from some knowledge of management accounting;
- MBA and similar courses where study of management accounting is required, although not at a specialist level;
- A and AS level business studies students may benefit from this book as background reading to their studies.

While the principal intended audience for the book comprises students taking a formal course of instruction at college or university, it is also intended that the book should lend itself to self-study by anyone who is interested in extending their knowledge of basic accounting. This could include people who are starting, or thinking of starting their own businesses, and who realise that they will need accounting information. Also, the book could be useful for people who are already engaged in business but who are aware that they do not quite understand how management accounting works.

The overarching aim of the book is to develop understanding of management accounting. It is not, primarily, a book about how to produce management accounting information. Some of the chapters do, indeed, require students to prepare fairly straightforward management accounting statements. However, the principal purpose of this approach is to aid understanding; it is often easier to understand how accounting figures hang together if you have had some experience of working them out for yourself.

Special notes for the suspicious

Accounting and finance are often regarded as particularly difficult parts of the business curriculum. Lecturers in accounting are quite frequently presented with some quite seriously ingrained negative attitudes in their non-specialist students. Dealing with some of the most frequently encountered:

'Accounting is boring and it's not relevant to what I'm doing anyway'

Students who are primarily interested in the discipline they have chosen to study often have difficulty in appreciating why they should have to study accounting. A fashion student, for example, is likely to be much more interested in creative outcomes and in developing his or her own skills and deeper appreciation of the creative process. It is, however, the case that people who are successful in making careers in fashion (and other creative endeavours) have to be very much alive to the business environment in which they work. People who have forged successful careers in the creative arts are often surprisingly well-tuned in to all the business and accounting aspects of what they do.

'Accounting should be left to the accountants'

Students in other business disciplines who are looking forward to careers in, perhaps, retail management or marketing sometimes feel that accounting should be left to the accountants. It is one of the contentions of this book that accounting is, on the contrary, much too important to be left to the accountants. Business managers owe it to themselves to be able to interpret the reports that accountants present to them; they are vital aids to understanding what is going on in the business. Business managers should be in a position to question accountants from a position of strength about the information that is being presented to them. If they are not sufficiently knowledgeable to do this they risk being quite seriously restricted in their understanding of their business and their ability to make sound decisions.

It is important to appreciate that accounting is not an exact science. Accounting has emerged in its present day form, after many centuries of development, because there has been a need for it. It is, essentially, about communication between people and so it is vulnerable to all the impediments which hinder proper communication. For example, people sometimes tell lies and accounting can be used, very effectively, to tell lies. Accounting is often imprecise and its imprecision can be easily exploited by the unscrupulous. After studying this book, students should be more aware of the strengths and limitations of accounting as a means of communication.

'Accounting is all about maths, and I'm no good at maths'

Accounting undeniably involves dealing with numbers. However, the study of accounting rarely involves much beyond simple arithmetic. Specifically, the principal prior skills required of students of this book are the ability to add, subtract, multiply, divide and to calculate a percentage. Towards the end of the book, students will be required to draw simple line graphs and to calculate compound interest. Most of these are skills that are covered at Key Stages 2 and 3 (for students who have come through the UK primary and secondary education system recently). There is nothing in this book (or indeed in many accounting textbooks) that requires knowledge of mathematical techniques beyond GCSE level.

What the study of accounting does involve, however, is the ability to understand what the numbers signify. This is a skill which some students find relatively difficult to acquire. The book, therefore, spends a lot of time from early on in developing that kind of understanding. It cannot be emphasised too frequently that this book is about developing understanding of accounting information.

'I won't be able to understand all the jargon'

Accounting is no different from many other spheres of fairly advanced human endeavour in that it has its own terminology. Jargon is often baffling to the uninitiated, but, inevitably, some of the jargon simply has to be learned. In this book, the author has tried to ensure that all unfamiliar terms are fully explained in the most straightforward terms possible. There is a glossary towards the end of the book which explains a lot of the more unfamiliar terminology so that students do not have to go hunting back through the book to find the original explanation.

Structure and features of this book

The book is divided into two parts. The five chapters in the first part provide an introduction to accounting and finance for business. Topics covered include sources of finance for business, business start-ups, some essential facts about companies and the role of accountants in business. Course tutors may choose to lecture on these topics, or, where time is limited, they may ask students to read these chapters as background material.

The second part of the book deals with management accounting. From chapter 6 onwards, most chapters involve the study of some accounting techniques (and therefore the use of some manipulation of figures) but the overall objective is always to encourage understanding of management accounting statements and principles.

All chapters, apart from Chapters 1 and 5, contain at least one case study. These are often quite extensive, covering many aspects of the material covered by the chapter. Several of the cases incorporate more general business problems, so as to illustrate the close link between the management of a business and the accounting information that is used to inform management decision making and control.

All chapters include an extensive range of exercises so that students can test their knowledge and understanding. Students are often worried and may become demotivated if the end-of-chapter exercises are too difficult. Therefore, the book aims to provide a good range of tests covering both the simple and more complex points presented in the chapter. If students wish to test their understanding with even more exercises, further examples are provided on the book's dedicated website (see overleaf).

About half of the end of chapter exercises contain answers within the book. Answers to the remainder can be supplied by course lecturers who have obtained the Lecturer's guide (see overleaf).

Supplementary material

In addition to the material presented in the book, the following supplementary material is available:

Dedicated website

The website can be found at www.thomsonlearning.co.uk/gowthorpema2. The lecturer section is password protected and the password is available free to lecturers who confirm their adoption of the book. Lecturers should complete the registration form on the website to apply for their password. The following material is available:

For students and lecturers (open access)

- Multiple Choice Questions for each chapter
- Answers to Case Studies within the text
- Related Weblinks
- Additional Questions with Answers

For lecturers only (password protected)

- Answers to specific lecturer examples within the text
- Downloadable PowerPoint slides
- Additional Lecturer Questions with answers
- Comprehensive Teaching Notes
- Testbank of Multiple Choice Questions
- Additional Case Studies

Walk-through Tour

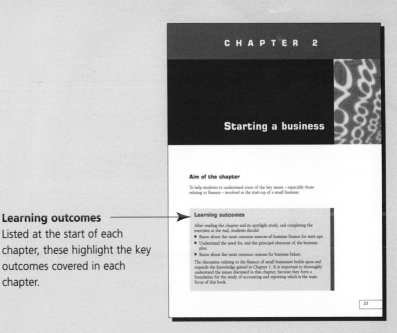

Learning outcomes
Listed at the start of each chapter, these highlight the key outcomes covered in each chapter.

Examples
Examples are dispersed throughout the text to illustrate the practical application of key concepts.

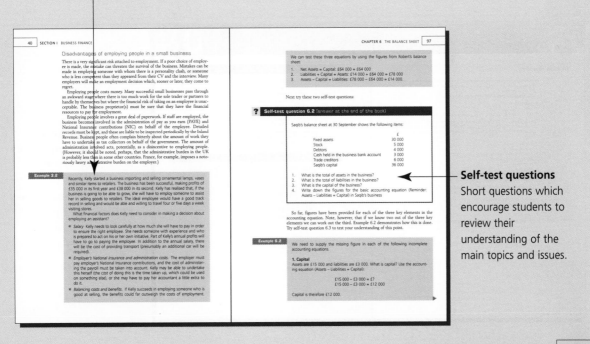

Self-test questions
Short questions which encourage students to review their understanding of the main topics and issues.

Spotlights

Mini cases which focus on decisions which have proved to be crucial for successful businesses.

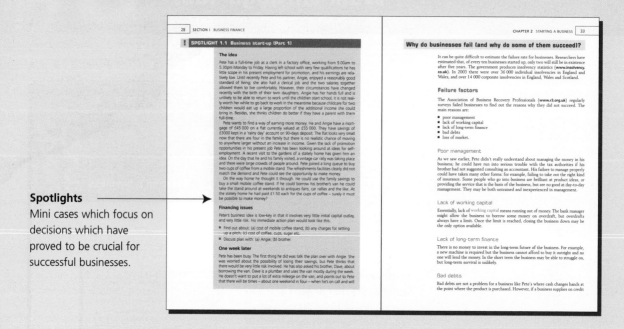

Chapter summary

The end of each chapter has a summary of the main points and key concepts covered.

Website summary

Website summary sections direct students and lecturers to the companion website where additional resources are available to enhance understanding of specific topics.

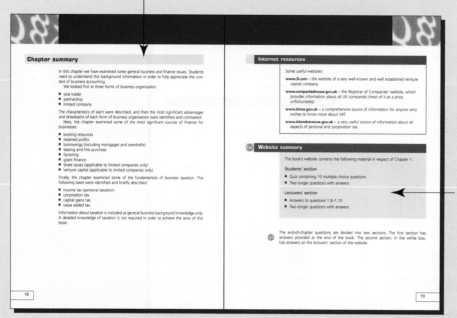

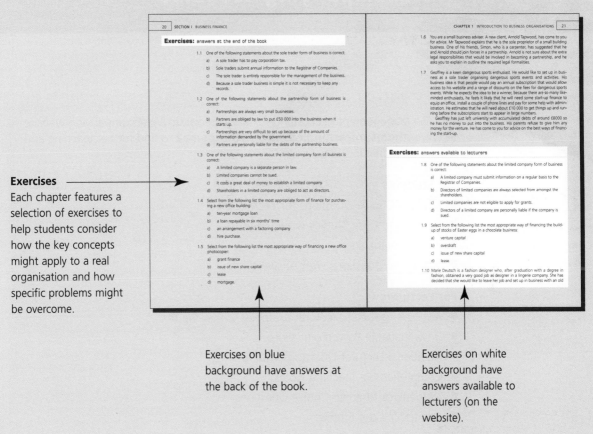

Exercises

Each chapter features a selection of exercises to help students consider how the key concepts might apply to a real organisation and how specific problems might be overcome.

Exercises on blue background have answers at the back of the book.

Exercises on white background have answers available to lecturers (on the website).

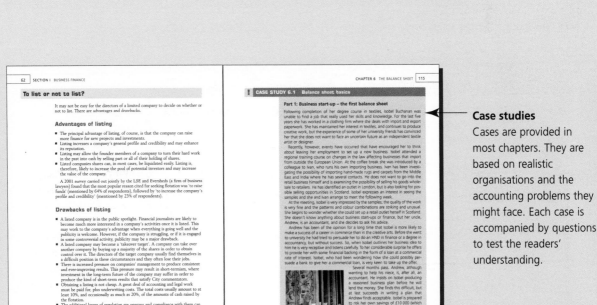

Case studies

Cases are provided in most chapters. They are based on realistic organisations and the accounting problems they might face. Each case is accompanied by questions to test the readers' understanding.

Accompanying Website

Visit the *Management Accounting for Non-Specialists* 2/e accompanying website at **www.thomsonlearning.co.uk/gowthorpema2** to find further teaching and learning material including:

For Students
- Multiple Choice Questions for each chapter
- Answers to Case Studies within the text
- Related Weblinks
- Additional Questions with Answers

For Lecturers
- Answers to specific lecturer examples within the text
- Downloadable PowerPoint slides
- Additional Lecturer Questions with answers
- Comprehensive Teaching Notes
- Testbank of Multiple Choice Questions
- Additional Case Studies

Business finance

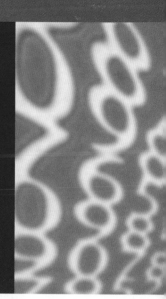

Introduction

This section of the book examines issues in business finance relevant to different sizes of organisation. The first four chapters provide an introduction to issues in business financing. They should be especially useful for those students who are new to the study of business and accounting. Chapter 1 provides a general introduction to business organisations and their financing, examining characteristics of the different forms of business commonly found in the UK and elsewhere, and discussing sources of finance. Chapter 2 is concerned with business start-ups. Using a detailed case study, it examines some of the relevant financing and other problems that face the entrepreneur. Chapter 3 examines some of the problems and opportunities that face the growing business, and includes a description of some of the stages involved in business expansion. Chapter 4 examines the financing of limited companies, and extends the basic Chapter 1 coverage into a more detailed look at business financing via the stock market.

Chapter 5 aims to equip students with an understanding of the reasons why people need accounting information, the nature of accounting information and the role of the accountant. It provides an introduction to the rest of the book which is concerned with the acquisition of the skills that prospective business managers and proprietors need in order to be able to understand the information that accountants present to them.

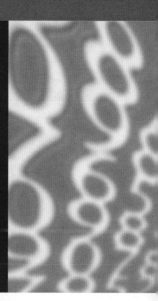

Introduction to business organisations and finance

Aim of the chapter

To introduce the most common forms of business organisation and to discuss the principal sources of finance for those organisations.

Learning outcomes

After reading the chapter and completing the exercises at the end, students should:

- Understand the differences between the sole trader, partnership and company forms of business organisation, including the advantages and drawbacks of each type.
- Know about some of the different sources of business finance available to commercial organisations.
- Know in outline about some important features of the business environment including the various ways in which tax is charged on businesses.

This chapter provides an introduction to the business environment and its financing. It is useful to know about the features discussed in this chapter as a background to the development of more detailed knowledge of accounting and finance in business which occupies most of the book.

The book focuses on the role of accounting and finance in commercial organisations. Accounting is also important for not-for-profit organisations and the public sector, but these are beyond the scope of this book.

Forms of business organisation

There are three common forms of business organisation: sole trader businesses, partnerships and limited companies. Other forms of organisation are encountered occasionally, but we will concentrate in this book on the three common ones. All three types of organisation are run with a view to making profits.

Sole trader businesses

A sole trader operates a business himself or herself, keeping any profits that are made (after deduction of tax). This is a useful form of business for certain types of trade or profession. For example, a plumber, carpenter, financial services adviser, tax adviser, writer or night-club singer could each operate as a sole trader business. Each of these offers a service to the public; each receives money in exchange for performance of the service. After deduction of the various expenses that are involved in running the business, any sum that is left over is the profit, all of which can be kept by the sole trader.

Example 1.1

Having finished his apprenticeship, Yasin sets up in business as a plumber. He pays for a listing in *Yellow Pages*, subscribes to a plumbers' trade association, installs a phone in his flat and waits to be contacted by members of the public and other businesses who require plumbing services. If there is a demand for his services (and there almost certainly will be; it is notoriously difficult to find a plumber) he will soon be called upon. Yasin charges fees for his services out of which he must meet business expenses.

What are Yasin's business expenses? They will typically involve: cost of tools, expenses of running a van, telephone bills, advertising (the *Yellow Pages* listing) and small amounts of administrative expense, such as paying for an accountant to sort out his tax affairs.

In order to keep his business affairs in good order, he will need to keep receipts as evidence of his expenses, copies of the bills he makes out to his customers, and bank statements. It is important not to mix up the business income and expenditure with his own personal items. Yasin or his accountant will summarise all the income he has received from customers and all the expenses of running the business on an annual basis. Income less expenses equals the profit of the business.

At an early stage, the tax authorities take an interest in Yasin's business activities. He will have to pay tax based upon the calculation of his profit. Later in the chapter we will examine the tax regime in a little more detail.

Characteristics of the sole trader form of business

The sole trader is the only person responsible for the management of the business. Although he or she may employ other people as the business gets bigger, all the decision making and risk taking involved in the business rests on the shoulders of one individual. If the business runs into financial difficulties or faces other problems, the sole trader is on his or her own in addressing them.

Sole trader businesses tend to remain fairly small. For people who are self-employed in the types of trade or profession mentioned earlier, this form of business can work very well. However, if the business is of a type that is likely to grow very much bigger, the sole trader form of organisation will need to be replaced by a partnership or limited company structure, which allows more than one person to act as manager.

If a sole trader overstretches himself or herself financially, perhaps by borrowing too much, or if losses rather than profits are made, he or she is liable for all the consequences as an individual. For example, a lender would be entitled to pursue repayment of a loan even to the point where the sole trader would have to sell personal property to repay it. In extreme cases, this can result in personal bankruptcy.

The sole trader business is relatively informal and easy to set up. The business does not require registration of a separate legal entity and so it is quite likely that no legal costs will arise. In the initial stages, at least, the principal administrative issues are likely to arise with the Inland Revenue authorities. A competent chartered accountant can mediate between the individual and the Inland Revenue to ensure that the correct amount is paid, and that tax does not become a problem.

Partnerships

A partnership is a business run by two or more people with a view to making a profit. Typically, partnerships are fairly small businesses, but there are certain types of business activity in which very large partnerships are operated. Professional partnerships, such as those between solicitors, may develop to be very large businesses indeed. There is a legal restriction limiting the number of partners in most types of partnership to 20; however, professional partnerships (solicitors, accountants, surveyors or architects for example) are exempt from the restriction. The very largest partnerships are such big businesses that people who have barely met each other are in partnership together.

Many different trades and professions may be run through the medium of a partnership; apart from the professions noted above, doctors, pharmacists, business consultants, shopkeepers, builders, hairdressers and almost any other type of trade or business activity could be run via a partnership.

Example 1.2

Winston and Winona are computer games enthusiasts. They both work as local government administrative officers and are bored with their jobs. They decide to start a business selling computer games; they will rent shop premises for retail sales, but will also run a mail order service from the room behind the shop. The business is established as a partnership with a business name of WW Wizard Games. The two partners decide that, as they will both be working full-time in the new business, they will share all the profits from the business equally.

▶

As in the case of Yasin in Example 1.1, it will be necessary to keep some records of the business activities. It makes good sense to do so as it will contribute to good relations with the tax authorities. However, unlike the case of the sole trader, Yasin, there are some legal requirements governing the records that have to be kept by the business, and the way in which the business operates. Partnerships are covered by the Partnership Act 1890. This is a relatively straightforward piece of legislation that sets out a basic structure of legal relationships between partners, minimum record-keeping requirements and ways of resolving disputes between partners. For example, the Partnership Act states that profits will be shared equally between partners unless they make some other agreement between themselves. Winston and Winona have agreed in any case to share profits equally; this is a common arrangement where all partners are contributing equally to the success of the business. However, they could share profits in any way that seems appropriate.

Apart from the basic legal structure set out in the Partnership Act 1890, partners may decide to draw up a formal, legal agreement between themselves. Typically this would set out the details of the financial and legal arrangements that are to operate; it might, for example, state that Partner A will receive 60% of the profits of the business while Partners B and C each receive 20%. It may also deal with the actions to be taken in the event of a dispute between the partners. Not all partnerships bother to have a formal agreement of this type set up, but it can prove to be very useful if relationships turn sour.

Characteristics of the partnership form of business

The success of a partnership depends to some extent on the quality of the relationships between partners. Sometimes, people who are friends, or who are related to each other, set up a business partnership together. The pressures of running a business can sometimes place an intolerable strain on what has previously been a good relationship. On the other hand, where partnerships work well, they can be highly productive, especially if the partners have a range of skills that complement each other. Winona, in Example 1.2, is perhaps very good at selling over the counter, but lacks the attention to administrative detail that is required to run the mail order side of the business. If Winston is a good administrator, he will complement Winona's skills, and between them they will perhaps be able to run a successful business.

As well as sharing in the running of the business, the partners are likely to be able to command more resources to put into the business. At the start-up stage, each may have savings or other resources (such as equipment) which they can put into the business. If the partnership needs to borrow money, it may be in a better position to do so than the sole trader.

If the partnership loses money, or cannot repay loans, lenders are able to recover money owed by requiring the partners to sell items of property that they own personally. In this respect the partnership is no different from the sole trader, and the partners face the consequence of bankruptcy in the worst cases.

Each partner is liable under the law for the actions of his or her partners. If Winona makes a business decision that turns out badly and the partnership is left owing a large amount of money, both Winona and Winston are liable for the consequences of the decision. Winston could not claim that he knew nothing about the decision; he would still be equally liable with Winona. (It really is important for partners to know and trust each other thoroughly.)

A partnership business is not difficult to set up. However, partners should be prepared to go to the additional trouble and expense of having a clear partnership agreement drawn up with the help of a solicitor. It will make potential disputes in the future easier to resolve.

Limited companies

A limited company is a legal arrangement for regulating the ownership of business. A company is regarded as a separate person for the purposes of the law; so, for example, a company, unlike a partnership, can enter into a legal contract. This means that, if the other contracting person sues, he or she sues the company, not the owners of the company. The company itself becomes liable for its unpaid debts, overdrafts and so on.

This legal construction is an extremely important feature of the business world, in the UK and in many other countries. Because the company itself enters into contracts, takes out loans and so on, its owners are protected from any adverse consequences of the action. This is the concept of limited liability. It is an extremely useful and helpful device that protects shareholders from personal loss if the business runs into trouble.

Setting up a company (the process of incorporation) involves some legal formalities that must be followed strictly. It is therefore more difficult than setting up a sole trader business. However, the difficulties should not be overstated: there are specialist company registration firms, which, for a modest fee, take care of all the formalities. It need cost little more than £150 to set up a company.

After the company is incorporated, there are certain regular legal formalities that must be complied with. More details are given in the following sub-section.

Example 1.3

Winston and Winona decide to set up their business as a limited company, rather than as a partnership. The business is registered in the name of WW Wizard Games Limited. They divide ownership of the business between them; each owns exactly 50% of the shares in the business. Winona and Winston are both shareholders. Both are involved in the day-to-day management of the business and, as well as being **shareholders**, are also **directors**.

Characteristics of the limited company form of business

Shareholders are liable only for the amount that they have paid into the company in exchange for shares. This is the maximum amount which they can lose if the company is, for example, sued for not repaying its loans on time.

The legal formalities involved in setting up and running a limited company are more complex than for partnerships and sole traders. The directors of a limited company are responsible for making available to the public a certain amount of financial information about the activities of the company on a regular basis. They must do this via the Registrar of Companies, which is an agency responsible for the collection of data relating to companies. Any member of the public can obtain information about a limited company by visiting one of the offices of the Registrar of Companies or through its website (**www.companieshouse.gov.uk**). Regular filings include accounting information. Information that could remain private ina sole trader or partnership organisation must be made public by limited companies.

In small companies, shareholders (who are the owners of the company) and directors (who are responsible for managing it) are the same people. However, in larger companies it is frequently the case that most shareholders have nothing to do with the management of the company. Day-to-day management can be left in the hands of directors who are professional managers. Shareholders in very large companies often have virtually no contact with the company or its managers.

Sole traders, partnerships and limited companies contrasted

When setting up a business from scratch, the founder or founders must consider carefully which form of business organisation is most suitable for them. Usually, it is sensible to take professional advice on the matter as it can be advantageous for tax purposes to choose one form over another. Leaving tax to one side for the time being, the following are the principal advantages and drawbacks of the three different types of organisation.

Sole trader – advantages

- It is easy to start up as a sole trader.
- There are no legal formalities on start-up.
- The sole trader is self-reliant; he or she does not risk getting involved in the personality clashes that can occur where more than one person is managing a business.
- The sole trader does not have to share the profits from the business with anyone else.

Sole trader – drawbacks

- A sole trader bears all of the consequences of legal action against the business for unpaid debts and unfulfilled contracts. His or her personal property may have to be sold to meet business debts.
- A sole trader organisation remains small-scale.
- The sole trader bears the brunt of any losses or business difficulties.
- There is no co-manager with whom problems can be shared.
- If the sole trader is weak in some aspect of business expertise (such as ability to sell, to manage people or to keep track of business records) the business may suffer because there is no one available with complementary skills.

Partnership – advantages

- In a partnership, management is shared and the business can benefit from the complementary skills that the partners bring to it.
- Business decisions do not have to be taken alone.
- Business risks are shared, as are any losses that the business makes.

Partnership – drawbacks

- Partners are responsible in law for the consequences of each other's actions.
- Partners face unlimited liability; they must bear all of the consequences of legal action against the partnership. Their personal property may have to be sold to meet unpaid business debts.
- The profits of the business are shared between all the partners whereas a sole trader keeps all the profits for himself or herself (but note that a partnership business, which combines the skills of two or more people, should be able to generate higher profits than a sole trader).

Limited company – advantages

- The most significant advantage conferred by company status is the limitation of personal liability. Shareholders can invest in a business knowing that they will not be pursued for further contributions once their shares have been paid for.
- The limited company legal structure allows for shareholders to appoint professional managers as directors.
- A limited company's shares can be used to spread the ownership of the business among many people.
- Shares can be sold and bought so that transfer of ownership is relatively easy and straightforward.

Limited company – drawbacks

- Setting up a company requires adherence to a set of strict formal legal requirements, and will sometimes require professional advice.
- Regular filing of financial information with the Registrar of Companies is a legal requirement; this involves additional administration and means that members of the public have access to information that would remain strictly private in a partnership or sole trader organisation.

Finance for business

When starting a business the founder or founders must find a source of finance to pay for the setting-up costs, any equipment that is needed and, probably, for the expenses of the business for the period during which it is getting established. Most established businesses will also require finance from time to time to pay for such items as:

- Buying major items of equipment or land and buildings.
- Expanding the scope of the business (for example, opening new offices or conducting research into new product feasibility).
- Helping the business through difficult periods such as temporary recessions or decreases in sales.

In this section of the chapter we will examine the principal sources of finance that may be available to a business. Some are more appropriate than others for particular purposes.

Existing resources

When a business starts up, the founder(s) will almost certainly make an initial contribution of their own resources. This may be in the form of cash they have saved, or won, or been given. It could be in the form of motor cars or vans, premises or some other item of resource. Such initial contributions are known in accounting terms as capital introduced. We will examine financing business start-ups in much more detail in Chapter 2.

Where partners contribute to the setting up of a business, they may contribute unequal amounts depending on the resources they have at their disposal. In such cases, it may be decided between the partners that those who contribute more will receive an extra share of the profits to compensate.

Example 1.4	

Jakes, Jones and Jessop form a partnership to conduct legal business. The total capital introduced by the partners is £190 000, constituted as follows:

Jakes – office building valued at £100 000

Jones – cash of £50 000

Jessop – cash of £30 000 plus office equipment valued at £10 000

The partners decide between them that they will allocate a 10% return on each of these contributions out of the profits made by the business, before dividing the profits equally between them. The business makes £49 000 in profits in its first year, which will be allocated between the partners as follows:

	Jakes £	Jones £	Jessop £
10% on Jakes' capital: £100 000 × 10%	10 000		
10% on Jones' capital: £50 000 × 10%		5 000	
10% on Jessop's capital: £40 000 × 10%			4 000

Remaining profit split equally between the partners:
£49 000 − (10 000 + 5 000 + 4 000) = £30 000.

	Jakes	Jones	Jessop
Split equally	10 000	10 000	10 000
Total	20 000	15 000	14 000

The introduction of capital is possible at any point subsequent to the foundation of the business. Whenever the business needs more resources the founders may be able to make a further contribution.

Retained profits

As a business grows it makes profits. The owners of the business usually take out part of the profits as their reward for investing in it. However, they are not obliged to take out all the profits; they may leave some in the business to be invested to produce growth and further profits. The amount of profit left in the business is referred to as retained profits. This can be a very good source of funds for further investment as it is not dependent on any outside person or organisation.

Borrowed money

When thinking about potential sources of finance, borrowing may be one of the first possibilities that springs to mind. However, borrowing is not always the most appropriate source of finance for a business. In some circumstances it simply may not be obtainable. Many business start-ups would not be able to borrow money because no organisation would be willing to take the risk of lending it. Lenders need to know that: (a) the money they lend will be paid back eventually; and (b) the business will be able to pay a reasonable rate of interest on the borrowing. In order to do so the business needs to stand a good chance of being profitable.

The cost of borrowing

The cost of borrowing is the interest that must be paid on a regular basis to the lender of the money. Large institutional lenders may agree to lend money to the business but they will expect to receive interest payments on time and without fuss.

The risk/return relationship

Banks and other lenders do not always charge the same rate of interest. They make an assessment of how risky the lending is — i.e. how likely it is that the borrower will fail to repay. If the loan is perceived as more risky than average, the lender will either refuse to lend, or will charge a high interest rate on the lending. Sometimes, it may only be possible to borrow at extremely high interest rates.

Security

Sometimes banks and other lenders will not lend unless the loan is secured. A mortgage is a familiar example of a secured loan – familiar because at some point in their lives a lot of people take out a mortgage to buy a house or flat. Businesses often take out commercial mortgages to assist in the purchase of property in the form of real estate.

Overdrafts

Overdraft facilities may be obtainable through the business's bank account. An overdraft is most likely to be made available to a business if it can prove that the extra funds are needed only in the short term and that the business is fundamentally sound.

Example 1.5

Christmas Glitter Limited is an established business making Christmas lights and decorations. The period from July to the beginning of October each year is spent in frantic activity in the factory in order to build up the stocks of goods for sale in the company's three most important trading months — October, November and December. A lot of money is needed in July to October; materials have to be purchased and paid for, and staff costs are heavy because a lot of overtime is worked. At this time of year the business usually requires an overdraft. The company's bank manager is quite happy to provide overdraft facilities during this period because she knows from experience that by mid-November the company will have paid off the loan.

This is an example of a seasonal shortfall in cash, caused purely because of the nature of the business. A short-term facility like an overdraft tides the company over until it starts to generate cash.

It should be noted that an overdraft is a short-term solution. It is technically repayable on demand; this means that the bank can demand immediate repayment of the overdraft at any time. In practice, however, banks rarely demand immediate repayment.

Leasing and hire purchase

When a business makes a large purchase of an item that will be used over the medium to long term, it has to pay out a lot of cash at one time. Sometimes it makes sense to look at alternative ways of financing such a major item.

Under a leasing arrangement the business (the lessee) pays a regular amount to a lessor in exchange for the use of an item such as a piece of machinery. The lease often extends over a period of years. The lessor, usually a financial institution, pays for the machine, which is delivered to the lessee's premises and will, typically, remain there throughout its useful productive life. The lessor organisation is the legal owner of the machine but will probably never even see it. The lessee never owns the machine, but will use it, often for years, in the business.

Short-term leases are sometimes taken out on items such as photocopiers and cars. The items may be replaced regularly and each time this happens a new lease is negotiated. Again, the lessee never actually owns the item in question.

Hire purchase is a similar arrangement to the longer-term leasing described above, with the difference that, once the final agreed payment is made, under the terms of the agreement ownership passes to the purchaser business.

Factoring

Many businesses sell on credit – that is, they supply goods or services for which they are paid after a period of a month or two. The delay in receiving cash can be costly; if it is extended for too long the business may run into difficulties. Factoring is a way of speeding up the receipt of cash.

Example 1.6

Noone & Belfast Limited is a business that supplies major retail stores with home furnishings. The stores are slow to pay and sometimes the company has to wait up to three months to receive money that is owed to it.

The directors of Noone & Belfast decide to investigate a factoring arrange-ment. At the end of most months the company is owed about £200 000 by various stores that have bought goods but have not yet paid for them. The direc-tors approach a factoring company which proposes the following arrangement:

- They will pay Noone & Belfast 80% of the amount owed to them at the next following month end (i.e. £160 000).
- The factoring company will do all of the administration work connected with collecting the debts.
- Each time Noone & Belfast are ready to bill a customer for goods supplied to them the factoring company will pay the company 80% of the amount billed.
- The remaining 20% less a handling charge will be paid over when the factor receives the amount due from the customer.

The advantages of this arrangement for Noone & Belfast are that they receive a one-off large amount of cash (£160 000), and thereafter, they will receive 80% of the invoice value as soon as they bill a customer. They will also be able to devolve most of the administrative work connected with collecting debts to the factor.

In exchange for the cash supplied up-front by the factoring company, and for the administrative work, there will be a handling charge. This could be 2–3% of the total amount billed; obviously the factoring company needs to be able to make a profit out of the arrangement.

Although the arrangement costs money, it may well be worth considering for Noone & Belfast Limited.

Grant finance

Businesses may be able to obtain grants from the government, local authorities or other agencies and funding bodies. Usually, grants would be awarded only in quite specific circumstances. For example, a local authority trying to encourage the growth of local business might allow companies moving into the area a rent-free period in local authority business units. Although this is not a grant of cash it is a saving on the expense of rental, and it may well entice businesses into the area.

Grant finance is very advantageous in that it usually does not have to be repaid. However, there may be strings attached. In the example above, a business taking advantage of the rent-free period might have to undertake to stay in the area for a further minimum period of time of, say, three years.

Financing companies: Share issues

A company (but not a partnership or sole trader business) can raise additional finance by issuing more shares for cash. If the company is doing well, it can offer existing and potential shareholders a sound investment opportunity.

In Chapter 4 we will examine share issues in much more detail.

Financing companies: Venture capital

Medium-sized companies may be able to seek finance from venture capitalists. A venture capital company invests for limited periods in growing companies in order to give them a short to medium-term financial boost. Usually, the venture capitalist buys into the shares in the company, and will often provide management expertise as well.

Example 1.7

Hawthorn and Hayward Limited has been in business for five years, and has experienced very rapid growth during the whole of that period. The company's directors are now looking to expand into European markets and are seeking both additional finance of around £250 000 and specific expertise to help them. They approach a venture capital organisation, Bizexpand, for help.

Bizexpand's adviser explains that his organisation would buy shares in Hawthorn and Hayward in exchange for a cash sum of £250 000. Bizexpand would consequently become a significant shareholder in the company. In addition, one of Bizexpand's specialist staff would take up a directorship in Hawthorn and Hayward. The new director would be appointed because of his or her expertise in opening up European sales markets.

The arrangement is planned to last for between two and three years. At the end of a maximum period of three years, Bizexpand would sell its holding of shares (hopefully at a handsome profit) and the specialist director would move on.

Investment by a venture capitalist can be very helpful to a growing company, because it usually combines a sizeable input of cash together with advice and expertise in areas that will benefit the company.

Short-, medium- and long-term finance

It is important for businesses to match their needs for finance with the most appropriate form of finance. Using an overdraft to buy a new office building, for example, would be highly inappropriate. Taking out a ten-year commercial mortgage, on the other hand, would probably be the most sensible course.

Table 1.1 categorises the different sources of finance discussed earlier into short-term, medium-term and long-term sources.

Table 1.1

Terms of sources of finance	Short-term	Medium-term	Long-term
Existing resources	✓	✓	✓
Retained profits	✓	✓	✓
Borrowings	✓	✓	✓
Mortgage			✓
Overdraft	✓		
Short leases	✓		
Long leases and hire purchase		✓	✓
Factoring	✓		
Grant finance	✓	✓	✓
Share issues		✓	✓
Venture capital		✓	✓

Fundamentals of taxation

Taxation is a fact of life for most people and businesses. In this section we will take a brief look at the most common taxes levied on the different types of business which we examined earlier in the chapter.

Income taxes (personal taxation)

Sole traders and partners in business partnerships make profits (they hope) which are chargeable to tax. The tax that is levied is not a specific business tax; it is charged according to the individual's own circumstances at income tax rates.

Example 1.8

Cerise and Cherry are partners in a discounted clothing business. Under their partnership agreement Cerise takes 60% of the profits and Cherry takes 40%. In the tax year 20X5–20X6 the partnership profits are £30 000. Neither partner has any other source of income.

Cerise will be entitled to 60% of the profits: £30 000 × 60% = £18 000

Cherry will be entitled to 40% of the profits: £30 000 × 40% = £12 000

Each partner will include her share of the profits in her personal tax return. Each woman will be liable for income tax on her share less any attributable personal allowances. National Insurance contributions will also be payable.

Corporation tax

As the name implies, this is a tax levied on companies. Directors are paid a salary for working in the company, and they will pay income tax and National Insurance on the amounts they earn (just like any other employee). The company itself, however, is liable to corporation tax on its profits.

The company's profit is calculated (income less expenses = profit) and then corporation tax rates are applied. In recent years in the UK, corporation tax rates have tended to fall. Currently, in the 2004–2005 tax year, the basic corporation tax rate is 30% with a small companies' rate of 19%.

Capital gains tax

If an item such as an office building is sold at a profit, capital gains tax is likely to be charged. Capital gains tax applies to both individuals and companies, and so would be levied on sole traders, partnerships and limited companies.

Value added tax

Value added tax (VAT) is the UK's principal form of indirect tax; it is a tax on the purchase of goods. As private individuals we frequently pay VAT on goods and services that we purchase; we have no choice in the matter, and because prices are charged inclusive of VAT we do not usually even notice that we are paying the tax.

What about VAT from the point of view of a business? Businesses act as collectors of VAT, which they pay over on a regular basis to the government authority that collects it, the Customs and Excise. The operation of VAT is demonstrated in Example 1.9.

Example 1.9

Palfrey and Bennett Limited is a retail business that sells men's clothing from a series of high street outlets. The company adds a charge of 17.5% (the standard rate of VAT) to all the items that it sells. The company's customers pay the tax.

At the end of the three-month period ending 31 March 20X5, Palfrey and Bennett completes a VAT return. Total sales before VAT for the three-month period are £100 000. VAT at 17.5% is £17 500. The amount of £17 500 is known as output tax.

Palfrey and Bennett has itself, however, paid VAT on the purchases it makes. During the same three-month period it has bought goods totalling £70 000 before VAT. VAT at 17.5% is £12 250. The amount of £12 250 is known as input tax.

The quarterly liability to the Customs and Excise is calculated as follows:

Output tax for the quarter	17 500
Less: Input tax for the quarter	12 250
VAT payable	5 250

The company must complete a VAT return immediately following each quarter. In this case, by the end of April 20X5 it must send the VAT return to the Customs and Excise together with payment of £5250. The Customs and Excise authority is very strict indeed about deadlines.

Each of the businesses supplying Palfrey & Bennett will also be obliged to fill in VAT returns and make payments to the Customs and Excise. People in business often complain about the large administrative burden imposed by accounting for VAT. However, once a business has set up systems to cope with VAT, filling in the VAT return is usually straightforward.

Very small businesses are not obliged to register for VAT. However, if total sales for a year exceed £58 000 or are expected to exceed that amount, it is compulsory to register for VAT.

This section has provided only a very general introduction to the taxation of businesses. For the purposes of this book it is regarded as general background business knowledge. Detailed knowledge of tax is not required for any part of the material that will be covered in the rest of the book. In almost all cases, the exercises ignore the effects of taxation in order to avoid adding an unnecessary layer of complication. However, readers should bear in mind that the effects of taxation can be a significant factor in the real world.

Chapter summary

In this chapter we have examined some general business and finance issues. Students need to understand this background information in order to fully appreciate the context of business accounting.

We looked first at three forms of business organisation:

- sole trader
- partnership
- limited company.

The characteristics of each were described, and then the most significant advantages and drawbacks of each form of business organisation were identified and contrasted.

Next, the chapter examined some of the most significant sources of finance for businesses:

- existing resources
- retained profits
- borrowings (including mortgages and overdrafts)
- leasing and hire purchase
- factoring
- grant finance
- share issues (applicable to limited companies only)
- venture capital (applicable to limited companies only).

Finally, the chapter examined some of the fundamentals of business taxation. The following taxes were identified and briefly described:

- income tax (personal taxation)
- corporation tax
- capital gains tax
- value added tax.

Information about taxation is included as general business background knowledge only. A detailed knowledge of taxation is not required in order to achieve the aims of this book.

Internet resources

Some useful websites:

www.3i.com – the website of a very well-known and well established venture capital company.

www.companieshouse.gov.uk – the Registrar of Companies' website, which provides information about all UK companies (most of it at a price, unfortunately).

www.hmce.gov.uk – a comprehensive source of information for anyone who wishes to know more about VAT.

www.inlandrevenue.gov.uk – a very useful source of information about all aspects of personal and corporation tax.

The end-of-chapter exercises are divided into two sections. The first section has answers provided at the end of the book. The second section, in the white box, has answers on the lecturers' section of the website.

Website summary

The book's website contains the following material in respect of Chapter 1:

Students' section

- Quiz containing ten multiple choice questions
- Two longer questions with answers.

Lecturers' section

- Answers to exercises 1.8–1.10
- Two longer questions with answers.

Exercises: answers at the end of the book

1.1 One of the following statements about the sole trader form of business is correct:

a) A sole trader has to pay corporation tax.

b) Sole traders submit annual information to the Registrar of Companies.

c) The sole trader is entirely responsible for the management of the business.

d) Because a sole trader business is simple it is not necessary to keep any records.

1.2 One of the following statements about the partnership form of business is correct:

a) Partnerships are always very small businesses.

b) Partners are obliged by law to put £50 000 into the business when it starts up.

c) Partnerships are very difficult to set up because of the amount of information demanded by the government.

d) Partners are personally liable for the debts of the partnership business.

1.3 One of the following statements about the limited company form of business is correct:

a) A limited company is a separate person in law.

b) Limited companies cannot be sued.

c) It costs a great deal of money to establish a limited company.

d) Shareholders in a limited company are obliged to act as directors.

1.4 Select from the following list the most appropriate form of finance for purchasing a new office building:

a) ten-year mortgage loan

b) a loan repayable in six months' time

c) an arrangement with a factoring company

d) hire purchase.

1.5 Select from the following list the most appropriate way of financing a new office photocopier:

a) grant finance

b) issue of new share capital

c) lease

d) mortgage.

1.6   You are a small business adviser. A new client, Arnold Tapwood, has come to you for advice. Mr Tapwood explains that he is the sole proprietor of a small building business. One of his friends, Simon, who is a carpenter, has suggested that he and Arnold should join forces in a partnership. Arnold is not sure about the extra legal responsibilities that would be involved in becoming a partnership, and he asks you to explain in outline the required legal formalities.

1.7   Geoffrey is a keen dangerous sports enthusiast. He would like to set up in business as a sole trader organising dangerous sports events and activities. His business idea is that people would pay an annual subscription that would allow access to his website and a range of discounts on the fees for dangerous sports events. While he expects the idea to be a winner, because there are so many like-minded enthusiasts, he feels it likely that he will need some start-up finance to equip an office, install a couple of phone lines and pay for some help with administration. He estimates that he will need about £10 000 to get things up and running before the subscriptions start to appear in large numbers.

Geoffrey has just left university with accumulated debts of around £8000 so he has no money to put into the business. His parents refuse to give him any money for the venture. He has come to you for advice on the best ways of financing the start-up.

Exercises: answers available to lecturers

1.8   One of the following statements about the limited company form of business is correct:

a)   A limited company must submit information on a regular basis to the Registrar of Companies.

b)   Directors of limited companies are always selected from amongst the shareholders.

c)   Limited companies are not eligible to apply for grants.

d)   Directors of a limited company are personally liable if the company is sued.

1.9   Select from the following list the most appropriate way of financing the build-up of stocks of Easter eggs in a chocolate business:

a)   venture capital

b)   overdraft

c)   issue of new share capital

d)   lease.

1.10   Marie Deutsch is a fashion designer who, after graduation with a degree in fashion, obtained a very good job as designer in a lingerie company. She has decided that she would like to leave her job and set up in business with an old friend from college who also trained as a designer. Marie has heard that it is more sensible to set up as a limited company because it would mean that she and her friend would not be personally liable for the debts of the business. However, she says she is sure that there must be some strings attached, and would like you to tell her about any disadvantages in limited company status.

CHAPTER 2

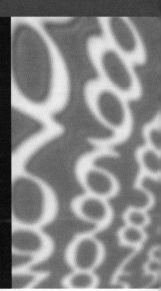

Starting a business

Aim of the chapter

To help students to understand some of the key issues – especially those relating to finance – involved in the start-up of a small business.

Learning outcomes

After reading the chapter and its spotlight study, and completing the exercises at the end, students should:

- Know about the most common sources of business finance for start-ups.
- Understand the need for, and the principal elements of, the business plan.
- Know about the most common reasons for business failure.

The discussion relating to the finance of small businesses builds upon and expands the knowledge gained in Chapter 1. It is important to thoroughly understand the issues discussed in this chapter, because they form a foundation for the study of accounting and reporting which is the main focus of this book.

Financing the small business

All businesses have to start somewhere. They mostly start small and are usually based upon a bright idea that occurs to one person, or sometimes, to a small group of people. The idea may be brilliant but impractical in business terms, or it may have occurred to lots of other people so there will be a high level of competition in the market, or it may be so good and original that it is going to make its owner a millionaire.

The basic business idea may arise out of a need for a product or service that cannot, apparently, be found, or cannot be found at the right price.

Example 2.1

Julie has a full-time job. She has two children, aged five and seven, at the village school which closes at 3.15pm each day, two hours before the end of her own working day. Julie cannot be there to collect the children, and no other member of the family is available at that time to help out. After trying various unsatisfactory arrangements for having the children collected, she concludes that the only way to solve the problem is to set up a business to run an After School Club on the school premises, so that the children of working parents can play in properly supervised conditions.

In this example, there is a perceived need for a service that does not currently exist. Provided that the need is shared by a sufficient number of people, and that the service can be provided economically, there is a business opportunity here.

Sources of finance for a new business start-up

In Chapter 1 we examined sources of business finance in outline. Below we look in more detail at some typical sources of finance that might be used to finance the start-up of a new business.

Any business start-up is likely to require an investment of money in order to make it work. Money is needed for some or all of the following:

- purchase of equipment
- supporting the owner and family while the business gets going
- paying for premises
- paying for staff
- expenses like business rates, insurance, running costs of cars, etc.

It can be very difficult to make realistic estimates of some of these costs. Later in the chapter we will begin to look at how to estimate costs. For the moment we will assume that some money and/or other kinds of resources are going to have to be contributed to the business in order to get it started. (Other kinds of resources could include, for example, use of a car or van that is already owned by the individual starting the business, or a contribution of free labour by members of the family.)

Where does the money come from?

Existing cash resources

Existing cash resources may be available in the form of savings and windfalls. In fact, the arrival of an unexpected windfall may even provide the impetus for the starting up of a business.

Example 2.2

Tim wins £120 000 on the National Lottery. He has always wanted to have a retail business, but has never had enough spare cash to be able to seriously consider setting one up. Now, because of this windfall, he has enough money in hand to be able to give up his job, and to invest in the lease of premises and the purchase of stock that he needs to get his business off the ground.

This scenario can probably be dismissed as completely unrealistic (although, after all, somebody has to win). More likely is the case where the prospective business person has some savings, or is made redundant and receives a sizeable sum of cash or is conveniently left some money in a will.

Also possible, depending upon the nature of the business, is self-financing through part-time work. In practice, many small businesses are financed in this way.

Example 2.3

Sasha completes her degree in fine art, producing several very good pieces of work at her degree show. Two of the pieces sell, and Sasha is offered an exhibition at a local art gallery. However, even though she may be comparatively successful in her working life as an artist, it is highly unlikely that she will ever earn enough from her work to be able to provide herself with a decent living. Very few artists earn much at all. Sasha takes a job for 15 hours per week in an art materials shop. This pays just enough to allow her to spend enough time producing her work for the exhibition, although she is very hard up indeed.

Family or friends

If the prospective business person has no resources it is possible that his or her family may be prepared to support the business in its early stages. Sometimes this can be through a handy injection of cash, or the loan or gift of an item of equipment. Very often, a supportive partner will agree to cover living costs from his or her salary during the early stages of the business.

It should be clear that the chances of obtaining this kind of financial support will depend upon the previous record and good standing of the individual.

Example 2.4

George wants to start a business supplying animal feed. He needs approximately £25 000 for renting premises, buying a second-hand goods vehicle and enough stock to get the business going. However, he is well known in the family as an unreliable spendthrift with an unfortunate tendency to lie and cheat. He has borrowed small sums of money from his parents and brother in the past and has failed to repay them. In the circumstances they are unlikely to be prepared to lend him anything at all.

Even if finance can be obtained in this way, there may be a downside. If the businessman borrows from his nearest and dearest, and then loses the lot in a reckless business start-up, family relationships can be scarred or even terminated. Business failure can, and often does, contribute to the breakdown of long-term relationships.

Grant finance

Grants can be an excellent source of start-up finance, as they usually do not need to be repaid. However, they are available only for quite specific purposes and will almost never serve to finance all of the expenses of a start-up. Also, once a grant is given, the granting authority will normally keep quite a close check on the progress of the business.

The chances are high that grant finance will not be available, but it is well worth checking just in case. Grants may be available for quite specific purposes. For example, in areas of high unemployment it may be possible to obtain a grant for employing local people.

In Example 2.1 involving Julie's childcare business (which is a real-life example), grant finance was obtained successfully. The business would have gone ahead without it, but at the time the government was making generous grants available to any business creating additional childcare places, and a grant was obtained to cover the cost of providing equipment and for the first year staffing costs. However, although the grant was 'free' in the sense that a cheque for several thousand pounds was obtained and did not have to be paid back, there were strings attached. The progress of the business was monitored frequently by a local business agency and this involved the keeping of quite detailed monthly accounts, and attending monitoring meetings.

Commercial borrowings

Generally speaking, anyone proposing to start up a small business will be reluctant to borrow money from external sources, such as banks, if it can possibly be avoided. There are several sound reasons for this reluctance. First, banks charge commercial rates of interest on loans. This can add substantially to the costs of a business start-up and can make the difference between potential success and failure.

Secondly, bankers will not lend to just anyone. In fact, they usually will not lend to anyone who does not have a record of success in business. This is not a problem if you are embarking on start-up number ten, with nine successful businesses to your credit, but, realistically, most people without a good track record in business are likely to face a polite refusal when they ask for a start-up loan.

Thirdly, bankers want to know that their loans will be repaid. They will maximise the likelihood of repayment by insisting upon security for the loan. This means that an arrangement is made so that, if the loan is not repaid on time, the bank can take an item, or items, of at least equal value from the business or the individual in settlement of the debt. The bank will usually insist upon a legally binding agreement, known as a charge, to ensure that the loan gets repaid.

Example 2.5

Des starts up in business with a bank loan of £50 000. He owns his own home, and, to cover its interests, the bank requires a legal charge over Des's house. The business goes bust after two-and-a-half years, still owing the bank the original £50 000 plus £3000 in unpaid interest. Because the bank has the legal charge, the house must be sold to meet the debt, and Des and his family will, effectively, be evicted and may be made homeless. Bankers are only human, and an individual bank manager may try very hard to find an alternative course of action. Nevertheless, the charge is a legal document, and the bank is quite within its rights to insist upon repayment via the sale of the house. After all, Des went into this with his eyes open; he knew the risks and should be prepared to take the consequences.

If security is not available in any other form, bankers may ask for a guarantee from someone who is sufficiently wealthy to repay the loan if the business fails.

Example 2.6

Suleman wants to borrow £25 000 from the bank for a business start-up. He owns virtually nothing himself, so there is no question of setting up a legal charge as in Des's case. However, his father is a successful businessman who considers it very likely that his son has inherited his business ability. He signs a guarantee for Suleman's loan. If the business fails, still owing the money to the bank, then the bank will require Suleman's father to settle the debt.

This type of arrangement is fine, provided that the guarantor (that's the person giving the guarantee) thoroughly understands the possible consequences if the business fails. In Example 2.6, Suleman's father is an experienced businessman who knows exactly what he is agreeing to when he signs the guarantee. However, there have been unfortunate cases where the guarantor has not understood that he or she stands to lose a very large sum of money if the business goes bad.

A secured loan is less risky, from a bank's point of view, than an unsecured loan. The nature of the loan and the value of the security tends to affect the interest rate. The greater the risk, the higher the rate of interest. Therefore a loan made by a bank on good security will carry a lower interest charge than an unsecured loan.

We are now going to examine an example of a business start-up in an extended case study that divides into two parts. The first part looks at a very low-key start-up requiring little finance.

The idea

Pete has a full-time job as a clerk in a factory office, working from 9.00am to 5.30pm Monday to Friday. Having left school with very few qualifications he has little scope in his present employment for promotion, and his earnings are relatively low. Until recently Pete and his partner, Angie, enjoyed a reasonably good standard of living; she also had a clerical job and the two salaries together allowed them to live comfortably. However, their circumstances have changed recently with the birth of their twin daughters. Angie has her hands full and is unlikely to be able to return to work until the children start school; it is not really worth her while to go back to work in the meantime because childcare for two children would eat up a large proportion of the additional income she could bring in. Besides, she thinks children do better if they have a parent with them full-time.

Pete wants to find a way of earning more money. He and Angie have a mortgage of £65 000 on a flat currently valued at £80 000. They have savings of £3000 kept in a 'rainy day' account on 90-days deposit. The flat looks very small now that there are four in the family but there is no realistic chance of moving to anywhere larger without an increase in income. Given the lack of promotion opportunities in his present job Pete has been looking around at ideas for self-employment. A recent visit to the gardens of a stately home has given him an idea. On the day that he and his family visited, a vintage car rally was taking place and there were large crowds of people around. Pete joined a long queue to buy two cups of coffee from a mobile stand. The refreshments facilities clearly did not match the demand and Pete could see the opportunity to make money.

On the way home he thought it through. He could use the family savings to buy a small mobile coffee stand. If he could borrow his brother's van he could take the stand around at weekends to antiques fairs, car rallies and the like. At the stately home he had paid £1.50 each for the cups of coffee – surely it must be possible to make money?

Financing issues

Peter's business idea is low-key in that it involves very little initial capital outlay, and very little risk. His immediate action plan would look like this:

- Find out about: (a) cost of mobile coffee stand; (b) any charges for setting up a pitch; (c) cost of coffee, cups, sugar etc.
- Discuss plan with: (a) Angie; (b) brother.

One week later

Pete has been busy. The first thing he did was talk the plan over with Angie. She was worried about the possibility of losing their savings, but Pete thinks that there would be very little risk involved. He has also asked his brother, Dave, about borrowing the van. Dave is a plumber and uses the van mostly during the week. He doesn't want to put a lot of extra mileage on the van, and points out to Pete that there will be times – about one weekend in four – when he's on call and will need the van. Pete agrees to pay his brother a reasonable charge for the hire of the van. This will reflect the mileage covered, and also the fact that there will be an additional insurance charge because the van is being used for a business other than plumbing.

Pete has looked at the cost of coffee machines. He cannot afford one of the bigger models, but has discovered he can save some cash by buying a second-hand reconditioned model. This would cost about £2000. For £100 he can buy sufficient coffee, plastic cups and so on to get started, but he doesn't know quite how long they'll last. He does some homework on possible venues, and discovers that the charges for pitches vary quite a lot. However, there is a small garden show due to take place only about 20 miles away, and the organisers are asking only £35 for the pitch that Pete wants.

He talks it through with Angie again. She is still worried. It isn't just the possible loss of the savings; Pete has succeeded in convincing her that if he can't make a go of the business the machine can always be sold on again, and the potential loss is small. She spends all week alone with the twins while Pete is out at work, and she doesn't want to have to cope alone for much of the weekend as well. Pete doesn't really have an answer to this objection, but suggests that she might get her mother or sister to come and stay to take the pressure off. Pete and Angie have an argument over this, but it concludes with her saying that he might as well try it out for a couple of months to see what happens. The next day Pete goes out and buys the coffee machine and arranges to borrow the van from his brother for the day of the garden show.

What are Pete's chances of success?

Factors in Pete's favour include the following:

- He doesn't have to borrow money, and the start-up is very low cost.
- The business idea is simple and will fit in with his existing job.
- He has the support (although not wholehearted) of his immediate family.

Factors working against Pete include:

- He hasn't investigated the business idea thoroughly. What about the competition? Owners of competitor stands might object to a newcomer.
- He hasn't attempted to estimate how much profit the business might make, or thought very clearly about how much he will charge per cup of coffee.
- He should probably have done more research on possible venues.
- Angie may be going to find it very difficult to cope alone at weekends. In addition, Pete doesn't seem to have considered the fact that his plan means that he will see very little of his family, and also that he is committing himself to working six or seven days a week.

Summary

Not all of the above factors relate to finance. We would need to know a lot more (and so would Pete) to be able to assess realistically his chances of success. From a financial point of view, Pete is unlikely (unless he's particularly unlucky or incompetent) to lose a lot of money. However, he should really be thinking more carefully about the business start-up than appears to be the case. It is clear from the case study that Pete's attitude to risk is more relaxed than Angie's. This could be an advantage, up to a point, in that he won't waste time and energy in worrying too much about the progress of the business. However, past a certain point, his attitude could lead to recklessness.

The business plan

Spotlight 2.1 shows a business start-up that has not been properly thought out. Pete should have produced a business plan. If he were seeking financing in the form of a loan or a grant he would certainly have to produce a quite detailed plan. However, even though he is not looking for finance it would be well worth his while to produce a plan. It would help him to clarify his ideas about the business, and give him some idea of its chances of success.

The business plan normally includes most or all of the following elements:

- Description of the business concept.
- Detailed description of the product or service that the business will offer.
- The market for the product or service, including market research and analysis of the competition.
- Profile of entrepreneur. A personal profile detailing relevant experience (including possibly a CV) and an analysis of personal strengths and weaknesses.
- Initial investment required. Type and cost of equipment, premises and similar items.
- Details of other people involved. If the plan is to employ people straight away, details are required of how they will be recruited and how much it will cost to employ them.
- Insurance requirements. Any relevant legal issues.
- Professional advisers. Details of the type of professional advice that may be required and how much it is likely to cost.
- Detailed financial projections. A budget will be required for at least the first year, showing the projected profit and cash flow.

The 'budget' as a statement of anticipated future income and expenses. 'Profit' is the amount left over after all the expenses of a business have been taken away from income. 'Cash flow' is the movement of cash in and out of the business.

Comparing the information in Spotlight 2.1 with the requirements of the business plan, we can see that Pete has some of the information he needs, but should really do a lot more investigative work before starting the business. The second part of the case study follows Pete's first 18 months of trading.

SPOTLIGHT 2.1 Business start-up (Part 2)

Pete's business after 18 months

Despite the absence of a proper plan for his business, Pete has managed to muddle through the first 18 months and has succeeded in making some money. He met several unexpected problems and had some bad luck:

- The coffee business is dependent on the weather. At Pete's first venue, the garden show, the temperature was very high and the ice cream vans did excellent business. Pete, on the other hand, had a disappointing day and didn't even manage to cover the costs of the pitch.

- Because Pete hadn't investigated the market he didn't understand how important the position of his pitch would be. The best pitches at a lot of venues are taken by experienced vendors and people like Pete lose out. However, he started attending smaller events and found that he could make more money that way; sometimes his is the only coffee stand, and he has had some excellent days' takings.

- Pete was involved in an accident when driving Dave's van to a venue. The immediate result of this was that he lost a day's takings, but the longer-term problem was that Dave refused to lend him the van again once it was repaired. Pete has therefore had to hire a van and it has cost him a lot of extra money.

- Pete didn't keep proper control over the cash coming in from the business. At the end of each day he put all the banknotes in his wallet, mixed up with his own money, and would use them for spending money. From time to time he would bank any surplus in his and Angie's joint bank account. After several months in business Dave persuaded him to go to see his accountant, Norris. Norris told Pete that he must keep the money from the business separate from his own money, and must count up and record each day's takings. Norris has sorted things out now, but he's just presented Pete with a bill for £550. He tells Pete that £300 of this cost came about through having to sort out the mess that resulted from Pete not keeping proper records.

The new plan

Despite these problems Pete loves running his own business. He really enjoys chatting with the people he meets at the venues, and he and Angie both like having the extra income. He likes the feeling of not having a boss telling him what to do, and he even enjoys the risk and uncertainty of running his own business.

Pete decides that he wants to give up the clerical job and go into full-time self-employment. He decides that he wants to open a coffee shop in the town centre. Pete is more confident now and he's sure he can make a go of it.

There's a small shop to let on the edge of the main town centre shopping area; Pete rings the commercial estate agent who is dealing with the premises and finds that he could take out a five-year lease at a rental of £7500 per year. The shop would need refurbishment, but Pete's brother Dave (who has got over the trauma of having his van wrecked and is now on good terms again) knows a lot of people in the building trade who would do a good job at minimum cost.

▶

Pete gets home from work and tells Angie about his idea. Angie is extremely unhappy about it; she becomes very agitated, loses her temper and starts shouting. She has got used to Pete working most weekends, and the extra money is really useful. If they were careful they could think about moving house sometime next year. She can now see that Pete really wasn't risking much in setting up his coffee business 18 months ago. But now, it seems crazy to her that Pete should even think about giving up his job to take on such a big risk as a proper coffee shop.

Financing issues

Pete has a great deal more to think about this time. He will need to find some external finance for this venture. Norris, the accountant, says that he can help him prepare a business plan to present to the bank manager, and that Pete should start thinking about the type of costs involved in setting up this venture.

Pete comes up with the following list of costs:

- rent
- refurbishment costs
- new equipment (coffee machinery, tables, chairs, crockery and so on)
- insurance
- business rates
- advertising
- wages (he will need to employ somebody else part-time for the busiest times of the week)
- coffee and other catering supplies
- electricity, water and phone bills.

He shows this list to Norris who says 'Well, so far so good, but there are some other things you haven't thought of. What about legal fees for setting up the lease? And I'll be putting in a bill for advice on your business plan, as well as the charges for doing your tax return. Also, if you get a bank loan for the start-up there will be a charge for interest.'

Other issues

Pete has a lot more work to do before he can decide whether or not this new business idea will work out. What about the competition? Are there other coffee shops in the area? Will there be a demand for food or snacks, as well as for coffee? Is the coffee shop really in the right location to attract customers? How much money does the business need to make to cover costs and to ensure that there is enough for the family to live on? Also, how is he going to persuade Angie that it's a good idea? If he can't get her support should he go ahead with the new business?

This second business idea of Pete's is very much more risky than the first. He's managed to make money out of the first business, although he's muddled through rather than following a proper plan. He's made quite a few mistakes, but he's learned something about running a business and has found that he enjoys being self-employed. However, if he takes on this business and it fails, what's going to happen to him and his family?

We'll follow Pete's progress in a future chapter.

Why do businesses fail (and why do some of them succeed)?

It can be quite difficult to estimate the failure rate for businesses. Researchers have estimated that, of every ten businesses started up, only two will still be in existence after five years. The government produces insolvency statistics (**www.insolvency.gov.uk**). In 2003 there were over 36 000 individual insolvencies in England and Wales, and over 14 000 corporate insolvencies in England, Wales and Scotland.

Failure factors

The Association of Business Recovery Professionals (**www.r3.org.uk**) regularly surveys failed businesses to find out the reasons why they did not succeed. The main reasons are:

- poor management
- lack of working capital
- lack of long-term finance
- bad debts
- loss of market.

Poor management

As we saw earlier, Pete didn't really understand about managing the money in his business; he could have run into serious trouble with the tax authorities if his brother had not suggested consulting an accountant. His failure to manage properly could have taken many other forms: for example, failing to take out the right kind of insurance. Some people who go into business are brilliant at product ideas, or providing the service that is the basis of the business, but are no good at day-to-day management. They may be both untrained and inexperienced in management.

Lack of working capital

Essentially, lack of working capital means running out of money. The bank manager might allow the business to borrow some money on overdraft, but overdrafts always have a limit. Once the limit is reached, closing the business down may be the only option available.

Lack of long-term finance

There is no money to invest in the long-term future of the business. For example, a new machine is required but the business cannot afford to buy it outright and no one will lend the money. In the short term the business may be able to struggle on, but long-term survival is unlikely.

Bad debts

Bad debts are not a problem for a business like Pete's where cash changes hands at the point where the product is purchased. However, if a business supplies on credit (that is, ships the goods to the customer before payment is received) and a big customer will not or cannot pay up, that can result in failure.

Loss of market

This can happen when a competitor business sets up successfully and takes away some of the market share. For example, a florist's business two streets away from a hospital will probably do well. However, if a rival florist opens up in a shop right next door to the hospital this will almost certainly result in a major impact on the existing florist's business.

This list is all very depressing, especially for anyone who is seriously thinking about setting up a business. However, many businesses do succeed and prosper. The factors that tend to lead to success include adequate financing, a cautious approach to risk-taking, existing management experience and sheer good luck.

Chapter summary

This chapter has covered some of the important elements of starting a business. We have seen that financial considerations are just part (although an important part) of the decision to start a business.

We have established a foundation for the study of business finance and accounting. The rest of Section One of the book deals with the financing of larger businesses. After that we will turn to a more detailed study of accounting matters.

Internet resources

Some useful websites:

www.businesslink.gov.uk – answers some frequently asked questions about small businesses in the UK.

www.dti.gov.uk – the website of the Department of Trade and Industry containing vast amounts of useful information about all aspects of business in the UK.

www.r3.org.uk – the website of the Association of Business Recovery Professionals.

www.about.com/business – A US site providing useful advice about a range of business issues, including start-ups.

www.startbusiness.co.uk – includes a very useful guide to the contents of a business plan.

www.insolvency.gov.uk – includes a lot of information about business failure in the UK.

 The end-of-chapter exercises are divided into two sections. The first section has answers provided at the end of the book. The second section, in the white box, has answers on the lecturers' section of the website.

Website summary

The book's website contains the following material in respect of Chapter 2:

Students' section

- Quiz containing ten multiple choice questions
- Two additional questions with answers.

Lecturers' section

- Answers to exercises 2.3 and 2.4
- Two additional questions with answers.

Exercises: answers at the end of the book

2.1 Erika is planning to become a self-employed graphic designer working from a small one-room office in a new development in the middle of town. You are a small business adviser and she has asked you for help in producing her business plan. You decide to prepare a list of questions to ask Erika at your first meeting, based on the major headings that you would expect to see covered in the business plan.

2.2 Ben has a degree in public relations and a huge list of useful contacts in the aerospace business, which he has established over a period of several years while working for Amis & Lovett, a large PR agency. He would like to set up his own PR agency. He plans to employ a new graduate and a secretary immediately in order to avoid being regarded as a 'one-man band'. He is confident that his savings (£45 000) will tide him over the first couple of months while he finds enough work to get started. List the main risks that you see in Ben's plan for the new business start-up.

Exercises: answers available to lecturers

2.3 Ashok has been left £100 000 by his grandma in her will. He plans to start a haulage business and will use part of the money to purchase an HGV. He already has an HGV licence. His wife will run the administration side of the business, initially from home, until they can afford to lease an office. Advise Ashok on the principal types of expense that you think he will face in running his haulage business.

2.4 Choose any two of the following businesses and, for each, write a list of the main expenses you think would be involved in running them as a profit-making business.

a) Childcare facility catering for children from three months to five years.

b) University cafe serving light snacks and lunches.

c) Internet-based travel agency.

d) Advertising agency.

e) Firm of estate agents.

CHAPTER 3

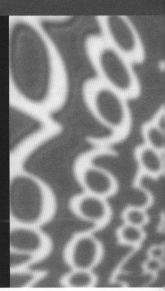

The growing business

Aim of the chapter

To assist in understanding some of the problems and opportunities that face the growing business, especially those related to finance.

Learning outcomes

After reading the chapter and its spotlight study, and completing the exercises at the end, students should:

- Know about some of the important stages in business expansion.
- Understand some of the problems and opportunities presented by business growth, including issues related to employment, developing the business organisation and moving into new markets.
- Know about the typical money management issues that face the proprietors of successful and growing businesses.
- Appreciate that business growth inevitably involves risk.

Introduction

In Chapter 2 we looked at some of the evidence about business survival. The evidence is not particularly encouraging in that the majority of new businesses will fail. In this chapter we will look at those businesses which survive and, to a greater or lesser extent, prosper. Prosperity and growth bring problems of their own. Sometimes established businesses are simply unlucky: perhaps key staff leave, a competitor offering a cheaper product or service becomes established, or some unforeseen event takes place such as accident or illness of the business proprietor. Sometimes, on the other hand, problems arise that the proprietor(s) of the growing business are simply unable to handle, such as growth that proceeds too rapidly or inability to cope with changing circumstances.

However, although problems may arise, there are also increased opportunities arising from growth. If a business does really well its original owners may be able to sell their stake and realise large amounts of cash. If the original objective in setting up the business was to become seriously rich, such owners achieve their ambition. For owners who decide to remain involved in the business, new opportunities may arise for business expansion. As a business grows and builds up a track record of success it becomes easier for it to borrow money in order to fuel further growth. Often, people who start and run successful businesses thrive on the new challenges and would not choose to give up their involvement even if they were able to retire early with large sums of cash.

In this chapter we will examine the phases of growth from a small to medium-sized business, charting some of the major milestones in business development. Financial management issues are often significant in the development of the growing business, and we will look at several relevant examples.

Stages in business growth and expansion

Employing people

In the previous chapter we examined a sole trader business. Many businesses do not grow past the point where they generate an income for one person and his or her dependants. A self-employed tradesperson, such as a plumber, small builder or garden designer may have no particular need or wish to expand the business to the point where employing another person becomes necessary. However, some business people will see the need for expansion, and employing another person is often the first step towards expansion.

Advantages of employing people in a small business

There is an opportunity to increase the skills base of the business. As we noted in the last chapter, one of the reasons why businesses fail is because of poor management. A sole trader is particularly vulnerable to this type of problem; he or she has to marshal a range of skills including selling abilities, financial management skills, organisational ability, self-discipline and so on. If any one of these is missing the business may fail. One way around the problem of missing skills is to either go into partnership with someone whose skills are complementary, or, in some cases, to employ a person who can contribute skills lacking in the proprietor.

Employing people is likely to increase the volume of trade in goods or services. Two pairs of hands can achieve more than one. If the right person is employed, he or she may be able to contribute to the profitability of the business.

Example 3.1

Kingsley is a self-employed furniture designer who undertakes commissions for the provision of original, well-designed furniture for businesses. He started up in business two years ago, and he has been very successful in generating work. He now has more than he can easily cope with. He is working seven days a week from early morning until late at night and his relationships with friends and family are suffering. Also, he has received some unpleasant letters recently from suppliers, including a threat from the electricity utility company to cut off his supplies unless he pays his bill within seven days.

It is pretty clear that Kingsley needs help. Administering a small business can take a disproportionately large amount of time. While Kingsley may not be ready to take on a full-time administrator, he should examine the possibility of employing a part-timer who can keep control of the paperwork. This would, presumably, free up part of Kingsley's time so that he could get on with more productive work.

The other area in which he probably needs help is in the design work. This is a much more difficult issue to resolve than the administration. People award Kingsley design commissions because they like his work. If he delegates some of the work to an assistant the design values may suffer. Unless Kingsley is prepared to carry on working all hours, he will have to make a decision on whether he keeps the business very small by turning down any commissions that he cannot manage himself, or, alternatively, whether he is prepared to share the design work with someone else. The first course of action involves a risk; if he turns down too much work the supply of commissions may dry up altogether. The second course of action also involves a risk; will the quality of work suffer? Also, does Kingsley have the necessary management skills to control the work of one or more designer employees?

Disadvantages of employing people in a small business

There is a very significant risk attached to employment. If a poor choice of employee is made, the mistake can threaten the survival of the business. Mistakes can be made in employing someone with whom there is a personality clash, or someone who is less competent than they appeared from their CV and the interview. Many employers will make an employment decision which, sooner or later, they come to regret.

Employing people costs money. Many successful small businesses pass through an awkward stage where there is too much work for the sole trader or partners to handle by themselves but where the financial risk of taking on an employee is unacceptable. The business proprietor(s) must be sure that they have the financial resources to pay for employment.

Employing people involves a great deal of paperwork. If staff are employed, the business becomes involved in the administration of pay as you earn (PAYE) and National Insurance contributions (NIC) on behalf of the employee. Detailed records must be kept, and these are liable to be inspected periodically by the Inland Revenue. Business people often complain bitterly about the amount of work they have to undertake as tax collectors on behalf of the government. The amount of administration involved acts, potentially, as a disincentive to employing people. (However, it should be noted, perhaps, that the administrative burden in the UK is probably less than in some other countries. France, for example, imposes a notoriously heavy administrative burden on the employer.)

Example 3.2

Recently, Kelly started a business importing and selling ornamental lamps, vases and similar items to retailers. The business has been successful, making profits of £35 000 in its first year and £38 000 in its second. Kelly has realised that, if the business is going to be able to grow, she will have to employ someone to assist her in selling goods to retailers. The ideal employee would have a good track record in selling and would be able and willing to travel four or five days a week visiting stores.

What financial factors does Kelly need to consider in making a decision about employing an assistant?

- *Salary.* Kelly needs to look carefully at how much she will have to pay in order to ensure the right employee. She needs someone with experience and who is prepared to act on his or her own initiative. Part of Kelly's annual profits will have to go to paying the employee. In addition to the annual salary, there will be the cost of providing transport (presumably an additional car will be required).

- *Employer's National Insurance and administration costs.* The employer must pay employer's National Insurance contributions, and the cost of administering the payroll must be taken into account. Kelly may be able to undertake this herself (the cost of doing this is the time taken up, which could be used on something else), or she may have to pay her accountant a little extra to do it.

- *Balancing costs and benefits.* If Kelly succeeds in employing someone who is good at selling, the benefits could far outweigh the costs of employment.

Suppose the total cost of employment is £30 000 per year; provided the employee can generate additional business that makes more than this amount in profit then it makes good business sense for Kelly to employ him or her. There may be other less obvious benefits: if Kelly gets flu and has to spend a week in bed the business, at the moment, grinds to a halt until she is better. If she could depend upon an employee, the business could be kept going more or less as normal.

Developing the business organisation

As a business grows and starts to employ more people, the way in which it is organised becomes more of an issue. There is a tendency in most business organisations to establish manageable units according to the functions they carry out. For example, in a typical manufacturing organisation it may be appropriate to establish separate departments for marketing, production, despatch, design, personnel, accounting and general administration. In the early days of the business only one or two people will be employed in each function, and the business proprietors are likely to retain firm control over all of the operations of the business. However, as the business grows, it becomes increasingly difficult for its owners to control every aspect of its functions. It is important for proprietors to be able to recognise when this stage has arrived, and to be prepared to delegate control to others.

Professional management

People who have started up successful businesses are often very reluctant to concede any part of their control to others. However, in most cases, it eventually becomes necessary to employ professional managers – people who have the experience and knowledge to manage functions such as marketing and personnel. Conflict sometimes ensues between the managers and the founders of the business as they disagree about the right way to manage change and growth.

Communication issues

As the business grows and departmental structures emerge, a range of communication problems can arise. Departments develop their own identities, and can, if not properly managed, become narrow in outlook, fighting territorial battles with other departments to protect their own status. Where this type of 'in-fighting' occurs, the overall objectives of the business tend to be forgotten.

Growth in bureaucracy

As we have already noted in this chapter, a certain amount of unavoidable record-keeping and administration is imposed on businesses by government regulation. As businesses grow and organisational functions separate, the business itself starts to require more complex records. An accounting department is usually required in order to keep the financial records straight. Some kind of authorisation and control procedures are inevitably required, but a great deal of management skill is needed to make sure that the generation of paperwork does not get out of hand. Organisations with excessive administration procedures may ultimately fail because they have become too inwardly focused. For example, staff become demotivated by the requirement to produce what they see as excessive paperwork. Perhaps the need for prompt and thorough organisational reporting starts to take priority over activities such as production quality control and establishing new sales contacts.

Moving into new markets or products

Expansion and growth of a successful business usually involves moving into new areas. Sometimes, this means expanding the range of products and/or services on offer, or new opportunities may arise to expand the market that the business serves. Clearly, there is always a risk involved in taking this kind of action. Some examples of typical business expansion decisions are examined in the following sub-sections.

Borrowing to finance expansion

Expanding a business involves additional costs, which can be substantial. The managers responsible for making the decision on whether or not to expand the business need to think carefully about all of the costs and potential benefits involved. Borrowing is often an attractive option, but the risks should be properly weighed up. The next example looks at a typical expansion decision.

Example 3.3

Lucinda and Lister are sole (and equal) shareholders and directors of L & L Limos Limited, a company that runs a small fleet of limousines for hire for weddings and by celebrities visiting the local area. Each year the business has gradually expanded its total sales as its reputation for reliability has grown. There is no direct competitor for their service in their own town, and, increasingly often, the firm is asked to undertake business in neighbouring towns and cities. Quite often the directors have to turn business away because all of the available cars are booked. Expanding the fleet and taking on new drivers seems like an increasingly attractive option.

How could this expansion be financed? The following costs would be involved: (a) the purchase or leasing costs of new vehicles; and (b) the employment of drivers, plus related costs. Also, the expansion might incur additional administrative costs (because more bookings would be made, more invoices would be generated and so on), and perhaps additional premises costs. The limos have to be housed securely in garage premises, and it might be necessary to expand the space available.

The directors need to look at the costs involved and think about financing. Several options may be open to them:

■ *Investment in new vehicles.* Buying the limos outright involves a substantial capital outlay and it might be preferable to lease the vehicles. However, if the directors want to borrow to finance outright purchase of the new limos they may well be able, as an established business, to obtain a bank loan quite easily. If they do not wish to take the risk of borrowing, they may be able to lend their own savings to the company.

■ *Investment in other costs of expansion by using existing resources* If there is spare cash available in the business, financing the expansion could be a good use for the funds.

■ *Financing via a flexible overdraft facility.* The directors need to prepare a cash flow budget that will reveal any points in the year at which short-term finance may be needed to cover shortfalls.

The directors face the risk that they have misjudged the market. If they invest in expansion and the demand for services is less than they thought, they may severely damage the future prospects of the business. Another risk is that, if they borrow money, interest rates could rise and become more of a burden on the business.

Amalgamating businesses to create expansion

Amalgamation of two or more businesses can be an attractive route to growth. For example, the managers of a business may decide that they wish to expand their business to a different city or area of the country. Starting up a new branch from scratch may be difficult, perhaps because the competition is well established. In such circumstances it often makes sense to try to join forces with a similar business in the area. Similarly, where a business wishes to expand the range of services it offers, the least-cost option may be to amalgamate with an established business.

Example 3.4

Linus, Lonsdale & Co is a firm of accountants established about ten years ago by Peregrine Linus and Paula Lonsdale. The business has always made a profit, and in recent years profitability has tended to improve. At a recent society of accountants' local meeting they met a sole practitioner, Liz, who is looking for an opportunity to merge her practice with another. She finds it difficult to cover the range of services that people expect from an accountant these days, and would like to take her own business into a partnership arrangement with another small practice. She specialises in capital gains tax and inheritance tax advisory services.

Bringing the two firms together would create a larger firm with three partners. If their range of skills is complementary the larger practice could, potentially, provide a better service to clients than at present. Also, a larger firm is in a better position to take on larger businesses as clients.

An amalgamation of businesses like this would probably involve some costs (for example, it might be necessary to enlarge the premises) but these would probably be fairly modest. The combined business could be more effective and better placed to expand in the future.

What risks are involved? The principal risk for the two firms is that the amalgamation does not work because of differences in style between the partners. The three partners must be able to get along harmoniously and, ideally, should have skills that complement each other. In a small firm it is very difficult to ignore major personality clashes.

Takeovers

In the previous example the amalgamation under consideration would involve the owners of the two businesses entering into partnership together. All of them would retain an ownership interest in the expanded firm. Takeovers, by contrast, involve buying out the interests of most, or all, of the existing owners. Where a business decides to attempt a takeover of a limited company (the 'target company'), for example, the shareholders in the target company are approached to see if they are willing to sell their shares. Where there are few shareholders this process can be relatively straightforward. If both buyer and seller(s) are willing, and a suitable price can be agreed, the takeover can go ahead. The result will be an expanded business, but the original holders of the shares will no longer have any financial or other interest in it.

The next example looks at a typical proposed takeover. Some of the business risks involved in takeovers are explored.

Example 3.5

Lupine Leisure Limited is a very successful manufacturer of sportswear. The company has grown rapidly since it was established five years ago, and it has built up a substantial cash surplus. The company's managing director, Lex Lupine, is highly entrepreneurial and is full of ideas for expanding the company's range of interests. The company's goods sell in a competitive market where big discounters and retailers are able to put pressure on suppliers to cut prices. Lex is unhappy with the margins that the company makes. He would like to break through into the retail market so that the company would control not only manufacturing but also the retailing of the products.

The options available to the company are to:

- Finance the opening and management of a small chain of retail stores.
- Acquire a small chain of retail stores (Lex has his eye on a particular chain that he thinks is ripe for takeover).

In both cases the medium-term plan would be to build aggressively upon a small-ish local network of stores to expand rapidly into neighbouring areas and, within five years, have nationwide representation. (Lex likes to think big.) When Lex presents the options to the other directors, he points out the advantages of the takeover approach: 'The beauty of it is that we can do this very quickly. We don't have to look around for suitable retail stores, and then arrange leases and employ managers and staff and so on. If we buy the chain it's all set up and in place. We can then concentrate on improving the overall management – we'll keep the decent managers and get rid of the rest – and we'll be in prime position to take up all the profit that's going.'

There are several potential risks in this situation. First, Lex may have misjudged the situation. He is seeking to integrate the supply of goods with their retailing, but the expansion into another area of the supply chain may not work well. The directors of Lupine Leisure are clearly good at running a manufacturing company; they may not have the necessary skills and experience to run a retailer successfully.

Secondly, there is a risk that, because of lack of knowledge, the company could pay too much for the retailer. If the retailer is a takeover target it may be because of some inherent weakness in its operations.

Thirdly, Lex wants to 'keep the decent managers and get rid of the rest'. However, what often happens in such situations is that the managers in takeover targets become concerned about their future prospects in the new, larger organisation. The good managers, who have portable skills and can easily get new jobs, tend to leave. The managers who stay may be the people who cannot easily transfer, perhaps because they are near to retiring age, or because they simply do not have the requisite skills and experience to attract another employer.

Finally, because of the apparent attractions of the scheme to take over the retailer, the directors of Lupine Leisure may not be giving sufficient thought to alternative uses for the company's cash resources.

Making money

As we have seen, the evidence is that most business start-ups do not succeed. However, those that do succeed may flourish and make money for their proprietors. In this section we will look at some of the issues and problems related to money management that arise for the owners of successful businesses.

Extracting cash

How do business people actually take money out of their businesses? We saw in the previous chapter, in the case study concerning Pete, that business resources must be kept strictly separate from personal resources. A business must be able to declare its profits for taxation purposes, and in order to do that, must have an orderly system of record-keeping. The business entity concept of accounting describes the necessary separation of the business and its proprietor.

Sole traders and partners in partnerships take money (and sometimes goods) out of the business in the form of drawings. Sole traders and partners usually need to take drawings from their businesses to pay their normal living expenses.

Where the business is set up as a company, the situation is slightly different. Directors are employees of the business and usually receive a salary for their work, just like any other employee. Where the directors are also shareholders they receive cash in the form of a dividend, which may be paid once or twice annually. Many companies have just one or two shareholders and directors who are the same people. The proprietors of such companies usually receive cash, therefore, in two forms: salaries and dividends. There are tax advantages to be gained by getting the balance of salaries and dividends just right; usually the business's accountant advises on the correct combination.

Managing cash within the business

One way of helping the business to grow is to keep past profits to fund future growth. Most business proprietors, therefore, aim to keep a balance between the amount of cash they remove from the business and the amount that is left in to fund growth. Spare cash in the business should be put to good use to help create future wealth – if it lies more or less dormant in a low interest bearing bank account, it is not being well used. Business proprietors and managers need to manage the position carefully so as to ensure that the business does not run short of cash when it is needed, but also that it is properly used to optimise the overall profitability of the business.

Exit strategies

Although people starting new businesses rarely bother thinking about it, it is important at some stage to start thinking about the most effective way of exiting a business. Serial entrepreneurs, whose principal interest is in start-ups, may be the exceptions to this generalisation; they will often have a vision of the length of time they wish to devote to the business before bailing out and starting on a new venture. However, all proprietors of successful businesses will need at some stage to evolve an exit strategy by addressing some of the following questions:

- When do I want to retire/leave?
- Who should take on the business when I go?
- How am I going to prepare for the transition to new management?
- Should I just sell my stake in the business?
- Is it saleable?
- Who is likely to buy it?

The problem is one of turning business wealth into hard cash which can be taken away by the retiring proprietor. This is more feasible for some kinds of business than for others. Businesses that manufacture or trade in goods, which have machinery, premises and a good brand name may be quite easy to sell. For example, earlier, in Example 3.5, we looked at the possibility of buying a chain of retail shops in preference to setting up shop businesses from scratch. As well as the shops, the fittings, the stock and so on, the retail chain would have a recognised brand name and, probably, some degree of customer loyalty. Factors such as loyalty and brand name are brought together under the general heading of goodwill in business terminology. Goodwill refers to all those intangible factors that are hard to quantify, but which add value to a business. Brand names, in particular, are powerful and valuable signifiers of a set of attributes to which customers are attracted.

By contrast, businesses that rely upon the particular skills and expertise of their proprietor may have little value once the proprietor decides to leave the business. In service businesses, there may be little left apart from desks and chairs once the proprietor (along with any remaining cash) is removed. For this type of business there is a particular challenge in building it up to the point where it can be continued without the original founder. The founder of the business may not want to let go of an enterprise that he or she has nurtured from day one, but part of ensuring the business's longer-term survival is to ensure that effective successors are identified and that they are given the space and opportunity to develop the business.

Some of the issues explored in this chapter are examined in the following spotlight study.

SPOTLIGHT 3.1 A successful business in danger

In this spotlight study we will examine some of the problems that can face even a successful business. The business context is that of a partnership, but some of the problems could also be found in a sole trader or company structure.

Chris and Anwar have been in partnership for over eight years running a computer consultancy business. Both men are in their mid-40s. They first met up almost 30 years ago at Sixth Form College where they studied computing at A level and founded a computer programmer's club. After that, they went to different universities and then gradually lost touch. However, almost ten years ago they met up again at a school reunion and started talking about their dissatisfaction with their respective jobs. At the time Anwar was employed in computer sales; although his job was well paid with high levels of commission, he really felt the time had come to run his own business. Chris had had various programming and consultancy jobs but he, too, was unhappy at the time because of an unsympathetic boss.

A year or so after their chance meeting, Chris and Anwar had taken the plunge into self-employment. Eight years on they remain the sole partners in the business, but now they employ nine consultants, three secretaries and a bookkeeper. The business has been successful and profitable almost from day one; the partners have complementary skills and have continued to work harmoniously together. Anwar is the public face of the firm; he has a 'larger-than-life' personality, is immensely sociable and extrovert, and has been able to build up a huge range of useful contacts in many industry sectors. The firm has never been short of work; in fact, the consultants all have to put in long hours to fulfil the existing contracts. Chris is the details man; he organises the provision of consultancy time to ensure that the contract requirements are met and is in charge of the management of all administrative matters. His technical knowledge is more advanced than Anwar's and he is involved hands-on in every contract the firm takes on. Despite having such different personalities, Chris and Anwar get along very well both personally and in business. They see each other socially, their families get along well and their sons go to the same school.

Now, however, the business has reached its first major crisis. About a year ago, Anwar suffered a fairly serious heart attack. He was advised to cut back on his hours of work, to give up smoking and to lead a much healthier life. It's been a huge struggle, but he's managed to kick the smoking habit; cutting back on work, however, has been much more difficult. Anwar loves his work; he cannot imagine life without it. Chris has encouraged him to leave earlier, to take on less and not to work so much at weekends. The trouble is, though, that the business is so absorbing and there's always so much to do that he hasn't really noticed that Anwar is putting in just as many hours as before.

One morning Anwar doesn't come into the office and Chris gets a phone call from the hospital. Anwar has suffered a much more serious heart attack; he will need major surgery and there is no question of him returning to work for many months. For the first time, Chris is really on his own.

A couple of days later, Marcia, one of the firm's best consultants, drops into Chris's office to tell him that she's leaving. She's got a good offer from one of the business's competitors. The initial salary is less than she's getting at the moment, but she's been promised a partnership position in a year's time. She says she's sorry to have to add to Chris's troubles by leaving at this point, but she has been in negotiations with the rival firm for a couple of months now. Chris tries to persuade her to stay, but Marcia's made her mind up. As she explains: 'The thing is, Chris, I've been here five years, and you and Anwar have never so much as mentioned me joining the partnership. I know I've done well here financially, but I'm still just an employee and I always will be as far as you're concerned.'

Chris is completely taken aback by this development. He really doesn't know what to do. Neither he nor Anwar has ever thought about inviting someone else to join the partnership. They've just assumed that the staff must be happy because they're earning so much money.

There's another problem, too. For the last three or four years, the business has been severely short of office space. The consultants spend most of their time out of the office visiting and working at clients. However, they all need some office space for the time they spend designing and planning solutions to clients' problems, liaising with equipment suppliers, and dealing with general administration. There has been a severe shortage of desk and storage space, and the business records are in a mess. Three months ago, Anwar and Chris started looking around for office premises to buy. Almost immediately they found the perfect solution – a three-storey office block not far from the existing offices. There would be enough space for all the staff on the first two floors, and the third floor could be let to provide some investment income. The purchase is going to be financed partly in cash, and partly by a mortgage secured on the value of the property. The partners are due to exchange legally binding contracts on the office building next week.

Later on Chris starts thinking seriously about the future for the first time. What's going to happen if Anwar doesn't get better, or if he can't return to work full-time? How will he, Chris, manage? He knows he doesn't have the skills or the sheer force of personality to take on Anwar's role as the public face of the firm. He shrinks at the thought of going out actively looking for business. He doesn't enjoy taking people out to lunch, like Anwar does, and he knows that he's no good at selling. He's always been a 'backroom' person.

What about the future of the firm? If Marcia leaves to become a partner elsewhere, perhaps the other consultants will follow her example and go too. What about the new office building? Should he go ahead and buy it on behalf of the firm?

Chris now thinks that perhaps he and Anwar should have thought about this sooner. And another thing: even assuming that Anwar's operation proves to be completely successful, and he's able to return to work full-time, what should they do about the future? One day they'll want to retire from the firm with a large enough amount of money to allow them a very comfortable retirement. What's the firm actually worth? Would he and Anwar be able to sell it?

The worst thing is that, for the first time since they set up the business together, Chris feels that he cannot discuss the business with Anwar. It wouldn't be fair to burden him with the problems when he's so ill.

Chris is very much in need of advice. What action should he take, both immediately and in the medium term?

Spotlight discussion

The partnership between Chris and Anwar has been very successful up till now; it appears to be based upon a sound working relationship that is enhanced by the partners' complementary skills. Anwar deals with the aspects of the business that require good people skills, while Chris is more of a technician and administrator.

Now, however, the partnership and therefore the business, is in danger. While the immediate problem relates to Anwar's state of health and the question mark over his future contribution to the business, there is an emerging problem with staff that has been building up, it appears, over a long period of time. High salary levels have not, evidently, been enough to keep Marcia committed to the business. She wants to be involved in running the business, and to be entitled to a profit share, and she is prepared to take the risk of leaving in order to put herself in the running for a partnership position. If Marcia feels like this it is quite possible that some of her colleagues feel the same way, and they may also be thinking about leaving.

One major problem that faces Chris is that he cannot take significant decisions without the involvement of his partner. Ideally, he needs to wait until Anwar returns, or at least, is sufficiently well to discuss the problems facing the business. The decision to buy the new premises, however, was taken jointly by them both, and Chris probably ought to go ahead with that. If the basic property investment is sound, it is unlikely that the partnership would lose money in the long run. Chris will probably have to organise the details of the move into the new premises himself, but then he would probably have handled that area of work in any case.

Decisions have to be made in the near future on the following:

- Employing someone to replace Marcia.
- Possibly employing someone to take over parts of Chris's work while he stands in for Anwar.
- Reallocating parts of Anwar's work to other consultants.

In the medium term decisions must be made on the following:

- Creating an employment and incentive structure in the firm that will allow it to retain staff.
- Agreeing on ways in which the ownership of the firm can be spread more widely, with a view to easing the retirement of the two existing partners and allowing them to withdraw the value of their equity from the firm.

If Anwar is unable to return to a full-time role within the business, the problems become even more pressing. Chris knows that he doesn't have the right mix of skills to take his partner's place. If the firm is to survive, he must ensure that Anwar's role in the firm is taken over by someone else. This may mean, ultimately, appointing from outside, merging with another similar firm, or allowing the firm to be taken over.

What is the business worth to Anwar and Chris? The spotlight study is a good illustration of how an apparently successful business could easily fade away as a result of an unforeseen event. This is a service business that depends for its survival on the partners and the quality of the staff they employ. Without the people, the business has very little substance or worth.

If the partners want to be able to take cash out of the business when they retire they need to plan their exit strategy carefully. The strategy will almost certainly involve admitting other people into the partnership. New partners admitted to an established business usually have to buy their way in, either by contributing a share of their salaries over a period of years, or by contributing a lump sum. These contributions compensate the existing partners for giving up part of the ownership and control of the business. If the strategy is managed well it provides several advantages:

- The partners who originally established the partnership are compensated for the share of the business which they transfer to new partners.
- Gradually, the skills base of the partnership can be broadened, making it more resilient to changing circumstances.
- The possibility of joining the partnership provides an incentive for staff.
- The business can survive even if the original partners leave it.

Risk

Risk has been mentioned at several points in this chapter. Each of the business decisions outlined in the examples involves taking a risk; this is an unavoidable factor in running a business. For example, a business may have to make a momentous decision about whether or not to invest several millions of pounds in a new factory. This type of decision clearly involves potentially major risks. Getting it wrong could bring about the downfall of the business.

All business people have to take risks. Sometimes their decisions prove to be wrong. More rarely, the decisions prove to be disastrously wrong. Successful businesses minimise their risks as far as possible, but risk cannot be eliminated. Financial analysis can help business managers to understand the range of possible consequences of their decisions. Later in the book we will examine the financial dimensions of decision making.

Chapter summary

In this chapter we have discussed the problems and opportunities presented by business growth. Specifically, we examined the advantages and drawbacks, and the most significant risks involved in employing people, developing a more complex business organisation and expanding the business into new products and markets.

We examined three approaches to business expansion:

- borrowing to finance expansion
- amalgamating businesses to create expansion
- takeovers.

Next, we looked at the issues involved in making money in a successful business, and ways in which proprietors of businesses actually extract money for their own use, including drawings by sole traders and partners, and dividends and salaries receivable by company shareholders and directors. This section concluded by examining exit and succession management by the proprietors of smaller businesses.

The spotlight study developed several of the issues discussed in the chapter, in particular the problems involved in managing a successful service business constituted as a partnership. The study involves consideration of problems relating to the following areas:

- complementary skills in a partnership
- personnel management
- succession management
- broadening ownership
- exit strategies.

The chapter concluded by considering the element of risk that is inherent in all business decisions.

 The end-of-chapter exercises are divided into two sections. The first section has answers provided at the end of the book. The second section, in the white box, has answers on the lecturers' section of the website.

Website summary

The book's website contains the following material in respect of Chapter 3:

Students' section

- Quiz containing five multiple choice questions
- Two additional questions with answers.

Lecturers' section

- Answers to exercises 3.3 and 3.4
- Two additional questions with answers.

Exercises: answers at the end of the book

Note: the principal objective of the following exercises is to set students thinking about some of the financial and other issues involved in business growth and development. No specific knowledge of particular types of business is required to answer these questions. Use imagination and common sense to think through the problems.

3.1 Nancy is a self-employed hairdresser. She runs a salon with the assistance of one untrained employee who takes bookings, tidies and sweeps up, and makes tea and coffee for the clients. Nancy would like to expand the business; this would involve employing a fully trained stylist. There is sufficient space in Nancy's existing premises for another person to work.

Advise Nancy on the costs, risks and potential benefits involved in employing a stylist.

3.2 Oleander Enterprises Limited is a small holiday company run by its two principal directors and shareholders, Libby and Lisa. The company organises exclusive (and expensive) holiday tours of French chateaux. During the four years since it was set up the company has gone from strength to strength. It now employs six people and it makes substantial annual profits. The company has a cash surplus and the directors have been considering ways of using the surplus to expand the business, possibly by starting up operations in new countries. Recently, the directors have been approached by Loretta, the managing director of another holiday company, Oxus Orlando Limited, which organises holiday tours in Turkey. Loretta is the principal director and shareholder of Oxus Orlando. She would like to sell her company and retire on the proceeds. Advise Libby and Lisa on:

1. The advantages and drawbacks of expanding by buying into another company.

2. The type of information they will require in order to be able to make a decision on whether or not to buy Oxus Orlando.

Exercises: answers available to lecturers

3.3 Norman and Naylor Partners is a business that runs corporate events. Sam Norman and Sally Naylor founded the business about five years ago and it has been very successful. The partners share profits equally. It now employs five full-time staff and calls upon a pool of up to 40 additional staff who can be employed part-time for specific events. Sally is several years older than Sam, and would now like to pull out of the business. She plans to take out her share of the value of the business with a view to buying and running a vineyard in Italy.

Identify the business problems and risks that Sam must deal with as a result of Sally's decision. What are the financial implications (in broad terms) for the partners?

3.4 Lionel is an experienced chartered surveyor with many years of experience. He is employed by a large property company where he receives a good salary and a performance-related bonus. He has recently been approached by an old friend, Leo, who is one of three partners in a firm of surveyors. The other two partners are nearing retirement age and they have decided that they need to bring in some 'new blood'. The partnership has been in operation for nearly 20 years and has carved out a sizeable niche in commercial property management. Leo tells Lionel that the partnership has been valued by a business valuation specialist at £1 200 000, a figure that includes goodwill of £500 000. If Lionel accepts the invitation to join the partnership he will be required to pay £300 000 in cash for a quarter share of the business. In exchange he will be entitled to 25% of the profits made by the partnership in the future.

1. Explain to Lionel what is meant by the term 'goodwill'.

2. Advise him on the type of information he will need to examine in order to be able to make a decision on whether or not to buy into the partnership.

3. Identify the main elements of risk involved in Lionel's decision.

CHAPTER 4

Large businesses

Aim of the chapter

To understand the context in which large businesses operate and in particular, the financing of quoted companies and the decision on whether or not to finance expansion of a company via a stock exchange flotation.

Learning outcomes

After reading the chapter and its spotlight study, and completing the exercises at the end, students should:

- Understand the operation of the UK stock market.
- Understand the reasons why companies choose to have their shares publicly quoted, and understand the fundamentals of what is involved in listing.
- Know about the advantages and drawbacks of operating as a listed company.
- Understand the need for information about listed companies, know about the principal sources of information concerning them, and be able to obtain relevant information.

Before we begin, a note about financial jargon. In this chapter we will examine several important aspects of the financing of companies, especially via the issue of shares. This will involve assimilating quite a lot of financial jargon and terminology. Remember to consult the glossary at the end of the book where necessary.

The jargon used in the financial news on television and radio, and in the financial press, can be very off-putting for the novice. However, once some basic items of terminology have been learnt, it soon becomes possible to read and understand the financial news. After a short time, it ceases to be such an effort, and may even, believe it or not, become interesting.

Sources of finance for companies

As explained in Chapter 1, there are many possible sources of finance that businesses may be able to obtain. Some of these, however, are available only where the business is structured as a company.

Issue of shares

Upon the initial formation of a company, ordinary share capital is issued to the first shareholders of the company. In the case of small businesses, the number of shareholders is usually low, often no more than one or two people. As companies grow, they may issue more shares to other people. Private companies (companies with 'limited' after their name) are not permitted to issue shares to the general public or to have their shares quoted on a stock market. Public limited companies (companies with 'plc') after their name, on the other hand, are permitted to issue shares to a wider public. Some plcs are quoted on a stock market and so are able to issue their shares widely to the general public. It is important to note that not all plcs are quoted companies, but that only plcs (and not private companies) may have their shares quoted on the stock market.

The ordinary shares of companies are often referred to as equity shares. They have a nominal value such as £1.50p or 25p; this is the basic denomination of the share. Shares that are quoted on a stock market have a share price representing a market value that is, usually, greater than nominal value. For example, a listed company has 5 000 000 shares with a nominal value of 50p each and a market value of £3.75. This gives the company a total nominal value of $5\,000\,000 \times 50\text{p} = £2\,500\,000$; this is the nominal value of its issued share capital. The total market value of the company (its market capitalisation) is $5\,000\,000 \times £3.75 = £18\,750\,000$.

Rights of shareholders

Ordinary (equity) share capital entitles its owners (shareholders) to a vote which they can exercise at the general meetings of the company. Usually, the only general meeting of a company is the annual general meeting (AGM) at which shareholders vote on such matters as appointment of directors, appointment of auditors, and on whether or not to accept the annual accounts that are presented at the meeting. In almost all cases, AGMs are extremely dull affairs, often poorly attended, but occasionally something interesting happens at the AGM of a major company, triggering a report about the AGM in the financial press.

The other principal right of shareholders is to receive dividends. Dividends are paid out to shareholders, often on a regular basis; they constitute the income received by shareholders on their investment. Very large companies usually have two regular payment dates each year for dividends (an interim dividend and a final dividend). The company's directors decide upon the level of dividend to be paid out; it is usually expressed as an amount in pence per share: for example, 'the directors have declared an interim dividend of 5p per ordinary share in issue'.

Benefits of limited company status

The liability of shareholders in companies is limited. That means that, even if the company fails, the shareholders cannot be called upon to contribute any further cash.

Because the capital of limited companies is split up into many shares, it is possible for a shareholder to sell a very small proportion of the total share capital of the company to another person. This can be useful where, for example, the original shareholders of a company have decided that they wish to spread the share ownership more widely, perhaps to other family members.

Usually, if a business becomes really large, a limited company is the only realistic business vehicle for it. It allows for multiple shareholders, each owning perhaps a very small proportion of the total business. Sole traders, for obvious reasons, usually own very small businesses. Similarly, partnerships, except in a few special cases, tend to be small or medium-sized businesses. The special cases tend to be professional firms (such as firms of accountants, lawyers, architects or other professionals) where very large partnerships do exist. In most cases, however, if a business grows to be very large, it will be in the form of a company.

Sometimes, the directors of a company may choose to raise finance by obtaining a listing on the stock exchange. This involves selling shares to a wider public than family, friends and business associates. In the next two sections we look at various aspects of the operation of the UK stock market.

The UK stock market

A stock market is a place where stocks are traded. So, what are the stocks referred to in the term 'stock market'? The UK stock market trades in, principally, the shares of quoted companies. Quoted companies comprise both UK based companies and overseas companies that have a quotation in the UK. The market also trades in British government bonds (these are known as 'gilts' or 'gilt-edged stock') and other types of shares and company bonds (also known as loan stock or debentures).

So, where is this 'place' where stocks are traded? In former times the principal stock market location in the UK was the trading floor of the London Stock Exchange. This was located in the City of London where the agents of people and organisations wishing to trade in stocks and shares met in person to arrange transactions. This physical location is no longer necessary following the far-reaching reforms and reorganisation of trading implemented over the last fifteen to twenty years. Transactions in shares now take place electronically.

The London Stock Exchange (LSE) is a powerful organisation that regulates the trading in shares and organises their listing. The LSE operates in two principal capacities: as a 'primary market' and as a 'secondary market'.

Primary market

The primary market function allows companies to raise capital via the LSE. In order to exploit the capital raising potential of the LSE new entrants to the market apply for a listing and, if successful, float the company on the stock market. This means that they are entitled to offer shares – either newly issued or existing shares – to the public.

Companies which already have a stock market listing may decide that they need to raise more finance. Such companies can issue more shares and sell them for cash.

Secondary market

The secondary market function allows trading in shares to take place between willing buyers and sellers. This is an extremely useful function providing for liquidity in shares. Liquidity means, in this context, that shares can be bought and sold easily. High liquidity is extremely attractive to investors; it means that they are not tied into their investment over long periods, but can liquidate (turn into cash) their investment whenever it suits them to do so. One of the problems of investing in unquoted companies is that it can be difficult (or downright impossible) to sell the investment to anyone else.

Organisation and operation of the London Stock Exchange

The LSE's market is split into two: the main market and the Alternative Investment Market (AIM).

The main market

The main market is the most important element of the market provided by the LSE. Companies on the main market have a full listing and are subject to the full range of regulation applicable to listed companies. In order to obtain a listing on the main market, companies normally have to have been in business for at least three years and to have a full record of accounts for that period.

The Alternative Investment Market (AIM)

AIM is a market that deals in shares of smaller and/or newer companies than those eligible to obtain a full listing. Many relatively small companies choose to obtain a quotation on this market. Investing in these companies is potentially riskier than investing in companies with a full listing because: (a) the business venture may be inherently riskier; and (b) the shares of AIM companies are often relatively illiquid – that is, they may not be traded very often or in very large volumes. This could make a holding of shares in an AIM company relatively more difficult to sell. However, some AIM companies are highly successful; they may move on to a full listing once they have built up a trading record.

Share prices

There are over 2000 UK companies quoted on the LSE at any one time, plus several hundred overseas companies. Although many companies have been listed for years, the list is constantly changing as new companies come to the market (at a rate of some 200–300 per year), and existing companies leave (because they have failed and go into liquidation, or because they are taken over, or because their directors decide to de-list).

Shares in quoted companies have a market price that can fluctuate a great deal. Shares in the larger, better known companies are traded very frequently, and their price can change from minute to minute. It is possible to obtain share prices with a delay of approximately 15 minutes from many sources nowadays. One of the best and most reliable is the LSE's own website (**www.londonstockexchange.com**). Shares in smaller companies, especially those on AIM, may be traded infrequently – i.e. their trading volume is low. Prices for such shares may remain relatively static with long periods of inactivity.

Share prices will tend to rise when a company is doing well, or when some piece of good news is announced (for example, the company has obtained new business or it has sacked an incompetent director). Conversely, bad news often results in a fall in share price. However, sometimes movement in share prices has relatively little to do with individual companies' activities and is the result of general market sentiment. For example, in the early part of 2000 share prices were generally high, but they fell during the middle of the year as the dotcom bubble burst. This 'bursting of the bubble' affected dotcom companies most severely but there was a more general loss of faith in high technology companies and in the market in general. There was a huge general drop in share prices following 11 September 2001. This affected all companies, but those involved in aerospace, insurance or tourism were particularly badly affected.

Stock market regulation

All companies are subject to regulation. The Companies Acts contain many legal stipulations about, for example, the internal constitutional arrangements for companies, the appointment and remuneration (that is, payment) of directors, the filing of accounts with the Registrar of Companies and the form and content of accounts. In addition there are other sources of regulation, including **accounting standards** which contain detailed requirements about specific items in the financial statements. However, listed companies are subject to another level of regulation in the form of a detailed rule book that used to be controlled by the LSE but is now regulated by the Financial Services Authority (FSA). The rules include, for example:

- A requirement for listed companies to report, via interim financial statements, half-yearly as well as annually (and in some specific cases, three-monthly – also known as quarterly – reporting is required).
- A requirement to include, alongside the annual financial statements, a chairman's statement.
- Regulations about building up large holdings of shares.
- Regulations about notifying the market of major events or large transactions.

Stock market indices

The FTSE

Anyone who watches television news, or who listens to radio news, will have heard the (usually) brief reports about the financial markets which sound something like: 'Bad news on the financial markets. The Footsie 100 fell 13 points to close at 5345.5.' While the first sentence makes sense, the second sounds like gibberish to the financial novice. Let's pick the important pieces out of the statement. 'Footsie' is the usual verbal reference for 'FTSE' which stands for 'Financial Times Stock Exchange'. The FTSE organisation, which is owned by the London Stock Exchange and the *Financial Times* newspaper, runs a series of indices both for the UK stock market and worldwide.

The FTSE 100 is an index that rises and falls in line with the value of the top 100 listed UK companies. The index started originally with a value of 1000. Each of the 100 constituent companies figures in the index according to the relative size of its capital. The minute-by-minute changes in the value of the 100 companies' share prices are fed into the index calculations. For most interested observers, daily tracking of the index value tells them all they need to know, but it is possible for people and organisations who are deeply involved in investing to find the current value at any time during LSE trading hours.

So, if the index falls by 13 points, it reflects an overall, average fall for the day in the share prices of those companies that make up the index. Some of the companies' share prices may have gone up; some will have fallen; but, overall, the average movement for the day is slightly downwards.

The reported index total (5345.5) is only really helpful to a person who keeps a regular eye on the movements in share prices. The index figure on its own means very little.

Which companies are in the FTSE?

At regular intervals the FTSE committee reviews membership of the FTSE 100; the principal criterion for membership is size, which, of course, fluctuates. The committee also reviews membership of the other principal stock market company classifications, and there are indices for the following:

- FTSE 250 – these are the 250 companies that are next in order of size after the FTSE 100.
- FTSE 350 – these are the FTSE 100 and FTSE 250 together.
- FTSE All-Share – the FTSE 100 and FTSE 250 plus a group of smaller, but still significant companies classified as FTSE SmallCap.
- FTSE Fledgling – these are fully listed companies that do not qualify in size terms for the FTSE SmallCap.

- FTSE TechMark – these are companies listed on the TechMark part of the LSE, which is a separate market introduced in 1999 for shares of high tech companies.

Information about the current values of all of these indices, and the rules that operate for their calculation, can be found at the FTSE website: (**www.ftse.com**).

Flotation and other types of share issue

Floating a company

As noted earlier, between 200 and 300 companies become publicly quoted each year. The process is time-consuming (it can easily take up to a year to organise and carry out) and may deflect directors' attention from running the business. A great deal of professional advice is required in order to conduct a successful flotation. Corporate finance advisers, stockbrokers (usually referred to simply as 'brokers'), lawyers and professional accountants are involved in ensuring that the process is successful.

Flotation for most companies involves a placing of the shares. This means identifying prospective buyers (usually institutional investors such as pension schemes, life assurance companies, venture capitalists, investment trusts and asset managers), and arranging to sell a portion of the shares. In the case of a placing, there is no invitation to the general public to buy into the new shares. An offer for sale, by contrast, does involve a general invitation to the general public and the institutions to buy shares in the company. It involves preparation of a detailed prospectus containing a great deal of information about the history and prospects of the company.

In either case, once the shares are floated they can be bought and sold in the secondary market. However, in most cases of smaller companies coming to the market for the first time, the principal or only buyers of the new shares are likely to be half a dozen or so of the well-known institutional investors.

Other types of share issue

New issues

Once a company has been floated successfully it may issue further blocks of shares in order to raise new capital. If there is sufficient demand for the shares, the new issue is likely to be successful.

Rights issues

It is commonly the case that, where a listed company wishes to raise cash via a new issue of share capital, it will do so via a rights issue. A rights issue is an offer to existing shareholders to purchase additional shares. It is usually expressed in terms such as 'a one-for-three rights issue'. This would mean that for every three shares already held in the company, the shareholder could buy one additional share. Taking up the rights issue allows an individual shareholder to retain the same percentage shareholding as before, as the following example illustrates.

Example 4.1

Wendover Household Goods plc has a total issued share capital of £1 000 000 £1 shares, the current market price of which is £5.30 each. It requires a fresh injection of capital to finance the building of a new factory to produce the company's revolutionary range of cleaning products. Wendover's corporate finance advisers tell the directors that the best way of raising the money is via a rights issue. They suggest an issue of one-for-four at £4.40.

An issue of one share for every four held will result in the issue of an additional 250 000 £1 shares. Each of these will be sold for £4.40, resulting in a cash inflow for Wendover of £1 100 000 if all the rights are taken up.

Jeannie Lemmon is one of Wendover's principal shareholders. She holds 170 000 of the issued shares. How much will Jeannie have to pay if she takes up the rights issue? She will have the opportunity to buy $170\,000 \div 4 = 42\,500$ shares. She will have to pay, therefore, $42\,500 \times £4.40 = £187\,000$ if she decides to take up the rights issue.

As in Example 4.1, it is usually the case that the rights issue price will be pitched below the current market value of the share in order to make it attractive to shareholders. If the rights issue fails (in that existing shareholders do not take up the issue) then it would be possible to try to raise additional capital by a placing or an offer for sale. However, existing shareholders could be assumed to have a particular interest in the company; if they are not interested in investing more money in the company, it is even less likely that outsiders will wish to do so.

Mergers and acquisitions

Where a full-scale effort is made by one company to purchase a majority of another company's shares, this is referred to as a takeover bid. What happens is that the bidding company offers to purchase shares from existing shareholders at a stated price. The existing shareholders do not have to accept the offer, so it has to be pitched at a price that will make it sufficiently attractive to induce a large number of the existing shareholders to sell. Takeovers are a common feature of the stock market environment. A hostile bid refers to a bid by one company that is rejected by the target company's directors. Not all takeovers, however, are hostile.

The consequences of a successful takeover bid are often far-reaching. The purpose of a takeover, in principle, is to allow a better quality management to take on the control of the operations of the target company. Ideally, takeovers should lead to improved efficiency and better returns for shareholders of the company that is taking over the other. In practice, it appears that takeovers do not always have the desired effect.

Mergers and acquisitions (M&A) is a general term referring to any bringing together of companies either by agreement or as a result of a hostile bid. Both 'mergers' and 'acquisitions' have specific meanings for accountants, but it is beyond the scope of this book to examine those meanings.

To list or not to list?

It may not be easy for the directors of a limited company to decide on whether or not to list. There are advantages and drawbacks.

Advantages of listing

- The principal advantage of listing, of course, is that the company can raise more finance for new projects and investments.
- Listing increases a company's general profile and credibility and may enhance its reputation.
- Listing may allow the founder members of a company to turn their hard work in the past into cash by selling part or all of their holding of shares.
- Listed companies shares can, in most cases, be liquidated easily. Listing is, therefore, likely to increase the pool of potential investors and may increase the value of the company.

A 2001 survey carried out jointly by the LSE and Eversheds (a firm of business lawyers) found that the most popular reason cited for seeking flotation was 'to raise funds' (mentioned by 64% of respondents), followed by 'to increase the company's profile and credibility' (mentioned by 23% of respondents).

Drawbacks of listing

- A listed company is in the public spotlight. Financial journalists are likely to become much more interested in a company's activities once it is listed. This may work to the company's advantage when everything is going well and the publicity is welcome. However, if the company is struggling, or if it is engaged in some controversial activity, publicity may be a major drawback.
- A listed company may become a 'takeover target'. A company can take over another company by buying up a majority of the shares in order to obtain control over it. The directors of the target company usually find themselves in a difficult position in these circumstances and they often lose their jobs.
- There is increased pressure on companies' management to produce consistent and ever-improving results. This pressure may result in short-termism, where investment in the long-term future of the company may suffer in order to produce the kind of short-term results that satisfy City commentators.
- Obtaining a listing is not cheap. A great deal of accounting and legal work must be paid for, plus underwriting costs. The total costs usually amount to at least 10%, and occasionally as much as 20%, of the amounts of cash raised by the flotation.
- The additional layers of regulation are onerous and compliance with them can be very expensive. It is usually necessary to employ additional staff.
- Movements in the company's share price can be worryingly difficult to explain or predict.

In the LSE/Eversheds' survey referred to earlier, the principal drawbacks to being a public company were identified as 'additional reporting requirements and associated costs' (mentioned by 57% of respondents) and 'volatility of share price, often with little correlation to business fundamentals' (mentioned by 18% of respondents).

The role of information in stock markets

Information is the lifeblood of stock markets. People, including those who represent the institutions that buy shares (for example, pension funds and insurance companies), need to have some assurance that they are buying shares that have some underlying value.

Sources of information about listed companies' shares

Published financial statements

All companies, whether listed or unlisted, are required to produce annual accounts for the benefit of shareholders. They are also required to file certain information (although not the full accounts in all cases – there are various exemptions for small and medium-sized companies) with the Registrar of Companies. However, the reporting requirements are more onerous for listed companies. All listed companies must produce an annual report, which has to be made available to interested parties. These are often very long and elaborate documents, running to many pages and involving high quality paper and design work. In addition to the full annual report, listed companies produce interim financial statements, which report results for the six-month period immediately following the year-end.

The reporting requirements mean that investors, potential investors and anyone else who is interested can obtain information about a company at approximately six-monthly intervals. It takes time, however, to compile this information. Most listed companies publish an annual report, at the earliest, some three to four months after the company's year-end.

How reliable is the information? There have been many cases of investors and others being misled by financial statements that were inaccurately or fraudulently prepared. All large companies are required by law to have an annual **audit** of their financial statements carried out by an independent firm of auditors. Although the audit process is not foolproof, and although it in no way guarantees accuracy, it does provide investors with some assurance that the financial statements are fairly stated.

The internet

The internet has emerged in the last few years as a very useful source of information about listed companies and their activities. Although not all listed companies have websites (and the law in the UK does not, currently, require them to have websites), most do.

There is no standardisation of content on websites, but, typically, a corporate website includes:

- Information about the activities of the business (this is often very extensive).
- The latest annual and interim financial statements.
- An archive of annual and interim financial statements.
- E-mail contact details.
- A constantly updated share price (sometimes via a link into the stock exchange's own website).
- Links into other useful websites.

A company's website can be a very useful source of information. However, the quality of website construction and content varies enormously. Some are out of date, dull, difficult to access and badly designed.

Many companies listed on stock exchanges outside the UK also have websites. Before the late 1990s it was often very difficult to obtain information about overseas companies; by contrast, nowadays, it can be very easy. Most US companies have extensive websites and it is becoming increasingly common to find good corporate websites among continental European companies.

As well as companies' own websites, there are many other sources of information available nowadays. The Hemscott Group website (**www.hemscott.net**) provides information about all UK based companies listed on the London Stock Exchange, including companies listed on the Alternative Investment Market. Some of the information is available by subscription only, but a large amount is freely available.

The financial press

The best and most extensive coverage of company activity and general financial news available in the UK is undoubtedly provided by the *Financial Times* (FT), which is published six times a week. Anyone who reads the FT thoroughly on a daily basis before long will be a fount of financial knowledge. Most business and accounting students will find that making a conscientious attempt to read the FT fairly thoroughly once a week will add considerably to their general financial knowledge.

Some Sunday papers and broadsheet daily papers (e.g. *The Times* and *The Guardian*) contain good coverage of financial and accounting issues.

The spotlight study for this chapter examines various aspects of the flotation decision.

! SPOTLIGHT 4.1 Going public

The directors of Gropius & Garner Productions plc are about to hold one of the most important board meetings in the company's history. A few months ago the founding shareholders, Brendan Gropius and Amelia Garner, suggested to the board that it was time to think about 'going public', by obtaining a listing on the stock exchange.

Brendan Gropius is the company's managing director, and Amelia Garner, who is a chartered accountant, is the finance director. They founded the company, which produces television commercials and documentaries, nine years ago. Since its foundation, the company has produced strong results; it has grown very rapidly and now employs almost 150 staff. The shares are currently held as follows:

- Bernard Gropius, 40%
- Amelia Gardner, 30%
- Sigmund Gropius (Bernard's cousin), 15%
- Karl-Heinz Muller (Amelia's brother-in-law), 15%.

As well as Bernard and Amelia, Sigmund and Karl-Heinz also hold directorships. There is one further member of the board who does not hold any shares: Judy Segal, who has overall responsibility for the production of commercials and documentaries.

Bernard and Amelia propose that 300 000 of the 700 000 shares currently in issue should be sold. Each director would sell shares in proportion to his or her total shareholding as follows:

Director	Shares currently held	Shares to be sold (3/7)	Shares remaining
Bernard (40%)	280 000	120 000	160 000
Amelia (30%)	210 000	90 000	120 000
Sigmund (15%)	105 000	45 000	60 000
Karl-Heinz (15%)	105 000	45 000	60 000
Total	700 000	300 000	400 000

In addition to the 300 000 existing shares that would be sold, the company would issue a further 200 000. The directors have been advised by their corporate finance advisers that they could probably raise around £10.50 per share on flotation, after taking into account all the costs of issue.

There are two principal reasons for the proposal to obtain a listing:

1. Bernard and Amelia are both paid large salaries for their work as directors of the company. However, they are both interested in selling a substantial part of their shareholding now, while share values in the market generally are high. The sale would allow each of them to realise a substantial amount of cash, which they could then invest elsewhere. They would both like to plan for an early retirement in about 5–8 years time.

2. The company plans to move into children's entertainment programmes because there are very substantial profits to be made from this area of the market in programmes. This will require a substantial investment of resources. Borrowing money to fund the expansion would be a possibility, but both Bernard and Amelia feel that the time is right for a flotation.

Judy Segal, the sole director without a shareholding, is concerned about the proposal. She can see, of course, that her fellow directors all stand to gain substantial sums by selling their shares, but she is not sure that the flotation will be advantageous to the company in the longer term. She would like the company to remain as an independent operator, and she has been alarmed by a spate of recent takeover announcements in the business press. She fears that, once floated, the company could be swallowed up rapidly by one of the bigger companies.

Bernard assures her that there is no particular reason why Gropius & Garner should become a takeover target. The company is well managed and has a good record of producing profits even in difficult times. He can see nothing but advantages from the move.

Discuss the advantages and drawbacks of stock market flotation for the company, taking into consideration the following questions:

- Would the company be at risk of becoming a takeover target?
- Are Bernard and Amelia being unreasonable in wanting to cash in their shares?
- Is Bernard correct in seeing only advantages in the flotation?

Spotlight study solution and discussion

In order to assess the advantages and drawbacks of the proposed flotation, it would be sensible first to assess the financial impact of the deal.

Would the company be at risk of becoming a takeover target?

A company is usually only at risk of becoming a takeover target if more than 50% of the voting shares are available for purchase. This deal involves the issue of a further 200 000 shares. Added to the existing 700 000 shares, this gives a prospective total of shares in issue of 900 000. How many of the shares will be retained by the current directors?

Holdings now (before flotation)	700 000
To be sold on flotation	300 000
Retained after flotation	400 000

So, the directors will hold 400 000 of 900 000 shares (i.e. less than half of the issued share capital). If another person or company wished to take over Gropius & Garner it would be technically possible to do so. Judy's concerns are, therefore, realistic in the circumstances.

In total, 500 000 shares will be sold. If the corporate finance advisers' estimates are approximately correct, this would mean that 500 000 × £10.50 could be raised, i.e. £5 250 000. The sale of the shares belonging to the directors will raise 300 000 × £10.50 = £3 150 000 and new capital raised for investment in children's programming will be 200 000 × £10.50 = £2 100 000.

How much money will the directors make?

- Bernard holds 40% of the shares currently in issue, and so he will be entitled to 40% of the proceeds of the directors' shares: 40% × £3 150 000 = £1 260 000.

- Amelia holds 30% of the shares currently in issue, and so she will be entitled to 30% of the proceeds: 30% × £3 150 000 = £945 000.

- Sigmund and Karl-Heinz each hold 15% of the shares currently in issue, and so will each be entitled to: 15% × £3 150 000 = £472 500.

Clearly, all the directors (except Judy) stand to make substantial sums out of the flotation. All will retain large holdings of shares in the business, and so they could potentially make more money out of selling more shares in the future.

Is it unreasonable of Bernard and Amelia to want to sell their shares?

Flotation on the stock market is a common way for founders of a company to turn part or all of their investment into cash. As both Bernard and Amelia are thinking ahead to retirement, the proposal to float the company makes perfect sense from their point of view.

Is Bernard correct in only seeing advantages in the flotation?

Because Bernard stands to gain a substantial sum of cash from selling part of his shareholding he is, perhaps, not very likely to dwell on the potential drawbacks of the flotation. However, Judy has pointed out one significant drawback in the form of a potential takeover bid. If the company were taken over the existing management might not be able to hold on to their lucrative directorships. Even if they did, they would find that they no longer have complete control over the company's activities.

Other possible drawbacks include:

- Increased public attention which is not always welcome. Following flotation the company would find itself subject to much more media interest than before.

- The company would have to start producing interim financial statements as well as a full annual report, and there are various other forms of additional regulation that would come into play. A listed company incurs additional costs in complying with regulation.

- There might be pressure from the City to produce better and more consistent results.

Most of these drawbacks are unavoidable. The company could help to minimise the possibility of takeover by floating rather fewer shares than originally intended. If 400 000 of 900 000 shares were to be made available, this would leave a majority in the hands of the four shareholder/directors. The company could, of course, still be vulnerable if one or more of the four were persuaded to sell all or part of their holding.

Chapter summary

The chapter started by examining some aspects of the financing of companies by the issue of shares, including the rights of shareholders, and a brief reprise of some of the benefits conferred by limited company status.

The role of the UK stock market as both a primary and secondary market was then discussed. A brief description of the main market and the Alternative Investment Market was included, followed by an introduction to stock market regulation. The FTSE indices were then briefly described and discussed.

Flotation of companies, new issues in established listed companies and rights issues were described. There are advantages and drawbacks to listing on the stock market, and these were detailed and discussed.

Finally, the important role that information plays in stock markets was flagged, and some of the principal sources of information about companies were described, including published financial statements, various internet resources and the financial press.

The spotlight study examined a company contemplating a listing. This involved assessment of the financial consequences of listing, both in terms of rewarding the company's founders and in raising fresh capital for investment.

Internet resources

Some useful websites:

www.ftse.com – explains the operation of the FTSE indices and reports regularly updated values for the main indices.

www.fsa.gov.uk – the website of the Financial Services Authority.

www.hemscott.net – provides a large quantity of useful information about UK based companies listed on the London Stock Exchange.

www.londonstockexchange.com – provides information about all companies currently listed on the LSE (including current share prices) and about the activities of the exchange itself. For example, at the time of writing, the website contained the LSE/Eversheds' survey report referred to earlier in the chapter.

Links to individual company's websites are often provided through the Hemscott site and through the LSE site referred to above. If there is no obvious link it is worth contacting the company by phone (phone numbers are obtainable from the Hemscott data) to ask if they have a corporate website.

The end-of-chapter exercises are divided into two sections. The first section has answers printed at the end of the book. The second section, in the white box, has answers on the lecturers' section of the website.

Website summary

The book's website contains the following material in respect of Chapter 4:

Students' section

- Quiz containing ten multiple choice questions
- Three additional questions with answers.

Lecturers' section

- Answers to exercises 4.5 to 4.8
- Three additional questions with answers.

Exercises: answers at the end of the book

4.1   Ashton Longton plc, a listed company, has issued share capital of £8 000 000 comprising shares of £1 nominal value. The current quoted price per share is £3.85. What is the company's market capitalisation?

4.2   The Alternative Investment Market is a market for:

a)   companies that do not currently wish to proceed to full listing

b)   companies that promote alternative lifestyles

c)   British government securities

d)   overseas companies without a trading history.

4.3   Warminster Toys plc has a total issued share capital of £3 000 000 in 50p shares. The company decides to make a rights issue of one-for-five at a price of £5.42 per share. To take up the rights the holder of 50 000 shares will have to pay:

a)   £27 100

b)   £135 500

c)   £54 200

d)   £271 000.

4.4   Yolande Brighton is the managing director of Brighton Bestwines plc, a company that supplies the licensed trade. The company has been very successful but has now reached the point where it needs to expand its warehousing capacity if it is to continue growing. The directors have been contemplating applying for a quotation on the Alternative Investment Market (AIM). The company will issue a further 500 000 shares (it already has 1 000 000 shares in issue). It hopes to be able to sell the shares at around £2.50 each. The directors have invited you to their board meeting to discuss the flotation. They are keen to raise the finance, but one or two of them are wondering about potential drawbacks to being quoted on the AIM, and they would like you to give them an outline of any possible problems they face. Prepare a list of potential drawbacks for discussion at the meeting.

Exercises: answers available to lecturers

4.5   Amery Chorlton plc, a listed company, has issued share capital of £4 000 000 comprising shares of 25p nominal value. The current quoted price per share is 98p. What is the company's market capitalisation?

4.6   Interim financial statements are:

a)   first drafts of the final financial statements of listed companies

b)   provisional financial statements that are awaiting audit

c)   half-yearly financial statements produced by listed companies

d)   audited financial statements awaiting directors' approval.

4.7 Willoughby Wooster plc has a total issued share capital of £1 000 000 in 25p shares. The company decides to make a rights issue of one-for-two at a price of £2.70 per share. To take up the rights the holder of 30 000 shares will have to pay:

a)   £40 500

b)   £10 125

c)   £20 250

d)   £7 500.

4.8 Tatiana, a friend of yours, has recently been left approximately £50 000 of listed company investments in her grandmother's will. She has been trying to read the *Financial Times* in order to see what is happening to her investments. She has found some information about three of them:

1.   Turtlehammer plc rose to 215p on speculation of a hostile bid from a competitor, but fell back to 210p by the end of the day's trading.

2.   The share price of Teddington Tilmain plc has risen by 26p following the announcement that it has obtained an important new export contract.

3.   Tolson Tortellini plc has announced today that it is making a rights issue of one-for-four at £2.30.

Tatiana frankly admits that she doesn't understand any of this. She asks you to explain each of the pieces of news in terms that she can understand. She would like to know if any of it is likely to be good news for her. Also, she would like you to tell her if the *Financial Times* is the only source of information about her investments.

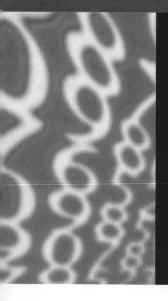

The role of accounting in business

Aim of the chapter

To understand the reasons why people need accounting information, the nature of accounting information and the role of the accountant.

Learning outcomes

After reading the chapter and completing the exercises at the end, students should:

- Understand why accounting information is produced.
- Be able to identify the principal groups in society who need and use accounting information.
- Know about the principal characteristics and features of accounting information.
- Understand the distinction between financial accounting and management accounting.
- Know about the functions that accountants perform in the production of accounting information.
- Appreciate the reasons why business managers should be able to understand accounting reports.

information held at Companies House, the information is potentially available to a very large number of people. In fact, the financial information of most companies remains undisturbed because there are very few people who are interested in it, apart from the shareholders. The company's shareholders are informed, in any case, of the financial condition of the company because they are entitled to receive a full set of annual accounts.

However, it is possible that other groups of people, apart from the shareholders, could be interested in the information. People or organisations who have been asked to lend money to the company are likely to be interested in its financial status. People who are affected by a company's existence (for example, those living near the premises of a chemical company that regularly breaches environmental legislation) may also take an interest. Later in this chapter we will consider the different categories of people who might be interested in a company's financial information.

Companies are required to submit tax returns and VAT returns, and financial reports must be made available to the Inland Revenue and Customs and Excise in the same way as for sole trader and partnership organisations.

Separation of ownership and management

In smaller companies the shareholders and directors are often the same people. Because they are engaged in the day-to-day management of the business, directors who are also shareholders really do not need annual financial information to tell them what is going on. They have access to as much internal financial information as they need.

However, the position is different for shareholders who are not directors. In large companies, most of the shareholders are remote from the activities of the business; they receive dividends and an invitation to the annual general meeting (AGM) of the business, but have no other contact with it. If they are shareholders in a listed company, they will be able to follow movements in the share price by consulting the financial press, but they are not entitled to the regular detailed internal financial information that the directors use in managing the business.

The relationships between the company, the directors and the shareholders are depicted in Figure 5.1. The diagram demonstrates the separation between the ownership of the company and its management. Shareholders appoint directors

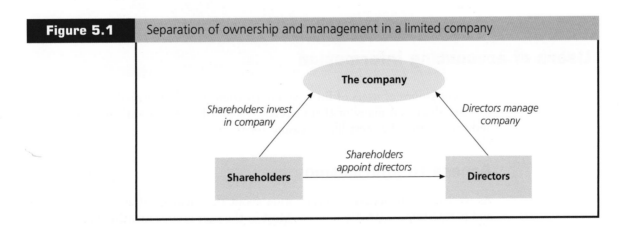

Figure 5.1   Separation of ownership and management in a limited company

(who in larger companies are professional managers) to manage the company on their behalf: the directors act as agents of the shareholders, or (to use an old-fashioned term) as stewards on their behalf. The stewardship function requires directors to act in the best interests of the company at all times. In order to demonstrate good stewardship, they should report on a regular basis to shareholders – hence the requirement in company law that full annual financial statements are sent to shareholders.

Clearly, where shareholders are remote from the management of their company there is potential for the directors to take action that benefits themselves rather than benefiting the shareholders. This is one of the potential problems of the agency, or stewardship, relationship. For example, a current, and recurring issue, is that of directors' remuneration in very large companies. Criticisms are often voiced in the press of the very large increases in salary and substantial bonuses that directors award themselves. Shareholders are in a position to take action if they do not approve of directors' remuneration packages (via their votes at the AGM) but, in practice, they rarely challenge the directors.

If directors wish to manipulate financial information they are well placed to do so. How can shareholders be sure that the annual financial information they receive has not been distorted in some way? The mechanism that is used in company law is the requirement for audit by an independent auditor. Until recently, all companies, whatever their size, were required to have an audit of their annual financial statements. The requirements have, in recent years, gradually been relaxed by the government so that smaller companies are now exempt from regular audit. However, shareholders in exempt companies can still require an audit if they wish for the reassurance it provides.

Accounting information within the business

With the exception of the very large professional partnerships permitted by law, all larger businesses in the UK are constituted as limited companies. As a company grows in size, its management needs ever larger quantities of internally generated accounting information in order to keep control of the business and to make good quality decisions. Larger companies, especially those involved in the complexities of, say, manufacturing or banking, tend to produce highly complex and sophisticated information for use by management.

Users of accounting information

Different groups of users of financial information can be identified. In this chapter we have discussed many of them already. Table 5.1 lists the principal user groups and summarises the most likely reasons for their interest.

Access to information

As we have seen, access to information about the financial affairs of sole traders and partnerships is strictly limited. Most of the user groups identified in Table 5.1

Table 5.1

Principal groups of users of financial information

User group	Reason for interest in financial information
Shareholders	To assess the performance of management in their role as stewards of the company
	To use the information to make decisions on whether or not to sell the investment in the shares of the company, or perhaps whether to buy more shares in the company
Potential shareholders	To make decisions on whether or not to invest in the shares of a company
Investment analysts	To assess the performance of the company in order to be able to advise their clients on investment strategy
Lenders and potential lenders	To assess the ability of the business to make repayments and to meet regular interest payments
Employees and trade unions	To assess the viability of the business and the extent to which it is likely to be able to (a) continue to offer employment; (b) increase pay and improve employees' conditions
Suppliers	Where suppliers offer credit terms, they need to be able to assess the likelihood of being paid promptly
Special interest groups	In the case of an environmental activist group, for example: to assess the extent to which the company has set aside funds for environmental clean-up operations
Government: tax collecting agencies	To assist in the assessment and collection of taxes
Government: other agencies	To assist, for example, in the collection of national statistical information
Financial journalists	To obtain information about a company's activities and profitability which will be of interest to the journalist's readers
Academics and students	To assist in the study of business activity
Customers	To assess the likelihood of the business continuing in existence, and continuing to supply the goods or services required by the customers
The general public	Anyone, not covered by any of the categories above, who has an interest in the activities of the company

would not be able to gain access; the exceptions are the government agencies concerned with the assessment and collection of tax, and lenders who are likely to be in a position to be able to demand financial information would not normally be available.

Because company financial statements are made publicly available, however, all these categories of users have access to them. In many cases the user groups are making important decisions on the basis of the information, answering questions such as:

- Should I sell my shares in this company?
- Should my bank be making an overdraft facility available to this company?
- Is the company doing well enough to make it safe for me to carry on working for it?
- How risky is it to supply goods on credit to this company?
- How well are the current management looking after my interests as a shareholder?

Company accounting information is called upon to be useful to a wide range of users in making decisions. In the next section of the chapter we look at the characteristics of useful financial information.

Characteristics of useful financial information

Ideally, financial information produced by businesses should have the following key characteristics:

- *Relevant*: to the decision being made. For example, the information should be prepared shortly after the events being reported so that it is not out of date by the time it is used.
- *Reliable*: the information should be properly prepared and free from error or bias in its preparation.
- *Comparable*: where financial statements from more than one period are concerned, the information should be prepared on the same basis, so that it is comparable.
- *Understandable*: the information in the financial statements should be capable of being understood.

In practice, it is not always possible to achieve information that fulfils all of these characteristics. In large and complex businesses collecting accounting data and processing it into a set of financial statements is a time-consuming process. By the time it is published (usually three to four months after the year-end date in a very large company) circumstances may have changed and the information may be of limited use for decision making. Also, the information that is reported is all historical – i.e. it relates to events that have already occurred. The extent to which past events are a reliable guide to the future is questionable in a fast-changing business environment.

Accounting information should be understandable, but, again, this is not always easily achievable. The financial statements of very complex organisations tend, inevitably, to reflect that complexity. People who are reasonably knowledgeable about business matters should be able to comprehend financial statements, but even their ability to understand is sometimes tested by the complex financial statements of major listed companies.

Financial accounting and management accounting

There are two distinct strands to accounting in organisations. Financial accounting refers to the processes and practices involved in providing users external to the business with the information that they need. Companies, because they provide a relatively large amount of information to outside users relative to partnership and sole trader entities, tend to devote substantial resources to financial accounting. This type of accounting is also referred to as financial reporting, and both terms are used in this book. Management accounting is the accounting that a business organisation carries out for its own internal uses. It assists management in controlling the business and in making decisions.

Both financial and management accounting use information generated by the accounting system of the business. Clearly, the accounting systems of businesses are likely to vary enormously depending upon the complexity and size of the business organisation. However, all accounting systems have certain characteristics in common. The flow of information in an accounting system and its relationship to financial accounting and management accounting is demonstrated diagrammatically in Figure 5.2.

Figure 5.2 The production of financial reports and management accounting reports

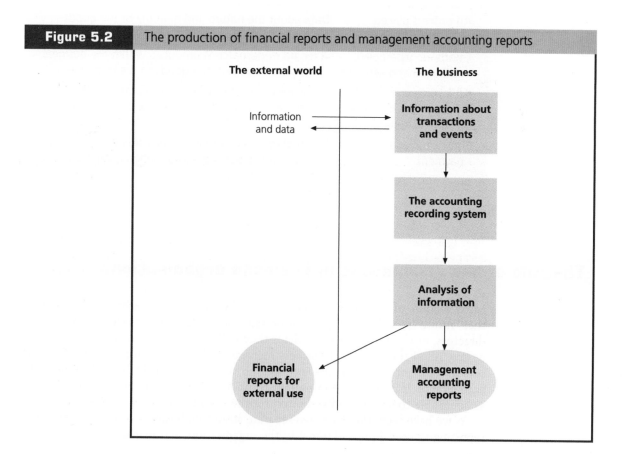

Data and information about events and transactions flow in and out of the business. For example, when a business makes a sale of goods to a customer that it supplies on credit (i.e. the customer is not obliged to pay cash straight away) the events and information flows set out in Table 5.2 take place. At each stage details about the event are 'captured' by the accounting recording system. Periodically, data that shares common characteristics (e.g. all sales invoices) are analysed and the analysis is used to produce reports for both financial and management accounting purposes.

The principal purpose of this book is to assist business and other non-accounting students to understand the important elements of management accounting reports. Therefore, we are not concerned with the details of data capture, recording and analysis for accounting purposes. These areas are the province of accountants. Unless students are so captivated by the accounting and financial understanding they glean from this book that they decide to change direction and become accountants, detailed knowledge of accounting systems really is not necessary. However, it is helpful to have some outline understanding of the way accounting information is gathered in order to produce the reports.

Table 5.2	Events and information flows relating to the sale of goods	
Event	**Information flow**
An order is placed	Data about the nature and quantity of the goods required flows into the business and is recorded
Goods are assembled, packaged and sent out	A record of despatch is produced within the business and is sent out with the goods to the customer
An invoice is raised through the business recording system	The invoice is sent out from the business to the customer – information leaves the business
The customer sends payment	Information is received in the business and is recorded. The cheque is banked – information again flows out of the business

The role of the accountant in business organisations

Many readers of this book will be aiming for a career in business management. In their future lives they will perhaps be sales or production managers, or personnel directors, or chief executives. Perhaps they will at some stage own their own businesses. All of these types of business manager and business proprietor work alongside accountants and use the information, often on a daily basis, produced by accountants. It is therefore important to understand what accountants do, as well as being able to understand and interpret the reports that they produce.

As we have seen, there are two separate strands in business accounting: financial reporting to user groups external to the organisation, and management accounting for reporting to managers within the organisation. This variation in function is reflected in the organisation of the accounting profession and in the training of accountants.

The accounting profession

The accounting profession includes the following types of accountant: independent accounting practitioners and accountants in business.

Independent accounting practitioners work outside industry and business in professional practices. These are the accountants who provide taxation and accounting services to a wide range of businesses. If they are registered auditors, they are authorised to carry out the audits of companies and other organisations.

Accountants in business are the accountants with whom business managers work in organisations. Broadly, they are either financial accountants or management accountants, depending upon whether they specialise in the external or the internal provision of accounting information.

Professional accountants may have one or more accounting qualifications. These days almost all professional accountants have a university degree, although it is not necessarily in accounting or a related subject (the author of this book, for example, is a chartered accountant with a degree in Russian). After university they enter into a period of three or four years training with an employer during which they take some very tough examinations. Not everyone who embarks on accountancy training will manage to qualify because the examinations are so demanding.

The following are the principal professional accounting bodies in the UK which have their own qualification systems:

- ICAEW: the Institute of Chartered Accountants in England and Wales (members have the letters ACA or FCA after their names).
- ICAS: the Institute of Chartered Accountants of Scotland (members have the letters CA after their names).
- ACCA: The Association of Chartered Certified Accountants (members have the letters ACCA or FCCA after their names).

The members of these organisations are found in both professional independent accounting practice and in business. Students of ICAEW and ICAS usually train in professional accountancy firms. Students of ACCA are found in both professional and business environments. Usually those who go into business specialise in financial accounting and reporting rather than in management accounting.

Finally there is CIMA: the Chartered Institute of Management Accountants (members have the letters ACMA or FCMA after their names). As the name of this organisation implies, its members work principally in management accounting, and its students train exclusively in the business environment.

People who have trained as accountants are often found at the most senior levels in business organisations. It is not unusual in the UK to encounter chief executives and senior directors who started their careers as accountants before moving into more general business management.

Why do business managers have to understand accounting reports?

As we have seen earlier in the chapter, and in the four previous chapters in this section of the book, accounting information is necessary to business organisations. To summarise, accounting is used to provide:

- Financial reports about companies for a range of user needs.
- Management reports in all types and sizes of business organisation to assist management to: control business operations; plan for the future; make decisions; and find out how the business is performing.

In business organisations where there is more than one manager, decisions tend to be taken collectively by directors or partners. It is very often the case that accounting information feeds into business decision making. In order to be able to make informed decisions non-financial managers must be able to understand the financial information that accountants present to them.

Accountants occupy a service function in the business, but the service they provide is a very important one. Poor financial reporting and control can be the downfall of an otherwise successful business.

Chapter summary

This chapter has provided a framework of information about accounting, which underpins the remainder of the book. First, the need for accounting information was examined in the context of three different types of business organisation: sole trader; partnership; and limited company. Each organisational type needs to make some information available to people or organisations outside the business. In addition, accounting information is needed to assist management in running the business.

The provision of information to outsiders is a much more important issue for limited companies than it is for partnership or sole trader organisations. The general public has access to company financial information through the medium of the Registrar of Companies. As well as filing information at Companies House, companies are also obliged by law to make annual accounting information available to their shareholders. The chapter explained the important issue of the separation between the ownership and management of limited companies, which is especially noticeable in larger companies.

There is a long list of potential users of accounting information: shareholders, potential shareholders, investment analysts, lenders and potential lenders, employees and trade unions, suppliers, special interest groups, the government, financial journalists, academics and students, customers and the public at large.

The chapter went on to discuss the characteristics of useful financial information: it should be:

- relevant
- reliable
- comparable
- understandable.

The distinction between financial accounting and management accounting was described and discussed, and then the role of the accountant in business organisations was described. There are several different professional accountancy qualifications and the main ones were noted.

The chapter concluded with a brief discussion of why business managers need to be able to understand accounting reports.

The end-of-chapter exercises are divided into two sections. The first section has answers provided at the end of the book. The second section, in the white box, has answers on the lecturers' section of the website.

Website summary

The book's website contains the following material in respect of Chapter 5:

Students' section

- Quiz containing five multiple choice questions
- Two additional questions with answers.

Lecturers' section

- Answers to exercises 5.5–5.8
- Two additional questions with answers.

Exercises: answers at the end of the book

5.1 One of the following statements about the regulations governing a sole trader business is correct:

a) A sole trader does not need to supply any accounting information about his or her business to anyone.

b) A sole trader must employ an accountant.

c) Sole trader businesses are exempt from completing VAT returns.

d) A sole trader must submit a tax return annually.

5.2 One of the following statements about the regulations governing limited company businesses is correct:

a) All limited companies are obliged by company law to have an annual audit.

b) A limited company must send annual accounts to all of its shareholders.

c) All shareholders have unlimited access to their company's management accounting information.

d) The general public can access information about a company only by applying in writing to the directors.

5.3 Podgorny & Weaver Limited is involved in the wholesale supply of fashion goods to retailers. The company directors have a monthly meeting to discuss strategy and to make decisions. The directors are presented with the following reports prepared by the company accountant each month:

- List of amounts owed by the retail businesses that the company supplies.

- Summary of the value of fashion goods items currently held in stock.

- Summary of the orders received during the month.

- Profit and loss account for the last month.

Explain how the directors would be able to make use of each of the reports listed in order to improve the management of the company.

5.4 A group of environmental activists is interested in the activities of Burnip Chemicals plc, a company that has been regularly fined in the past for emitting toxic waste into the river running past the factory premises. What kind of information would the activist group be seeking about the activities of the company? To what extent are the annual financial statements likely to be helpful to them?

Exercises: answers available to lecturers

5.5   One of the following statements about the regulations governing partnership businesses is correct:

a)   Partnerships are obliged to have an annual audit of their financial statements.

b)   Partnerships must prepare annual financial statements as the basis for the calculation of tax.

c)   At least one of the partners is obliged to hold a bookkeeping qualification.

d)   Each partner must submit his or her own VAT return.

5.6   Which of the following statements is correct? The stewardship function requires directors of limited companies to:

a)   Act at all times in the best interests of the company.

b)   Allow shareholders to see detailed accounting records upon request.

c)   Hold regular monthly meetings to answer shareholders' questions.

d)   Consult the shareholders over particularly difficult management decisions.

5.7   Ponderosa & Smythe plc is a shoe manufacturing business, specialising in children's shoes. The finance director has just received the following letter from a shareholder who has recently bought some shares in the company:

'Dear Mr Pershore

I have just read a most interesting article in the *Financial Times* about the decline in the market for children's shoes. The article suggests that, because of demographic changes, the market will decline by 3–4% each year over the next ten years. In the circumstances I think our company should branch out into women's shoes. I would like the directors to discuss this at the next board meeting. Could you please send me a copy of the sales budget for the coming year, so that I can see whether or not you have taken the declining market properly into account.'

What are the principal points that the finance director should make in response to this letter?

5.8   Mohsin, a bank manager, is looking at an application for a loan from Boxer Burstall Limited, a local company. The company has included a copy of its most recent annual accounts, which are for the year ending 31 December 20X6. The accounts show that a modest profit has been made in the year. It is now March 20X8.

1.   What type of information will Mohsin be looking for from the annual accounts to help him in making a decision on whether or not to lend the money?

2. How relevant is the accounting information that the company has provided to Mohsin's decision?

3. Is Mohsin entitled to request any further information?

SECTION TWO

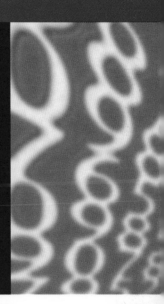

Management accounting

Introduction

This section of the book is concerned with the provision of accounting information for use within the business. Such information is used to assist managers in controlling a business and in making decisions. This type of accounting is usually known as management accounting. The eight chapters in this section of the book aim to equip students with the skills to understand management accounting information and to be able to use it to guide and manage business operations.

Chapter 6 introduces management accounting by contrasting it with financial accounting, and by observing some of its principal features. The purposes and uses of management accounting are examined in the context of a case study set in a successful business.

Chapters 7, 8 and 9 examine various aspects of planning and control within the business. Chapter 7 aims to achieve an understanding of cost components in business, while Chapter 8 examines the important process of budgeting. Chapter 9 examines standard costing systems, together with the calculation and interpretation of variances between planned and actual outcomes. These three chapters will equip a student with the knowledge and skills to both prepare and understand some of the important management accounting statements.

The following three chapters, 10 to 12 inclusive, are concerned with various aspects of decision making in business. Chapter 10 concentrates on the use of marginal costing and analysis in making a range of business decisions. The nature of cost behaviour is examined, and then the principles are applied to specific areas such as break-even analysis and decisions on, for example, whether or not to undertake certain types of contract. Chapter 11 looks at an area that is highly significant for all businesses: how to price products and services. The chapter commences with a brief introduction to the economics of supply and demand, and examines competition issues in the market. The rest of the chapter is devoted to examining the various approaches to price setting that are taken by businesses in practice. Chapter 12 examines capital investment decision making. Various methods of investment appraisal are introduced and explained, and the advantages and drawbacks of each are discussed.

Finally, Chapter 13 looks at ways in which performance is measured and reported within the firm. Reporting performance in larger firms presents particular problems, and the nature of reporting by divisions within organisations is examined. The uses of both financial and non-financial measures of performance are examined.

In Chapter 6 a Spotlight study is used as a means of explaining important principles. All of the other chapters in the section conclude with a case study that examines some of the important features that have been explained within the chapter.

@ Extra case studies

A number of additional case studies are available on the lecturers' section of the website. A case study on activity-based costing is available for use by students who have gained a good understanding of the costing principles covered in Chapter 7. A further case study (Piers) can be used once Chapter 8 on budgeting has been fully assimilated. There is an additional case study on capital investment appraisal (Ortega Ruiz plc) that can be undertaken following study of Chapter 12.

CHAPTER 6

Management and cost accounting information

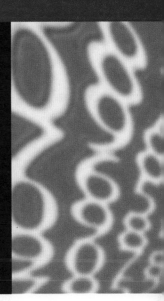

Aim of the chapter

To establish the need for accounting information geared towards users within the business, and to introduce some of the basic terminology and ideas such as planning, control and decision making.

Learning outcomes

After reading the chapter and completing the related exercises, students should:

- Appreciate the need to generate accounting information for use within the business organisation.
- Understand the range of uses for internal accounting information.
- Understand some basic terminology such as planning, control and decision making.

This is a relatively short chapter, which sets the scene for the areas considered in detail in subsequent chapters. Much of this chapter is taken up with the illustrative spotlight study that helps to explain the need for accounting information within the organisation.

Contrasting financial accounting and cost and management accounting

In Chapter 5 we briefly examined the role of financial accounting in reporting the results and position of business enterprises. As explained in that chapter, financial accounting is useful to a potentially wide range of users, including the managers and proprietors of businesses.

However, there are limitations in the usefulness of the periodic financial statements. These include:

- lack of timeliness
- orientation to past events.
- high levels of aggregation.

Lack of timeliness

It takes time to produce financial statements for external users; they may not become available until six months or so after the year-end. Most businesses produce financial statements only once a year. Taking these two factors together, it means that the most recently available financial statements may be up to 18 months out of date.

Orientation to past events

Conventional financial statements report on events in the past; they do not tend to look forward into the future, and rarely contain any element of forecast information.

High levels of aggregation

Financial reports produced for the benefits of users external to the business pull together a lot of information into relatively few descriptions and figures.

Most external users of the information (for example, creditors, customers and potential investors) have to resign themselves to these limitations. Even if they want more information, they are not usually entitled to it. Business managers are in a different position; they have the resources of the business at their disposal and consequently they have access to a great deal of potentially useful information that can be used to help them run the business.

Cost and management accounting refers to the provision of information resources that business managers can use to help run the business.

Some features of cost and management accounting

Lack of regulation

Cost and management accounting is accounting that is internal to the business only. The nature and content of financial reporting, especially for limited companies, is heavily regulated, but, by contrast, there are no regulations relating to cost and management accounting. Accounting information is generated for internal use in whatever form, and in whatever quantity, is most appropriate for the business.

Orientation towards past *and* future

We noted above that financial reporting information is oriented towards events that have already occurred. Cost and management accounting draws upon past events for information but is also oriented towards the future. It considers such questions as, for example:

- How much profit is the business likely to make next year?
- How much additional business are we likely to pick up if we lower our prices by 5%?
- Should we close down a part of the business that is making losses?
- We need a new machine in the factory. Should we buy it or lease it?
- How much does this product actually cost to produce?
- Which divisions in the business are, relatively speaking, more profitable?

Timely production

The overriding objective of the production of cost and management information is that it should be useful. Management can set up systems that produce useful information quickly. For example, in most businesses it will be useful to have monthly sales figures reported as quickly as possible. Such figures do not necessarily have to be completely accurate. Also, they do not necessarily have to be accompanied by other profit and loss information (which would probably slow up the production of information). There is no reason why simple sales figures could not be available a day or two after each month-end. Managers would thus be in a position to respond to changes in the figures very quickly, as illustrated in the following example.

Example 6.1

Duckworth Failsafe Limited produces household alarm systems in do-it-yourself installation kits. Until recently there have been two types: the Standard and the De-Luxe systems. This year, from 1 January, the company has introduced the Super-De-Luxe, which has much more sophisticated circuitry and an extra alarm box for external installation. The gross margins on the three types are 38%, 40% and 46% respectively, and the company is keen to promote sales of the higher specification products.

Each month the sales director holds a meeting with the sales force on about the fifth or sixth of the month. On 5 April 20X4 he holds a meeting at which he discusses the sales figures (in units) for January, February and March, which are as follows:

	Standard	De-Luxe	Super-De-Luxe	Total
January	2 038	1 604	213	3 855
February	2 175	1 598	344	4 117
March	2 240	1 634	28	3 902

At the meeting he asks his staff why they think that sales of the Super-De-Luxe, after a promising start in January and February, have nosedived in March. A couple of the sales reps tell him that Duckworth's principal competitor has brought out a de-luxe system that is not only cheaper than Duckworth's but which also has some extra features. 'We can't compete with it on either price or quality' says one of the reps.

The sales director now has quite a lot of information to take with him to the next main board meeting: concrete evidence in the form of the sales figures of problems with the Super-De-Luxe sales, and some reasons for the drop in sales. The information he has available does not *solve* the problem, but the rapid provision of figures has at least allowed him to *identify* that a problem exists. It is then up to the board of directors to discuss the problem and possible solutions to it.

Frequent reporting

In Example 6.1, sales of alarm systems were reported internally once a month. This is clearly a much more frequent basis of reporting than the annual financial reporting undertaken by businesses. Indeed, it is common for businesses to organise their internal management reporting on a monthly basis; monthly management accounts are produced for distribution to directors and managers. However, it is possible to produce internal cost and management information as frequently as necessary. In larger businesses some elements of internal information may be reported as frequently as once a day. For example, very large retailers are likely to produce sales figures daily for the business as a whole, for individual stores and for regions or divisions.

Cost accounting and management accounting

Both cost accounting and management accounting are referred to in the context of the production of information for internal purposes. Is there a difference between cost accounting and management accounting?

- *Management accounting* describes the process of collecting, collating and reporting information that is of use to the managers of a business for making decisions, for monitoring past performance and for making the most efficient use of resources.
- *Cost accounting* describes the process of identifying and accumulating the costs of business operations in a way that is helpful in valuing stock and in

identifying the costs and profitability of different departments or divisions of a business.

There is a considerable overlap in the terms, and indeed, they are often used interchangeably. In this book we will not attempt to demarcate the terms rigorously. 'Management accounting' will be used as a general term to cover the production and uses of information within a business. We will refer to 'cost accounting' in areas where we are specifically considering the identification and accumulating of costs. However, there is no need to be concerned about precision in the usage of either term.

The purpose and uses of management accounting

The spotlight for this chapter sets the scene for considering the principal uses of management accounting information. Through consideration of the spotlight study and the discussion of it, we will identify some of the principal uses of information prepared for internal use within a business.

SPOTLIGHT 6.1 Management accounting – pros and cons

Eight years ago Paco set up a greetings card company, Calder Calloway Cards Limited. The company buys in card designs from freelance designers and then prints, assembles and packs the cards for sale to retailers. Paco started out on a small scale; he and his brother Pedro bought up some card designs at low prices from struggling art students, printed them in runs of about 1000 and then went round card shops selling them in small quantities. The business did very well, largely due to the brothers' flair in spotting good, commercial, card designs, and their abilities as salesmen.

Initially, Paco owned 60% of the company, Pedro owned 30% and the remainder of the shares were held by other family members. However, the company gradually needed more capital to expand and the brothers sold off some of their

shares to a couple of wealthy private investors, Walter and Jennifer. Pedro, although he still owns some shares and remains as a director of Calder Calloway, has moved on to start another business in selling advertising space. The private investors do not take an active part in the management of the company, but they are both very experienced and Paco quite frequently uses them as sounding boards for new ideas. Over the last two years they have both tried to persuade Paco to hire some expert managers. About a year ago, Walter and Jennifer had a meeting with Paco which proved to be a turning point. Although Paco lost his temper and accused them of trying to ruin his business, he was eventually brought round to accepting that the company had grown too big for him to manage alone.

Jennifer: Look, Paco, you're the boss, and we're not trying to dictate to you, but the company's just too big and complex now to be run by just one person. You need some help if you're going to be able to stay on top of things.

Walter: And it *is* getting out of hand. I'm concerned to see that the gross profit margin for 20X6 has fallen yet again – that's the third year running. Just how are you planning to tackle that little problem?

During 20X7 Paco accepts the inevitable, and uses the services of a recruitment consultancy to appoint a sales director, Tracey, and a production director, Karim, both of whom have a lot of relevant experience. The first formal meeting of the new board is on 1 February 20X8, exactly a week after the two new directors took up their appointments. Paco's plan was that they would have a few days to settle into their new responsibilities and then the board would be in a position to have an effective formal meeting to discuss ideas about future plans for the company.

Both new directors have submitted details of some new ideas for consideration at the meeting. Tracey's list includes:

- Introduce a commission scheme for the sales force [who are currently on fixed salaries] based on the extent to which their actual performance exceeds budget performance.

- Concentrate sales efforts on the more profitable ranges of cards.

Karim's list includes:

- Invest in some new printing equipment. The existing equipment is out-of-date; it keeps breaking down and staff report that the printing is often of such poor quality that a lot of **work-in-progress** has to be simply thrown away.

- Employ some designers to work full-time for the company. This would help to ensure that the company had a constant stream of new designs, and would help to establish a corporate design approach, which is lacking under the present haphazard system of buying in designs.

The directors' discussion of these points proceeds as follows:

Paco: Well, this idea about the commission could work, but I don't quite see what you mean about actual performance as opposed to budget performance . . .

Tracey: I mean the sales budget in terms of the number of units you're budgeting to sell in a given period. You could break the overall number down into an expected sales volume for each person in the sales force; if he or she exceeds that they get rewarded by a commission. You can make the scheme as complex as you like, really. In one company I worked for they had a 'seller of the month' scheme. If you won it three times the company paid for a luxury weekend break . . . that kind of thing.

Paco: But we don't have a sales budget. . . . People just sell what they can . . . it's always worked that way in the past and we've done pretty well. . . .

Tracey: Well, I was wondering why I got blank looks when I asked to see the sales budget. . . . Are you telling me you don't set budgets?

Paco: This is a very successful company. We don't need to bother with a lot of extra paperwork.

Karim: Well, what about management information generally? Don't you have any management accounting systems at all?

Paco: Well, no, why would we? It would just mean employing a load of expensive beancounters. I've got no time for accountants. The bookkeeper does an excellent job and the accountant comes in to do the final accounts once a year, and keep us out of trouble with the Customs and Excise and the Inland Revenue. That's good enough for me.

Tracey: But if that's the case we really can't consider either of my suggestions, can we? I want to concentrate on selling the more profitable ranges of cards, but how am I going to find out which ones are more profitable if we don't have any information?

Paco: Er . . .

Karim: And what about production? I can't make a decision about buying a new machine unless I can compare projected costs of using the new machine with the costs of the existing set up. Please tell me, at least, that you monitor the design costs. If we're going to employ designers I need to compare the costs of employing them against the costs of buying in a lot of separate designs.

Paco: Oh, well, the annual costs are all included in the profit and loss account, you see. Here's the draft profit and loss account for 20X7 – the accountant's just finished it. He'll do a summary one to send to Companies House, but this one's really quite detailed – look, there's a figure for design costs – I'm not quite sure what's in it, but I expect it includes all the costs of paying for the designs.

Tracey: But what puzzles me is how you keep on top of what's going on in the business. How do you know what your production costs are? How can you tell if they're getting out of hand? Did you know, before Karim told you, that a lot of the production simply goes to waste?

Paco: Look, I know what you're saying. You want me to fill the place up with overpaid accountants who'll waste a lot of time and money telling me things I know already. . . . When you work in a business long enough you get a feel for what's going on. I don't need a lot of management reports to tell me that.

The meeting degenerates into a prolonged argument. Tracey and Karim try to persuade Paco that a business the size of Calder Calloway needs a sound system of management information. Paco, on the other hand, is opposed to spending

▶

(he uses the term 'wasting') money on gathering information that won't tell him anything that he doesn't already know.

What are the arguments for and against the provision of management information for a company like Calder Calloway Cards Limited? What kind of management information is required? Why is it needed?

Spotlight solution and discussion

The situation outlined in the spotlight is by no means unusual. The founder of a company who remains in control through a period of growth is often unwilling to accept that the nature of the business has changed. The approach to business management, which worked so successfully when the business was small, may not be appropriate once it has grown past a certain point. The investors, Walter and Jennifer, have managed to persuade Paco to bring in additional management expertise, but the new directors clearly face a struggle if they are to bring Paco round to their way of thinking about management information.

Tracey and Karim's point of view

In order to illustrate the need for management information in the company we will look at the four proposals made by the new directors:

1. *Introduce a commission scheme for the sales force based on the extent to which their actual performance exceeds budget performance.* A system of commission to reward the sales force can often be an effective way of motivating staff to increase sales. However, management needs to be sure that the scheme is set up in such a way that it does not cost more than the additional profit that can be generated from extra sales, and that it is fair to all staff and sets achievable targets (if the targets are too high staff are likely to be demotivated). This proposal will require a decision, based upon an informed analysis of the existing costs involved in running the sales force and upon future projected figures. Various types of commission scheme are possible, and a range of options could be considered.

2. *Concentrate sales efforts on the more profitable ranges of cards.* We know from the details in the case that the company's gross profit margin has been falling. It might make sense to concentrate on the more profitable ranges of cards, but, as Tracey points out, in order to do so the directors need to know which ranges are most profitable. There is no management information on this point, making it very difficult to plan and make realistic decisions for the future. This is a good example of the need for detailed costing information.

3. *Invest in some new printing equipment.* This is another proposal that involves a decision. There may be several possible courses of action here, and information will be needed on all of them before an informed decision can be made. The directors really need to know quite a lot about the costs of running the existing production facility; the extent and cost of the wastage that appears to be taking place; and the projected costs of alternative production facilities. Until and unless this type of information is

made available, the directors will find it impossible to reach a properly informed decision.

4. *Employ designers to work full-time for the company.* This is another proposal that involves the directors in decision making. As Karim says, they need to compare the costs of employing designers with the costs of buying in work from freelance designers. There are several aspects to this type of decision, not all of which are related to cost. For example, employing a team of designers might lead to a stronger corporate approach to design. On the other hand, the designs might become predictable and repetitive over time if they are being produced by the same team.

These proposals all involve, to a greater or lesser extent, decision making. Managers and directors of businesses need relevant information to feed into the decision-making process, so that they can make fully informed appraisals of alternative courses of action. It is quite clear that the directors of Calder Calloway do not have information to hand that will permit them to do this. Their ability to plan and to control the business is severely constrained because of the lack of management information.

In short, management information can help managers in planning, controlling and decision making.

Paco's point of view

Is there anything to be said for Paco's point of view? He does not appear to accept the need for any formalised source of management information, and thinks he can continue to run the business by instinct as he did in its early days. This is not a realistic approach.

However, Paco's views have some validity in that the cost of provision of management information is an important factor. Managers need to have enough relevant information upon which to base their decisions, but the process of providing information must, itself, be controlled. Sometimes organisations are criticised for having excessive bureaucracies and too much paperwork. Sometimes, accountants get the blame for being responsible for pushing too much paper around the organisation.

Calder Calloway, however, is an organisation that clearly lacks relevant information, and Paco should be persuaded to implement some systems that will provide what is necessary in order to plan, control and make decisions effectively.

An important final point

In their enthusiasm to get started in their new jobs and to make a positive impact on the company, both Tracey and Karim have produced lists of ideas for consideration. This is premature; they are rushing into action without considering the longer-term strategy of the business. What are the objectives of the business? What are its priorities in the mid to long term? What strategic decisions need to be made in order to achieve the objectives? These issues need to be thrashed out and decided at board level – the directors are ultimately responsible for deciding on where the business should be going. Then, and only then, is it appropriate to consider the detailed aspects such as those suggested by Tracey and Karim.

Determining business objectives

Determining the overall objectives of a business is not necessarily a straightforward process. Naturally, all businesses within an essentially capitalist system need to make a profit (eventually, and preferably sooner rather than later), and profitability is likely to be an important objective for business managers. However, there are others. Objectives could be expressed in some of the following ways:

- 'We want to be the market leader in plumbers' fittings.'
- 'This company aims to be the best travel agent in the business.'
- 'We aim to operate according to the highest ethical standards at all times.'

Let's look at a few real-life examples of what companies say about their objectives:

- *GUS plc* (formerly Great Universal Stores): 'GUS is committed to creating long-term shareholder value by focusing on businesses with above average growth potential and establishing leadership positions in its chosen markets.'
- *GlaxoSmithKline plc*: 'Our global quest is to improve the quality of human life by enabling people to do more, feel better and live longer.'
- *Pearson plc*: 'In all we do, we aim to be brave, imaginative and decent.'

Strategic decisions

Moving on a stage from the overall business objectives towards more detailed considerations, business managers need to make strategic decisions that will assist in attaining the objectives.

Examples of the type of strategic decision that needs to be made by senior management include:

- *Positioning in market*: should the business aim to go up-market or down-market in its provision of goods and services? For example, a supermarket business could aim to compete with the 'no frills' operators such as Aldi, Netto and Kwiksave, or could aim to provide expensive high margin goods in competition with Marks & Spencer.
- *Sourcing of goods*: a decision that often has to be made in business is where to locate production operations. Should they be moved overseas to locations where labour costs are lower?
- *Moving into international markets*: should a business that is based in one country's market take the risk of moving into other areas?

The management accounting process

The spotlight discussion earlier illustrated several key points about the process of management accounting, and its link with the functions of management. In this section we will summarise what we have learned so far about management and its need for information.

- *Setting business objectives*: The primary functions of management are: (a) to identify the objectives of the business; and (b) to direct the activities of the business so as to meet the objectives.
- *Assess alternatives and make decisions and make plans*: Management needs information about the alternative actions it could take. Having assessed the available information, management takes decisions and makes detailed plans for the future.
- *Monitoring outcomes*: Management uses information to assess the extent to which its plans have succeeded and its business objectives have been met.
- *Control and redefine objectives and plans*: On the basis of a comparison with planned and actual outcomes it may be necessary to redefine the overarching objectives of the business and the detailed plans that are geared towards achieving the objectives.

Management information is needed at each of these stages, to carry out the essential functions of planning, control and decision making.

Because this is not a textbook about management, we will not consider the setting of strategic objectives in the chapters that follow. We are principally concerned with accounting and finance in business and we will be looking at the provision of management accounting information to assist with planning, control and decision making.

Chapter summary

First, financial accounting and cost and management accounting were contrasted. Financial accounting is of limited usefulness as a source of management information because of factors such as:

- lack of timeliness
- orientation to past events
- high levels of aggregation.

Some of the key features of cost and management accounting were described. These include:

- lack of regulation
- orientation towards past *and* future
- timely production.

The spotlight for the chapter illustrated the need for management accounting information in a growing business. Management accounting should provide relevant information to feed into decision making, and should allow managers to plan effectively and to control the activities of the business.

Finally, the stages involved in the management accounting process were summarised. Decision making, planning and control functions are undertaken by managers as part of their primary functions of identifying and meeting the overall objectives of the business.

 The end-of-chapter exercises are divided into two sections. The first section has answers provided at the end of the book. The second section, in the white box, has answers on the lecturers' section of the website.

Website summary

The book's website contains the following material in respect of Chapter 6:

Students' section

- Quiz containing five multiple choice questions
- Two longer questions with answers.

Lecturers' section

- Answers to exercises 6.4–6.6
- Two longer questions with answers.

Exercises: answers at the end of the book

Note that because this chapter is a relatively short introduction to management accounting, there is only a limited number of end-of-chapter exercises. The intention is that the exercises should be answered in fairly general terms, drawing upon both common sense and imagination. Students have to try to think their way into the situations described in order to specify the kind of management information that would be useful. The objective behind the questions is to get students accustomed to thinking about typical decisions that have to be made in business.

If this book is being studied as part of a taught course, any of the questions that follow could be used as a basis for class discussion.

6.1 Cueline Limited manufactures furniture at factory premises held on a lease. The lease is due to end next year, but it could probably be renegotiated. The company's directors are also considering the possibility of buying freehold premises. What items of financial information would be useful to the directors in reaching a decision?

6.2 Putt plc owns several shops selling golfing and other sporting equipment. It operates principally in the area around London. The company's directors will be meeting next month to discuss a proposal for a major change in business strategy. The sales director has observed that gross margins on golf-related items are much higher than those on other stock lines, and he is proposing that the company should in future sell only golfing equipment. What items of information, financial and non-financial, are likely to be useful to the directors in assessing the pros and cons of the proposed change in strategy?

6.3 Bulstrode, Barker and Bennett is a successful firm of solicitors operating in a small town. Bulstrode died some years ago, Barker has retired, but Dexter Bennett still works in the business as senior partner. There are three junior partners, and Dexter has called a meeting of the partners to discuss the decisions they should make on the following proposals:

a) The conveyancing department is very busy. Would it make economic sense for the firm to employ another solicitor in that department?

b) The firm currently specialises in conveyancing and litigation work. The town's principal specialist in divorce work has just retired, and Bennett thinks there is an opportunity to pick up some extra business. He knows a highly experienced divorce specialist who is currently working for a large firm in London. She could be persuaded to move if she were offered a position as a junior partner.

What information are the partners likely to need (both financial and non-financial) in order to reach the right decisions on these proposals?

Exercises: answers available to lecturers

6.4   Cyclostyle Limited makes metal parts for bicycles. The metal press machine, which has been used in the business for several years, is now reaching the end of its useful life. The directors are looking at two replacement options. One is a German machine at a cost of £54 000. The other is a British machine at a cost of £38 500.

What items of information, financial and non-financial, are likely to be useful to the directors in deciding between the two machines?

6.5   Preedy Price Limited is a small fashion company run by two sisters, Anne Preedy and Amelia Price. They have been very successful in marketing a range of very exclusive and expensive knitwear through small specialist retail outlets. The company has been approached by a large retailer, Shield & Flagg plc, which would like to market a cut-price version of some of the sisters' exclusive designs. Shield and Flagg's buyer assures the sisters that this would be a very good opportunity for them to make high volume sales and to make a lot of money. She estimates that volumes of up to 35 000 garments per year are quite feasible. The maximum number of garments the sisters have produced and sold in one year to date is 5600.

Production could be handled by some of Shield & Flagg's regular knitwear production factories, or the sisters could set up their own large-scale production facilities. In order to make the launch of the new lines successful, however, stocks of around 20 000 items would have to be available in advance of the items going on sale in Shield & Flagg's 35 stores around the country.

What factors (both financial and non-financial) should the sisters take into consideration in deciding whether or not to take up this new opportunity?

6.6   Denver runs a restaurant business, operating from rented premises in the centre of a large town on the outskirts of London. His business has been relatively successful; he has succeeded in making a small profit each year, but he feels that he could do better if he expanded the business.

Denver is a sole trader and the only person with whom he can really discuss business strategy, in complete confidence, is his accountant, Dylan. He has arranged a meeting with Dylan to discuss possible future directions for the business. He starts the meeting by explaining some of the ideas he's had to improve the business:

The fundamental point is that I need to expand the number of covers. I can't do this in my current premises at Hanover Road, and I would need to move. There's a freehold building for sale on Cross Street with a restaurant on the ground floor. If I bought that I could have half as many covers again as I have now. I could sell my house and then move into the upper part of the building. That would help to keep the mortgage down to a reasonable level.

I've also been wondering about making some fairly major changes to the menu. My net profit margin, as you know from the annual accounts you've just prepared for me, is only about 6%. I would like to cut out the less profitable menu items. I think I know which ones are less profitable but I can't be sure.

As you know, I'm open six evenings a week at the moment. I'm wondering about starting weekend lunches as well, but I don't know whether I could make enough money to justify keeping the place open.

Advise Denver on the type of information – financial and non-financial – he needs in order to make decisions on the three points above (the advice can be given in fairly general terms).

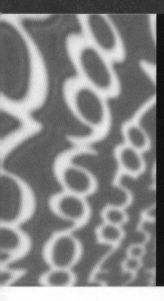

CHAPTER 7

Costing

Aim of the chapter

To achieve an understanding of some of the principal components of cost in business, and of the terminology and classifications used in costing, and to be able to apply this understanding to numerical examples.

Learning outcomes

After reading the chapter and completing the related exercises, students should:

- Recognise and understand a range of basic costing terminology.
- Be able to classify costs into direct and indirect costs.
- Understand the build-up of materials, labour and production overheads into full production cost.
- Be able to apportion costs between cost centres.
- Be able to calculate and apply suitable overhead absorption rates.
- Understand the basic principles of activity-based costing.

Costing in business

Costs are incurred in obtaining goods or services that will be used for the benefit of the business in achieving its overall objectives. Traditional costing techniques were established from the time of the Industrial Revolution onwards in the context of large manufacturing organisations. Such organisations were typically engaged in 'heavy' industrial activities, exploiting large amounts of investment in machinery and using a lot of labour.

Nowadays, of course, the nature of many industries has changed radically. More efficient production methods have focused on reducing the element of labour required in production and in using labour more efficiently. Heavy industry is no longer so economically significant (a factor that is especially noticeable in the more developed economies of the world) and recent years have seen the rapid growth of service industries. Such industries do not use capital in the form of large factories full of machinery. They rely for their economic success on exploiting ideas, employing the time and energies of creative people. This element of 'human capital' has become increasingly important in all types of industry.

Contrast, for example, a steelworks and an advertising agency. The steelworks uses physical objects in the form of fairly simple tools and machinery located in a very large space, plus physical labour, to transform iron ore via physical processes into steel. The emphasis is on *physical* transformation. The principal costs involved in such a process are the costs of raw material, the depreciation charges for the physical assets consumed and the cost of employing people to do the work.

By contrast, the advertising agency is about the transformation of mental processes and ideas. A team of creative people work together to produce ideas. The more successful of the ideas will gain a kind of physical form in due course when they are turned into newspaper and television advertisements, but the physical processing of the ideas is likely to be done by other firms and individuals outside the agency. The advertising agency itself is primarily a medium for the generation and transmission of ideas. The labour involved is not physical but mental. The principal costs involved in running an agency are the costs of paying staff salaries and benefits and providing them with computers, telephones and other communication media. There are some costs related to physical assets consumed (for example, the people have to be accommodated; they take up physical space in buildings) but these are likely to be relatively insignificant in a 'knowledge' business like an advertising agency.

In this chapter we will examine some basic features of traditional costing techniques. Many of these are related to examples in manufacturing industry where the techniques were developed. However, costing and management accounting techniques are also useful in service and knowledge-based industries. Some of the examples in this chapter and subsequent chapters in Section Two will illustrate the application of management accounting in non-manufacturing environments.

Cost classification: Direct and indirect costs

In a manufacturing environment there are three basic components of cost:

- materials cost

■ labour cost
■ production overheads.

Materials and labour cost are both direct inputs into the manufacturing process. Production overheads are indirect inputs. They are costs involved in running a production facility but which are not themselves identifiable with individual items produced. These costs are often classified as direct (direct materials, labour and any other direct expenses) and indirect (overheads). If in doubt about whether a cost is direct or indirect, ask the question: 'Can this cost be traced directly to the product?'

The following example will help to illustrate the point.

Example 7.1

The spotlight study for the previous chapter was set in a greetings card company. Think about what is involved in producing a greetings card:

1. A design is produced.
2. The design is printed on to card in a run of an appropriate size – say 1000 cards per production run.
3. The card is cut and folded.
4. Other processes such as embossing, gilding and over-printing may be required, depending upon the design.
5. The cards are matched with envelopes of suitable size.
6. Each card and envelope is individually packaged in a cellophane wrapper.

What are the direct and indirect costs involved in this process?

Direct costs

Direct materials
Materials costs include the cost of card, ink, possibly metal-leaf, envelopes and cellophane and, perhaps, a label.

Direct labour
Labour is required to set up and operate the printing machine (likely to be a computerised process, but one which will involve some input of time), to operate the machine that cuts and folds the card, and to package the card together with the envelope (this last may be a completely manual process)

Direct expense
There is another expense involved in the process: that of the card design. If this is outsourced (i.e. individual designs are bought in from freelance designers), as in the Chapter 6 example, there is a clearly defined direct expense. Suppose the company pays the designer 100 for the design under an agreement that allows it to produce 1000 cards from the design, each card bears a cost of 10p in respect of design costs.

Indirect costs

Indirect production costs (overheads)

Indirect production costs include all of those costs of running the production facility that cannot be directly identified with units of production. These would include such items as:

- factory rental
- production supervisors wages
- factory cleaning costs
- maintenance and repair of factory and machinery.

Other indirect costs (overheads)

As well as indirect costs incurred in running the production facility, there are many other costs involved in running a business, for example:

- administration salaries
- rental of the office
- depreciation of the office computer
- salespersons' salaries.

Total cost

All of the costs taken together add up to the total cost of running the business, summarised as follows:

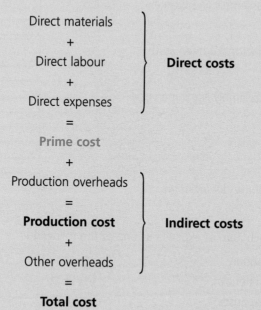

Direct materials
+
Direct labour   } **Direct costs**
+
Direct expenses
=
Prime cost
+
Production overheads
=
Production cost } **Indirect costs**
+
Other overheads
=
Total cost

Note that the terms 'indirect costs' and 'overheads' mean the same thing. Either term can be used.

? **Self-test question 7.1** (answer at the end of the book)

Beeching Plumstead Limited has a factory which produces babies' pushchairs. The following is a list of some of the costs which the company incurs:

Canvas material

Metal spokes for wheels

Spare parts for sewing machine repairs

Advertising expenditure

Machine oil

Electricity bill for factory

Wages of assembly line workers

Wages of factory canteen staff

Wages of assembly line supervisor

Secretary's salary

Delivery vehicle depreciation

Classify each item of expense as one of the following:

- direct labour
- direct materials
- direct expenses
- indirect production overheads
- other indirect overheads.

In the next example, we will fit some figures into the structure.

Example 7.2

Julienne Jack Limited is a company that produces socks from a small rented factory space. In the month ending 31 August 20X4 it incurs the following costs:

	£
Depreciation of knitting machines	420
Knitting machine repair	68
Machine operators' wages	6 330
Wool	4 850
Sticky labels for socks	93
Plastic ties for sock pairing	133
Factory rental	1 230
Electricity costs – factory	216
Electricity costs – office	38
Part-time secretary's wages	540
Office stationery and supplies	21
Factory cleaner's wages	123
Telephone – office	83
Delivery costs	436
Other office costs	214
Other factory costs	130

Rearrange the information given above into a cost statement for August 20X4.

Julienne Jack Limited: Cost statement for the month ending 31 August 20X4

	£	£
Direct materials		
Wool	4 850	
Sticky labels for socks	93	
Plastic ties for sock pairing	133	
		5 076
Direct labour – machine operators' wages		6 330
Prime cost		11 406
Production overheads		
Depreciation of knitting machines	420	
Knitting machine repair	68	
Factory rental	1 230	
Electricity costs – factory	216	
Factory cleaner's wages	123	
Other factory costs	130	
		2 187
Production cost		13 593
Other overheads		
Electricity costs – office	38	
Part-time secretary's wages	540	
Office stationery and supplies	21	
Telephone – office	83	
Delivery costs	436	
Other office costs	214	
		1 332
Total costs		14 925

Cost classification: Product and period costs

Another way of looking at costs is to classify them as product or period costs.

- Product costs are those related to production of goods or services for sale by the business. Using the terminology we have already established, product costs include direct and indirect production costs.
- Period costs are those costs that are incurred in the period of account for example, salaries of sales and marketing personnel.

Note that the principle of accruals or matching operates in management accounting, just as in financial accounting. For example, cost of sales used in management accounting must be adjusted for opening and closing stock. In a manufacturing business, this means bringing forward opening stock and carrying forward closing stock, both valued at production cost. Next we will consider product costs in more detail.

Costing of products and services

In order to keep track of costs, to be able to plan and control business activity and to be able to value work in progress and finished goods stock, it is usually necessary, especially in manufacturing industries, to allocate costs to products. Work-in-progress and finished goods stock are carried forward to the next accounting period at production cost (i.e. including materials, direct labour and production overheads costs). This accumulation of costs is known as absorption costing.

Where the cost information relates to a single piece of work chargeable to one client the accumulation of costs may help in establishing the price at which the goods or services are to be invoiced. In costing terminology this is known as job costing.

Often in manufacturing industries goods of a generic type are produced to replenish general stocks of finished goods. Costing information is gathered for each type of product manufactured. In costing terminology this is known as product costing.

Sometimes in manufacturing industries it is appropriate to produce goods in batches or production runs of convenient sizes. Costs are allocated to each batch or run. In costing terminology this is known as batch costing.

All product and service costing involves the allocation of costs to cost units. A cost unit is an item of production or a group of products or a service for which it is useful to have product cost information. Three examples of cost units follow, each illustrating a different type of costing method.

| **Example 7.3** | Gulam, a conveyancing solicitor, spends time on work for various different clients in the course of a day. Each piece of work for a client represents a cost unit. For example, Gulam's client, Maisie, is moving house and is also selling a commercial |

property. Each of these two matters represents a cost unit. Each of the matters Gulam deals with has its own unique code; for example, Maisie's house move is coded 0376 and her commercial property sale is coded 0375. During the day Gulam keeps a time record of each unit of five minutes that he spends on each matter. On a particular day, extracts from his time records look like this:

Name: Gulam		**Date**: 14 October 20X4	
Time	*Time units*	*Client and code*	*Details*
2.05–2.15	2	Maisie 0376	Phone call to discuss possible completion dates
2.15–2.30	3	Bryan 0412	Dictate letter re Land Registry search
2.30–2.40	2	Maisie 0375	Dictate letter to commercial agents

This form serves as a computer input document. At the end of the day, all the solicitors in Gulam's firm submit their time sheets, and the details are input to the computer system. In respect of the day recorded above, two time units of five minutes each will be logged to each of Maisie's file codes. The time is costed by the computer at Gulam's charge-out rate – so, if his charge-out rate is £60 per hour, each file will receive a charge of £10 (i.e. 10 minutes at £1 per minute) in respect of the solicitor's time spent on 14 October 20X4. Other types of cost will be logged against the codes; for example, the cost of Land Registry searches and similar fees.

Once the conveyancing is successfully concluded Gulam will be able to generate an invoice to send to Maisie from the information that is logged on the computer.

This example illustrates job costing applied to a service environment.

Example 7.4

Peirce Waterworth Limited manufactures a range of components for the motor industry. The company keeps a constant stock of its 100 or so most popular lines so that it can respond immediately to orders. For example, once stocks of component XL046, an air filter, fall to 50 units, production is scheduled to replenish the stocks of the component. The input of materials is logged, and the number of hours and minutes that people spend operating the machines. These are charged to production of the XL046 and the stock value is built up by successive inputs of materials, labour and overheads.

This example illustrates product costing.

Example 7.5

In the example of the greeting cards company used earlier (see Example 7.1), a production run of 1000 cards was assumed. This is likely to be quite a reasonable size for a cost unit. Treating each individual card as a cost unit would involve a pointlessly detailed set of calculations. Given that the 1000 cards are identical and are all produced in one run, the cost unit in this case will be the run of 1000 cards. Having established the costs for the cost unit, the cost of an individual card is easily calculated by dividing total costs by 1000.

This example illustrates **batch costing**.

In the next three sections of the chapter we will examine the allocation of the three broad areas of cost – materials, labour and production overhead – to cost units. This is illustrated in the context of a manufacturing environment.

What follows may appear complicated. Students should try to bear in mind the overall objective of identifying the materials, labour and production overhead components of a cost unit.

Materials costs

Raw materials are bought in and a stock maintained as necessary in order to ensure that shortages, which would slow up production, do not occur. Direct materials are issued to production in appropriate quantities and the cost is allocated to the appropriate cost unit.

How do we establish the cost of raw materials transferred into production? The answer to this question is not, perhaps, as straightforward as it seems, especially where there is a fairly large volume of identical items moving in and out of stock, and where prices are changing. Businesses usually employ one of three principal valuation conventions in dealing with this matter: first in, first out; last in, first out; and weighted average cost.

- *First in, first out (FIFO).* This convention assumes that the items that have been in stock the longest are the first to move out into production. (Note that this is a theoretical assumption for valuation purposes only – it may not be borne out by the actual physical movements in stock.)
- *Last in, first out (LIFO).* This convention assumes that the items that have come into stock most recently are the first to move out into production. (Note that this is a theoretical assumption for valuation purposes only – it may not be borne out by the actual physical movements in stock.)
- *Weighted average cost (AVCO).* Under this convention the value of each individual item of stock is a weighted average of the value of all items in stock.

In practice in the UK, FIFO and AVCO are widely used. LIFO tends not to be used because it is an approach to valuation that is not approved by the accounting standards in the UK (although it is approved in some other parts of the world).

| Example 7.6 | Potts Pilchard Limited runs a business manufacturing pencils. These are placed in presentation boxes that hold 48 pencils. The boxes are purchased from the same |

supplier in batches of between 100 and 200. The stock record for February 20X3 shows the following details of deliveries into stock and transfers to production:

Date	Deliveries into stock
3 February	120 units purchased at £1.50 each
18 February	160 units purchased at £1.55 each

Date	Transfers to production
6 February	95 units
21 February	80 units
26 February	70 units

Stock at 1 February was 25 units which cost £1.50 each. Examining each of the three approaches to valuation in turn:

First in, first out (FIFO)

Date	Deliveries into stock Units	£	£	Transfers to production Units	£	£	Balance Units	£
1 Feb							25	37.50
3 Feb	120	1.50	180.00				145	217.50
6 Feb				95	1.50	142.50	50	75.00
18 Feb	160	1.55	248.00				210	323.00
21 Feb				50	1.50	75.00	160	248.00
				30	1.55	46.50	130	201.50
26 Feb				70	1.55	108.50	60	93.00
Cost of transfers to production						372.50		

At the end of the month the closing balance of stock is 60 units. Because of the assumption that the first items to enter stock are the first to leave it, closing stock is valued on the basis of the latest price at which stock was purchased (in this case £1.55).

Last in, first out (LIFO)

Date	Deliveries into stock Units	£	£	Transfers to production Units	£	£	Balance Units	£
1 Feb							25	37.50
3 Feb	120	1.50	180.00				145	217.50
6 Feb				95	1.50	142.50	50	75.00
18 Feb	160	1.55	248.00				210	323.00
21 Feb				80	1.55	124.00	130	199.00
26 Feb				70	1.55	108.50	60	90.50
Cost of transfers to production						375.00		

At the end of the month the closing balance of stock is 60 units (just as before). Because of the assumption that transfers to production are always of the most recently arrived stock, closing stock is valued on the basis of the earlier prices at which stock was purchased. Note that where prices are rising (as in this case) LIFO gives a comparatively lower closing stock value.

Weighted average cost (AVCO)

	Deliveries into stock			Transfers to production			Balance		
								AVCO	
Date	Units	£	£	Units	£	£	Units	£	£
1 Feb							25	1.50	37.50
3 Feb	120	1.50	180.00				145	1.50	217.50
6 Feb				95	1.50	142.50	50	1.50	75.00
18 Feb	160	1.55	248.00				210	1.538	323.00
21 Feb				80	1.538	123.05	130	1.538	199.95
26 Feb				70	1.538	107.67	60	1.538	92.28
Cost of transfers to production						373.22			

At the end of the month the closing balance of stock is 60 units (as before), but the closing stock valuation is £92.28. It is usual to find that the AVCO value lies somewhere between the FIFO and LIFO value.

Summary

Method	Transfers to production £	Closing stock £	Total £
FIFO	372.50	93.00	465.50
LIFO	375.00	90.50	465.50
AVCO	373.22	92.28	465.50

Note that the total cost involved is identical in each case. What differs between the methods is the allocation of the total cost incurred between transfers to production and closing stock.

Why does the method of stock valuation matter? Remember the basic formula for cost of sales:

Opening stock
Add: purchases
Less: closing stock

If opening or closing stock values change, cost of sales changes, and so do the figures for gross or net profit. In a time of rising prices FIFO produces a higher profit figure than LIFO.

? **Self-test question 7.2** (answer at the end of the book)

Bryanston Buckley Limited is a manufacturing company. It buys in stocks of a component, X, which it uses in production. Stocks of component X at 1 March 20X6 were 55 units at £3 each. The following movements in stock took place in March: (a) on 10 March 160 units of X were purchased for £3.20 each; (b) 35 units of X were transferred to production on 12 March, and a further 70 were transferred to production on 25 March.

What is the closing stock value calculated under each of the following conventions?

a) FIFO

b) LIFO

c) AVCO.

Labour costs

Earlier, in Example 7.3, we looked at the case of a solicitor booking his time to various different jobs. In a production costing process, direct labour time must also be booked to the production process. This is often a quite elaborate procedure involving careful observation and record-keeping. A production operative may work on a range of different cost units during a day, and a method must be found of ensuring that the work is accurately booked. If errors are made product costs will be misstated and incorrect decisions may result.

The following are some of the complexities that may arise in respect of the identification and allocation of direct labour:

- *Employee performs a combination of direct and indirect labour tasks*. An employee may spend part of his or her time on a production line engaged in specific aspects of production that can be allocated to cost units. However, in addition he or she may have more general tasks, such as cleaning machinery, sweeping up, engaging in routine maintenance and so on. Therefore, it may be necessary to allocate time between direct and indirect labour tasks.
- *Variation in methods of payment*. There are several ways of paying employees. Usually there is a basic rate element, but in addition there may be special payments for working overtime or unsocial hours. Sometimes, for example in garment production, direct labour employees are paid piece rates for work (a fixed amount, say, for each shirt sewn); in addition they may be paid a bonus for achieving a particularly high level of output.
- *Idle or non-productive time*. If a machine breaks down or there is some other kind of hitch in the production process employees may not be able to be employed in productive activity. This is sometimes known as idle time. Employees are entitled to be paid for the time, but how should it be treated?

It is often the case that the management accountant takes into account all of the complexities of labour costs, averages them, and produces an hourly rate for each grade of labour, which can then be applied to all direct labour time spent in production.

Example 7.7

This example demonstrates the allocation of direct material and labour costs to a particular job (remember the job costing method described earlier in the chapter).

Barker and Clyde Limited produce machine parts for the airline industry. They have an order from an aircraft manufacturer for 150 units of component BYA570. This work is assigned job code V477848. This involves the following transfers from stores:

650 kg of material V, valued at AVCO, which is currently £3.60 per kilo
125 kg of material G, valued at AVCO which is currently £5.50 per kilo.

Three grades of direct labour are involved:

Grade 7, which is to be recorded at the rate of £5.50 per hour
Grade 13, recorded at the rate of £7.60 per hour
Grade 14, recorded at the rate of £7.80 per hour.

The cost accountant collects information about direct labour time spent from the factory and summarises it on to computer input forms, which identify the job codes, labour grade and hours spent.

When the job is completed the computer record shows the following summary for prime cost:

Job No: V477848; Date: 12.11.X3 Component No: BYA 570; Supervisor: Ashton;

Quantity: 150 units

	£	£
Direct material		
Material V (650kg × £3.60)	2 340.00	
Material G (125kg × £5.50)	687.50	
		3 027.50
Direct labour		
Grade 7: 26.5 hours booked @ £5.50 per hour	145.75	
Grade 13: 12 hours booked @ £7.60 per hour	91.20	
Grade 14: 3.75 hours @ £7.80 per hour	29.25	
		266.20
Prime cost		3 293.70

This information allows us to calculate prime cost per component:

$$\frac{£3\ 293.70}{150} = £21.97$$

? **Self-test question 7.3** (answer at the end of the book)

Harvey & Cork Limited produces photograph frames in batches of 500. The following materials and labour are booked to batch number 30453A:

■ 100 kg of metal @ £4.50 per kilo

- Paint: 2 litres of blue @ £6.80 per litre
- Glass: 500 pieces at 30p each
- 22 hours of direct labour at A grade (charged at £4.80 per hour)
- 19 hours of direct labour at B grade (charged at £6.00 per hour).

Prepare a batch costing record to show the prime cost of batch no. 30453A. What is the cost per picture frame?

Production overheads

Allocation of production overheads is one of the most difficult problems for the management accountant. Production overheads are part of the overall production cost, and it is usually necessary to allocate them in order to produce useful information for management and for stock valuation. However, as we have seen, they are not directly identifiable with cost units. Where production goes through several stages, the first step in dealing with production overheads is usually to allocate them to cost centres.

Allocation to cost centres

Often, production is organised methodically into cost centres to which costs can be allocated. Cost centres are functions or areas into which costs can be organised.

Example 7.8

Choremaster Limited produces industrial cleaning machines. There are three distinct stages in the production process:

metal machining
brush fitting
paint and finishing.

The metal machining shop has its own full-time production supervisor. The other production supervisor employed by the company splits her time in a 60:40 ratio between the brush fitting shop and the paint and finishing shop. The cost of employing each supervisor, including benefits and employer's National Insurance, is £17 360 per annum. (Note that production supervisors' salaries are part of the company's indirect production overheads.)

What is the allocation of supervisors' salaries to each of the three production areas?

	£
Metal machining	17 360
Brush fitting (60% × £17 360)	10 416
Paint and finishing (40% × £17 360)	6 944

Apportionment to cost centres

In Example 7.8 the indirect cost of supervisors salary could be allocated because precise information was available about the use of the supervisors' time. Where indirect costs cannot be allocated, they must be apportioned. Cost apportionment often involves some fairly arbitrary decisions about the split of costs between cost centres.

We will expand the Choremaster Limited example to illustrate what is involved in cost apportionment.

Example 7.9

Choremaster Limited incurs the following indirect production overheads in the year ending 31 December 20X7:

	£
Factory rent	33 970
Production supervisors' salaries	34 720
Canteen costs	13 440
Cleaning and other indirect labour	8 885
Factory rates	12 480
Insurance	8 760
Electricity – factory	10 770
Building maintenance	2 490
Machine maintenance and repair	3 423
Depreciation of machinery	12 220
Depreciation of canteen fixtures and fittings	1 792
Total	142 950

The indirect production overheads have to be apportioned between the three production areas: metal machining, brush fitting and paint and finishing.

Usually, different methods of apportionment are used depending upon the nature of the cost. Some common approaches to apportionment are listed below:

Type of cost	Typical method of apportionment
Factory rent, rates, insurance, building maintenance, electricity, indirect labour and cleaning	Floor area
Depreciation of machinery	Machinery value
Canteen costs	Number of employees
Machinery maintenance and repair	Number of call-outs
Production supervisors' salaries	Number of employees

It is important to note that these methods of apportionment do not constitute precise rules. Much depends upon the nature of the expense and the amount of detail that can be collected about how it is incurred. In the case of Choremaster Limited, for example, we know that the production supervisors' salaries can be allocated neatly across the three departments. In other companies, it might not be possible to make such an allocation, and a basis of apportionment (such as number of employees, as suggested in the table above) would be more appropriate.

We need some further information in order to be able to apportion Choremasters costs. This is given in the table below:

	Total	Metal machining	Brush fitting	Paint and finishing
		Cost centre		
Floor area (sq metres)	10 000	6 000	2 000	2 000
Number of employees	28	17	6	5
Machinery value	122 200	103 000	8 400	10 800
Maintenance & repair call-outs	7	6	0	1

We can now apportion costs to each cost centre, as follows. Factory rent is apportioned to each cost centre on the basis of floor area. For example, the part of cost to be apportioned to the metal machining cost centre is:

$$\frac{6\ 000}{10\ 000} \times £33\ 970 = £20\ 382$$

Brush fitting:

$$\frac{2\ 000}{10\ 000} \times £33\ 970 = £6\ 794$$

Paint and finishing:

$$\frac{2\ 000}{10\ 000} \times £33\ 970 = £6\ 794$$

(Note that £20 382 + £6 794 + £6 794 = £33 970, i.e. all of the cost is apportioned.)

We can use the same approach to apportioning all the other costs

		Total	Metal machining	Brush fitting	Paint and finishing
			Cost centre		
	Basis	£	£	£	£
Factory rent	Floor area	33 970	20 382	6 794	6 794
Production supervisors' salaries	Actual	34 720	17 360	10 416	6 944
Canteen costs	Employees	13 440	8 160	2 880	2 400
Cleaning and other indirect labour	Floor area	8 885	5 331	1 777	1 777

	Basis	£	£	£	£
Factory rates	Floor area	12 480	7 488	2 496	2 496
Insurance	Floor area	8 760	5 256	1 752	1 752
Electricity – factory	Floor area	10 770	6 462	2 154	2 154
Building maintenance	Floor area	2 490	1 494	498	498
Machine maintenance and repair	Call outs	3 423	2 934	—	489
Depreciation of machinery	Machinery value	12 220	10 300	840	1 080
Depreciation – canteen	Employees	1 792	1 088	384	320
Totals		142 950	86 255	29 991	26 704

Self-test question 7.4 (answer at the end of the book)

Swift Metals Limited produces machine parts. Its factory space is divided into three areas: preparation, tooling and finishing. These three functional areas are used as cost centres. Swift's management accountant has asked you to prepare a schedule showing the apportionment of the company's production overheads between the three cost centres for the year ending 31 December 20X4.

The production overhead totals are as follows:

	£
Factory costs (rental, insurance, cleaning etc.)	700 000
Canteen costs	18 496
Machinery depreciation	17 650
Machinery maintenance and repair	2 961
Supervisory salaries	23 358
Total	762 465

- Factory costs are to be apportioned on the basis of floor area.
- Canteen costs and supervisory salaries are to be apportioned on the basis of number of employees.
- Machinery depreciation is to be apportioned on the basis of the net book value of machinery used in each cost centre.
- Machinery maintenance and repair is to be apportioned on the basis of the number of call-outs.

Relevant data is included in the following table:

| | Total | Cost centre | | |
		Preparation	Tooling	Finishing
Floor area (square metres)	20 000	7 000	9 000	4 000
Number of employees	34	16	12	6
Machinery value	176 500	26 000	112 000	38 500
Maintenance & repair call-outs	9	2	6	1

Prepare the overhead apportionment schedule for the management accountant.

Overhead absorption

In the previous section of this chapter we examined the allocation and apportionment of costs to cost centres. This allows us to say, for example, that overheads of £29 991 were allocated to Choremasters brush fitting cost centre, but we are no closer to identifying the total production overhead cost of an individual cost unit.

We need to find some way of transferring overhead costs to cost units. Traditionally, the way this has been done in manufacturing industries is via **overhead absorption**, a method of allocating an appropriate portion of production overheads to cost units. A logical way of doing this might be on the basis of the number of units of production. Suppose that Choremaster Limited produces 5400 cleaning machines in the period during which it incurred total production overheads of £142 950. The total production overhead attributable to each cleaning machine could then be calculated as:

$$\frac{£142\,950}{5\,400} = 26.47 \text{ (to nearest penny)}$$

So £26.47 becomes the **overhead absorption rate** applied to each machine in respect of production overhead. It would be added to the materials and direct labour costs for each cleaning machine to arrive at a total production cost per machine. Note that this is a 'blanket' overhead rate; it is appropriate where a business produces only one product. Where there is more than one product the overhead absorption procedures become more complicated.

In this example, the information could only be calculated accurately once the accounting period was over and total costs could be summed and allocated to cost centres. Management accounting information, as we have seen, needs to be produced very quickly in order to be useful, and a retrospective exercise in overhead absorption is not likely to be very helpful. For this reason, overhead absorption is done in practice on the basis of figures budgeted in advance; a budgeted overhead absorption rate is calculated and then applied to production. (Note that we will examine budgeting in more detail in the next chapter.)

The next example will demonstrate some of the techniques involved in calculating overhead absorption rates and will examine three possible approaches to overhead absorption: number of units of production; machine hours; and labour hours.

Example 7.10

Rutland Stamp Limited produces large metal storage containers in one size only. The production process involves three stages:

1. *Cutting department*: large metal sheets are cut into standard sizes, and are shaped and drilled.
2. *Assembly department*: the standard pieces are attached together by screwing and welding.
3. *Painting and finishing*: the containers are smoothed down and spray painted.

Each department is treated as a cost centre.

The management accountant is working out appropriate overhead absorption rates for the next financial year (the year to 31 December 20X7). She estimates that total production overheads will be £136 000, allocated as follows between the cost centres:

	£
Cutting	£56 000
Assembly	£48 000
Painting and finishing	£32 000

Total production in units for 20X7 is estimated at 16 000 containers. The management accountant has also worked out budgeted materials and labour costs per container, as follows:

Prime cost of container	£
Direct materials (metal, fixings, paint)	15.50
Direct labour	
Cutting: 10 minutes (@ £6 per hour)	1.00
Assembly: 1 hour 30 minutes (@ £6 per hour)	9.00
Painting and finishing: 20 minutes (@ £4.50 per hour)	1.50
Total prime cost	27.00

Note that the cutting department processes are mostly mechanised; there is a relatively low input of labour. Assembly processes, by contrast, are mostly manual. The extent to which processes are labour intensive influences the choice of overhead absorption method, as we will now see.

The management accountant now needs to work out an overhead absorption rate to be applied to each of the three cost centres. She will use three different rates, one for each department, and each worked out on a different basis.

Cutting department: Overhead rate per machine hour

Where manufacturing processes depend more upon machines than upon labour input, it is usually most appropriate to work out an overhead absorption rate based upon machine hours available. The number of machine hours is estimated by reference to factory working hours and number of machines. For example, in this case, suppose that the accountant estimates that a total of 16 000 hours of machine time will be available over the next year. The cutting department overhead for the year is estimated at £56 000. The estimated overhead absorption rate for the cutting department for 20X7 will therefore be:

$$\frac{56\ 000}{16\ 000} = £3.50 \text{ per machine hour}$$

For every machine hour used in production £3.50 will be charged in production overheads.

How many machine hours will be used to produce one container? Assuming that all of the available machine hours (16 000) are required to produce 16 000 containers, each cost unit uses up 1 machine hour, and therefore £3.50 will be included in the production cost of a container.

Assembly department: Overhead rate per labour hour

In this department the manufacturing processes are labour intensive. The accountant estimates that 24 000 direct labour hours will be used in this department in 20X7. The assembly cost centre overhead for the year is estimated at £48 000. The estimated overhead absorption rate for the assembly department for 20X7 will therefore be:

$$\frac{48\ 000}{24\ 000} = £2.00 \text{ per labour hour}$$

How many assembly labour hours will be used to produce one container? Each container requires 1 hour 30 minutes in labour time. Therefore 16 000 containers would therefore require 24 000 hours (which just happens to be the number of direct labour hours available in this department). The overhead to be absorbed in respect of assembly for each cost unit will be 1.5 × £2.00 – i.e. £3.00.

Painting and finishing: Rate per unit of production

The painting and finishing cost centre overhead for 20X7 is estimated at £32 000. This will be spread over an estimated 16 000 units of production (cost units). The estimated overhead absorption rate for the assembly department for 20X7 will therefore be:

$$\frac{32\ 000}{16\ 000} = £2.00 \text{ per unit}$$

Finally, we will work out an estimated total production cost per unit, as follows:

Production cost of container	£	£
Direct materials (metal, fixings, paint)		15.50
Labour:		
Cutting: 10 minutes (@ £6 per hour)	1.00	
Assembly: 1 hour 30 minutes (@ £6 per hour)	9.00	
Painting and finishing: 20 minutes (@ £4.50 per hour)	1.50	
		11.50
Production overhead		
Cutting	3.50	
Assembly	3.00	
Painting and finishing	2.00	
		8.50
Total production cost		35.50

Overhead absorption rates: Some other approaches

The example of Rutland Stamp Limited demonstrated the use of three different approaches to calculating overhead absorption rates: rate per unit, rate per machine hour and rate per labour hour. There are some other possibilities.

Percentage of direct labour

The overhead absorption rate would be calculated as follows:

$$\frac{\text{Production overheads}}{\text{Direct labour cost}} \times 100$$

The next example explains how the overhead absorption rate is calculated and applied on this basis.

Example 7.11

Suppose that the fabrications cost centre of Millom Sunter Limited uses two grades of direct labour. Grade A is paid at £6.70 per hour and Grade B is paid at £5.90 per hour. The production estimates for the 20X8 accounting year require 30 000 hours of Grade A and 28 000 hours of Grade B labour. The management accountant has already carried out an allocation and apportionment exercise, which resulted in estimated production overheads of £208 000 for the fabrications cost centre in 20X8. What is the overhead absorption rate to be used for fabrications? Direct labour equals:

Grade A: 30 000 hours × £6.70 = 201 000
Grade B: 28 000 hours × £5.90 = 165 200
366 200

Overhead absorption rate for fabrications:

$$\frac{\text{Total budget production overheads}}{\text{Direct labour cost}} \times 100 = \frac{208\ 000}{366\ 200} \times 100 = 56.8\%$$

(to one decimal place)

So, 56.8% of the direct labour charge for any batch, job or cost unit will be added to represent production overheads.

Taking the example a little further, Millom Sunter Limited manufactures components for the shipbuilding industry on a job costing basis. The job cost card for an order of 120 units of component 177Z2A is as follows:

Component No: 177Z2A; Quantity: 120 units	£	£
Direct materials		370.00
Direct labour		
Grade A: 25 hours @ £6.70	167.50	
Grade B: 39 hours @ £5.90	230.10	
		397.60
Prime cost		767.60
Production overheads		
56.8% × direct labour cost = 56.8% × 397.60		225.84
Total production cost		993.44

Percentage of direct materials cost

This approach to overhead absorption works in the same way as the percentage of direct labour cost. An overhead absorption rate is worked out in advance by using budget figures. Production overheads for an individual job, batch or product are then calculated by reference to the input of materials cost.

Both this method and the percentage of direct labour cost method can be particularly useful where a range of different products is made. It must be recognised, however, that there are no fixed rules about which method to use. The ultimate test to be applied to all management accounting information is whether or not it is useful in managing the firm. Management should use the methods and techniques that they find most efficient and effective in achieving the overall objectives of the business.

Many new techniques and ideas have been explored in this chapter. The case study at the end of the chapter brings together some of the key features of the material covered.

Activity-based costing (ABC)

As discussed at the beginning of this chapter, very significant changes have taken place in the business environment since the Industrial Revolution. Manufacturing industry has become relatively less important in the developed world, with service industries playing a correspondingly more significant part in economic development.

Traditional absorption costing techniques (which have been the subject of most of this chapter) are based upon a model of industry where the principal costs were associated with the employment of direct labour hours and/or machine hours. However, as industrial processes have become increasingly mechanised the prime importance of direct labour hours has been correspondingly reduced. Machine-based processes have, themselves, often become streamlined and more efficient, using less energy and other types of resource. There has been a consequent reduction in the input of machine hours in many types of process. At the same time, the relative importance of indirect overheads in many businesses' cost structures has tended to grow. So, increasing amounts of indirect overhead have been allocated to shrinking numbers of machine hours or direct labour hours. This results in questionable allocations of costs – if the overhead absorption rate is £60 per direct labour hour (not an unreasonable scenario, in practice), then every additional minute spent on the production of a cost unit will result in the burden of £1 extra in overhead allocation.

During the 1980s firms began to experiment with alternative approaches to costing. A very important alternative to traditional absorption costing has emerged – activity-based costing (ABC) – the adoption of which has been gradually spreading throughout the world. The basic principle of ABC is that cost units should bear the cost of the activities they cause. Costs are driven by activities that take place in the business environment – activities which include, for example:

- ordering materials
- storing materials
- setting up production runs
- testing the quality of production
- organising production.

The next example illustrates ABC by contrasting it with traditional absorption costing.

Example 7.12

Sallis Weller Limited produces two products: product X and product Y. Until now, it has adopted traditional absorption costing techniques, transferring overheads to production via an overhead absorption rate based on direct labour hours. The company's managing director has recently read an article about ABC, a revolutionary costing technique. He asks the finance director to organise a comparison by applying ABC alongside normal absorption costing for a month.

Using absorption costing

During November 20X6 the company produces 2000 units each of product X and product Y, and incurs the following indirect production overhead costs:

	£
Factory cleaning	2 000
Power	16 000
Factory rental	23 000
Factory insurance	5 000
Supervisory salaries	12 000
Canteen charges	3 000
Machinery depreciation	21 000
Machinery maintenance	5 000
Production consumables	6 000
Other indirect labour costs	12 000
Other factory costs	8 000
Total	113 000

Total direct labour hours for the month are 5000, resulting in an overhead absorption rate of:

$$\frac{113\ 000}{5\ 000} = £22.60$$

Relevant details for the two products are as follows

	Product X	Product Y
Hours of direct labour (per unit)	1	1.5
	£	£
Direct materials (per unit)	17.50	12.00
Direct labour (per unit)	7.00	10.50
Prime cost	24.50	22.50
Overhead		
1 direct labour hour × £22.60	22.60	
1.5 direct labour hours × £22.60		33.90
Production cost per unit	47.10	56.40

Using ABC

ABC involves the identification of key activities and their drivers. The finance director carefully examines the activity bases of the factory operations and establishes five basic activities that take place:

machining
finishing
materials ordering
materials issue to production
scheduling, control and quality testing of production.

The fundamental cost driver for each activity, together with quantities, is established as follows:

Activity	Cost driver	Total	Product X	Product Y	£
Machining	Machine hours	3 000	2 000	1 000	45 000
Finishing	Direct labour hours	5 000	2 000	3 000	25 000
Materials ordering	Number of orders placed	25	16	9	4 000
Materials issue to production	Number of materials issues made	75	47	28	12 000
Scheduling etc	Number of production runs	36	22	14	27 000
					113 000

This table shows that the production of X involves more activity in several respects than that of Y. Materials ordering appears more complicated (more orders have to be placed) and the number of production runs is far greater.

The final column of the table shows the results of the finance director's reclassification of the total of £113 000 indirect production overheads for the month. The individual items for rental, insurance, supervision, etc. have been apportioned between the five activities.

At this stage, all the information is in place to allocate overheads to each of the products by activity. An amount of cost per unit of cost driver can be calculated as follows:

Activity				Cost amount
Machining	$\dfrac{\text{Overhead}}{\text{Machine hours}}$	$=$	$\dfrac{45\ 000}{3\ 000}$	$= £15$ per machine hour

$$\text{Finishing} \quad \frac{\text{Overhead}}{\text{Direct labour hours}} = \frac{25\ 000}{5\ 000} = £5 \text{ per labour hour}$$

$$\text{Materials ordering} \quad \frac{\text{Overhead}}{\text{Materials orders}} = \frac{4\ 000}{25} = £160 \text{ per order}$$

$$\text{Materials handling} \quad \frac{\text{Overhead}}{\text{Issues to production}} = \frac{12\ 000}{75} = £160 \text{ per issue}$$

$$\text{Scheduling etc.} \quad \frac{\text{Overhead}}{\text{Production runs}} = \frac{27\ 000}{36} = £750 \text{ per run}$$

Then the overhead is allocated between products X and Y:

	Product X	£	Product Y	£
Machining	2 000 × £15	30 000	1 000 × £15	15 000
Finishing	2 000 × £5	10 000	3 000 × £5	15 000
Materials ordering	16 × £160	2 560	9 × £160	1 440
Materials handling	47 × £160	7 520	28 × £160	4 480
Scheduling etc.	22 × £750	16 500	14 × £750	10 500
Total		66 580		46 420

Per unit	66 580/2 000	33.29	46 420/2 000	23.21
Prime cost per unit (as before)		24.50		22.50
Production cost per unit ABC		57.79		45.71
Production cost per unit – traditional		47.10		56.40

The example illustrates the very large differences that can emerge when costing under the traditional method is compared with ABC. In this example, product Y appeared to cost more under the traditional method than product X. Following the application of ABC the positions reverse. Traditional methods of allocation ignore the detail of the activities that actually take place on the factory floor. Where production processes are more cumbersome because of, for example, the necessity for more frequent ordering of materials, such factors should be taken into account in costing.

It is argued that the application of ABC results in significant improvement in the quality of information obtained from the costing system, and consequently, in better control and planning of activities. However, as even this relatively straightforward example has shown, it is a system of considerable complexity. A great deal of information has to be collected and administered, and the system is costly to implement.

Chapter summary

This chapter has covered a great deal of ground and has introduced several new techniques and ways of thinking about business costs. It is important to work through the examples carefully, referring back to the content of the chapter where necessary.

First, we examined cost classification, classifying costs under the headings of direct material, direct labour, production overheads and other overheads. Some basic principles of costing of products and services were introduced, including examples of job costing, product costing and batch costing. The three basic elements of product cost – materials, labour and production overheads – were then dealt with in turn.

The principal issue with materials costs is the value at which they are allocated into production (and, in consequence, the closing stock value of unallocated items). Examples were used to demonstrate the first in first out (FIFO), last in, last out (LIFO) and weighted average (AVCO) methods.

Direct labour costs were then examined, and the application of direct labour hourly rates in job costing was demonstrated by means of an example.

The rest of the chapter was devoted to the complexities of accounting for production overheads within the costing systems of businesses. Detailed topic coverage included allocation and apportionment of production overheads to cost centres, and common methods of overhead absorption, including the calculation of overhead rates per machine hour, per labour hour, per unit of production, as a percentage of direct labour cost and as a percentage of direct materials cost.

Finally, an alternative to traditional absorption costing methods was explained: activity-based costing (ABC). ABC is being adopted more widely now because of its superior information content. However, as the chapter example indicated, ABC is not without its problems; it can be complex and expensive to adopt.

The end-of-chapter exercises are divided into two sections. The first section has answers provided at the end of the book.

 The second section, in the white box, has answers on the lecturers' section of the website. Finally the chapter contains a case study that examines many of the elements of costing that have been covered here.

Website summary

The book's website contains the following material in respect of Chapter 7:

Students' section

- Quiz containing ten multiple choice questions
- Six additional questions with answers
- Answer to the case study at the end of this chapter.

Lecturers' section

- Answers to end-of-chapter exercises 7.8 to 7.15
- Five additional questions with answers
- The website contains an additional case study 'Harwell & Peacock plc' which relates to Activity-Based Costing.

Exercises: answers at the end of the book

7.1 Paige Peverell plc produces plastic casings for telephones. The following is a list of some of the costs which the company incurs:

Plastic moulding machine depreciation	
Sales office fixtures and fittings depreciation	
Plastic materials	
Advertising expenditure	
Depreciation of factory building	
Electricity bill for factory	
Wages of assembly line workers	
Wages of factory canteen staff	
Wages of assembly line supervisor	
Secretary's salary	
Delivery vehicle depreciation	
Factory consumables	
Royalty payable per item produced to telephone designer	
Mobile phone bill – sales director	

Classify each item of expense as one of the following:

  direct labour

  direct materials

  direct expenses

  indirect production overheads

  other indirect overheads.

7.2 ArtKit Supplies Limited manufactures metal paint tins for the artist's supplies industry. The company operates from a small rented factory unit. In the year ending 31 August 20X3 it incurs the following costs:

	£
Sundry factory costs	2 117
Hinge fittings for boxes	960
Secretarial and administration salaries	12 460
Delivery costs	1 920
Machine operators' wages	18 250
Machinery repair	176
Factory cleaning	980
Lacquer paint for boxes	1 600
Rental of factory	6 409
Finishing operative's wages	10 270
Sundry office costs	904

Salesman's salary	18 740
Metal	18 006
Electricity – factory	1 760
Office supplies	2 411
Depreciation – machinery	1 080
Office telephone	1 630

Rearrange the information given into a cost statement for the year ending 31 August 20X3.

7.3 Porter Farrington Limited imports components for input into its production process. In May 20X4 the following deliveries into stock and transfers to production take place in respect of component PR430:

Date	Activity	Units
1 May	Balance of stock @ £3.00 per unit	30
2 May	Delivery of stock @ £3.30 per unit	50
18 May	Transfer to production	(40)
31 May	Balance of stock	40

What is the value of closing stock, assuming that Porter Farrington Limited adopts the FIFO convention?

a) £123

b) £126

c) £120

d) £132.

7.4 Clement is a sole trader who owns a small factory. He and his team of skilled workers produce high quality furniture to order. He has been given an order for a set of 12 dining chairs by a luxury hotel chain. Clement keeps a job card record for each order on which he records prime cost details. This order (Code ref: 3223) has had the following materials and labour booked to it:

Direct materials	Booked
Mahogany	18 pieces
Seat padding	12 pieces
Leather cloth	6 metres

Direct labour	Booked
Grade 1	115 hours
Grade 2	86 hours

Mahogany is purchased at £36 per piece (average price), each piece of seat padding costs £3.50 and the leather cloth is £42.00 per metre.

Clement employs two grades of labour: grade 1, for which direct labour cost is £8.50, and grade 2, for which direct labour cost is £9.25.

Produce a job cost record for Job No. 3223 calculating: (a) total prime cost, and (b) prime cost per chair.

7.5 Jersey Brookfield & Co. Limited is a manufacturer of soap powders and detergents.

Each of the products moves through two stages: bulk production and then packaging. In the year ending 31 December 20X2 Jersey Brookfield incurred production overheads which it plans to allocate and apportion as follows between the two departments:

	£	Basis of apportionment
Factory building depreciation	5 670	Floor area
Factory rates	11 970	Floor area
Factory insurance	7 980	Floor area
Canteen costs	18 876	No. of employees
Supervisory salaries	29 480	No. of employees
Other indirect labour	18 275	Machinery net book value
Machinery depreciation	21 500	Machinery net book value
Cleaning	17 850	Floor area
Electricity	30 290	Actual
Building maintenance	5 040	Floor area
Total	**166 931**	

The following information is relevant for the apportionment of overheads:

	Total	Bulk production	Packaging
Floor area	10 500 sq. m.	6 000 sq. m.	4 500 sq. m.
Employees	22	10	12
Machinery NBV	215 000	146 000	69 000
Electricity	30 290	18 790	11 500

Produce a schedule apportioning the overheads between the two departments (cost centres).

7.6 Barley Brindle Limited produces a single product, Product B. One unit of Product B has a prime cost of £10.20, which includes one hour of direct labour @ £6.20, and each unit uses 0.5 hours of machine time. Estimated production of B in 20X8 is 60 000 units and total production overheads are estimated at £218 000.

Calculate the overhead recovery rates (to the nearest penny) for 20X8, based on:

i)   direct labour hours

ii)   machine hours

iii)   units of production.

7.7 Washington and Middlewich Limited produce two types of metal shelving in their factory – one for domestic use, and one, which is produced to a higher quality standard, for commercial use (in factories and hotel kitchens, for example).

Each shelf unit passes through two processes: first, metal machining and second, painting and finishing (P&F). Commercial shelving is made of stronger material, has extra bracing bars and is given an additional coat of paint in the painting shop. Cost structures for the two products are as follows:

Domestic shelves			Commercial shelves		
	Department	£		Department	£
Materials	Machining	18.00	**Materials**	Machining	27.00
	P&F	3.30		P&F	4.60
		21.30			31.60
Direct labour	Machining 0.75 hours × £6	4.50	**Direct labour**	Machining 1 hour @ £6	6.00
	P&F 1 hour @ £6	6.00		P&F 1.5 hours @ £6	9.00
		10.50			15.00
Prime cost		31.80	**Prime cost**		46.60

Production overheads are estimated at the following apportioned amounts for next year:

	£
Machining	172 490
Painting and finishing	116 270

The company plans to produce 6 000 units of each product next year.

Calculate overhead absorption rates based upon:

i)   percentage of direct materials cost

ii)   percentage of direct labour cost.

Discuss which basis of overhead absorption might be preferable for each cost centre.

Exercises: answers available to lecturers

7.8   Monkseaton Purnell Limited produces motherboards for PCs from a range of bought in components. The following is a list of some of the costs that the company incurs:

Depreciation of factory work benches	
Bank interest charges	
Administration salaries	
Sundry factory expenses	
Factory insurance	
Supervisor's salary	
Assembly operatives' wages	
Managing director's salary	
Production office computer depreciation	
Purchase of silicone chips	

Factory rental	
Depreciation of sales representatives' cars	
Purchase of circuit boards	
Factory cleaning	

Classify each item of expense as one of the following:

   direct labour

   direct materials

   direct expenses

   indirect production overheads

   other indirect overheads.

7.9   Brisbane Melbourne Limited manufactures a range of containers for cosmetics in metal and plastic. In the year ending 31 December 20X4 the company incurs the following costs:

	£
Selling department sundry expenses	1 899
Metal	21 444
Depreciation of factory building	1 500
Factory cleaning	6 440
Metal moulding machine: operators' wages	12 222
Factory power	8 370
Finishing operative's wages	10 240
Sales department salaries	39 434
Security guard to factory	4 290
Dyes and paint	2 490
Sundry factory expenses	4 284
Depreciation of office building	1 100
Telephone charges	4 338
Factory canteen costs	12 234
Plastics	63 570
Distribution costs	18 777
Factory insurance	6 960
Plastics machine: operators' wages	15 249
Machinery depreciation	3 950
Administrative salaries	21 496
Stationery and other office admin. supplies	2 937
Other administrative expenses	6 422
Depreciation of office fixtures and fittings	1 929

Rearrange the information given into a cost statement for the year ending 31 December 20X4.

7.10   Wensleydale Woollen Waistcoats Limited (WWW Ltd) buys in wool to manufacture into waistcoats on its weaving machines. The stock card for wool code 78X4A shows the following movements in June 20X3:

Date	Activity	Kg
1 June	Balance of stock @ £2 per kilo	38
2 June	Issue to production	(8)
6 June	Delivery into stock @ £2.10 per kilo	50
20 June	Issue to production	40

There were no other transactions in the month.

What is the value of the issue to production on 20 June if WWW Ltd uses the AVCO stock valuation convention?

a)   £82.50

b)   £84.00

c)   £80.00

d)   £81.00.

7.11   Ribble & Vance Limited produces components to order for specialist motor manufacturers. An order for 100 components (code 1187AB6) was received from one of Ribble & Vance's principal customers. A job code, X4721, was assigned and over the following month various items of direct material and labour were booked to the job:

Item	Booked
Material J	21.4kg
Material Q	3.7kg
Grade IV labour	16 hours
Grade VIII labour	8 hours

Material J was booked out of stores on 21 September 20X0. The store card for material J contains the following details for September 20X0:

Date	Activity	Kg
1 September	Balance of stock @ £14.30 per kg	28.7
8 September	Delivery of stock @ £14.20 per kg	30.0
18 September	Transfer to production job code X4692	(20.6)
21 September	Transfer to production job code X4721	(21.4)

Ribble & Vance Limited apply the FIFO method of stock valuation. Material Q costs £2.75 per kg. Grade IV direct labour cost equals £4.78 per hour and grade VIII direct labour cost equals £8.21 per hour.

Produce a job cost record for Job No. X4721, calculating (i) total prime cost and (ii) prime cost per component.

7.12   Curtis Bedford is managing director of the family business, Bedford Bowler Limited. The company manufactures children's wooden train sets. Recently Curtis has been on a course about costing and he is keen to apply his new knowledge to the business. Thinking through the production process, he can identify three principal cost centres: machining, assembly and painting, and packaging.

Curtis's accountant supplies the following summary of production overheads incurred by the business to the most recent year-end, 31 December 20X6. Curtis adds a note of what he thinks is the most appropriate method of apportionment between cost centres.

	£	Basis of apportionment
Factory rental	21 105	Floor area
Packaging machine leasing charges	5 500	Actual (see note)
Cleaners wages	17 991	1/3 to each cost centre
Factory rates	6 930	Floor area
Electricity – factory	8 280	Actual
Supervision	21 456	No. of employees
Machinery maintenance and repair	4 472	Call-outs
Machinery depreciation	12 250	Net book value
Total	97 984	

Note: the packaging machine leasing charges relate only to machinery used in the packaging cost centre. There is no other machinery in the packaging department.

The following information is relevant for the apportionment of overheads:

	Total	Machining	Assembly	Packaging
Floor area	6 300 sq.m.	2 500 sq.m.	1 700 sq.m.	2 100 sq.m.
Employees	18	5	9	4
Machinery NBV	61 250	35 000	26 250	—
Electricity	8 280	3 905	1 892	2 483
Call outs	8	5	3	—

Produce a schedule apportioning the overheads between the three departments (cost centres).

7.13 A manufacturing business, Oakshield Carver Limited, organises its production into four cost centres. In the coming financial year the company plans to produce 115 000 items of product. Further details of its plans are included in the following table:

Cost centre	Production overhead £	Machine hours	Direct labour hours
Machining	297 000	80 000	3 000
Assembly	136 000	20 000	6 000
Finishing	121 500	15 000	9 000
Packaging	76 000	5 000	2 000
Totals	630 500	120 000	20 000

Calculate the overhead recovery rate for each department on the following bases:

i) machining – machine hours

ii) assembly – units of production

iii)   finishing – direct labour hours

iv)   packaging – units of production.

7.14   The facts are as in Exercise 7.13. The prime cost and timing details for one unit of production are:

	£
Materials	14.20
Direct labour	18.00
Prime cost	32.20

Each unit uses two hours of machine time in the machining department and 1.5 direct labour hours in the finishing department.

Calculate the total production cost for one unit of the company's product, using the overhead absorption rates calculated in Exercise 7.13.

7.15   Activity-based costing (ABC) is a costing system that was developed in the 1980s as a result of an increasing awareness in businesses of the deficiencies of traditional approaches to production overhead absorption.

i)   Describe the principal deficiencies in the traditional product costing system that ABC seeks to correct.

ii)   Describe the key features of ABC.

iii)   Identify and comment upon a significant advantage *and* a significant disadvantage associated with the implementation of an ABC system.

CASE STUDY 7.1 Dealing with overheads

Gemma Entwistle is the managing director of Entwistle Garden Equipment Limited. She inherited the business from her parents, Jeff and Hilda, when they retired two years ago, and she has put a lot of work into making improvements and in trying to improve efficiency. Jeff and Hilda manufactured a single product, a deluxe garden seat made of high quality hardwood, which has been a consistently good seller throughout western Europe. The company sells to garden centres and wholesalers.

Last year, after conducting some market research, Gemma made the decision to expand the range of products offered. When studying horticulture at college she developed a new mini-greenhouse design and she has decided to put that into production first because it uses the same range of production facilities as the garden seats. The two products use different wood qualities and the garden seats are much more carefully finished, but essentially the processes involved are very similar.

The factory facilities are split into two sections: (a) cutting and turning and (b) assembly and finishing. In the first section wood is cut by machine, drilled and shaped ready for assembly; most of the production activity is machine work. In the second section the pieces are assembled and fixed, the wood is polished and varnished and brass fixings attached. The range of tasks in this section is more diverse, and more labour intensive.

One of Gemma's innovations is to improve the quality of management information, which was generally more or less non-existent when her parents ran the business. She brought in a consultant to advise on systems developments and, following his recommendation, she now employs a part-time management accountant. Currently, towards the end of 20X1, the management accountant, Bernice, is looking at the likely costs for 20X2.

The basic prime cost structure for each of the two main products is as follows:

	Greenhouse £
Direct materials	12.00
Direct labour	
Cutting and turning dept; 1 hour @ £6.00 per hour	6.00
Assembly and finishing dept: 2 hours @ £7.00 per hour	14.00
Prime cost	32.00

Note that in the cutting and turning department two machine hours are required for each greenhouse, while in the assembly and finishing department 0.5 of a machine hour is required for each greenhouse.

	Garden seat £
Direct materials	15.00
Direct labour	
Cutting and turning dept: 1.50 hours @ £6.00 per hour	9.00
Assembly and finishing dept: 3 hours @ £7.00 per hour	21.00
Prime cost	45.00

Note that in the cutting and turning department 2.5 machine hours are required for each garden seat, while in the assembly and finishing department 0.5 of a machine hour is required for each garden seat.

The greenhouses currently sell to retailers for £85.00 each and the garden seats sell for £103.00.

Bernice has estimated production overheads for 20X2. These have to be split between the two departments and she suggests to Gemma that the following bases of apportionment would be appropriate:

Overhead	Total for 20X2 £	Basis of apportionment
Factory rental	75 000	Floor area
Factory insurance	7 600	Floor area
Cleaning	8 900	Floor area
Canteen	11 100	Number of employees
Factory rates	9 500	Floor area
Electricity	22 500	Actual (because separately metered)
Machine maintenance	16 464	Number of call-outs
Machinery depreciation	30 000	Net book value
Canteen depreciation	3 500	Number of employees
Supervisors' wages	57 936	Actual
Other factory costs	23 000	Floor area
	265 500	

Bernice establishes the following information for the apportionment:

Basis of apportionment	Total	Cutting and turning	Assembly and finishing
Floor area (square metres)	5 000	3 500	1 500
Direct labour employee numbers	25	8	17
Electricity (actual)	22 500	15 200	7 300
Supervisors' wages (actual)	57 936	29 716	28 220
Machinery net book value	300 000	250 000	50 000
Maintenance call-outs	21	18	3

Bernice decides to calculate overhead absorption rates based upon (i) machine hours and (ii) direct labour hours. The totals anticipated for 20X2 for machine hours and direct labour hours by department are:

	Cutting and turning	Assembly and finishing	Total
Machine hours	22 500	5 000	27 500
Direct labour hours	12 500	25 000	37 500

Gemma aims to produce and sell 5000 units of each product in 20X2. Gemma and Bernice require the following information:

a) Totals for overheads apportioned to each department (cost centre).

▶

b) Overhead absorption rates for each department based upon (i) machine hours and (ii) labour hours.

c) A calculation of the total amount of overhead absorbed using the two different methods if 5000 units of each product are produced and sold in 20X2.

d) A calculation of the gross profit for each greenhouse and garden seat on the assumption that selling prices remain the same, using i) the overhead absorption rate based on machine hours and ii) the overhead absorption rate based on labour hours.

e) A recommendation as to whether machine hours or labour hours should be used as the basis for overhead absorption.

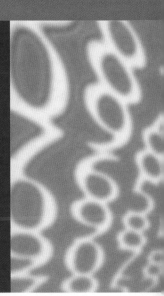

CHAPTER 8

Budgeting

Aim of the chapter

To understand the reasons for, and the processes involved in, setting a budget in a business organisation, and to be able to prepare and evaluate budget statements.

Learning outcomes

After reading the chapter and completing the related exercises, students should:

- Understand the role of budgeting in planning and controlling business organisations.
- Be able to prepare straightforward budget statements for a small business.
- Know about the stages involved in setting a budget for a larger business organisation, and appreciate some of the behavioural issues that may arise.
- Be able to evaluate actual outcomes against budget plans.

What is a budget?

A budget is a plan, expressed in financial and/or more general quantitative terms, which extends forward for a period into the future. Budgets are widely used in organisations of all types and sizes. In this chapter we will concentrate on the use of budgets in profit-oriented businesses, but it should be recognised that budgets are used in all kinds of organisations, including, for example, schools, health trusts and charities. Also, it is possible (and often desirable) to prepare personal expenditure budgets to ensure that spending does not exceed income, or as a basis for negotiating borrowing such as a mortgage.

Budgeting forms part of a broader planning process. In Chapter 6 we examined the broad context of management control accounting and its links with the functions of management. The summary from that chapter is repeated below:

- *Setting business objectives*: The primary functions of management are: (a) to identify the objectives of the business; and (b) to direct the activities of the business so as to meet the objectives.
- *Assess alternatives and make decisions and make plans*: Management needs information about the alternative actions it could take. Having assessed the available information, management takes decisions and makes detailed plans for the future.
- *Monitoring outcomes*: Management uses information to assess the extent to which its plans have succeeded and its business objectives have been met.
- *Redefine objectives and plans*: On the basis of a comparison with planned and actual outcomes, it may be necessary to redefine the overarching objectives of the business and the detailed plans that are geared towards achieving the objectives.

The budgeting process falls largely into the second stage of the management process outlined above. Having established strategic objectives, management assesses the alternative actions that could be taken in order to meet those objectives. Having decided upon the action or actions that will best meet the objectives, taking into account any relevant constraints, managers must then formulate more detailed plans.

Often in larger organisations there will be a strategic (or long-range) plan reaching forward into the future over, for example, a three to five-year period. Within that plan, budgets are prepared, often on an annual basis, for the 12 months ahead. Example 8.1 illustrates the relationship between strategic objectives, long-range planning and an annual budget.

| Example 8.1 | Referring back to the Chapter 6 spotlight, let us reconsider Calder Calloway Cards Limited. To recap, the company, during its first eight or nine years of life, had had no formal management planning or control systems. With the appointment of two new directors it became clear that the haphazard approach to management that had been adequate in the early years would no longer suffice. During 20X8 Paco, the managing director, accepts the need for a more formal planning and management control process. He and his fellow directors meet |

several times with a view to deciding upon a set of strategic objectives for the business. They also decide to recruit a management accountant to help in the formal process of budget setting and evaluation.

The directors determine the following key strategic objectives:

- To grow the company to the point where it is a credible competitor with the largest producers in the greetings card market.
- To produce cards of high quality with a distinctive company design identity.

Out of these two key objectives a long-term plan develops. The directors decide that the plan should cover the next five years. It is a written document that identifies the strategy for achieving the key objectives. An extract from it includes the following principal actions (together with more detailed actions for achieving the key action):

- Increase sales by at least 30% per annum
  - Recruit new members of the sales team
  - Encourage and motivate by use of commission and reward schemes
  - Identify new outlets.
- Reduce unit costs and increase gross profitability to 45% within five years
  - Improve and expand production facilities by investment in 'state of the art' printing machinery
  - Implement a system of capital expenditure control and evaluation
  - Improve production logistics.
- Improve, and keep improving, the quality of the product
  - Recruit quality supervisor
  - Improve supervision
  - Implement a Total Quality Management system to motivate all staff.
- Create a distinctive design identity for the company's products
  - Recruit a design team under the strong leadership of a design director who will be a full member of the board of directors
  - Identify and recruit staff at an appropriate level and remuneration
  - Identify key elements of design policy in conjunction with design director.

Some of the points are likely to be acted upon within the next 12 months; others will produce action over the longer term.

The directors, working together with the new management accountant, will produce a budget for the next 12 months. This will identify financial and other quantitative measurements that represent the changes proposed. The immediate financial implications of the plan will be recognised in the budget. For example:

- *Personnel budget*: it seems likely that recruitment of the design team will take place within the next 12 months. Costs of recruitment and of the new salaries will be included in the budget. Consequential savings (for example, in respect of the payments made to freelance card designers) will also be estimated and their effect taken into account. The personnel budget will be expressed both in terms of numbers of staff and financial costs.
- *Capital expenditure budget*: a detailed budget taking account of the effects of likely short-term decisions will be required. For example, if the production director, Karim, decides that a printing machine should be scrapped and

▶

should be replaced during the year with a new machine costing around £20 000, the decision has an impact on production speed and quality, volume of production, cash (£20 000 has to be found) and depreciation.

■ *Sales budget*: if the company aims to increase sales by at least 30% the budget should reflect this aim. The planned increase involves extra costs (for example, in recruiting additional staff, in creating and implementing a ommission scheme and in planning a campaign to expand into new sales outlets).

All of these implications (and more) must be reflected in the budget for the following financial year.

Budgeting is not, as the example implies, a simple process. However, if the business sets its strategic objectives sensibly, the budget, to some extent, emerges naturally from higher level management decisions.

The budget process

In this section we will examine the kind of process involved in setting a budget for a medium to large-sized organisation that is organised into departments. Budget setting in a small organisation is likely to be more straightforward in that it involves communication between fewer parties. In a very small organisation it may be that only the proprietor of the business is involved in setting the budget. As usual, we will initially examine the process by means of an example.

Example 8.2

Arbus Arbuthnot plc manufactures and sells cosmetics and skincare products. It operates in a highly competitive market in which there is a culture of constant scientific development. The company's basic strategic objective is to improve market share by the development of improved products, innovating more quickly and effectively than the competition. Each year the research and development department finds new ways of improving products (for example, by changing the feel and consistency of a skin make-up).

Stage 1: Discussing the sales budget

The most important constraint on the company's activities is, generally, the level of sales. The sales budget is set first (as is the case in most commercial organisations operating in a competitive environment) and all other budgets are developed from it.

In June 20X3 the budget process gets under way to set the budget for the accounting year that runs from 1 March 20X4 to 28 February 20X5. The directors meet to talk about the sales budget. Their discussion is influenced by the fact that a new improved face cream has recently been introduced by a competitor. Arbus Arbuthnot has responded to this by changing the advertising and packaging of their equivalent product, emphasising the scientific soundness of the formula. The directors feel that the advertising is likely to prove fairly effective, and they are optimistic about the sales projections for the coming year. They agree that the budget volume of sales (i.e. number of items sold in the various categories of product) should increase by an average of 5%, and that prices can be increased by 3%. They are aware, however, that their competitors are working on anti-ageing products for both men and women; in order to keep up with the market Arbus Arbuthnot is going to have to increase its research and development activities.

Stage 2: The production budget

The next stage is that the detailed analysis of the sales budget is used to project production requirements. If sales volumes are expected to increase by 5% it is reasonable to suppose that a corresponding increase in production will be required. However, other factors can influence the production budget; for example, if a special product promotion is planned, linked to an advertising campaign, it will probably be necessary to plan for additional production.

Stage 3: Communication of budget guidelines

At this point it is probably appropriate to broaden the scope of the budget process. The directors have made the strategic decisions relating to objectives and they have decided upon the broad general approach to be taken in the next following year's budget (e.g. an increase of 5% in sales volume, some price increases and so on). Budgeting guidelines will then be communicated to the various departments around the company.

Stage 4: Submission of departmental budgets

Individual departments or divisions can now be asked to submit their budgets for approval. These should be prepared in accordance with the broad thrust of policy. The research and development department, for example, is clearly being directed to expand its activities; the head of R&D will probably revise personnel requirements and may start work on presenting a proposal for an expansion of laboratory facilities. The marketing department may respond to the call for a 5% increase in sales volume by planning additional marketing campaigns.

It is a generally accepted principle of budgeting that budgets are more likely to work if they involve the participation of all of the people who are expected to put them into operation. Such participation may involve a great deal of paper, meetings and discussion, but many organisations obviously feel that the process is worthwhile in order that participants feel that they can claim 'ownership' of the final budget.

Stage 5: Approval of budgets

A well-organised budget process will have a range of submission deadlines for parts of the budget. Once the departmental budgets have been submitted they can be coordinated and considered together to judge the extent to which they are reasonable and achievable given the inevitable operational constraints that apply to all businesses. For example, the head of R&D submits an ambitious budget based upon a planned expansion of numbers of personnel by 30%. He also requests capital expenditure of £1.5 million. These proposals may be quite reasonable in the context of management expectations (or perhaps the head of R&D is indulging in a spot of empire-building). Senior managers will accept, reject or modify such proposals and then return them to the originator. In some processes, budget proposals may be discussed and modified several times before the final budget is agreed.

Stage 6: Agreement of budget

Once the budget has been extensively negotiated and discussed, the final agreed version can be disseminated across the business and then people can get on with the business of implementing it. If the process has been genuinely participative and a feeling of 'ownership' has been achieved, the budget may prove to be a very useful co-ordinating and motivating tool. In the next section we summarise the benefits to be obtained from effective budgeting.

Benefits of effective budgeting

The principal benefits are summarised under the following four sub-headings.

Planning and coordination of operations and activities

Setting a budget concentrates the minds of all of the personnel involved on the objectives of the organisation and how they might best be furthered in the shorter term. This allows for coordinated, planned actions to take place, and should minimise the number of opportunities for 'off the cuff' decisions that are not necessarily in the best long-term interests of the organisation. The efficient coordination of activities becomes particularly important in a large organisation where individual departments or divisions may not have a sufficiently broad perspective on the overall objectives of the organisation. Decision making at a divisional level may make sense within the context of that individual division but may not be optimal within the context of the business operation as a whole.

Providing motivation

If the budget process is effective it may help to promote a sense of ownership of targets and objectives. Staff may feel motivated to work harder in order to achieve strategic and shorter-term objectives. However, if the budget process is not managed effectively the opposite effect can take hold. Some of the adverse effects of budgeting are discussed later in the chapter.

Control of operations and activities

Because a budget is (or should be) a carefully thought out plan, it should allow managers to control business activity. Once the budget has been set and approved it should be carefully monitored, with actual outcomes being compared to the budget. Where necessary, action should be taken, quickly, in order to correct any aspects of the operations that are not functioning as planned.

Basis for performance evaluation

A budget provides a yardstick by which group or individual performance can be judged. For example, each division in a major company may have sales targets set for it. Those divisions that regularly exceed targets may be rewarded by opportunities for new investment, by bonuses for staff, or at least by not being closed down or sold off. Individual performance may also be rewarded on the basis of evaluated budget out-turn. For example, a company where each division has a sales manager could reward the sales manager of the best performing division by means of an individual bonus or promotion.

Some problems with budgeting

The problems which are encountered with budgeting in practice are mostly linked to human behaviour. Some of the problems that can arise are highlighted in the following sub-sections.

Demotivational budgets

Although the budgeting process as described earlier in the chapter is intended, ideally, to encourage participation and 'ownership', the practical effect may not be as intended. If the budget process is essentially authoritarian with little or no effective participation, middle managers and staff may feel resentful and disinclined to work to budget.

Setting unrealistic targets

Unrealistic targets may add to the demotivational effect. If senior management set an over-optimistic budget for sales volume increases, staff may simply decide that it is not worth even trying to achieve the targets. Faced with an apparently hopeless task, they may withdraw their interest and enthusiasm and may even start to think about changing their employment.

Budgetary slack

Where managers and staff are closely involved in the budget setting process, they may try to give themselves an easy life by setting low targets for achievement. Senior managers need to be aware of the possibility that staff will attempt to build in budgetary slack.

An incremental approach

Often, in practice, incremental budgets are set. This would involve, for example, taking last year's total for each budget heading or the actual performance figures and adding 5%. This is a thoughtless and superficial approach to budgeting, which, usually, would fail to link the budget to strategic objectives of the business. (It also fails to recognise that not all costs increase at the same rate.) At its worst it positively encourages misuse of resources and overspending. If a department head knows that budgets are set by adding 5% to this year's actual spending, then he or she is much more likely to overspend in order to ensure a bigger allowance next year.

Use it or lose it

In many organisations managers feel it necessary to spend every last penny of budget allowance; they know that if they do not spend up to budget the unused allowance will be taken away from them in future years. This approach does not lead to the best possible strategic use of resources.

Name, blame and shame

It is important that responsibility for budgets and their outcomes is clearly identified. Managers should be answerable only for variations that are under their control. For example, sales figures are affected by sales returns. Failure to achieve target sales because of high levels of sales returns may or may not be the fault of the sales staff. If they have been selling too aggressively the high level of returns may be attributable to them. If, on the other hand, the goods are being returned because they are substandard as a result of a failure in the production quality inspection process, the responsibility does not lie with the sales staff.

Finally, it is worth noting that setting budgets is a costly process. Some organisations have dispensed with the type of traditional budgeting described in this chapter because the costs are perceived to outweigh the benefits gained.

The spotlight below illustrates a budget process which could result in problems and less than optimal performance.

SPOTLIGHT 8.1   A budget dispute

Brunswick Carlton plc is a producer of domestic dishwashing machines. The company has gradually lost market share in recent years and its profitability has tended to decline, although it has not yet actually reported a loss. The chief executive has recently retired at the age of 70 and his successor, Clive Neil, has just been appointed. Also on the board is Shahera Patel, sales director, Bryn Edwards, production director and Clare Burnhope, finance director. At a recent meeting the directors agreed that the key strategic objectives for the business should be to regain lost market share and re-establish the company as an innovator and market leader.

The directors meet again to discuss the budget for the coming year. Shahera has just presented a proposal for the sales budget that includes a modest increase in machines sold; last year the actual number of machines sold, including export sales, was 164 000. She has had a meeting with the sales force, all of whom have worked for the company for many years and have a lot of experience of the market. They say that the market's very competitive at the moment and they don't feel that they'd be able to sell significantly higher volumes unless there was a real improvement in the product. On the basis of her discussions she has budgeted a sales volume of 168 000. She feels that selling prices should remain the same because of the level of competition in the market.

Clive does not respond well to the sales budget proposals:

Clive: We decided last week that we're going to reposition this company and regain the market share that's been dribbling away over the last five years. At a rate of an extra 4000 machines a year it'll take forever. Anyway, the size of the overall market is still increasing by about 8% a year, so we should be aiming higher than 4000 just to stand still. I'm sorry to say it, Shahera, but the trouble is that your sales people have grown complacent and lazy – they're just not prepared to put their backs into making new contacts. We need to set them a real challenge that they can get their teeth into and if they can't make their figures we'll recruit people who can.

Shahera: Well, fair enough, but what sort of figure did you have in mind?

Clive: If we said 200 000 machines next year, that'd be a bit over a 20% increase. It should be quite achievable given the 8% growth in the market that's forecast anyway. There's a lot of movement in the housing market, you know, and when people move house they often buy a new dishwasher. The sales are there for the asking.

Bryn: Yes, but if we sell 20% more we've got to produce 20% more, and I don't quite see how we can do that unless we can expand our production facilities. We're working flat out as it is on the shop floor, and we'd need to spend a lot more on product development to make any significant improvements to the product.

Clare: And if we have to expand production facilities we'll need to finance additional capital expenditure and working capital.

Clive: It looks to me as if you've all become a bit complacent. What this place needs is a real shake-up – a culture change – I'm only interested in 'can do' and all you're giving me is a lot of reasons why we *can't* do things. We're going to play this one my way, whether you and the sales staff and the shop floor workers like it or not. I was brought in here to make changes and that's exactly what I'm going to do. We'll call it 200 000 in sales volume for next year, and that's final.

▶

The spotlight study requirement is to discuss the likely effects on the budget process and the effectiveness of Clive's decision to radically increase the sales volume budget for the next year.

Spotlight study discussion

Clive is not encouraging a participative approach by his autocratic insistence on a very high sales volume target. The other directors are likely to feel resentful of the fact that he is disregarding their objections (which they may genuinely feel to be valid). However, Clive may not actually care very much about what the others think, especially if his hidden agenda is to drive them out of the company.

The orthodox approach to budgeting is that it should be participative in nature; people should be allowed their say and should be able to claim ownership of the agreed budget. Participation, it is argued, leads to higher levels of motivation and identification with the strategic objectives of the business. However, in this case, there may well be an element of complacency among the long-standing directors and the workforce. Market share and profitability have been decreasing over a long period, and it may be that only radical action will turn around the gradual decline.

Clive may be right; the sales force may indeed have become lazy. They may have been setting themselves easy targets for years, building in budgetary slack. However, presented with a budget of 200 000 units of sales, they may simply decide that it's not worth even trying to hit such a high target. Even if Clive is correct and this level of sales is achievable by the company in the short term, he and the other directors are probably going to have to work out a strategy for enthusing the sales team. Given that the sales director, Shahera, herself, is apparently happy with a very low target increase, Clive appears to be facing some major difficulties.

From the information given about the company, it seems that some fairly radical shake-up is required. However, Clive's abrasive and confrontational approach may not achieve the results he wants.

Preparing the budget: Principal types of budget

Budgets are often prepared for a budget period of one year. However, the budget period can extend over a shorter, or, occasionally, a longer period. Often, the annual budget is further split into quarters, months or even weeks.

Another, related type of budget is the rolling budget. The budget is initially prepared for an appropriate budget period (probably one year). With each month that elapses, another month is added on to the end of the budget, so that at any given time there is a full 12-month budget. For example, a company sets a budget for the 12 months between 1 September 20X3 and 31 August 20X4. At the end of September 20X3 another month (September 20X4) is added on to the end of the budget. At the end of October 20X3 the budget for October 20X4 is added on, and so on.

As we have seen, the starting point for most budgets is the sales budget. Within most businesses of any size, related budgets will be required for areas such as production, research and development, administration and capital expenditure. Once the budget process is complete a full set of interrelated budgets (the master budget) is available for use within the business.

Figure 8.1 sets out some of the principal budgets that will be required in a manufacturing business.

Figure 8.1 presents the sales budget in a central position, signifying its importance to all other budgets. The sales budget links in directly to the production budget, which, in turn, drives budgets for raw materials, direct labour and production overheads. The link with other costs is a little more tenuous, as denoted by the broken lines. However, all of these costs are related to some extent to the general volume of activity generated by the business. All functional areas in the business may have needs for capital expenditure, which is shown in the figure in a separate

| Figure 8.1 | Principal budget areas within a manufacturing business |

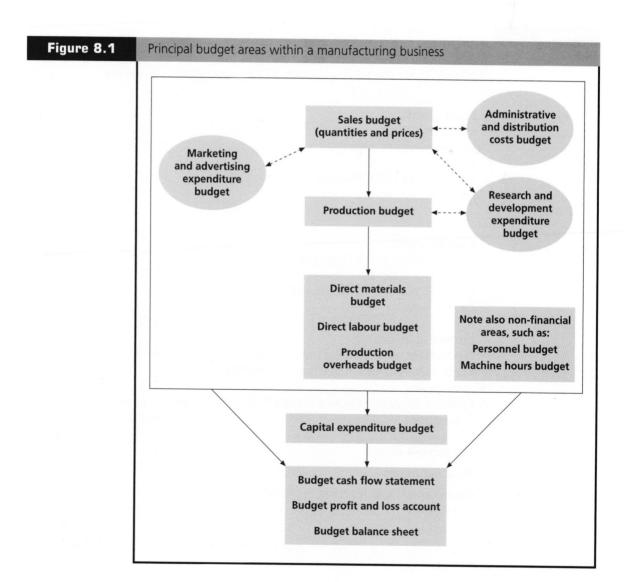

box below. Finally, all of the budget information (sales, production, expenses and capital expenditure) is brought together in the form of three principal budgeted statements: the budget cash flow statement; budget profit and loss account; and budget balance sheet.

Setting the budget: A practical example

In this section we will examine the mechanics of budget setting using a simple example based on a company that manufactures only one product. Even though the setting is deliberately simplified the example produces many interlinked numbers. Students will need to work through it thoroughly in order to understand how the various elements fit together.

Example 8.3

Macey Nelson Limited manufactures a single product: vacuum cleaners. The company is in the process of preparing a budget for the six months ending 30 June 20X6. The balance sheet at 31 December 20X5 is as follows:

	£	£
Fixed assets		
Machinery at cost	96 000	
Less: accumulated depreciation	(38 400)	
		57 600
Office fixtures and fittings and computer	15 000	
Less: accumulated depreciation	(3 000)	
		12 000
		69 600
Current assets		
Stocks: finished goods (200 units)	15 000	
Stocks: raw materials	3 750	
Debtors (December 20X5 sales, all on credit)	40 000	
Cash at bank	8 000	
	66 750	
Current liabilities		
Creditors for raw materials (1 month's purchases)	10 000	
Creditors for production overheads (1 month's purchases)	9 000	
Creditors for administrative expenses (1 month's purchases)	4 000	
	23 000	
Net current assets		43 750
Total net assets		113 350
Share capital and reserves		
Share capital		20 000
Reserves		93 350
		113 350

At the end of every month the figure for debtors equals the total sales for the month just ended (e.g. debtors at the end of December are December's sales). At the end of every month creditors equals the total purchases for the month just ended (e.g. creditors at the end of December are December purchases).

Macey Nelson's selling price and cost structure for one vacuum cleaner is as follows:

	£
Selling price	100
Raw materials	25
Direct labour	20
Prime cost	45

The business uses full absorption costing based upon the number of units planned for production.

The company's sales director produces a forecast for sales (in units) for the first six months of 20X6 on the basis of discussions he has held with fellow directors and with his sales team. The production director then works out projected production in numbers of units. Projections for sales and production in units, together with opening and closing stocks of finished goods for each month are as follows:

Month	Opening stock in units	Number of units: sales	Number of units: production	Closing stock in units
January	200	250	300	250
February	250	280	280	250
March	250	280	330	300
April	300	300	350	350
May	350	300	350	400
June	400	300	350	450
Total		1 710	1 960	

Production in July is estimated at 350 units.

Production is planned in such a way as to build up stocks of finished goods towards the autumn; this is to ensure that the company has sufficient stock to respond to a potential increase in demand following a major advertising campaign that is planned for the latter half of the year. At the beginning of each month the production director plans to have half of the raw materials in stock which will be required for the coming month's production schedule. In order to simplify the budgeting exercise it is assumed that there is no work-in-progress at each month-end.

Production overheads forecast for the first six months of 20X6 are:

	£
Factory rental	16 000
Supervisory salaries	12 450

	£
Other direct labour	6 250
Cleaning	3 900
Insurance	2 600
Power	5 800
Depreciation of machinery	4 800
Maintenance	1 000
Canteen costs	2 500
Business rates	2 800
Other factory expenses	700
Total	58 800

Production overheads accumulate evenly over the sixth-month period.

Monthly administrative costs total £4000, plus £250 of depreciation of office fixtures and fittings and computer. Each month's expenses are paid in the next following month (remember that this does not include depreciation, which is a non-cash adjustment).

No capital expenditure is planned for the six months ending 30 June 20X6 and there will be no disposals of fixed assets.

The requirement is to prepare the following budgets for the first six months of 20X6:

a) Raw materials purchases budget.
b) Budget overhead absorption rate.
c) Budget profit and loss account for each of the six months ending 30 June 20X6 and a summary budget profit and loss account for the six-month period.
d) Budget balance sheet at 30 June 20X6.
e) Budget cash flow statement for each of the six months ending 30 June 20X6.

a) Raw materials purchases budget

Each unit of product uses £25 of raw material, and we need to ensure that raw material sufficient for half of each month's production is available in stock at the beginning of the month. We can work out the opening and closing stock for each month, the utilisation of raw materials in production and hence (by means of a balancing figure) the amount of raw materials purchases each month:

First, opening stock:

	Calculation of opening raw materials stock	£
January	Given in balance sheet at 31.12.X5	3 750
February	50% × 280 (Feb. production) × £25	3 500
March	50% × 330 (Mar. production) × £25	4 125
April	50% × 350 (Apr. production) × £25	4 375
May	50% × 350 (May production) × £25	4 375
June	50% × 350 (June production) × £25	4 375

Each month's opening stock is the closing stock of the previous month. Closing stock in June is still required. We know that July production is estimated at 350 so the opening stock for July will need to be 50% × 350 × £25 = £4375 (remember that opening stock for July is the same as closing stock for June).

Utilisation of raw materials in production:

	Calculation of utilisation of raw materials in production	£
January	300 units × £25	7 500
February	280 units × £25	7 000
March	330 units × £25	8 250
April	350 units × £25	8 750
May	350 units × £25	8 750
June	350 units × £25	8 750

Bringing all this information together we can calculate the expected level of raw material purchases.

Opening stock + Purchases of raw materials – Raw materials used in production = Closing stock

This formula contains four pieces of information; we now know three of them so we can calculate the fourth. Purchases of raw materials is the balancing figure, which we can calculate for each month as follows:

Closing stock + Raw materials used in production – Opening stock

	Opening stock of raw material £	Purchases of raw materials £ (bal. fig.)	Raw materials used in production £	Closing stock of raw material £
January	3 750	7 250	(7 500)	3 500
February	3 500	7 625	(7 000)	4 125
March	4 125	8 500	(8 250)	4 375
April	4 375	8 750	(8 750)	4 375
May	4 375	8 750	(8 750)	4 375
June	4 375	8 750	(8 750)	4 375

b) Budget overhead absorption rate

Total production overheads for six months: £58 800
Total number of units to be produced: 1960.

Therefore the budget overhead absorption rate per unit is:

$$\frac{£58\ 800}{1\ 960} = £30 \text{ per unit}$$

We now know the total budgeted production cost per unit:

	£
Prime cost	45
Production overhead absorbed	30
Total production cost per unit	75

We need this information in order to calculate the budget profit and loss account for each of the six months in the budget period.

c) Profit and loss

Macey Nelson Limited: Budget profit and loss account for each month
January–June 20X6

	Jan £	Feb £	Mar £	Apr £	May £	Jun £
Sales	250 × £100 = 25 000	280 × £100 = 28 000	280 × £100 = 28 000	300 × £100 = 30 000	300 × £100 = 30 000	300 × £100 = 30 000
Cost of sales (= production cost	250 × £75 = (18 750)	280 × £75 = (21 000)	280 × £75 = (21 000)	300 × £75 = (22 500)	300 × £75 = (22 500)	300 × £75 = (22 500)
Gross profit	6 250	7 000	7 000	7 500	7 500	7 500
Administrative expenses (incl. depreciation)	(4 250)	(4 250)	(4 250)	(4 250)	(4 250)	(4 250)
Net profit	2 000	2 750	2 750	3 250	3 250	3 250

Macey Nelson Limited: Summary budget profit and loss account for the six months ending 30 June 20X6

		£
Sales	1710 units @ £100 each	171 000
Cost of sales	1710 units @ £75 each	(128 250)
Gross profit	1710 units @ £25 each	42 750
Administrative expenses	6 months × £4 250	(25 500)
Net profit		17 250

d) Budget balance sheet at 30 June 20X6

Workings are as follows:

1. Fixed assets

	At 31 December 20X5 £	Depreciation: six months to 30 June 20X6 £	At 30 June 20X6 £
Machinery			
Cost	96 000		96 000
Acc. depreciation	(38 400)	(4 800)	(43 200)

Net book value	57 600		52 800

Office equipment

Cost	15 000		15 000
Acc. depreciation	(3 000)	6 × £250 = £1 500	(4 500)
Net book value	12 000		10 500

2. Stock

Raw materials closing stock at 30 June 20X6 has already been calculated at £4375. Finished goods closing stock in numbers of units at 30 June 20X6 is 450 units. The production cost of each unit is £75, therefore closing stock of finished goods is:

$$£75 × 450 = £33 750$$

3. Debtors

Debtors at the end of June 20X6 equal the amount of sales for June – i.e. £30 000.

4. Creditors

Creditors for raw material purchases at the end of June 20X6 equal the amount of raw material purchases for June – i.e. £8750. Creditors for expenses included in production overheads equal the production overheads incurred in June.

	£
Total production overheads for six months:	58 800
Less: depreciation (not a purchased item)	(4 800)
	54 000

$$\frac{£54\ 000}{6} = £9\ 000$$

Creditors for administration expenses at the end of June 20X6 equal the administrative expenses incurred in June, which will be paid in July 20X6 – i.e. £4000 (excluding depreciation, which is not a purchased item).

5. Reserves

	£
Reserves at 31 December 20X5	93 350
+ Budget net profit for six months to 30 June 20X6	17 250
	110 600

We do not know the figure for cash at bank (until we have done the cash flow budget which is the next stage), but we know all the other figures in the budgeted balance sheet at 30 June 20X6.

Macey Nelson Limited: Budgeted balance sheet at 30 June 20X6

	£	£
Fixed assets (working 1)		
Machinery at cost	96 000	
Less: accumulated depreciation	(43 200)	
		52 800
Office fixtures and fittings and computer	15 000	
Less: accumulated depreciation	(4 500)	
		10 500
		63 300
Current assets		
Stocks: finished goods (working 2)	33 750	
Stocks: raw materials (working 2)	4 375	
Debtors (working 3)	30 000	
Cash at bank (balancing figure)	20 925	
	89 050	
Current liabilities		
Creditors for raw materials (working 4)	8 750	
Creditors for production overheads (working 4)	9 000	
Creditors for administrative expenses (working 4)	4 000	
	21 750	
Net current assets		67 300
Total net assets		130 600
Share capital and reserves		
Share capital		20 000
Reserves (working 5)		110 600
		130 600

e) Budget cash flow statement for each of the six months ending 30 June 20X6

We have already calculated most of the information we need. However, we still require calculations for payments made in respect of direct labour. Each unit produced requires direct labour valued at £20. Therefore, for each of the six months, payments for direct labour will be made as follows:

Month	Production (units)	Production × £20
January	300	6 000
February	280	5 600
March	330	6 600
April	350	7 000
May	350	7 000
June	350	7 000

	Jan £	Feb £	Mar £	Apr £	May £	Jun £
Opening balance at bank	8 000	19 000	18 150	18 925	18 425	19 675
Add: sales receipts	40 000	25 000	28 000	28 000	30 000	30 000
Less: payments for raw materials purchases	(10 000)	(7 250)	(7 625)	(8 500)	(8 750)	(8 750)
Less: payments for direct labour	(6 000)	(5 600)	(6 600)	(7 000)	(7 000)	(7 000)
Less: payments for overheads	(9 000)	(9 000)	(9 000)	(9 000)	(9 000)	(9 000)
Less: payments for admin. expenses	(4 000)	(4 000)	(4 000)	(4 000)	(4 000)	(4 000)
Closing balance at bank	19 000	18 150	18 925	18 425	19 675	20 925

Notes:
1. Each month we start with the opening balance of cash at bank. On 1 January 20X6 this is the amount of cash at bank in the balance sheet at 31 December 20X5.
2. We add in sales receipts (which, in this case, are the amount of the sales made in the previous month).
3. We take away payments for direct labour (which are made within the month in which they are incurred so there is no opening or closing creditor balance in respect of this item).
4. We take away payments for overheads and administrative expenses, which, in this case, are the amounts from the previous month.
5. At the end of each month we can calculate a budgeted closing balance at bank. This, in turn, becomes the opening balance of cash at bank in the following month.

Discussion

This has been a very long, complicated example, with lots of calculations. Most students will need to work through this several times before they are completely familiar with the idea of the various budgets and the figures used to illustrate them.

The type of budget calculations shown can be done more easily and speedily on a spreadsheet, once a basic model is set up. Use of a spreadsheet facilitates 'what if' type questions, and allows budget setters to consider the effect of changes in assumptions. It is recommended that students set up the information above into a spreadsheet in order to understand the calculations and the way in which the figures work together.

There are some numerical examples of budget setting (none of them are as complicated as the Macey Nelson example) at the end of the chapter. Students can try these examples on paper, using spreadsheets, or, preferably, using both methods in order to gain understanding of the calculations.

Application of budgets to other types of business

The long example of Macey Nelson Limited above illustrates the budgeting process in a manufacturing business. However, it should be appreciated that the budget process is just as important in other types of business such as service and retailing. Exactly the same principles apply, but the process is likely to be somewhat more straightforward where manufacturing processes are not involved. Some of the end of chapter examples apply what we have learned about budgeting to non-manufacturing environments.

Monitoring outcomes

The summary set out at the beginning of this chapter links some of the key functions of management with management accounting. So far in this chapter we have looked at the role of management in setting business objectives, in assessing alternatives and making decisions, and in making plans (budgets). The next logical stage in the sequence is that of monitoring outcomes. Management uses information to assess the extent to which its plans have succeeded.

In order to be able to monitor outcomes accounting data must be gathered on a fairly frequent basis so that management is in possession of sufficient relevant information. Where the budget for a period of 12 months is divided up into 12 monthly budgets, it is likely that information about actual outcomes will be gathered and presented also on a monthly basis.

It is important that managers build into their work patterns a regular disciplined routine of monitoring outcomes and taking any necessary action. After all, as we have seen earlier in the chapter, building a budget requires a very significant input of people's time and energy. These would be wasted if management then fails to monitor outcomes thoroughly. It should be noted also that monitoring itself is a costly process because it uses expensive management time. Business organisations should ensure that the procedures involved do not get out of hand; managers may spend too much time looking backwards in order to provide explanations for what has already happened.

Chapter summary

This chapter started off by looking at budgeting in the context of management activities and decision making. The need for strategic planning was briefly revisited, and an example illustrated the link between broad strategic planning and detailed actions leading to the construction of a budget.

Next, we examined the budget process by reference to a medium to large-sized organisation. The example in this section identified the crucial role of the sales budget and examined the way in which other budgets within a commercial organisation are linked to the sales budget.

The benefits of effective budgeting were discussed, and then various problems associated with budgeting were identified. The first case study for the chapter illustrated some of the tensions that operate at senior management level when there is disagreement about the budget.

The next section of the chapter was concerned with setting various linked budgets in the context of a manufacturing organisation. A comprehensive practical example was worked through to illustrate the practicalities of budget setting. Budgets were set for a six-month period, including budget cash flow statement, profit and loss account and balance sheet. The example demonstrated how all the figures fit together.

Finally, the last section of the chapter examined some of the techniques and issues involved in monitoring outcomes.

 The end-of-chapter exercises that follow are divided into two sections. The first section has answers provided at the end of the book. The second section, in the white box, has answers on the lecturers' section of the website. Finally, the chapter contains a case study that examines many of the elements of costing that have been covered here.

Website summary

The book's website contains the following material in respect of Chapter 8:

Students' section

- Quiz containing ten multiple choice questions
- Three additional questions with answers
- Answer to the case study at the end of this chapter.

Lecturers' section

- Answers to end-of-chapter exercises 8.8 to 8.14
- Five additional questions with answers
- The website contains an additional case study 'Piers'.

Exercises: answers at the end of the book

8.1 You are the newly appointed management accountant of Brewster Fitzpayne Limited, a small manufacturing company. The management accounting information used in the company has previously been at a low level in terms of both quantity and quality. The finance director of the company was himself appointed only a few months ago, and he has decided that, as a priority, the management information system should be improved. He is planning, with your assistance, to install a budgeting system, but he needs to persuade his fellow directors that this innovation will be of benefit to the company. He has asked you to draft a briefing paper to the board setting out the principal benefits of a system of budgetary control.

8.2 Buckle Purslane Limited uses a rolling budget system. The company's directors are currently preparing a sales and production budget for the month of March 20X7, which is just over one year away.

They have decided that sales of their single product should be budgeted at 12 000 units for March 20X7, with 14 800 units budgeted for April 20X7. The company's policy is to hold closing stock of finished goods at 75% of the next following month's sales level.

What is the production budget in units for March 20X7?

a)   8 100

b)   14 100

c)   9 900

d)   12 000.

8.3 Luminant Productions Limited produces light fittings from a small factory unit. The company's directors have just met to discuss the sales budget and related matters for the next quarter, and have come up with the following figures for projected sales:

	Units
July 20X6	8 600
August 20X6	8 200
September 20X6	9 000

Opening stock of finished goods at 1 July 20X6 is expected to be 6000 units. The directors feel that they keep too many units in stock and they intend to reduce stock to more reasonable levels over the next few months. They plan to reduce opening stock by 500 units each month after July 20X6.

Each light fitting unit uses £2 of raw materials. Raw materials stock at 1 July is estimated to have a value of £2800. The directors wish to increase that stock level slightly over the next few months, as there is a danger of running out of stock to transfer to production.

	£
Opening stock at 1 August should be:	3 000
Opening stock at 1 September should be:	3 100
Opening stock at 1 October should be:	3 200

Calculate for each of the three months:

a) The production budget (in units).

b) The raw material purchases budget (in £s).

8.4 Barfield Primrose Limited is the manufacturer of the renowned 'Primrose' ice cream maker, which retails at £199. Barfield Primrose sells to wholesalers at £145 per unit. The prime cost structure of the ice cream maker is as follows:

	Per unit
Direct materials	37.00
Direct labour	24.00
Prime cost	61.00

For the year ending 31 December 20X2, the finance director of Barfield Primrose estimates that production overheads will be incurred totalling £312 390. He plans to use an overhead recovery rate based upon budgeted machine hours. The budget for machine hours is 17 355 hours for the year, and each unit produced uses up 1.5 machine hours.

Administrative and selling cost budgets have been prepared and the directors have recently decided on the sales forecasts for the coming year. The forecasts for the first three months are as follows:

	Sales forecasts: units	Administrative and selling costs: £
January	620	18 400
February	610	19 250
March	640	18 900

Calculate a budget overhead recovery rate for use by the company during 20X2. Then prepare a budget profit and loss account for each of the three months January–March 20X2.

8.5 Reinhart has his own wholesale business selling goods to retailers. His sales are made entirely on credit. In respect of the sales in any given month he expects 75% to be paid for in the next following month, and 25% in the month after that. (So, for example, sales made on credit in March would be paid for in April as to 75% and May as to 25%.)

Budget data relating to four months of Reinhart's sales are as follows:

	£
November 20X4	25 000
December 20X4	26 800
January 20X5	21 000
February 20X5	21 300

Reinhart is preparing his cash flow forecast for the month of February 20X5. How much should he include as sales receipts?

a) £21 000

b) £21 250

c) £22 450

d) £21 225.

8.6 Skippy is about to set up in business as a tour operator, after several years of working in the travel industry. He is starting out on a small scale, working from a room in a friend's office. The friend has agreed to let him have the room rent-free for six months in order to get him started.

In his first quarter of operations, January–March 20X4, Skippy plans two tours, both coach trips to Austria. He advertises the trips in November and December 20X3, paying the cost of £3000 out of his own money. He also pays £2000 for a computer. He intends that both of these amounts should constitute his initial capital contribution to the new business. The computer will be depreciated over its estimated useful life of five years on the straight-line basis.

The revenue and cost structure of each trip is as follows:

	£
The trip will cost £530 per person. The coach carries a maximum of 60 people and Skippy expects an 80% load factor – that is, 48 people. So 48 × £530 = sales revenue per trip	25 440
Hotel costs = £42.50 per person for 7 nights half board accommodation: 7 × £42.50 × 48	14 280
Coach travel costs	2 600
Insurance bond	1 500

The first trip is planned for 17 February, and the second for 15 March. The sales revenue from the trips will be received in advance – receipts from trip one will be received in January, and from trip two in February.

The hotel requires a non-returnable deposit of 50% in advance, with the remainder paid at the end of the stay. Advance payments for trip one will be made in January, and for trip two will be made in February.

The coach costs must also be paid in advance: trip one will be paid for in January and trip two in February. The insurance bond for both trips will be paid in January.

Other costs are: phone – the bill for an estimated £360 will be paid in March; and sundry office costs – £200 paid in cash each month.

Prepare for Skippy:

i) A budget cash flow statement for the three months of January, February and March 20X4.

ii) A budget profit and loss account for the three months ending 31 March 20X4.

iii) A budget balance sheet at 31 March 20X4.

8.7 Referring to the information given in exercise 8.6, at the beginning of April 20X4 Skippy reviews the past three months. Bookings on the first coach trip to Austria were not as good as planned: he sold only 42 places on the coach. However, the second trip was very popular with sales of 50 places. The hotel charged Skippy based upon the actual, not the budgeted number of people. Coach and insurance costs remained the same.

Actual office costs were higher than budgeted: in January Skippy paid £230, in February £350 and in March £270. The phone bill of £455 was paid in March. Prepare a profit and loss account for the three months ending 31 March 20X4 showing columns for actual results, budgeted results and the variation between the two. Also prepare an actual balance sheet at 31 March 20X4 showing an extra column for the budgeted figures. Has Skippy's business performed better or worse than budget, overall?

Exercises: answers available to lecturers

8.8 It is widely recognised that budget setting can be mishandled in organisations and may result in some undesirable effects that work against an organisation's best interests. Write a short report that describes potential problems that may arise if budgeting is not handled properly.

8.9 Hillgate St. Martins Limited manufactures a single product. Its budget sales (in units) for December 20X4 are 9350. Opening stock of finished goods for the month is budgeted at 12 360 units and closing stock is budgeted at 13 475 units.

Each unit of finished goods stock uses 2kg of a raw material that is forecast to cost £3 per kilo. Opening stock of raw material at the beginning of December 20X4 is forecast at 18 000 kilos, but closing stock for the month should fall to 16 000 kilos.

What is the budget amount in £s of purchases of this raw material for December 20X4?

a) £56 790

b) £68 790

c) £49 410

d) £55 410.

8.10 Colney Brighouse Limited makes office furniture. The company's directors are preparing sales and production forecasts for January, February and March 20X4. Sales forecasts in units for its two principal products, tables and office chairs, are as follows for the relevant months:

	Tables	Chairs
January 20X4	13 000	28 000
February 20X4	15 000	31 000
March 20X4	16 000	35 000
April 20X4	18 000	36 000

Opening stock at 1 January 20X4 is forecast at 7500 (tables) and 19 000 (chairs). The directors have decided to aim for closing stock at the end of each month amounting to exactly 50% of the following month's sales requirements. Prepare the production budget for tables and chairs for January–March 20X4 (inclusive).

8.11 Corby Thirlwell Limited manufactures ornamental birdbaths made out of reconstituted stone. The company works on a rolling budget system, and its senior management is currently examining forecasts for the month of June

20X1. June is a big month for sales in the birdbath business, and the directors are optimistically forecasting sales of 3250 units. They intend to launch a sales incentive scheme to encourage the sales staff to sell more birdbaths; from the beginning of 20X1 each birdbath sold will result in a payment of £1.50 to the salesperson. The selling price of each birdbath is £65. The production cost structure of one birdbath is as follows:

Per unit	£
Direct materials	18.00
Direct labour	12.57
Production overhead recovery	13.86
Production cost	44.43

Administrative overheads for June 20X1 are forecast at £12 479, and selling and distribution overheads (excluding the cost of commission) are forecast at £10 220.

Prepare a budget profit and loss account for the month of June 20X1.

8.12 Roxanne's budgeted year-end accounts at 31 December 20X4 include a figure for debtors of £23 600. This represents:

	£
20% of November sales of £28 000	5 600
60% of December sales of £30 000	18 000
	23 600

This calculation is based upon the normal pattern of receipts for the business: 40% of sales on credit are paid for within the same month, and 40% are paid for in the following month, with the remaining 20% paid for in the month after that.

If January 20X5 sales are budgeted at £28 000. How much will be included for sales receipts in the cash flow forecast in January 20X5?

a) £28 800

b) £23 600

c) £24 000

d) £19 520.

8.13 Silas is starting out in business on his own, running a shop selling scuba diving gear. He has gained a lot of free publicity for his new venture by writing articles in specialist trade and enthusiasts' magazines, and he is well known as a leading expert on scuba diving. He is therefore fairly confident that he will be able to start selling in reasonable quantities straight away.

Silas is renting shop premises, and his principal start-up cost has been the cost of equipping the shop with stock. He has also invested in an electronic till, a computer for keeping track of stock and dealing with correspondence, and some general shop fixtures and fittings. His expenditure just prior to start up is:

	£
Stock	42 000
Computer	2 500
Till	1 000
Fixtures & fittings	3 500
Total	49 000

Silas also transfers £6000 from his own bank account into a new business bank account. He has sold his house to finance the new venture and is currently living in the flat above the shop.

In his first year in trading Silas plans the following sales and purchases of stock:

	Sales	Purchases
	£	£
April	1 500	2 250
May	4 500	3 750
June	8 250	6 750
July	9 000	7 500
August	12 000	7 500
September	12 000	7 500
October	12 000	6 750
November	10 500	6 750
December	12 000	6 375
January	7 500	6 375
February	9 000	5 625
March	10 500	6 000
	108 750	73 125

It is expected that most sales will be for cash, but 25% are planned to be made on credit to scuba diving organisations. Credit sales are expected to be settled in full in the month after invoicing.

Purchases of stock will be on credit, with payment made in full in the month following purchase. Closing stock at the end of March is budgeted at £42 045.

Silas has budgeted for the following expenses:

Expense item	£	Payment details
Rent	6 000	Payable in quarterly instalments in April, July, October and January
Insurance	1 200	Payable in April
Phone	600	Quarterly bills of £150 to be paid in June, September, December and March
Water rates	750	Payable in May
Business rates	1 500	Payable in April
Wages	1 800	£150 to be paid each month
Subscriptions	300	£150 in May and £150 in November
Sundry admin and other expenses	2 400	£200 to be paid each month

Silas plans to draw £1000 from the business in cash each month.

The computer will be subject to depreciation on a straight-line basis over four years. Fixtures and fittings and the electronic till have an estimated useful life of 10 years and will be depreciated on a straight-line basis. No residual values are expected at the end of the assets' useful lives.

Prepare the following statements for Silas:

i)   Budget cash flow statement showing the cash movement in each of the first 12 months of business.

ii)   Budget profit and loss account for the 12 months ending 31 March.

iii) Budget balance sheet at 31 March.

8.14 Working with the information from 8.13, put the cash flow information into a spreadsheet. Use the spreadsheet to perform 'what if' calculations to answer Silas's questions as follows:

i)   'What would happen to my estimated cash at bank balance at the end of March if my debtors took two months, instead of one month, to pay me? Would the bank account go overdrawn at any point in the year?'

ii)   'I think I may have underestimated my sundry admin expenses. What would happen to the cash at bank balance at the end of March if my expenses each month were £400 rather than £200?'

iii) 'What would happen to the end of March cash at bank balance if both of these things happened – i.e. debtors take two months to pay me, not one, and admin expenses increase to £400 each month? Would I have an overdraft at any point, and if so, what would be the maximum budget overdraft figure?'

CASE STUDY 8.1   Business start-up: Budget vs. actual

This case study picks up the story of Pete from Chapter 2. Pete started out in business in a very low-key way. Having managed fairly successfully to combine a small, part-time business venture together with full-time employment, he had more or less decided by the end of the Chapter 2 spotlight to become self-employed on a full-time basis, running a coffee bar.

This case study is divided into two parts. Part 1 requires the preparation of budget statements (cash flow, profit and loss account and balance sheet). Part 2 examines the monitoring process, and requires students to comment on Pete's progress in the first three months.

Part 1

Pete spends most of the 20X7 calendar year preparing to open his new business. Having identified premises that he can afford to rent, he then spends some time standing about outside counting the number of passers-by. The premises are on the edge of the main town centre, but are on a road that is used quite frequently by students going to college. Having studied the foot traffic, Pete is fairly confident that he will be able to attract passing trade. As regards competition, there are two other coffee bars in town. One is in the shopping centre, attached to a large department store. It attracts quite a high volume of business and always seems to be busy despite the fact that the coffee is really not very good. The other coffee bar is on the opposite side of town from Pete and he doesn't regard it as a serious competitor.

Pete's accountant, Norris, has been helpful in advising him on a business plan, and in forcing Pete to think carefully about costs. Together, they decide upon the assumptions and estimates set out below. These will be used to prepare a budget.

1. Volume of trade: Pete reckons that trade will increase as people get to know about his coffee bar, and about the good quality coffee he plans to serve. He estimates that he should attract somewhere between 70 and 90 customers on an average day once the business gets established. To be on the safe side he estimates 70 customers per day for the first month, 75 per day for the second and third months of trading, 80 per day for the fourth and fifth months of trading, 85 for the sixth month of trading and 90 thereafter. Each month contains, on average, 26 days when the coffee bar will be open.

2. Average spend per person: Pete estimates that most people will buy at least one coffee plus a posh Italian biscuit or cake. Average spend is estimated at £2.50.

3. Gross profit percentage is estimated at 72%.

4. Pete and Norris establish a list of expenses that the business will incur in its first year, and the estimated timings of their payment:

Category	£	Estimated timing
Legal fees	1 000	To be paid in month 1
Launch party	2 300	To be paid in month 1
Advertising	1 600	£1000 in month 1, £400 in month 3 and £200 in month 6

Category	£	Estimated timing
Wages	2 800	£233 or £234 per month
Rental of premises	7 500	£1 875 in months 1, 4, 7 and 10
Business rates	2 600	£2 600 in month 3
Water rates	860	£71 or £72 per month
Power, heat and light	800	£200 in months 3, 6, 9 and 12
Phone charges	400	£100 in months 3, 6, 9 and 12
Insurance	500	£500 in month 1
Accountant's fees	800	£400 in month 5 and £400 in month 12
	21 160	

Wages are payable to an assistant who will help Pete out on two days per week for 50 weeks of the year. He or she will be paid for 7 hours per day at a rate of £4.00 per hour.

5. The shop needs some refitting and decoration. The costs will be kept as low as possible because Pete and his brother Dave will do a lot of the work themselves. Estimated costs to be incurred before opening are:

	£
Refurbishment and decoration	5 000
Fixtures and fittings (tables, chairs, cups, saucers etc.)	3 000
Coffee machine	5 000
	13 000

Pete will use savings of £2000 to meet part of these initial costs. Dave offers to do the work for free, and also amazes Pete by producing a cheque for £3000 out of his own savings to put into the business. Pete is touched and pleased that his brother is willing to support him by putting up some money, but he insists on treating it as a loan. Dave accepts this, but says that he definitely doesn't want any interest.

The costs of refurbishing the premises and buying essential equipment will be treated as fixed assets, to be depreciated on a straight-line basis over five years, and on the assumption that there will be no residual value at the end of that time.

6. Norris points out to Pete that he had better make some allowance for drawings because Pete and his wife and children have no other regular income. After some discussion they fix upon £900 per month as being the minimum amount necessary to support the family.

7. It is assumed that all the set-up expenses will be incurred and paid for immediately before the start of business. Set-up expenses will amount to £13 000, but against that can be set off the contributions from Pete and his brother, totalling £5000, so the business will start off with a negative cash position of £8000.

8. In order to keep things simple the cash flow forecast should exclude the effect of any interest payable.

Required: prepare a cash flow forecast for Pete's first year of trading, a budget profit and loss account for the same period, and a budget balance sheet at the end of year 1.

Hint: because a coffee bar is a cash business there will be no debtors. Also, it can be assumed that supplies are bought and paid for straight away, so cost of sales will be the same as payments for suppliers.

Part 2

Pete and Norris visit the bank manager with a business plan that includes the cash flow forecast and budget profit and loss account for the first year, and the budget balance sheet at the end of the first year. After a long discussion, the bank manager agrees to make an overdraft facility of £15 000 available at a rate of 10% per year. However, the bank manager flatly refuses to make the overdraft available without security. Pete and his wife Angie rent their flat and have no property of their own. After consultation with members of his family, Pete persuades his mother to put her house up as security for the overdraft. Pete signs a lease for the new shop, and he and Dave start work immediately. Having taken a course in book-keeping at the local college, Angie starts keeping the accounts for the business.

After three months, Pete and Angie meet the accountant, Norris, to discuss the results of the first three months trading. They are rather worried that things are not going according to plan. The actual figures for each month are set out below:

Month	1 Actual £	1 Budget £	2 Actual £	2 Budget £	3 Actual £	3 Budget £
Receipts (sales)	2 604		2 998		3 016	
Payments						
Cost of sales	774		929		944	
Legal fees	1 200		—		—	
Launch party	1 907		—		—	
Advertising	980		—		—	
Wages	200		180		—	
Rental	1875		—		—	
Business rates	—		—		2 600	
Water rates	72		72		71	
Power, heat, light	—		—		190	
Phone charges	—		—		87	
Insurance	505		—		—	
Accountant's fees	—		—		—	
Additional expenses	250		300		424	
Drawings	900		900		900	
Total payments	8 663		2 381		5 216	
Opening balance	(8 325)		(14 384)		(13 767)	
Add: receipts	2 604		2 998		3 016	
Less: payments	(8 663)		(2 381)		(5 216)	
Closing balance	(14 384)		(13 767)		(15 967)	

▶

Pete explains to Norris that he's not had quite as many customers as anticipated, and also that they're just not spending very much per head. They're mostly students and are short of cash. They tend to buy a small coffee and a cheap biscuit. The higher margin posh Italian biscuits and cakes are just not selling. Also, each month there has been some kind of unexpected expense. In the first month, a man came into the coffee bar and introduced himself as a representative from the Performing Rights Society. Because Pete plays the radio all day long, and the coffee bar is treated as a public place, the PRS is entitled to an annual payment of £250. In the second month, Pete discovered that the person he was employing to help out two days a week had been stealing from the till. He worked out that she'd taken about £300 from the till. He sacked her straight away, and since then has managed without any help. Then, in month three, he and neighbouring tenants discovered that there were rats in the back yard. Pete's share of the bill for employing ratcatchers was £424.

Pete has tried to cut back on advertising, and has managed to keep phone and electricity bills under control, but he is worried about the state of the overdraft. During March, Pete rang the bank and persuaded the manager to stretch the overdraft facility to £17 000 but he knows he can't keep on doing this.

Required:

a) Complete the actual/budget statement for the first three months of trading by entering the first three months' budget figures into the statement given above.

b) Discuss Pete's first three months of trading, and comment on his business prospects for the rest of the year.

Standard costing, flexible budgeting and variance analysis

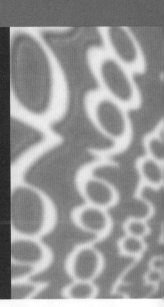

Aim of the chapter

To understand the nature of a standard costing system, the application of flexible budgeting in interpreting actual results against budgets and the detailed analysis of variances.

Learning outcomes

After reading the chapter and completing the related exercises, students should:

- Understand the use of a standard costing system in a manufacturing environment.
- Be able to compare actual results against flexed budgets.
- Be able to analyse and understand the range of possible reasons for the variances that emerge from comparison of actual with standard costs.

Identifying and attributing variances

In the previous chapter we examined the setting of budgets and the comparison of actual with budgeted results. Often the identification and analysis of the difference between actual and budgeted performance is quite straightforward. For example, suppose that a business budgets to spend £10 500 on business insurance on the basis that the previous year's charge was £10 000 and the general level of price inflation suggests that 5% would be a likely level of increase. The business's insurers, however, and in common with the rest of the insurance industry, raise charges by 10%. The actual bill for insurance totals £11 000, £500 more than was budgeted. Investigation of other insurers shows that it is not possible to obtain cover for less than £11 000. The adverse variance of £500 against budget in this case can be easily explained. It is a general price increase, not attributable to any internal factor such as poor purchasing or failure to control expenditure properly.

In practice, however, and especially in a relatively complex manufacturing environment, it can be difficult to track down the reasons for variances unless some quite detailed analysis is carried out.

Example 9.1

Sugden Harkness Limited, a manufacturing business, sets a budget based upon a sales forecast for July of 5000 units. Each unit of product is budgeted to use 3 metres of raw material (15 000 metres in total) at a cost of £4.20 per metre (15 000 × £4.20 = £63 000). The actual business performance statement for July shows that, although exactly 5000 units were sold, the total cost of the raw material element of cost of sales was £68 000. What has happened here? Clearly, raw material costs have increased; there is an adverse variance of £68 000 − £63 000 = £5000. The reasons, however, are not clear, unless further analysis is undertaken. It could be that:

- The price has increased to a level higher than the £4.20 budgeted.
- The production process has been less efficient than expected and has used more than 3 metres of raw material per unit of product.
- Both of these factors are present in some combination.

The management accountant of Sugden Harkness needs to be able to analyse the variance in more detail in order to be able to: (a) find out if there is a problem that needs attention; and (b) attribute responsibility for the adverse variance to the appropriate department or person.

The process of **responsibility accounting** ensures that problems are tracked to their source. Having correctly identified the source, it is then the responsibility of management to ensure that problems are dealt with via appropriate corrective action. As we saw in the previous chapter, one of the possible adverse consequences of a budgeting system arises where responsibility is incorrectly attributed, leading to resentment and demotivation. Sometimes, the reason for the occurrence of a problem seems obvious, but further investigation may be required to look beyond the apparently obvious and to uncover true causes and effects.

Taking the example of Sugden Harkness a little further, suppose that the adverse variance was found to be attributable to extra usage of the raw material.

This looks, on the face of it, as though it should be the responsibility of the production manager and his team. It may well result from inefficiencies in the use of raw materials (too much wastage, for example). However, the picture changes if we find out that the regular supplier of the raw material had increased prices, and that, in response to the increase, the purchasing manager had purchased inferior quality material but at the budget price. The poorer quality resulted in more wastage as the material was put through the production process. The adverse variance now appears to be attributable to the purchasing manager rather than the production manager.

Despite problems of this type in attributing responsibility for variances, variance identification and analysis are very common procedures in manufacturing industry. Variances are often identified and quantified by using a **standard costing** system.

Standard costing

Standard costing is a system of costing that can be used in business environments where a repetitive series of standardised operations are carried out. In such systems each element of production involves a consistent input of resources at prices that can be predicted with a fair degree of accuracy.

Standard costs are the budgeted costs of individual units of production. The standard cost is compared with actual cost in order to calculate an overall variance. This overall variance can then be broken down further in order to identify:

- The effects of variation in volume of the resource inputs.
- The effects of variation in price of the resource inputs.

Standard costing and variance analysis are widely used in industries where mass production is carried out. Managers in such industries are frequently presented with financial reports including information about variances, and it is important even for non-financial managers to understand something about the fundamentals of standard costing systems.

Establishing standard costs

As we saw in the previous chapter, establishing budget information can be a time-consuming and potentially expensive task. Standard costs may also require a substantial investment of time in research and observation. For example, in order to establish standard costs for the direct materials component of a product, it is necessary to examine two aspects: (a) the purchase price of the material inputs; and (b) the expected rate at which material is used in the product.

The purchase price may be variable depending upon the supplier used, quantities available, movements on commodities markets and so on. The standard cost will probably reflect a price that can be obtained with a reasonable amount of effort on the part of those responsible for materials purchasing. If too low a standard price is set, purchasers will not have to make much of an effort to better it. On the other hand, if the standard price set would be obtainable only rarely, then purchasers may become demotivated. The motivational and behavioural factors for this type of budgeting, in fact, are the same as those we examined in Chapter 8.

Establishing the rate of usage will require careful observation of the manufacturing process, probably on a number of separate occasions. Again, the rate of materials consumption adopted as the standard is likely to reflect a realistic achievable target, set neither too low nor too high. However, standard cost setters need to be wary of relying upon too many established precedents and practices. There may be a need to challenge lax and wasteful production procedures in setting standards.

Each element of cost of production is broken down and costed. Even for an apparently simple product, there may be many different elements of cost. Take a tin of beans, for example. Materials input per batch includes: beans, tomatoes, salt, sugar, flavourings, tins and labels. Each part of the processing involves labour and machine times, which must be timed to the second in order to produce accurate costs and forecasts.

For each product a standard cost card is built up. A simple illustration is given in the following comprehensive example.

Example 9.2

We will use a comprehensive example to illustrate the application of variance identification in a standard costing system. Although the basic facts in the example are straightforward there are several calculations. The whole example takes up several pages, because each step is explained in full. Students should work through it slowly and ensure that each point is understood before moving on. It will seem difficult, if not impossible, at first, but it does all hang together quite logically. Don't give up!

Sherborne Suggate Limited manufactures a specialised metal component that is sold to manufacturers of heavy lifting machinery. The standard cost card for one component is as follows:

	£	
Selling price	150.00	Per unit
Costs		
Direct materials	35.00	7kg of metal @ £5 per kilo
Direct labour	15.00	3 hours @ £5 per kilo
Prime cost	50.00	

The company's budget for January 20X3 is as follows:

	£
Sales: 1000 units @ £150	150 000
Costs	
Direct materials: 1000 units × (7kg × £5)	(35 000)
Direct labour: 1000 units × (3 hours × £5)	(15 000)
Production overhead	(50 000)
	50 000
Selling and administrative overhead	(20 000)
Net profit	30 000

The production overhead, as we have seen in previous chapters, is usually absorbed via an overhead absorption rate. For the purposes of this particular demonstration we will assume that the overheads are simply recorded, and also, that they remain at the same level regardless of changes in the level of production, i.e. they are fixed overhead costs. Later in the chapter we will examine overhead variances in more detail, but for the moment, we will simplify the overheads aspects of the question.

Simple comparison of budget with actual results

After the end of the 20X3 financial year, the management accountant identifies the variances between the budget and actual results.
    Actual results are as follows:

	£
Sales: 1 100 units @ £145	159 500
Costs	
Direct materials: 1 100 × (7.5kg × £4.50)	(37 125)
Direct labour: 1 100 units × (2.8 hours × £5.50)	(16 940)
Production overhead	(52 000)
	53 435
Selling and administrative overhead	(21 250)
Net profit	32 185

A very brief comparison of the statements shows us that the company has produced higher profits than expected. Good news, surely? Well, yes, but has the business made as much extra profit as might be expected, given that it has sold an extra 100 components? The answer to the question is not immediately obvious; it requires further analysis of the variances.

Flexing the budget

One problem with comparing the two statements shown above is that we are not really comparing like with like. The initial budget was produced on the assumption that 1000 units would be sold. The actual outcome is that 1100 units were sold. In order to make a more useful comparison, we need to adjust the budget to reflect the additional volume of sales. This is known as flexing the budget.
    The flexed budget profit and loss account (flexed to reflect the actual level of activity of 1100 units sold) is as follows:

	£
Sales: 1100 units @ £150	165 000
Costs	
Direct materials: 1100 × (7kg × £5)	(38 500)
Direct labour: 1100 units × (3 hours × £5)	(16 500)
Production overhead	(50 000)
	60 000

	£
Selling and administrative overhead	(20 000)
Net profit	40 000

The flexed budget shows the sales revenue that would have been expected from sales of 1100 units, and all the costs adjusted for the additional volume of sales. Remember that we are working on the assumption that production overheads do not increase in line with the volume of sales. Selling and administrative overheads, also, are assumed not to increase in line with the volume of sales; they are also regarded as fixed overhead costs. (Note: The distinction between variable costs and fixed costs will be examined in more detail later in the chapter.)

We now have three profit and loss statements: the original budget, the flexed budget and the statement of actual results. It will help at this point to place them side by side:

	Original budget £	Flexed budget £	Actual £
Sales	150 000	165 000	159 500
Costs			
Direct materials	(35 000)	(38 500)	(37 125)
Direct labour	(15 000)	(16 500)	(16 940)
Production overhead	(50 000)	(50 000)	(52 000)
	50 000	60 000	53 435
Selling and administrative overhead	(20 000)	(20 000)	(21 250)
Net profit	30 000	40 000	32 185

Calculating variances

The original budget net profit was £30 000. Actual net profit is £32 185. The overall variance is a favourable variance of £2 185. We will break this figure down into its constituent variances which will allow us to identify possible problem areas.

Sales profit volume variance

A key element of the difference is the sale of more units than originally anticipated. This variance is the difference between the original budget profit and the flexed budget profit: £40 000 − £30 000 = £10 000. It is clearly in the interests of the company to sell more components, and so this is a favourable variance.

Sales price variance

The actual profit is affected by the fact that, although extra sales have been made, the selling price is actually lower than budgeted. This variance is calculated as follows:

		£
Actual volume of sales at actual selling price: 1100 × £145		159 500
Less: actual volume of sales at budget selling price:		
1100 × £150		165 000
Sales price variance		5 500

This represents an undesirable outcome for the firm; it would have been better to sell at the higher, budgeted price, so this is an adverse variance.

At this stage, refer back to the three statements presented side by side, and note that we are comparing the flexed budget statement with the actual statement in order to calculate this variance.

Direct materials variances

Comparing the figure for direct materials in the flexed budget statement with the figure in the actual statement:

	£
Flexed budget for direct materials	38 500
Actual direct materials	37 125
	1 375

The actual amount is less than budget; this is a good outcome and so this is classified as a favourable variance.

We can analyse this variance further by looking at the budget input of resources against actual input. Management accountants are able to calculate two direct materials variances: direct materials price variance and direct materials quantity variance. These relate, respectively, to price effects and volume effects.

Direct materials price variance. We compare:

- The actual quantity of raw materials used at the price actually paid (actual price).
- The actual quantity of raw materials used at the price budgeted (standard price).

Using the same measure of quantity (actual) ensures that we isolate the price effect.

	£
Actual quantity at actual price	
7.5kg was used for each of 1100 components	
Actual quantity used is 7.5kg × 1100 = 8 250kg	
8250kg × price actually paid (£4.50)	37 125
Actual quantity at standard price	
8 250kg × standard price (£5.00)	41 250
Direct materials price variance	4 125

The business has paid less per unit for direct materials than it expected; this is therefore a favourable variance.

Direct materials quantity variance. We compare:

- The actual quantity of materials used at standard price.
- The standard quantity of materials used at standard price.

	£
Actual quantity at standard price	
Actual quantity used (already worked out) – 8 250kg	
Standard price per kg – £5	
Actual quantity at standard price = 8 250 × £5	41 250
Standard quantity at standard price	
Standard quantity: 7kg × 1 100 components = 7 700kg	
Standard price per kg – £5	
Standard quantity at standard price = 7 700 × £5	38 500
Direct materials quantity variance	2 750

The business has used more materials per component than budgeted; this is therefore an adverse variance.

In summary, the direct materials variances are:

	£
Direct materials price variance	4 125 (F)
Direct materials quantity variance	2 750 (A)
Direct materials variance	1 375 (F)

Note: 'F' stands for Favourable; 'A' stands for Adverse.

Direct labour variances

Comparing the figure for direct labour in the flexed budget statement with the figure in the actual statement:

	£
Flexed budget for direct labour	16 500
Actual direct labour	16 940
	440

The actual amount is more than budget; this is not a good outcome and so is classified as an adverse variance.

As with direct materials, we can break down this overall variance into two variances, one quantifying the price effect and the other quantifying the volume effect. These are traditionally known (respectively) as the direct labour rate variance and the direct labour efficiency variance.

Direct labour rate variance. We compare:

- The actual hours of direct labour used at the wage rate actually paid (actual rate).
- The actual hours of direct labour used at the wage rate budgeted (standard rate).

Using the same measure of hours (actual) ensures that we isolate the rate effect.

	£
Actual hours at actual rate	
Actual hours was 2.8 hours for each of 1 100 components:	
2.8 × 1 100 = 3 080 hours	
3 080 hours × rate actually paid (£5.50)	16 940
Actual hours at standard rate	
3 080 hours × standard rate (£5.00)	15 400
Direct labour rate variance	1 540

The business has paid more per hour for direct labour than it budgeted; this is therefore an adverse variance.

Direct labour efficiency variance. We compare:

- The actual hours of direct labour used at standard rate.
- The standard hours of direct labour used at standard rate.

	£
Actual hours at standard rate	
Actual hours used (already worked out) – 3 080 hours	
Standard rate per hour: £5	
Actual hours at standard rate = 3 080 × £5	15 400
Standard hours at standard rate	
Standard hours: 3 hours × 1100 = 3 300	
Standard rate per hour: £5	
Standard hours at standard rate = 3 300 × £5	16 500
Direct labour efficiency variance	1 100

The business has used fewer hours per component than budgeted; this is therefore a favourable variance.

In summary, the direct labour variances are:

	£
Direct labour rate variance	1 540 (A)
Direct labour efficiency variance	1 100 (F)
Direct labour variance	440 (A)

Production overhead variance

	£
Budget figure for production overhead	50 000
Actual figure for production overhead	52 000
Production overhead variance	(2 000) (A)

The company appears to have spent more than initially planned; therefore, this is an adverse variance

Selling and administrative overhead variance

	£
Budget figure for selling and administrative overhead:	20 000
Actual figure for selling and administrative overhead:	21 250
Production overhead variance	(1 250) (A)

Having calculated this long list of variances, they can now be presented in the form of a standard cost operating statement, as follows:

Sherborne Suggate Limited: Standard cost operating statement for January 20X3

	Total £
Original budgeted net profit	30 000
Sales profit volume variance	10 000
Flexed budget net profit	40 000

	Favourable £	(Adverse) £	
Other variances			
Sales price variance		(5 500)	
Direct materials price variance	4 125		
Direct materials quantity variance		(2 750)	
Direct labour rate variance		(1 540)	
Direct labour efficiency variance	1 100		
Production overhead variance		(2 000)	
Selling and administrative overhead variance		(1 250)	
Total	5 225	(13 040)	(7 815)
Actual net profit			32 185

What does this statement tell us? Remember that we started out with the simple observation that there was an overall favourable variance between budgeted profit and actual profit of £2185. The standard cost operating statement above allows us to identify the component parts of that overall variance, and to pinpoint the areas where problems may have arisen. There are several adverse variances:

- *Sales price variance.* Although the volume of sales has increased, the beneficial effect on profit is not as great as it might have been because the selling price has fallen. Of course, these two factors may very well be related; it could be that the company has made a deliberate attempt to boost sales by setting a lower selling price. If that was the intention, the objective appears to have been met.
- *Direct materials quantity variance.* It appears that the production process is less efficient in terms of usage of materials than was originally intended. There may be good reasons why this has happened; indeed, the problem

may be that the original standard set for quantity was too ambitious. Further investigation of the variance would probably be necessary. This adverse variance, however, is more than offset by a favourable direct materials price variance. Perhaps a special purchase of materials has been made, but, of course, if the quality is slightly poorer, it may be more difficult to use the materials efficiently.

- *Direct labour rate variance*. Production staff appear to have been paid at a higher rate than allowed for in the standard cost calculations. If this is a permanent change, the standard cost needs changing. If it is a temporary change, the reasons for it should be investigated. It is noticeable, however, that the direct labour efficiency variance is positive; perhaps higher paid staff are working more quickly, or perhaps the supervision process is more effective than originally anticipated.

While the standard cost operating statement certainly provides management with more information than a simple statement like 'profits have gone up', it does not, clearly, answer all the questions. However, it serves a useful purpose in directing management's attention to areas that may require investigation and in suggesting the kind of questions that should be asked.

Before moving on, try this self-test question, which runs through the same variance calculations as the example above.

? Self-test question 9.1 (answer at the end of the book)

Bridge and Blige Limited make metal casings for lawn mowers in one standard size. In February 20X6 the company's budget for sales and related costs is as follows:

	£
Sales: 800 units × £35	28 000
Costs	
Direct materials: 800 units × (2kg × £6)	(9 600)
Direct labour: 800 units × (1 hour × £7.50)	(6 000)
Production overheads	(4 000)
	8 400
Selling and administrative overheads	(2 300)
Net profit	6 100

The actual figures for February 20X6 are as follows:

	£
Sales: 900 units @ £36	32 400
Costs	
Direct materials: 900 units × (1.9kg × £5.50)	(9 405)
Direct labour: 900 units × (1.2 hours × £7.00)	(7 560)
Production overheads	(4 400)
	11 035

Selling and administrative overheads	(2 450)
Net profit	8 585

i) Prepare a flexed budget for 900 units for February 20X6.

ii) Calculate the full range of variances demonstrated in the Sherborne Suggate Limited example (Example 9.2).

iii) Prepare a standard cost operating statement that reconciles the difference between the budget net profit and the actual net profit figures shown in the statements above.

Overhead variances

The Sherborne Suggate example given above contained only very simple overhead variances. However, it can be useful to management to have access to rather more detailed analysis. It is customary in manufacturing businesses to draw a distinction between variable overheads and fixed overheads in the calculation of variances relating to production overheads.

Variable overheads are those that increase or decrease corresponding to increases and decreases in production. For example, the following costs would all tend to vary as production levels vary:

■ machine cleaning and repair costs
■ machine oil and consumables costs
■ quality inspection costs.

Many overheads, however, will be fixed. A production supervisor's salary, for example, is likely to stay the same whether she is supervising the production of 100 units per day, or 95, or 105. It would be a different matter if production changed radically and the number increased to, say, 1000. More production supervisors would have to be employed. However, it is safe to say that, provided variations in production levels are relatively small, many costs remain the same.

In Example 9.3 we will examine variable and fixed overhead variances by means of a demonstration. It is possible to break down overhead variances for activity and expenditure effects (as for materials and labour) but such a level of complexity is regarded as being beyond the scope of this book. We will, therefore, calculate only one overall variance for variable production overheads and one overall variance for fixed production overheads.

Example 9.3

Goldman Le Saint Limited produces a single product. Its budget for March 20X7 is as follows:

	£
Sales: 1000 units @ £80	80 000

	£
Costs	
Direct materials: 1 000 units × (4kg × £3)	(12 000)
Direct labour: 1 000 units × (3 hours × £5.00)	(15 000)
Variable production overheads: 1 000 units × (4 machine hours × £2.00)	(8 000)
Fixed production overheads: 1 000 units × (4 machine hours × £6.00)	(24 000)
	21 000
Selling and administrative overheads	(4 000)
Net profit	17 000

Note that in this example production overheads are split into variable and fixed production overheads – the first time that we have encountered such a split.

Both variable and fixed production overheads are recovered via overhead absorption rates based upon machine hours. The budget machine hours for March 20X7 are 4000 hours (1000 units × 4 machine hours per unit). The actual figures for March 20X7 are as follows:

	£
Sales: 900 units × £80	72 000
Costs	
Direct materials: 900 units × (4kg × £3.00)	(10 800)
Direct labour: 900 units × (3 hours × £5.00)	(13 500)
Variable overheads	(9 600)
Production overheads	(25 500)
	12 600
Selling and administrative overheads	(4 000)
Net profit	8 600

The first stage in calculating variances, as before, is to flex the budget for the actual level of sales activity. Flexed budget for 900 units:

	£
Sales: 900 units × £80	72 000
Costs	
Direct materials: 900 units × (4kg × £3.00)	(10 800)
Direct labour: 900 units × (3 hours × £5.00)	(13 500)
Variable overheads: 900 units × (4 hours × £2)	(7 200)
Fixed production overheads: 900 units × (4 hours × £6)	(21 600)
	18 900
Selling and administrative overheads	(4 000)
Net profit	14 900

As in the previous example, it will be helpful to set the original budget statement, the flexed budget statement and the actual statement side by side:

	Original budget £	Flexed budget £	Actual £
Sales	80 000	72 000	72 000
Costs			
Direct materials	(12 000)	(10 800)	(10 800)
Direct labour	(15 000)	(13 500)	(13 500)
Variable production overhead	(8 000)	(7 200)	(9 600)
Fixed production overhead	(24 000)	(21 600)	(25 500)
	21 000	18 900	12 600
Selling and administrative overhead	(4 000)	(4 000)	(4 000)
Net profit	17 000	14 900	8 600

The overall variance is:

	£
Original budget net profit	17 000
Actual net profit	8 600
	8 400 (A)

Sales profit volume variance

This variance is the difference between the original budget profit and the flexed budget profit: £17 000 − £14 900 = £2100 (A). The variance is adverse because the flexed budget profit is lower than the original budget profit.

Anyone who has managed to keep up so far will see that there are no variances for sales price, direct material, direct labour, and selling and administrative overheads. Once the budget is flexed, it becomes clear that sales prices, direct material and direct labour costs are exactly as would have been predicted if 900 units had been budgeted for. The example therefore isolates the changes in variable and fixed production overhead.

Variable production overhead variance

The variance can be calculated in the same way as, say, the total direct materials variance: by comparing the totals in the flexed budget statement with the actual statement:

	£
Flexed budget for variable overhead	7 200
Actual variable overhead	9 600
	2 400 (A)

Fixed production overhead variance

The overall variance can be calculated in the same way as, say, the total direct materials variance: by comparing the totals in the flexed budget statement with the actual statement:

	£
Flexed budget for fixed overhead	21 600
Actual fixed overhead	25 500
	3 900 (A)

We can now produce a standard cost operating statement for March 20X7:

Goldman Le Saint Limited: Standard cost operating statement for March 20X7

	Total £
Original budgeted net profit	17 000
Sales profit volume variance	(2 100)
Flexed budget net profit	14 900

	Favourable £	(Adverse) £	
Other variances			
Sales price variance	—	—	
Direct materials price variance	—	—	
Direct materials quantity variance	—	—	
Direct labour rate variance	—	—	
Direct labour efficiency variance	—	—	
Variable overhead variance	—	(2 400)	
Fixed overhead variance	—	(3 900)	
Selling and administrative overhead variance	—	—	
Total	—	(6 300)	(6 300)
Actual net profit			8 600

Before moving on, try Self-test question 9.2, which isolates the calculation of the variable and fixed production overhead variances.

? Self-test question 9.2 (answer at the end of the book)

Singh and Waterhouse Limited manufacture one style of storage shelving. The company's budget for April 20X8 is as follows:

	£
Sales: 1 800 × £45	81 000
Costs	
Direct materials: 1 800 units × (16 metres × £1.00 per metre)	(28 800)
Direct labour: 1 800 units × (2 hours × £5.00 per hour)	(18 000)

Variable production overheads: 1 800 units × (2 machine hours per unit × £1)	(3 600)
Fixed production overheads: 1 800 units × (2 machine hours per unit × £6)	(21 600)
Profit before other overheads	9 000

The actual figures for April 20X8 are as follows:

	£
Sales: 2000 units × £45	90 000
Costs	
Direct materials: 2 000 units × (16 metres × £1)	(32 000)
Direct labour: 2 000 units × (2 hours × £5.00)	(20 000)
Variable overheads	(3 800)
Production overheads	(23 400)
Profit before other overheads	10 800

You are required to:

a) Flex the budget for a sales level of 2000 units.

b) Calculate all variances.

c) Prepare a standard cost operating statement for the company for April 20X8.

Investigating the reasons for variances

Implementing a standard costing system represents a major investment of time and other resources for most businesses. The benefits of this investment will outweigh the costs only if full use is made by management of the information conveyed by variances. It is important, too, that the investigation of variances is carried out promptly. The examples in this chapter have all assumed that standard costs are being compared with actual on a monthly basis; this is a realistic assumption which reflects actual practice in industry. If the comparison were to be made annually or even quarterly, any underlying problems would persist for far too long. In order for management to be able to exert full control frequent and timely action is required.

Deciding which variances merit investigation

It is a matter of management policy to decide the level at which a variance becomes significant and worthy of further investigation. The following criteria will probably be important in deciding which variances merit investigation:

- *Significance in percentage or monetary terms*. For example, management may decide to investigate any variance, favourable or unfavourable, which is greater than 5% of the flexed budget total. Or they may use a monetary criterion, such as 'investigate any variance greater than £5000'.

- *Frequency of occurrence*. Variances may be individually minor, but cumulatively significant. For example, if there is a persistent adverse materials price variance across a range of different materials items, this may point to lax purchasing management.

Principal reasons for the occurrence of variances

Sales variances

Actual sales volume may differ from budget volume because of such factors as:

- greater than expected success of an advertising campaign
- improved efficiency and effectiveness of sales staff
- failure of a competitor
- entry of a new competitor into the market
- loss of sales staff, or loss of morale and motivation through poor management.

Sales prices may differ because of such factors as:

- lowering of prices to increase volume
- lowering of prices to respond to new competition
- increasing prices to take advantage of exit of competitor from the market
- fashion trends (it may be possible to charge higher prices for fashionable items).

Direct materials variances

Price variances may arise because of any, or a combination, of the following factors:

- successful negotiation for lower prices
- obtaining quantity discounts for large orders
- variation in material quality
- volatile market for material, leading to unexpected increases or decrease in price.

Quantity variances may arise as follows:

- better or worse quality of material than expected
- employment of higher or lower skilled workers than anticipated
- level of supervision/number of quality checks
- poor functioning of machinery.

Direct labour variances

Rate variances may arise in the following circumstances:

- The mix of labour differs from plan; for example, using more higher paid staff in production because of under-employment elsewhere in the factory.
- Unexpected increase in rate arising from the conclusion of negotiations over wage levels.

Efficiency variances may arise as follows:

- better or worse quality of material than expected
- employment of higher or lower skilled workers than anticipated

- level of supervision/number of quality checks
- poor functioning of machinery.

Overhead variances

Overhead variances may arise because of any of the following:

- non-controllable price changes because of events in the wider economy
- poor management control over costs
- improved management control over costs.

Last, but not least, variances may occur simply because the standard cost was incorrectly set. For example, if the standard cost for a particular item reflects the best possible cost achievable only in ideal circumstances, then it is unlikely to be met. The existence of variances may signal no more than the need to alter the standard cost. However, before this step is taken the variance should be thoroughly investigated to ensure that there is no other cause.

Chapter summary

This chapter has dealt with several important aspects of budgetary control in practice. First, standard costing and responsibility accounting were described. Then the principal part of the chapter was devoted to a detailed description of variance analysis, and the mechanics of variance calculation and reporting. The variances discussed are summarised in Figure 9.1.

The chapter then proceeded to discuss the investigation of variances. Criteria for investigation were briefly described, and then some of the principal causes of the different variances were identified.

The end-of-chapter exercises are divided into two sections. The first section has answers provided at the end of the book The second section, in the white box, has answers on the lecturers' section of the website. Finally, the chapter contains a case study that-covers many of the aspects of standard costing that have been covered here.

Figure 9.1	Summary of variances covered in the chapter

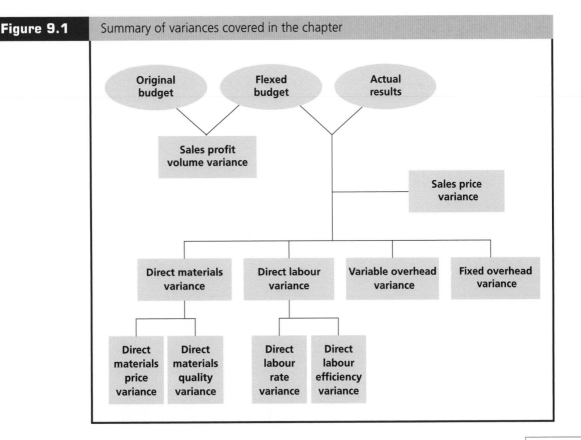

Website summary

The book's website contains the following material in respect of Chapter 9:

Students' section

- Quiz containing ten multiple choice questions
- Four additional questions with answers
- Answer to the case study at the end of this chapter.

Lecturers' section

- Answers to end-of-chapter exercises 9.11 to 9.19
- Five additional questions with answers.

Exercises: answers at the end of the book

9.1   Denholm Pargeter Limited is an engineering company producing a wide range of component parts for the aerospace industry. Its component XP04/H has the following budget sales and prime costs for March 20X1:

	£
Sales: 1 200 units × £30 per unit	36 000
Costs	
Direct materials: 1 200 units × (3kg × £1.20)	4 320
Direct labour: 1 200 units × (2 hours × £8.50)	20 400
Prime cost	24 720

The production manager wishes to assess the change to the budget on the basis that 1300 units are produced and sold.

You are required to flex the budget for component XP04/H for 1300 units.

9.2   Darblay Harriett Limited produces a single product – a wooden cabinet. The company's budget for November 20X9 is as follows:

	£
Sales: 2 000 units × £19.50	39 000
Costs	
Direct materials: 2 000 × (2 metres × £2.00)	(8 000)
Direct labour: 2 000 × (1 hour × £6.00)	(12 000)
Production overhead	(10 000)
	9 000
Selling and administrative overhead	(3 000)
Net profit	6 000

Darblay Harriett does not absorb production overheads using an overhead absorption rate. It may be assumed that all of its overheads are fixed in nature. If the company flexes its budget for 2600 units, what will be the revised net profit figure?

a)   £14 700

b)   £8 700

c)   £11 700

d)   £17 700.

The following information is relevant for questions 9.3 to 9.8.

Edwards and Sheerness Limited is in the motor parts industry. Its budget for July 20X2 is as follows:

	£
Sales: 2 500 units × £29.00	72 500

	£
Costs	
Direct materials: 2 500 × (3 kg × £3.00)	(22 500)
Direct labour: 2 500 × (1.5 hours × £4.40)	(16 500)
Production overhead	(17 000)
	16 500
Other overheads	(3 500)
Net profit	13 000

Edwards and Sheerness Limited does not absorb production overheads using an overhead absorption rate. It may be assumed that all of its overheads are fixed in nature.

The company's actual results for the month are as follows:

	£
Sales: 2 650 units × £28.00	74 200
Costs	
Direct materials: 2 650 × (2.8 kg × £3.30)	(24 486)
Direct labour: 2 650 × (1.7 hours × £4.20)	(18 921)
Production overhead	(16 900)
	13 893
Other overheads	(3 600)
Net profit	10 293

9.3   What is the sales profit volume variance for the month?

a)   £2 707 (A)

b)   £2 010 (A)

c)   £2 707 (F)

d)   £2 010 (F).

9.4   What is the sales price variance for the month?

a)   £640 (F)

b)   £640 (A)

c)   £2 650 (F)

d)   £2 650 (A).

9.5   What is the direct materials price variance for the month?

a)   £2 226 (F)

b)   £2 226 (A)

c)   £2 385 (F)

d)   £2 385 (A).

9.6   What is the direct materials quantity variance for the month?

    a)   £1 749 (F)

    b)   £1 749 (A)

    c)   £1 590 (F)

    d)   £1 590 (A).

9.7   What is the direct labour rate variance for the month?

    a)   £901 (A)

    b)   £795 (A)

    c)   £795 (F)

    d)   £901 (F).

9.8   What is the direct labour efficiency variance for the month?

    a)   £2 332 (F)

    b)   £2 332 (A)

    c)   £2 226 (F)

    d)   £2 226 (A).

9.9   Ferguson Farrar Limited is a manufacturing company. For the month of April 20X3 it budgeted for 4000 units of production, each to use 1.5 hours of machine time. Production overhead absorption rates were budgeted as follows:

    Variable production overhead = £4 per machine hour.
    Fixed production overhead = £8 per machine hour.

    The actual level of production in the month was 4200 units. The original production overhead budget, the flexed budget and the actual expenditure are shown in the following table:

	Original budget £	Flexed budget £	Actual £
Variable production overheads	24 000	25 200	26 250
Fixed production overheads	48 000	50 400	48 750
	72 000	75 600	75 000

    Calculate:

    a)   the variable production overhead variance

    b)   the fixed production overhead variance.

9.10   Grindleton Gears Limited is a manufacturing business that uses a standard costing system. If a variance exceeds 5% of the flexed budget total for that item, the management team investigates it, whether it is favourable or adverse. The company's flexed budget for February 20X4 is:

	£
Sales	123 470
Costs	
Direct materials	(28 250)
Direct labour	(29 900)
Variable production overheads	(8 640)
Fixed production overheads	(19 780)
Profit	36 900

The management team is presented with the following standard cost operating statement for the month:

	Total £
Original budgeted net profit	30 900
Sales profit volume variance	6 000
Flexed budget net profit	36 900

Other variances	Favourable £	(Adverse) £	
Sales price variance	1 030	—	
Direct materials price variance	—	(1 650)	
Direct materials quantity variance	—	(106)	
Direct labour rate variance	—	—	
Direct labour efficiency variance	200		
Variable overhead variance	1 400	—	
Fixed overhead variance	339	—	
Total	2 969	(1 756)	1 213
Actual profit			38 113

You are required to:

i) Using the company's own criterion, decide which variances should be examined.

ii) List reasons why the variances you have identified may have arisen.

iii) Calculate the actual figures for sales, direct materials, direct labour, variable overheads, fixed overheads and profit.

Exercises: answers available to lecturers

9.11 Dorchester Slugg Limited manufactures plastic refuse bins. Its monthly budget for August 20X6 is as follows:

	£
Sales: 4 000 units × £18	72 000

	£
Costs	
Direct materials: 4 000 (7kg × £1)	(28 000)
Direct labour: 4 000 × (0.5 hours × £6.00)	(12 000)
Production overhead	(10 000)
	22 000
Selling and administrative overhead	(4 000)
Net profit	18 000

Dorchester Slugg does not absorb production overheads using an overhead absorption rate. It may be assumed that all of its overheads are fixed in nature.

You are required to flex the budget for a sales and production level of 4500 units.

9.12 Dillinger Thompson Limited produces a line of leather bags. Although they vary slightly in design, the cost structure is the same for each bag. The company's budget for January 20X5 is as follows:

	£
Sales: 4 000 units × £22.00	88 000
Costs	
Direct materials: 4 000 × (1 square metre × £6.50)	(26 000)
Direct labour: 4 000 × (0.5 hours × £7.80)	(15 600)
Production overhead	(24 000)
	22 400
Selling and administrative overhead	(6 000)
Net profit	16 400

Dillinger Thompson Limited does not absorb production overheads using an overhead absorption rate. It may be assumed that all of its overheads are fixed in nature.

If the company flexes its budget for 3600 units, what will be the revised net profit figure?

a) £11 760

b) £17 760

c) £14 160

d) £7 600.

The following information is relevant for questions 9.13 to 9.18.

Estella Starr Limited produces garden sheds that are sold direct to the public in kit form. March is one of the company's best months for sales, and in March 20X3 the directors have set some ambitious targets. These are summarised in the following budget for the month:

	£
Sales: 900 units × £217.00	195 300
Costs	
Direct materials: 900 × (16 metres × £4.00)	(57 600)
Direct labour: 900 × (4 hours × £6.30)	(22 680)
Production overhead	(62 300)
	52 720
Other overheads	(10 600)
Net profit	42 120

Estella Starr Limited does not absorb production overheads using an overhead absorption rate. It may be assumed that all of its overheads are fixed in nature. The company's actual results for the month are as follows:

	£
Sales: 830 × £214.00	177 620
Costs	
Direct materials: 830 × (15 metres × £4.10)	(51 045)
Direct labour: 830 × (4.1 hours × £6.00)	(20 418)
Production overhead	(61 400)
	44 757
Other overheads	(8 950)
Net profit	35 807

9.13   What is the sales profit volume variance for the month?

   a)   £6 313 (A)

   b)   £8 946 (A)

   c)   £8 946 (F)

   d)   £6 313 (F).

9.14   What is the sales price variance for the month?

   a)   £2 490 (F)

   b)   £2 490 (A)

   c)   £15 190 (F)

   d)   £15 190 (A).

9.15   What is the direct materials price variance for the month?

   a)   £6 555 (A)

   b)   £1 245 (A)

   c)   £6 555 (F)

   d)   £1 245 (F).

9.16 What is the direct materials quantity variance for the month?

a) £3 320 (F)

b) £3 320 (A)

c) £7 800 (A)

d) £7 800 (F).

9.17 What is the direct labour rate variance for the month (to the nearest £)?

a) £360 (A)

b) £360 (F)

c) £1 021 (F)

d) £1 021 (A)

9.18 What is the direct labour efficiency variance for the month (to the nearest £)?

a) £523 (A)

b) £523 (F)

c) £340 (F)

d) £340 (A).

9.19 Feltham Finch Limited is a manufacturing company. For the month of August 20X4 it budgeted for 780 units of production, each to use four hours of machine time. Production overhead absorption rates were budgeted as follows:

Variable production overhead = £2.80 per machine hour.
Fixed production overhead = £7.60 per machine hour.

The actual level of production in the month was 760 units. The original production overhead budget, the flexed budget and the actual expenditure are shown in the following table:

	Original budget £	Flexed budget £	Actual £
Variable production overheads	8 736	8 512	8 476
Fixed production overheads	23 712	23 104	24 160
	32 448	31 616	32 636

Calculate:

i) the variable production overhead variance

ii) the fixed production overhead variance.

! CASE STUDY 9.1 Variance investigation: A surprise result

The case study for this chapter brings together all the different variance calculations in a comprehensive example. The first part of the case study requires a full range of variance calculations. The students' section of the website includes the solution to part 1. The solution is followed on the website by part 2 which develops the case a little further. In part 2, the identification of significant variance, and the subsequent investigation by managers, produce an unexpected outcome.

Part 1

Andrea Ellison is managing director of Francis & Follett Limited, an unlisted company that manufactures wooden bedframes. After a few difficult years in the last decade the company has managed to secure half a dozen contracts with major home furnishings retailers. This has significantly expanded the volume of trade and has allowed the company to repay its long-term loans. The company's accountant and business adviser suggested last year that it is now time to improve the quality of management control systems. Andrea and her brother, Phil, the sales director, are the two active directors in the business. In the past they have been able to keep tight control over the business by close supervision. However, as the business has taken on more staff, that kind of control has lessened.

Factory supervision is now under the control of a production manager, Faroukh, who was promoted to this position after several years as senior supervisor. The purchasing and stores function is managed by Perry, who has also been a trusted employee for many years.

A few months ago Andrea and Phil appointed a management accountant, Sylvie, who has worked hard to establish a budgetary control system in time for the start of the new financial year on 1 January 20X4. Sylvie has carefully monitored the production process with the help of Faroukh, and has established standard costs and times for all parts of the process. The annual budget is split into 12 monthly budgets, and actual performance is monitored each month. It is now the end of March 20X4 and the new system has been in place for three months.

The budget for March 20X4 is as follows:

	£
Sales: 1 600 units × £103	164 800
Costs	
Direct materials: 1 600 units × (12 metres × £2.50 per metre)	(48 000)
Direct materials: 1 600 units × 1 bag of metal components × £4.50	(7 200)
Direct materials: 1 600 units × 1 packaging box × £3.50	(5 600)
Direct labour: 1 600 units × (2.5 hours × £6.00 per hour)	(24 000)
Variable production overheads: 1 600 units × (1.5 machine hours per unit × £4)	(9 600)
Fixed production overheads: 1 600 units × (1.5 machine hours per unit × £10)	(24 000)
	46 400
Selling and administration overheads	(16 600)

	£
Net profit	29 800

The pieces for each bedframe are flat-packed in the factory. Each pack contains the necessary metal components for assembling the bedframe. Francis & Follett Limited buys in the components ready packaged in plastic bags.

Production overheads are absorbed on the basis of machine hours. Machine hours for March are budgeted at 2400 hours. Actual figures for March are as follows:

	£
Sales: 1 650 units × £103	169 950
Costs	
Direct materials: 1 650 units × (12.2 metres × £2.70 per metre)	(54 351)
Direct materials: 1 650 units × 1 bag of metal components × £4.50	(7 425)
Direct materials: 1 650 units × 1 packaging box × £3.50	(5 775)
Direct labour: 1 650 units × (2.4 hours × £6.00 per hour)	(23 760)
Variable production overheads	(10 050)
Fixed production overheads	(23 960)
	44 629
Selling and administration overheads	(16 420)
Net profit	28 209

Sylvie has prepared a standard form for the monthly and quarterly reporting of variances. The form is set out below with the variances filled in for January and February and a space for the March figures.

Francis & Follett Limited: Standard cost operating statements for the quarter ending 31 March 20X4

	January £	February £	March £
Budget net profit (original)	28 350	29 800	
Sales profit volume variance	1 450	1 450	
Flexed budget net profit	29 800	31 250	
Sales price variance	—	—	
Direct materials price variance	(3 904)	(3 934)	
Direct materials quantity variance	(360)	(413)	
Direct labour rate variance	—	—	
Direct labour efficiency variance	990	990	
Variable overhead variance	(592)	(460)	
Fixed overhead variance	776	750	
Selling and administration overhead variance	210	(26)	
Actual net profit	26 920	28 157	

Requirements are:

i) Prepare a flexed budget on the basis of sales and production of 1650 units for March 20X4.

ii) Calculate all relevant variances, and record them in the March column of the summary standard cost operating statement for the first quarter of 20X4.

Marginal costing for decision making

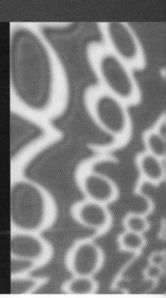

Aim of the chapter

To understand the key elements of marginal costing, including cost-volume-profit analysis and the use of marginal costing in making a range of business decisions.

Cost classification: Variable, fixed and semi-variable costs

It can be very useful for the purposes of decision making to classify costs according to their variability. Later in the chapter we will look at examples of business decisions, but for the moment we will simply consider the differences in cost behaviour between variable costs, fixed costs and semi-variable costs.

Variable costs

A fully variable cost is one that varies in line with the level of business activity. For example, direct materials costs tend to be fully variable.

Using a graph to show variable cost behaviour

Variable costs increase as the level of activity increases; the relationship between costs and activities is linear and can be plotted onto a graph, as shown in Figure 10.1.

As activity increases (e.g. the number of units of production) variable costs increase. The line on the graph begins at 0 because at this point zero activity = zero variable cost.

| Figure 10.1 | Graph of variable cost behaviour |

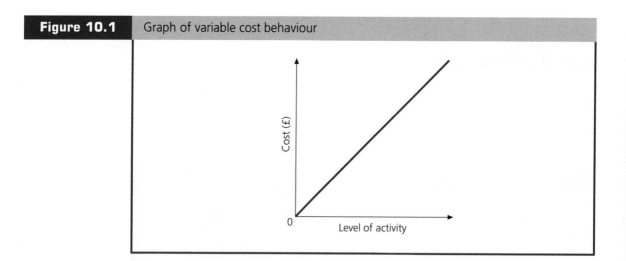

| Example 10.1 | |

Sparks Kitchenware Limited produces various types of kitchen equipment. A basic metal spatula requires 300 grams of metal at a cost of £1.00. The cost of metal to make two spatulas is exactly twice as much: 600 grams at a total cost of £2.00.

To make 10 spatulas, 3kg (300 grams × 10) of metal is required at a total cost of £10.00. For each additional spatula, the cost increases by £1 (i.e. the same amount every time). This is an example of a fully variable cost.

Earlier we noted that direct materials costs *tend* to be fully variable. When might they not be fully variable? Well, in practice, it is usually possible to obtain lower prices per unit of material as volumes increase. In the case of Sparks Kitchenware Limited, suppose that a quantity discount of 5% is available for purchases of metal in quantities over 100kg. This means that a higher volume of production will be relatively a little cheaper than a low volume. However, it is often quite realistic to make an assumption that direct costs are fully variable with the level of output.

We can plot the variable cost data onto a graph similar to that in Figure 10.1. The variable materials cost of the spatulas produced by Sparks Kitchenware Limited is shown at three different levels of activity in the following table (and see Figure 10.2).

Number of units produced	Variable cost total (£1 × number of units produced)
0	0
10	£10
20	£20

Figure 10.2	Sparks Kitchenware Limited: Variable materials cost graph

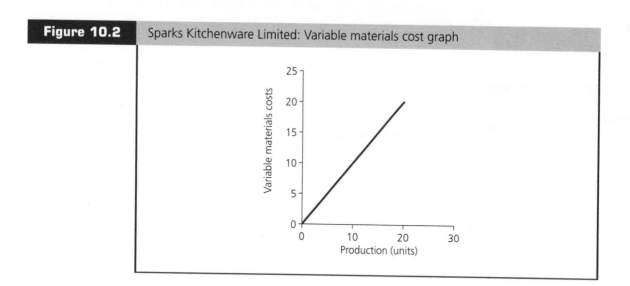

Fixed costs

A fixed cost is one that does not vary with the level of business activity.

Using a graph to show fixed cost behaviour

See the graph in Figure 10.3.

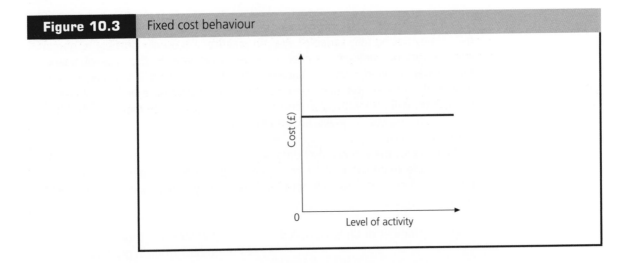

Figure 10.3 Fixed cost behaviour

Example 10.2

Sparks Kitchenware Limited rents a factory unit. It pays rent of £28 000 per year for the unit, and insurance of £4360 per year. These are both examples of costs that do not vary with the level of output of the factory. Whether 1 or 1 000 000 metal spatulas are produced, the cost of factory rent and insurance remains the same.

We can plot the fixed cost of factory rental (£28 000) onto a graph (see Figure 10.4).

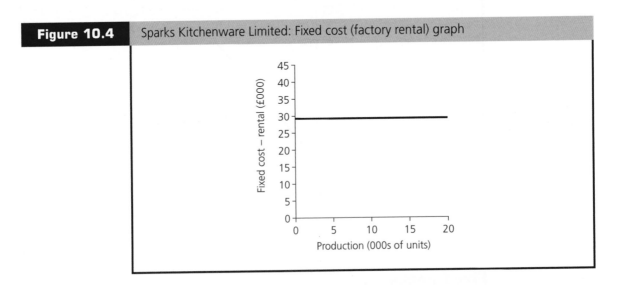

Figure 10.4 Sparks Kitchenware Limited: Fixed cost (factory rental) graph

Of course, even fixed costs vary eventually. Suppose that the maximum number of spatulas Sparks Kitchenware can produce in its factory is 1 million per annum. If the business is successful and expands beyond this level of production it will need to obtain bigger production facilities – so factory rent and insurance would go up. It is only possible to describe costs as fixed within certain levels of activity.

Stepped costs

Where a business reaches the level of activity where a fixed cost must increase, the increase is sudden (see Figure 10.5).

| **Figure 10.5** | Stepped cost behaviour |

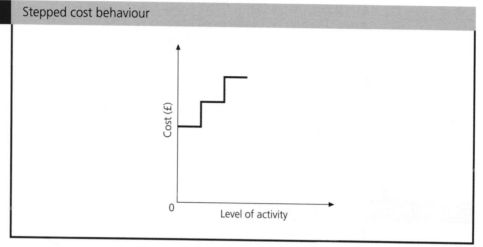

| **Example 10.3** | |

Sparks Kitchenware Limited employs production supervisors at an annual salary cost of £12 500 each. The company's health and safety policy requires a certain level of supervision in the factory, and so the directors have decided that a supervisor must be employed for every 10 machine operators. So, if the number of machine operators is 50, 5 supervisors will be employed at a total cost of (5 × £12 500) £62 500. If the number of machine operators rises to 51 the company's policy requires that 6 supervisors will be employed. The total cost rises to (6 × £12 500) £75 000. We can plot this stepped cost onto a graph (see Figure 10.6).

| **Figure 10.6** | Sparks Kitchenware Limited: Supervisors' salaries cost graph |

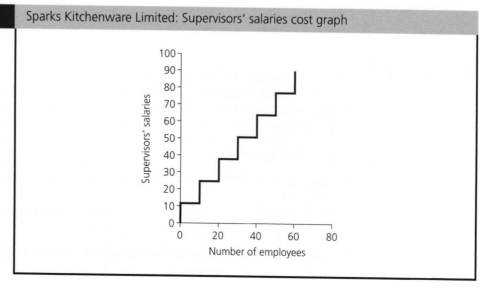

Semi-variable costs

A semi-variable cost is one that varies to some extent with the level of business activity; it has both fixed and variable elements.

For example, telephone bills have both fixed and variable elements. There is a line rental charge that is fixed; it remains the same regardless of the number of calls made. In addition to the fixed line rental, however, there is a variable element that depends upon the number of phone calls made.

Using a graph to show semi-variable cost behaviour

Figure 10.7 shows that, even at a zero level of activity, some cost is incurred; that is why the cost line starts part way up the vertical axis.

Figure 10.7	Semi-variable cost behaviour

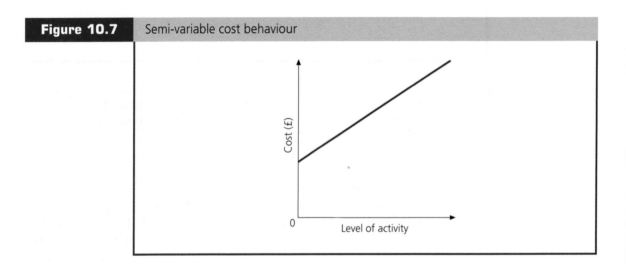

Example 10.4

Sparks Kitchenware Limited employs two sales staff. Each is paid a basic salary of £15 000 per year. In addition, each member of staff is paid a commission of 10% of sales value for every sale they make. Sales of £10 000, therefore, incur commission charges of £10 000 × 10% = £1000. Sales of £100 000 incur commission charges of £100 000 × 10% = £10 000.

Total sales salaries costs:

- Sales level of 10 000: £30 000 (basic salary) + £1000 (commission) = £31 000
- Sales level of 100 000: £30 000 (basic salary) + £10 000 (commission) = £41 000

We can plot the semi-variable cost of sales salaries onto a graph (see Figure 10.8).

| Figure 10.8 | Sparks Kitchenware Limited: Semi-variable cost (sales salaries) graph |

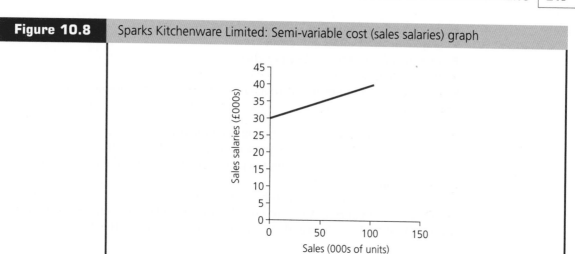

Typical cost behaviour in different business sectors

In some types of business there are few, if any, variable costs. Even in businesses where a substantial proportion of cost is apparently variable with levels of activity, the reality may be that the costs are fixed in nature. We will look at some examples to illustrate these points.

A manufacturer

Usually, the direct materials used in manufacturing production tend to be variable; a progressively larger amount of material is used as the level of activity increases. By the same token, we would expect direct labour to be a variable cost. However, in practice, an employer's obligations to employees under employment regulations are often such that the labour cannot necessarily be regarded as direct. In many of the examples in this section of the book we have assumed that the supply of direct labour, like water from a tap, can be turned on or off at the convenience of management. This assumption, in many circumstances, is unrealistic. While a long-term downturn in an industry is likely to result in reductions in employees, short-term reductions in activity do not result in workers being laid off.

Therefore, in determining whether or not labour is a variable cost, the circumstances must be examined carefully. For example, sometimes, especially in garment manufacture, workers are paid piece rates – i.e. a sum for each completed item. Where this forms the whole of a worker's pay, the cost is truly variable. In some cases, however, there will be a basic, fixed level of wages plus a piece rate. This arrangement constitutes a semi-variable cost.

A commercial airline

Very few of the costs involved in running a commercial airline are variable. There are some very significant fixed costs, though:

- depreciation of aircraft
- employment of pilots and cabin crew
- aircraft maintenance and safety charges
- airport charges
- interest costs (on borrowing money to finance the purchase or lease of the planes).

A commercial aircraft service running scheduled flights must run the advertised flights even if there are very few passengers (in fact, because the planes have to be in certain places at scheduled times, a plane is likely to make the flight even if there are no passengers at all).

Any variable costs are likely to be very minor indeed compared to the high level of fixed costs incurred. Variable costs would include, for example, the cost of drinks supplied free during flights (the fewer passengers the fewer the drinks served, by and large).

Restaurant

Running a restaurant usually involves incurring a high level of fixed costs. For example:

- premises rental
- cost of employing staff
- depreciation of equipment.

What about food costs? To some extent these are variable, but because of the perishable nature of many food items there may be a fixed element of cost involved. If food is not sold to customers it will have to be thrown away sooner or later.

Labour costs may be variable to some extent, depending upon the basis of employment. If the restaurant proprietor expects a quiet evening he may be able to reduce the level of waiting and kitchen staff to some extent, but he will have to schedule at least some staff. Even if no customers at all turn up, he will still have to pay the staff for their time, and this basic minimum of staff time would represent a fixed cost.

Holiday tour operator

A holiday tour operator incurs fixed costs such as rental of offices, employment of staff to take bookings and deal with ticket administration, and so on. However, some of the costs are likely to be variable with the level of bookings taken from the public. A total of 37 couples booking a resort holiday will require 74 flight tickets and 37 rooms. There could, however, be some fixed elements to these costs; for example, where the contract with a hotel owner stipulates that, say, a minimum of 30 rooms will be paid for each week by the tour operator, regardless of whether or not they are used. In a case like this, the tour operator is being obliged to share with the hotel owner the risk of unused rooms.

Clearly, categorising costs neatly into 'fixed' and 'variable' categories is not always as simple in practice as it may at first appear. In many businesses genuinely variable costs are rare.

Costing for decision making

In Chapter 7 we examined the features of absorption costing, and noted that this approach to costing, while useful for some aspects of planning and control, may be defective for decision making. We will re-emphasise this point by means of an example.

Example 10.5

Modena Mayhew Limited plans the following budget income and expenditure for May 20X7:

	£
Sales: 1000 units × £10 each	10 000
Costs	
Direct materials and labour	(4 000)
Production overheads, absorbed at £3 per unit	(3 000)
	3 000
Selling and administrative costs	(1 500)
Net profit	1 500

The business is not working to full capacity and it would be possible to produce more units of product. Modena Mayhew's sales director is approached by a contractor who wishes to order 100 units, to be produced and delivered in May; however, he wishes to negotiate a special price of £8.50 per unit. In order to help to decide whether or not to accept the order, the sales director needs information on the cost of a unit of product. What does it cost to produce one unit?

It might be tempting to take the total costs in the statement above (£4000 + £3000 + £1500 = £8500), divide by 1000 and come up with the figure of £8.50 per unit. However, this approach would be incorrect, unless *all* the costs were variable (and that is highly unlikely to be the case). Those costs that are fixed remain fixed unless the level of activity changes radically.

Really, the sales director needs to know the *additional* cost of manufacturing an extra unit of product. If we assume that all of the production costs and the selling and administrative costs are fixed (probably quite a reasonable assumption) and all the direct costs are variable, this means that the business is incurring £4000 of variable cost to produce 1000 units of product. Variable cost per unit of product is therefore:

$$\frac{4\ 000}{1\ 000} = \text{£4 per unit}$$

This is the additional cost that would be incurred by manufacturing the 1001st unit of product in May.
Comparing the two:

	£
Total cost per unit of product	8.50
Variable cost per unit of product	4.00

If the sales director incorrectly calculated that the additional cost of the 100 unit order would be £850 (£8.50 × 100) he would conclude that it would not make sense to accept the order because the sales revenue from it would be no greater than cost. However, if he takes the variable cost per unit, he may conclude that the order should be accepted.

To prove that it would, indeed, increase profit to accept the extra order, we will look at the May budget statement revised to include the additional 100 units at a selling price of £8.50 per unit:

	£
Sales: 1 000 units × £10 each	10 000
100 units × £8.50 each	850
	10 850
Costs	
Direct materials and labour (at £4 per unit for 1 100 units) (*variable cost*)	(4 400)
Production overheads, absorbed at £3 per unit originally budgeted (*fixed cost*)	(3 000)
	3 450
Selling and administrative costs (*fixed cost*)	(1 500)
Net profit	1 950

The revised budget profit is £1950, that is £450 higher than the original budget profit figure. The figures show that extra profit can be made by accepting the order, even at a lower price.

Marginal costing

A marginal cost in economics is the cost of one additional item. In the example given above we looked at the cost of making the 1001st unit of product. This is a marginal cost. Marginal costing is a piece of accounting terminology describing an approach to costing that excludes fixed costs. As we have seen, marginal costing provides a much sounder basis for decision making than absorption costing.

In the rest of the chapter we will look at some important aspects of decision making using marginal costing. First, it is necessary to introduce some more new terminology.

Contribution

Contribution refers to the amount that remains after variable costs have been deducted from sales. Referring back to the information in Example 10.5, the additional contribution per unit of product that would be made on the additional order for 100 units would be:

	£
Sales price per unit	8.50
Less: variable cost per unit	(4.00)
Contribution per unit	4.50

If contribution is a positive figure it contributes towards meeting the fixed costs of the business. Once sufficient contribution is made to cover all of the fixed costs, any remaining amount contributes to net profits.

Contribution can be calculated per unit, and can also be shown as a total (number of units sold × contribution per unit).

Break-even

The break-even point is the point at which no profit and no loss is made in a set of business transactions. For example:

	£
Sales: 10 000 units × £3	30 000
Less: variable costs: 10 000 units × £1	(10 000)
Contribution	20 000
Fixed costs	(20 000)
Net profit	Nil

? Self-test question 10.1 (answer at the end of the book)

Brinn Bartholomew Limited sells municipal litter bins for £250 each. The bins cost £97 in direct materials (all variable cost) and £36 in direct labour (all variable cost). In June 20X9 the company plans to sell 1400 bins. Its budgeted fixed costs for the month are £120 400.

- What is the company's budgeted contribution for June 20X9?
- What is the company's budgeted net profit for June 20X9?

Cost-volume-profit analysis

It is important to understand the relationships between the level of business activity, the different types of cost and profitability. The analysis of the interaction of these factors is known as cost-volume-profit analysis (CVP analysis). We will examine CVP relationships further, firstly by charting cost, volume and profit in graphical form, and then by using formulae to express the relationships between the factors. We will look first at the construction of break-even charts.

Break-even charts

Step 1

Earlier in the chapter we constructed graphs for each different type of cost. Developing that approach further, we can show both fixed and variable costs on the same graph (see Figure 10.9). An alternative presentation is shown in Figure 10.10.

Fixed costs, as we have seen, are those that remain at the same level regardless of the volume of activity. Variable costs increase steadily as the volume of activity increases. Showing the two together on a graph gives the result illustrated. The upper sloping line represents total costs. Where there is zero activity (i.e. no production or sales) the only costs incurred are fixed costs (which is why the total cost line starts part way up the vertical axis). As activity increases, so do total costs.

| **Figure 10.9** | Graph of total costs, split into fixed and variable |

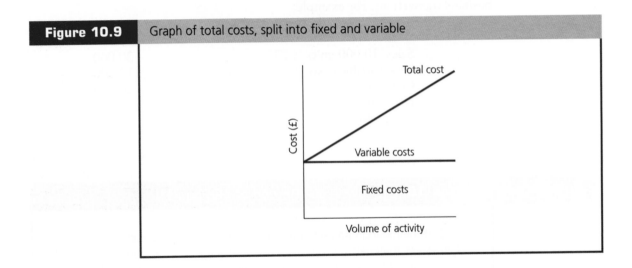

| **Figure 10.10** | Graph of total costs, split into fixed and variable (alternative presentation) |

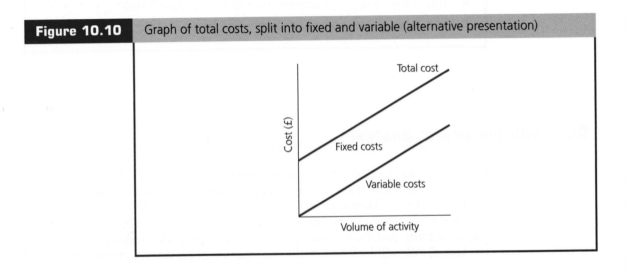

> Marshall Mexico Limited has the following cost structure for 20X7:
>
> Fixed costs: £50 000 up to 10 000 units of production.
>
> Variable costs: £5 per unit up to 10 000 units of production.
>
> Using either graph paper or a spreadsheet program graphing facility, plot these costs onto a single graph, showing lines for fixed costs and total costs. Identify the areas of the graph that represent fixed costs and variable costs.

Step 2

We will now add a further line to the graph, this time for sales revenue (see Figure 10.11). The addition of this line produces a break-even chart, which provides useful information about the activities of the business.

The point at which the total revenue crosses the total cost line is break-even point. We can see that break-even point occurs where:

$$\text{Total sales revenue} = \text{Total costs}$$

By dropping a line down from the break-even point to the horizontal axis of the graph we can read off the volume at which break-even point occurs; this is shown as a vertical dotted line in Figure 10.11. Charting a line between the vertical axis and the break-even point, we can read off the sales value at which the break-even point occurs; this is shown as a horizontal dotted line on the figure.

| **Figure 10.11** | Break-even chart |

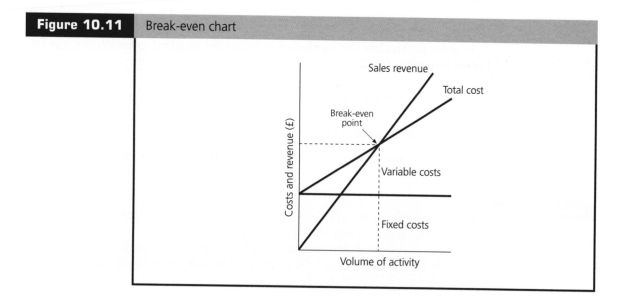

Self-test question 10.3 (answer at the end of the book)

> The facts are the same as for self-test question 10.2. Marshall Mexico Limited sells its product at £15 per unit. Taking the graph drawn for self-test question 10.2, draw a total revenue line and establish the break-even point. Drop a line down to the horizontal axis and find out the volume of activity at which break-even point occurs. Draw another line from the break-even point to the vertical axis and find out the sales value at which break-even point occurs.

Break-even analysis using formulae

There are drawbacks to using graphs for establishing the break-even point of a business:

■ The answer obtained tends to be approximate because of inaccuracies in drawing the graph.
■ It would be unnecessarily time-consuming to have to draw a graph each time analysis of break-even was undertaken.

Instead, we can work out break-even points using the relationships between sales and costs that we established earlier.

$$\text{Selling price per unit} - \text{variable costs per unit} = \text{Contribution per unit}$$

Remember that contribution per unit contributes towards meeting the fixed costs of the business. The point at which all the fixed costs of the business are met is break-even point. Beyond break-even point, the contribution contributes towards the net profit of the business. So, break-even point occurs where:

$$\text{Sales revenue} = \text{Total costs}$$

And also where:

$$\text{Contribution} = \text{Fixed costs}$$

In order to calculate the number of units of sales required to break even, the following formula is used:

$$\text{Break-even point (in units)} = \frac{\text{Fixed costs}}{\text{Contribution per unit}}$$

The break-even point in sales value can be calculated by:

$$\text{Break-even point (in units)} \times \text{Selling price per unit}$$

Example 10.6

Mulberry Piggott Limited manufactures and sells raincoats. It sells each raincoat for £30.00. Variable costs are £10.00 per coat.

In the year ending 31 December 20X5 the company expects to incur fixed costs of £60 000. How many raincoats will it have to sell to break even?

Sales revenue per unit = £30.00
Variable costs per unit = £10.00

Contribution per unit is, therefore, £20.00 (sales minus variable costs).

$$\text{Break-even point (in units)} = \frac{\text{Fixed costs}}{\text{Contribution}}$$

$$= \frac{60\,000}{£20} = 3000 \text{ units}$$

Break-even point in sales value:

$$3000 \text{ units} \times £30.00 = £90\,000$$

? Self-test question 10.4 (answer at the end of the book)

Neasden Northwich Limited sells its products at £20 per unit. Variable costs per unit are £6. The company expects to incur fixed costs of £70 000 in 20X6. Calculate the break-even point (in units) for 20X6.

Further applications of break-even analysis

Target profit

The break-even point, expressed in numbers of units or sales value, provides management with valuable information. However, managers may also want to know how many units they will have to sell in order to reach a specified profit target.

We can apply marginal costing to this type of problem quite easily, as it is a logical extension to break-even analysis. Remember that, once sufficient contribution is made to cover all of the fixed costs of a business, any remaining amount contributes to net profits.

So, we can extend the break-even formula as follows:

$$\text{Target sales in units} = \frac{\text{Fixed costs} + \text{Target profit}}{\text{Contribution per unit}}$$

Example 10.7

Using data from the Mulberry Piggott example:

sales revenue per unit = £30.00
variable costs per unit = £10.00
contribution per unit = £20.00
fixed costs = £60 000

The company's directors would like to know how many units would have to be sold to reach their target profit of £30 000. Applying the formula:

$$\text{Target sales in units} = \frac{\text{Fixed costs} + \text{Target profit}}{\text{Contribution per unit}}$$

$$\text{Target sales in units} = \frac{60\ 000 + 30\ 000}{20} = 4\ 500 \text{ units}$$

Expressed in terms of sales value:

$$4\ 500 \text{ units} \times £30 = £135\ 000$$

Showing profit on a graph

Up till now we have not focused specifically on the graphical representation of profit. Suppose that Mulberry Piggott can make and potentially sell up to 7000 raincoats per year without fixed costs changing. We can plot the following points on a graph:

Production level	Fixed costs £	Total costs £	Total revenue £
0	60 000	60 000	0
7 000	60 000	130 000	210 000
		(£60 000 + 7 000 × £10)	(7 000 × £30)

This gives the result shown in Figure 10.12. The areas of profit and loss are marked on the graph. Beyond break-even point, as production increases, the area between the revenue and total costs lines is occupied by profit. The first dotted line shows

Figure 10.12 Mulberry Pigott: Cost-volume-profit graph

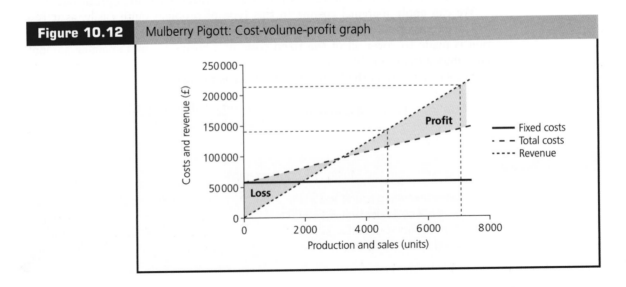

sales in units and in revenue to produce profits of £30 000 (as calculated above). The second dotted line shows the maximum activity level that is possible at a level of fixed costs of £60 000. Profits at this level (the difference between the total revenue and total costs lines) would be much higher than at a level of 4500 sales; we can prove this by doing the calculation of profit at the maximum activity level of 7000 units:

	£
Sales (7000 × £30)	210 000
Variable costs (7000 × £10)	(70 000)
Contribution	140 000
Fixed costs	(60 000)
Profit	80 000

Margin of safety

Margin of safety is the excess of planned or actual sales above the break-even point. In Example 10.6 we calculated the Mulberry Piggott break-even point in units as 3000 raincoats. If we suppose that the sales of 4500 units targeted by the directors (as in Example 10.7) are a realistic target, the margin of safety, expressed both in units and in sales value, is as follows:

	Units of sales	Sales £
Actual sales estimate	4 500	135 000
Break-even point	3 000	90 000
Margin of safety	1 500	45 000

The margin of safety can also be expressed as a percentage of the sales estimate:

$$\frac{1\ 500}{4\ 500} \times 100 = 33.3\%$$

Special decisions: Accepting contracts

In this section we look more closely at business decisions involving acceptance or non-acceptance of contracts on special terms. Marginal costing analysis can be useful in reaching the appropriate decision.

If an order or contract at a special price would produce a positive contribution to fixed costs, then the business should accept the order. However, there may be other factors to take into consideration.

Example 10.8

Solidago Solanum Limited manufactures sofas. Although the design details and fabric coverings vary, the basic design of the sofas is the same and they all sell for £1500 each. The company's factory can produce up to 1000 sofas per month, but in fact, production rarely exceeds 700 per month.

The sales director has just received a query from a potential new customer, Cuttpryce Limited. Cuttpryce is opening a chain of discount furniture stores and is examining potential sources of supply. The purchasing director of Cuttpryce offers to buy an initial consignment of 300 sofas at a price of £1200 each. The potential discount of £300 per sofa is so great that Solidago's sales director is tempted to refuse the order straight away. However, he consults his fellow directors over the decision.

The latest set of monthly management accounts shows the following summary:

Solidago Solanum Limited: Management accounts for July 20X4

	£
Sales (655 × £1 500)	982 500
Variable costs (655 × £895)	586 225
Contribution	396 275
Fixed costs	304 000
Net profit	92 275

What should the directors' decision be? Applying the basic decision rule: would the contract make a positive contribution to fixed costs?

Under the proposed contract:

	£
Selling price per sofa	1 200
Variable cost per sofa	(895)
Contribution per sofa	305

The contribution per sofa is positive, and so it appears that the contract should be accepted.

However, there are likely to be other relevant considerations. If it becomes generally known that Solidago sofas are available from Cuttpryce at £300 less than the normal retail price, why should anyone pay £1500? Acceptance of this new contract could have a significant impact on the rest of the company's business. If the company has a reputation for exclusivity and high quality, it could be damaged by association with a discounter.

The marginal costing analysis provides a useful starting point for discussion, but the decision made by the directors will have to involve many other relevant factors.

In industries where either the majority or all of the costs are fixed, the application of the decision rule explained above can lead to some apparently absurd prices. Where variable costs are virtually non-existent, selling price is more or less the same as contribution. This means that, potentially, even a very low selling price can make a positive contribution to fixed costs. This issue is explored in more detail in Chapter 11 which considers pricing decisions.

Special decisions: Major increases in activity levels

As we have seen, fixed costs remain fixed only up to certain levels of activity. If a business is considering major increases in levels of activity, it must take into account any likely increases in fixed costs.

Example 10.9

Spindrift and Schooner Limited is a small boat builder. It has operated successfully for many years from a boatyard that allows for production of 60 boats per year. In most years the company can sell all the boats it can produce. The selling price of each boat is £2600. Variable labour and materials costs are £985 per boat, and the fixed costs associated with running the business from the present boatyard are £48 200. Last year the company made a net profit of £48 700 on sales of £156 000.

The company's directors are meeting to discuss a proposal to increase the business's production capacity. A neighbouring property has become vacant and it would be possible to rent the additional space in order to produce more boats. The additional capacity in terms of production would be 20 boats. The sales director is confident that, with the growth in the leisure boating market, he will be able to sell the additional boats.

Variable costs per boat will remain the same. However, the expansion would produce an additional £26 500 in fixed costs. In a case like this, the increase in fixed costs has to figure in the decision making. The extra £26 500 is known as an *incremental* cost, and it must be compared with the *incremental* revenue that will be generated through higher sales. The basic decision rule is: if incremental revenue exceeds incremental costs, accept the project.

In this case we will assume that the sales director's confidence is justified and that he will be able to sell all of the additional 20 boats produced each year following the expansion:

	£
Incremental revenue	
Sales: 20 boats × £2 600	52 000
Incremental costs	
Variable costs: 20 × £985	(19 700)
Fixed costs	(26 500)
Incremental profit	5 800

Because the incremental profit is a positive figure it looks as though the business should increase its capacity. However, the directors might reflect that £5800 is a relatively small increase in net profit, and that the net profit percentage on these additional sales at 11.2% is substantially lower than the existing net profit percentage of 31.2%.

Special decisions: Limiting factors

So far, the only constraints on business activities which we have examined are the upper ceiling for production capacity and the restraint imposed by the market in terms of the amount of product or service that can be sold. However, there may be situations where other constraints operate. Such constraints are commonly known as limiting factors. For example, a product may require specialist labour for which there is a shortage, or a raw material which is in short supply.

Where a business produces more than one product, all of which require the input of resources whose supply is limited, management must come to a decision as to production priorities. The basic rule is that limited resources should be devoted to production of the products that produce the highest contribution per unit of limiting factor. This is not as complicated as it sounds, as Example 10.10 shows.

Example 10.10

Crosby and Crossthwaite Limited use the same production line to produce their three principal products, A, B and C. All three products use the same grade of labour, which is in short supply because of a booming local economy that has ensured virtually full employment.

The products have the following sales and variable cost values per unit sold:

	A £	B £	C £
Selling price	50	55	48
Variable costs	(28)	(28)	(24)
Contribution per unit	22	27	24

On the face of it, it would appear that the company should concentrate production on product B because it produces the highest contribution to fixed costs. However, the picture alters when we look at the input to each of the products of the scarce labour resource:

	A	B	C
Number of labour hours used	2	3	3
Contribution per unit	£22	£27	£24
Contribution per labour hour	£11	£9	£8

When we calculate the contribution per unit of limited resource, we can see that product A comes out ahead because it uses only two of the limited labour hours. The ranking of the three products is first A, second B and third C.

If there is sufficient demand for product A, it appears that the company should switch production entirely towards product A. However, demand for product A may be insufficient. We will examine the additional factor of demand in the next example.

Example 10.11

Using the same information as in Example 10.10, suppose that Crosby and Crossthwaite Limited can employ a maximum of 22 000 hours of labour in one year. Maximum annual demand for the three products is estimated at:

	A	B	C
Demand in units	8 000	6 000	8 000

How much of each product should the company plan to produce?

Taking product A first, 8000 units will use up 16 000 labour hours (at a rate of 2 hours per unit). The company should manufacture up to the maximum demand in respect of product A. This would leave 22 000 − 16 000 = 6000 labour hours available to manufacture something else. These hours should be used for the manufacture of product B, which is next in the limited resource rankings. Product B uses 3 labour hours per unit, so 6000 hours could produce 2000 units of product B.

The company's production plan is, therefore: product A 8000 units; and product B 2000 units.

Limitations of analysis based on marginal costing

Analysis based on marginal costing can be useful to management as a source of information for decision making. However, it has several significant weaknesses and limitations:

1. This type of analysis assumes that variable costs increase at a steady rate in line with activity. This assumption may not be valid in practice. As the level of business activity increases, variable costs per unit may tend to fall as the business takes advantage of discounts for purchasing larger quantities.

2. As we have seen, very few costs are truly variable. In some businesses only relatively trivial costs vary with the level of business activity. Providers of services, in particular, usually incur a mixture of principally fixed and stepped costs.

3. Fixed costs remain fixed only up to a point. Beyond a particular level of activity fixed costs will change. The level at which costs will change and the extent of that change may not be easy to estimate.

4. The examples used to illustrate the applications of cost-volume-profit analysis have all been based upon firms producing either a single product or a very limited range of products. In fact, most businesses provide a mixture of products or services. While it may be possible to identify variable costs for each product with a fair degree of accuracy, identification of fixed costs with a particular product is likely to be based upon quite arbitrary apportionment between products and activities.

5. All business decisions involve a complex range of factors. Marginal costing may help to point the way towards a decision, but there may be very good reasons in practice for ignoring the signposts offered by analysis based on marginal costing.

If the limitations of this type of analysis are not fully appreciated, it is possible for businesses to make serious mistakes in decision making.

Chapter summary

In this chapter we have explored costing for decision making. First we considered the nature of costs, and their classification. Using graphs, we illustrated simple cost behaviour, classifying costs as variable, fixed or semi-variable. Cost behaviour in a range of manufacturing and service environments was examined to illustrate the point that categorising costs is by no means straightforward in practice.

Having established some basic cost classifications we proceeded to examine the use of marginal costing in decision making. Cost-volume-profit analysis and the calculation of the break-even point for a business were introduced and then applied in several examples covering break-even point, target profit and the calculation of the margin of safety.

Finally, we examined decision making in the following areas:

- acceptance of contracts at special prices
- increasing activity levels where fixed costs increase
- production plans where there are limiting factors.

The end-of-chapter exercises are divided into two sections.

 The first section has answers provided at the end of the book. The second section, in the white box, has answers on the lecturers' section of the website. Finally, the chapter contains a case study that brings together many aspects of managerial costing.

Website summary

The book's website contains the following material in respect of Chapter 10:

Students' section

- Quiz containing ten multiple choice questions
- Six additional questions with answers
- Answer to the case study at the end of this chapter.

Lecturers' section

- Answers to the end-of-chapter exercises 10.13 to 10.22
- Seven additional questions with answers.

Exercises: answers at the end of the book

10.1 Billericay Ashworth Limited makes tennis racquets. In an average month it produces about 3000 racquets. The following are some of the costs the company incurs:

- *Cost of raw materials.* Each racquet uses £13.00 of raw materials.
- *Factory insurance.* The cost for a month is £800.
- *Telephone charges.* The company has several telephone lines. Its line rental charges per month are £1000. If no calls are made, the call charge is £0. On average 500 calls cost a total of £250 and 1000 calls, on average, cost £500. In most months about 1500 calls are made in the company.

You are required to:

i) Classify each of the above costs as one of the following:

- variable
- fixed
- stepped
- semi-variable.

ii) Using either graph paper or a spreadsheet program graphing facility, plot each of these costs onto a separate graph. Activity levels should be on the horizontal (*x*) axis and costs on the vertical (*y*) axis.

10.2 Classify each of the following costs as:

- variable
- fixed
- stepped
- semi-variable.

i) Sales staff members' mobile phone charges. There is a basic rental cost irrespective of the number of phone calls made, plus a charge for each phone call made, based on the number of minutes the call lasts.

ii) Factory machine oil.

iii) Metered water charges. The bill comprises a charge per unit for the number of units consumed.

10.3 For each of the following types of business, list at least two fixed and two variable costs that might typically be incurred:

- self-employed taxi driver
- solicitor
- shirt manufacturer
- beauty salon.

Try not to repeat the same examples of costs for the different businesses.

10.4 Porton Fitzgerald Limited manufactures wardrobes. The selling price of a wardrobe is £210. Each wardrobe costs £52 in direct materials (all variable) and £34 in direct labour (all variable). In April 20X4 the company expects to sell 450 wardrobes, and it has budgeted for fixed overheads of £43 200.

What is the company's budgeted contribution for April 20X4?

What is the company's budgeted net profit for April 20X4?

10.5 Fullbright Bognor Limited, a manufacturing business, has the following cost structure:

Selling price per unit: £85

Variable costs per unit: £41

The company's directors expect to incur fixed costs of £62 000 in the year ending 31 December 20X1. The maximum level of production which the company can reach is 3000 units per year.

You are required to:

i)   Draw a break-even chart recording: fixed costs; total costs; total revenue.

ii)   From the chart estimate the break-even point in units and in sales value for Fullbright Bognor for the year ending 31 December 20X1.

iii) Use the break-even formula to find the break-even point in units and in sales value for Fullbright Bognor for the year ending 31 December 20X1.

Remember that:

$$\text{Break-even point (in units)} = \frac{\text{Fixed costs}}{\text{Contribution per unit}}$$

10.6 Foster Beniform Limited makes mannequins for shop window displays. The company's directors are meeting to discuss sales budgets for 20X8. The business has struggled to make a profit in recent years, but the finance director has made strenuous efforts in the last year or so to reduce the level of fixed costs and the directors hope to be able to make a profit in 20X8. The production facilities can produce a maximum of 2000 mannequins per year.

The selling price of a mannequin is £55, with variable costs of production of £25 per unit. In order to be able to make plans for 20X8 the directors would like to know the break-even point in units if (a) fixed costs in 20X8 are £40 000; (b) fixed costs in 20X8 are £50 000.

You are required to:

i)   draw two break-even charts, one for each estimate of fixed costs, recording:

      – fixed costs
      – total costs
      – total revenue.

ii) From the charts estimate the break-even point in units and in sales value for Foster Beniform for 20X8 at each projected level of fixed costs.

iii) Use the break-even formula to calculate the break-even point in units and sales value at each estimated level of fixed costs for Foster Beniform for 20X8.

10.7 Gropius Maplewood Limited manufactures a single product that it sells for £150 per unit. Variable costs of each unit are £62, but are expected to rise at the beginning of 20X8 to £63; because of severe competition the company will not be able to pass on this increase in costs to its customers. Fixed costs for 20X8 are expected to be £90 000.

Break-even point for 20X8 is estimated (to the nearest whole unit) at:

a) 1 023 units

b) 1 429 units

c) 1 452 units

d) 1 034 units.

10.8 Gimball Grace Limited manufactures a single model of electric fan heater. Each heater sells for £21. Variable costs of manufacture are £7.50. Fixed costs of the business are estimated at £54 000 for the 20X3 financial year.

The net profit of the business in 20X2 was £36 500, and the directors hope to increase that by 10% in 20X3. How many fan heaters will they have to sell to reach their target net profit (to the nearest whole unit)?

a) 6 974

b) 4 000

c) 6 704

d) 7 374.

10.9 Garbage Solutions Limited makes wheelie bins. In the 20X1 financial year each bin will sell for £25, with variable labour costs of £3.20 per bin and variable raw materials costs of £4.20. Fixed costs are budgeted at £178 900. The company's directors have budgeted net profit of £83 150 in 20X1.

What is the company's margin of safety in units (to the nearest whole unit)?

a) 10 165

b) 9 448

c) 5 441

d) 4 724.

10.10 Harrison Haworth Limited makes rucksacks. It has developed and patented a highly effective waterproof material and a revolutionary design. These make the company's products very much sought after, and the rucksacks sell at a premium price of £68.50 to camping shops and hiking organisations. Annual sales are 20 000 rucksacks. Variable costs of manufacture are £29.00. The company's current level of fixed costs is £382 420.

Most of the company's sales are within the UK and Ireland, but there has been growing interest in Scandinavia and last financial year export sales to Norway and Sweden accounted for 10% of total sales.

The company has just received an enquiry from a Moroccan hiking organisation. The director of the organisation, Raoul, tried out one of the company's rucksacks on a recent hiking trip in the Atlas mountains, and is convinced that it's the best rucksack he's ever used. He would like to start supplying the rucksack in Morocco. However, he knows that there will be very few buyers in Morocco at the premium prices charged by retailers in the UK for Harrison Haworth's products. Raoul suggests that a reasonable price would be £50.00 and that the specification could perhaps be lowered, as the weather conditions are rather better in Morocco than in the UK and Scandinavia. He estimates that annual sales in Morocco would be around 1000 units. Harrison Haworth's production director modifies the design slightly, and estimates that the variable costs of the new design would be £26.30. You are required to advise the directors on whether or not they should accept the order, taking into consideration both financial and non-financial factors.

10.11 Inez & Pilar Fashions Limited is a fashion manufacturing and wholesale business operating from rented premises. The business is well established and has operated successfully for several years. However, Inez and Pilar, the company's directors, realise that they have reached maximum production capacity in their present building. They have an opportunity to expand into neighbouring premises. This would involve some minor reorganisation of production but could be achieved quite easily. Inez and Pilar have worked out that given extra production capacity their sales could increase, at an optimistic estimate, from the existing level of £310 000 per year to as much as £345 000. However, if there is a downturn in the economy the increase might be only £20 000.

Inez and Pilar estimate that variable production costs constitute 30% of sales value. If they take over the neighbouring premises there will be additional fixed costs of £15 000 per year.

You are required to advise Inez and Pilar on whether or not they should expand their production facilities, using calculations to support your arguments.

10.12 Juniper Jefferson Limited manufactures two models of baby buggy: the De Luxe and the Super De Luxe. There is currently a shortage of the special grade of aluminium required for the buggy frame. This is unlikely to be a long-term problem, but it will affect production over the next three months. The cost and selling price information for each model is as follows:

	De Luxe	Super De Luxe
	£	£
Selling price	150	165
Variable cost of raw materials		
Aluminium (at £8.50 per kg)	38.25	42.50
Other raw materials	12.50	15.00
Variable cost of labour	13.65	15.60

The company has 350kg of aluminium in stock and expects to be able to buy no more than a further 1000kg per month for the next three months.

You are required to:

i)   Calculate the contribution per unit of limiting factor for both models of buggy.

ii) Advise the directors on the production plan they should follow, assuming that:

a) demand for the De Luxe will be 800 units over the next three months, with demand for the Super De Luxe at 300 units over the same period; or

b) demand for the De Luxe will be 600 units over the next three months, with demand for the Super De Luxe at 400 units over the same period.

Exercises: answers available to lecturers

10.13 A tour operator, Colby Overland Limited, is organising a coach trip to Russia as one of its new season's forthcoming attractions. Two of the major costs incurred are described as follows:

i)   *Coach costs*. Each coach holds up to 40 passengers. The total cost of hiring a coach for the fortnight long trip is £14 000. The company will book only as many coaches as it needs. When the 41st holiday reservation is made, another coach is booked (and a further coach is booked upon receipt of the 81st holiday reservation, and so on). Because of constraints imposed by the limited availability of hotel rooms in Omsk, no more than four coachloads of passengers would be taken on the trip.

ii) *Hotel costs*. Each time a holiday reservation is made the company faxes the hotel in Omsk to make the extra booking. If no more rooms are available, the hotel refuses the booking and the tour is regarded as full. The hotel cost per passenger is £280.

Required:

i)   Using either graph paper or a spreadsheet program graphing facility plot each of these costs onto a separate graph. The number of holiday reservations should be shown on the horizontal (*x*) axis and cost on the vertical (*y*) axis.

ii) Classify each of the costs as one of the following:

   – variable
   – fixed
   – stepped
   – semi-variable.

10.14 For each of the following types of business, list at least two fixed and two variable costs that might typically be incurred:

- milk delivery business
- coffee bar
- stationery manufacturer
- cross channel ferry operator.

Try not to repeat the same examples of costs for the different businesses.

10.15 Vernon Xylophones Limited makes xylophones (no surprises there). The direct materials cost of a xylophone is £300; the direct labour process is intensive and costs £450 per xylophone. Both direct materials and direct labour are fully variable. Each xylophone sells for £1500. In August 20X2 the company expects to sell 120 xylophones, and it has budgeted for fixed overheads of £54 000.

What is the company's budgeted contribution for August 20X2?

What is the company's budgeted net profit for August 20X2?

10.16 Finch Fletcher Limited manufactures trumpets. Each trumpet sells for £350, and has variable costs of manufacture of £120. The company can produce no more than 1200 in a year. In the year ending 31 March 20X4 the company's directors expect to incur fixed costs of £172 000.
   You are required to:

   i)   Draw a break-even chart recording:
        – fixed costs
        – total costs
        – total revenue.

   ii) From the chart estimate the break-even point in units and in sales value for Finch Fletcher for the year ending 31 March 20X4.

   iii) Use the break-even formula to calculate the break-even point in units and in sales value for Finch Fletcher for the year ending 31 March 20X4.

10.17 Fallon Frodsham Limited manufactures and installs small prefabricated building structures that are sold to people who want to establish a home office using part of their gardens. Each prefabricated building sells at £13 000, including installation costs. The variable costs of manufacture are £7300 per building. The company's directors have set a sales target of 150 buildings for the 20X5 accounting year.

   i)   Using a break-even chart, estimate the maximum level of fixed costs the company can incur in 20X5 without making a loss, on the assumption that the sales target is met.

   ii) Apply the break-even formula to calculate the maximum level of fixed costs.

   Tutorial note: This question may require some thought. Known factors are total revenues (sales revenue per unit × number of units sold), and total variable costs (variable costs per unit × number of units sold). The point on the horizontal (*x*) axis at which break-even point is reached is also known (150 units). The line must be drawn from that point upwards to the point where it intersects with the total revenue line.

10.18 Gulf Gadgets Limited manufactures chess sets. Each chess set sells for £185. Variable costs of manufacture are £78. The company's directors are currently setting the budget for 20X9. Fixed costs are expected to be £65 000. The selling price of a chess set will rise to £187 and the variable costs of manufacture are expected to increase by 10%

Break-even point for 20X9 is estimated (to the nearest whole unit) at:

a)   607

b)   655

c)   642

d)   596.

10.19 Gecko Grimsby sells specialist aquaria. In the 20X4 financial year each aquarium sold for £1320. The variable costs of manufacture were £321 per aquarium and the total fixed costs incurred were £85 750.

If the selling price, variable costs and fixed costs are all expected to increase by 10% in the 20X5 financial year, how many aquaria (to the nearest whole unit) will the company have to sell to make net profits of £50 000?

a)   131

b)   144

c)   136

d)   124.

10.20 Gospodin Grimshaw Limited manufactures hiking boots for sale which it sells principally in Russia and other parts of eastern Europe.

Each pair of boots sells for £15. Variable costs are £5.50 per pair. Fixed costs are budgeted at £87 900 for the 20X6 financial year. The company expects to sell 15 000 pairs of boots in 20X6. What is its margin of safety in £s (to the nearest £)?

a)   £54 597

b)   £86 205

c)   £138 795

d)   £62 520.

10.21 Ince Pargeter Limited manufactures padded carrying cases for laptop computers. The market is currently buoyant, and the company's factory is working to capacity. The company has been offered the opportunity to compete for a contract for 10 000 cases per year at a selling price of £15 per case. This is below the company's usual selling price of £17.25. Variable costs of manufacture would be the same as for existing cases, i.e. £5.63. However, in order to be able to take on the contract the company would need to expand its production facilities. For technical reasons it would be impossible to expand production to increase capacity to produce exactly 10 000 additional units. The expansion of facilities would increase capacity to the point where 20 000 additional units could be manufactured. Ince Pargeter's sales director thinks it is possible that he may be able to obtain additional orders that will use up the spare capacity. If production facilities were expanded, fixed costs would rise from £283 000 to an estimated £390 000.

You are required to advise the company on whether or not it should expand its production facilities.

10.22 Jackson Demetrios Limited manufactures three different types of office desk. Type A has extra drawers, type B has a printer shelf and type C has a moveable footrest.

In the company's present factory, production facilities are limited and there is a restriction on the number of machine hours available. The directors have considered moving to larger premises, but they are unwilling to make the move just at the moment because of fears of a downturn in the office furniture market.

Cost and selling price information for each type of desk is as follows:

	Type A £	Type B £	Type C £
Selling price per unit	175	160	165
Variable materials costs			
Wood	37	35	35
Plastics	16	15	18
Screws and fixings	2	2	2
Variable labour costs	18	16	16
Machine hours required per unit	2.5 hours	2.0 hours	2.1 hours
Sales demand for 20X6	1 400	1 600	1 550

Machine hours available are 4000 hours during 20X6. You are required to:

i) Advise the directors on the most profitable production plan available to them without further expansion of the premises.

ii) Calculate the overall contribution to fixed costs (to the nearest £) if your recommended production plan is followed.

CASE STUDY 10.1 Decision making and disagreement

Arthur Wright has owned and run a manufacturing business, A & A Wright (Ranges) Limited for many years. The business makes high quality, old-fashioned kitchen ranges. There has been a resurgence of demand in recent years as these ranges have become fashionable again, and the business has performed quite well both in terms of sales and net profits. Arthur set up the business originally with his brother Albert, but Albert died at a comparatively early age leaving his share of the business to his widow Ella. Ella takes no active part in the business, and until very recently, the major decisions have been left up to Arthur.

Arthur would like to retire early at around 55, and, as he is now in his early 50s, he is planning to hand over the business to his son, Vinnie. Vinnie is now 23; he left university with a degree in business studies a few months ago and since then has been working with his father in the company. Arthur and Vinnie get along reasonably well outside work, but there have been several disagreements over operational details within the business. Arthur realises that Vinnie has his own ideas about how he wants to do things and knows they won't agree about everything, but he's been making all the decisions for the business ever since Albert died and he's finding it difficult to let Vinnie have a say in running things. From his point of view, Vinnie finds it frustrating that Arthur won't listen to him properly. He's got a lot of ideas about improving the marketing and the financial management of the company, but Arthur really doesn't seem interested.

The latest disagreement is over a potential sales contract. Vinnie has been approached by Jay Johnson Kitchens Limited, a company that installs up-market kitchens. Jay Johnson wants to order, initially, ten ranges, but at a substantially discounted price. Wright's list price is £1300 per range; sometimes Arthur allows discounts to long-standing customers, but never more than around £50. On average, Wrights sell for £1280 per range. Jay Johnson wants to pay no more than £1050. Jay tells Vinnie that he should accept the order because 'there'll be plenty more business coming your way so long as we get a decent price. I often order 20 or 30 at a time, you know; even if I don't need to use them all immediately, it's good to have all the colours in stock to show people. Still, if you don't want the business, there are other suppliers who will.'

Vinnie did an accounting course at college, and he remembers the textbook chapter on marginal costing and decision making particularly well. One of the problems he has with his father's approach to business is that Arthur simply won't treat management accounting information seriously. Vinnie, on the other hand, would really like to get a proper budgeting and standard costing system going, but he hasn't made any progress in persuading his father that it would be a good idea.

The two men discuss the Jay Johnson order:

Vinnie: I really think we should go with this, you know. I've done the figures, and it's clear that even at a price of £1050 there'll be a positive contribution to fixed overheads.

Arthur: I'll take your word for it, but you know, it isn't all about figures. There are other things besides figures to consider. I've always been prepared to negotiate on discount, but £250 per range is just out of the question. Look at Leonard's Kitchens, for example; they've been buying from me for years so I give them £30 discount on each range. Leonard's happy with that; he knows it's as good as he'll get from anyone else.

Vinnie: Yeah, but Leonard only orders three or four each month. Jay's asking for ten now, and who knows how many more he'll want if we give him the price he's asking for.

Arthur: But that's another thing. It's all very well getting the orders, but we've got a maximum production capacity in this factory of about 100 units a month. Sometimes, we're producing as many as 95. If we take this business and Jay starts ordering big numbers we'll not be able to do it.

Vinnie: Yes, well, I'm glad you've mentioned that, because I think we should be looking at increasing capacity anyway. This factory building's a disgrace – it's a nightmare trying to meet the health and safety regulations, and it costs a fortune to heat. We should be thinking about moving into one of those factory units they're building by the motorway.

Arthur: The trouble with you is you just want to change everything. All at once. No discussion. Your uncle Albert and I started with nothing, you know, and we built all this up ourselves. I'm still in charge here, and it'll be a while before I retire. Could be a very long while unless you develop a bit of common-sense.

Vinnie: 'You've never thought I was good for anything, have you? You don't want me to have this business, do you? You won't listen to any of my ideas, and anyway I'm sick to death of hearing about you and Albert. Give it a rest.

The discussion very rapidly degenerates into a nasty argument, the worst one yet.

Vinnie has prepared a brief summary of his costings. Establishing the average sales price was easy, but he's had to do a bit of guesswork on the variable costs. He meant to go through this calmly and rationally with Arthur, but that opportunity was lost when the discussion got out of hand. Here are Vinnie's figures:

A & A Wright Limited: Summary of 20X7 sales and costs

	£
Sales: 1 030 ranges at an average price of £1 280 per unit	1 318 400
Variable costs: estimated at £630 per unit	(648 900)
Contribution	669 500
Fixed costs: total costs of £1 240 300 less estimated variables of £648 900	(591 400)
Net profit	78 100

Contribution per unit on existing sales = 1 280−630 = £650.
Contribution per unit on Jay Johnson's order = £1 050−630 = £420.

Case study requirements

Discuss the following questions:

a) Are there any problems apparent from Vinnie's figures?

b) Is Vinnie correct in proposing to accept the Jay Johnson order? Is Arthur correct in wanting to refuse the order at such a low price? What about the other issues that Arthur and Vinnie raise in their discussion/argument?

CHAPTER 11

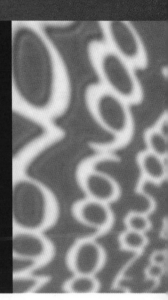

Pricing

Aim of the chapter

To understand the principal factors involved in setting selling prices by reference to a broad range of industry examples.

Learning outcomes

After reading the chapter and completing the related exercises, students should:

- Understand the interaction between supply and demand and the interdependence of price and quantity.
- Understand the various additional factors that play a part in pricing decisions.
- Understand the interface between pricing and costing, with especial reference to cost-plus pricing.
- Be able to apply knowledge of pricing issues across a range of industries and commercial activities.

The importance of pricing

So far, this section of the book has concentrated upon the various elements and classifications of cost with the aim of appreciating the importance of management accounting information that permits management to plan and control the business and make informed decisions.

In a commercial organisation, run with a view to profit, pricing is also of great importance. If prices are set too low to cover costs in the medium to long term, the business will suffer, and may even fail. In this chapter we will introduce some of the most important elements of decision making related to pricing.

The relationship between price and quantity

In fundamental economic terms, supply and demand are critical elements in the determination of prices. In a pure market environment, scarcity of supply of a commodity pushes up prices; lower available quantities command higher prices. Conversely, plentiful supply results in lower prices. There is, therefore, a theoretical interaction between quantity and price, which can be illustrated graphically (see Figure 11.1).

In the figure, three sets of lines have been drawn. Set #1 describes the supply of a lower quantity of goods; the relative scarcity is reflected in a higher price. Sets #2 and #3 describe a position of progressively higher supply which results in a relatively lower price. If a large number of price/quantity relationships are plotted the price/quantity relationship emerges. This is usually referred to as the demand curve.

The relationship described in the graph is an economist's representation of reality; it is an economic model of the relationship between price and quantity. How well does this neat graphical representation relate to reality? In practice, much

| Figure 11.1 | Demand |

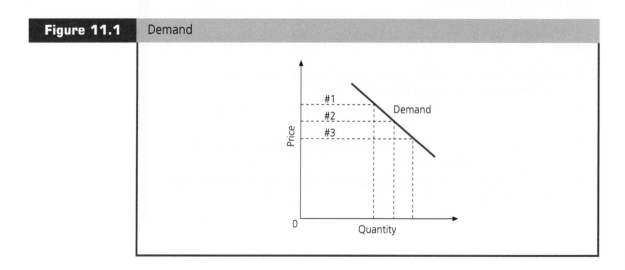

depends upon the nature of the commodity traded, the degree of competition in the market and the context in which it is supplied. It is possible to observe, in general terms, examples of such a relationship in the real world. For example, in the United Kingdom the price of strawberries in the summer months (when strawberries grown in the United Kingdom are available in large quantities) tends to be lower than in the winter months when the supply is smaller (because the only available strawberries are imported). However, it is usually quite difficult to observe the classic relationship between price and quantity in operation.

Elasticity and inelasticity

Demand is described by economists as elastic where:

- Customers are relatively indifferent about the product (because, for example, there are many identical or close substitutes in the market).
- The demand is highly sensitive to changes in price.

By contrast, demand is inelastic where:

- Customers place a high value on the product.
- Demand is relatively insensitive to price (i.e. it takes a substantial increase in price to have any effect on demand).

Problems in applying the economic model to the real world

The model represented by the graph in Figure 11.1 takes account of only two variables – price and quantity. However, in the real world other complexities frequently come into play. For example, the effects of:

- *Advertising*. If advertising is effective it can affect both demand and the price that people are willing to pay for a commodity or service.
- *Novelty*. A new product on the market can often command higher prices initially simply because of its novelty value.
- *Fashion*. An item that is widely perceived as more fashionable may be able to command a premium price.
- *Reputation*. A good brand name may command a premium price.

Sometimes, in practice, several of these factors interact.

Example 11.1

The Skoda story

'Classic. Comfort. Elegance. It can only be Skoda. Pardon me? Skoda?' (from an article by Malcolm Baylis: 'Have I got the name right?' at **www.carkeys.co.uk**, 29 December 1999).

Skoda, a company based in the Czech Republic, for many years manufactured cars that sold principally in eastern Europe. Sales in western Europe were low, because the company was dogged by a reputation for unreliability and drab design. However, once Skoda joined the Volkswagen Group of companies, the situation started to change.

Volkswagen cars have acquired a reputation for quality and reliability over a period of many years. Many people are willing to pay relatively high prices for this particular brand. Volkswagen re-engineered a new line of Skoda cars, using the same basic chassis design as for other VW group members (Seat and Audi included). Since the redesigned models have come onto the market Skoda sales and prices have increased, and the cars hold their value well on the second-hand market. In 1999 the author of the article quoted above noted that 'Skoda is no longer the cheapo car. The sales pitch today is not the price but definitely the quality, with company chiefs confident that quality will eventually see off the public's jibes that still, sadly, accompany the Skoda name.' Since then, a series of adverts has employed humour in what appears to have been a successful attempt to challenge the brand name problems head-on.

So, the demand for these cars, and their prices, have increased because of the public perception of a real change in quality. Although the Skoda brand name is still a disadvantage, advertising has effected a change in attitudes towards the company's products. A complicated mix of advertising, fashion, price change, quality change and change in brand reputation has resulted in higher sales volumes in western Europe.

In addition to the complex combinations of factors that affect price, there are other problems that arise in real-world attempts to apply the simple economic model:

- *Lack of information.* In most cases, it is very difficult to obtain accurate information as to the effect on prices of a change in demand, because these are theoretical effects. The model may be useful in helping to broadly predict the direction of price movements, but it is difficult to know with any degree of precision how much a change in price, for example, will affect demand.
- *Product range.* As noted, it is very difficult to obtain accurate information about the interaction of price/quantity/demand. This becomes even more difficult where large numbers of products are concerned. Most businesses produce a range of products or services, some of which may differ only slightly from each other. Management, in most cases, will simply lack the huge resources that would be required to accurately estimate demand over a range of conditions.
- *State of competition in the market.* The number and nature of competitors in the market will affect prices. These effects are examined in more detail in the next sub-section.

Competition in the market

The more suppliers in the market, the more competitive the environment. In such conditions, a state approaching 'perfect competition' is likely to exist. Because there are many suppliers, no individual supplier can set prices at a significantly higher level. Prices and supplies will easily reach an equilibrium state in which dramatic movements are unlikely to take place.

There may be special competitive conditions, however, in the markets for some products.

Special competitive conditions

Monopoly

A **monopoly** exists where only one supplier supplies the market with a particular good or service. The monopolist can take advantage of this unique position in raising prices to a high level. Regulation by the state often seeks to ensure that a monopoly position cannot arise. For example, proposed mergers between businesses are often carefully examined by regulatory authorities who have the authority to block any merger that would lead to a single, monopoly supplier in a market.

Oligopoly

An **oligopoly** exists where there are few suppliers (between, say, three and five) in the market for the supply of a particular good or service, and where market shares are fairly evenly spread out. An example of oligopoly exists in the provision of accounting services. Although there is a proliferation of accounting firms in the UK and worldwide, most of them are very small practices. There are only four major international firms that can genuinely compete for the business of accountancy advisory services to multinational corporations. Where oligopoly exists, there is a danger of reduced competition in the market and stagnation of prices. Regulators often take a keen interest in oligopolistic market conditions and will carefully assess the competitive implications of proposed mergers between members of an oligopoly. Nevertheless, oligopolies are found in many industries.

Cartel

A **cartel** is a price-fixing arrangement where a few major suppliers in a market agree between themselves to keep prices high. This is widely regarded as anti-competitive and in most market economies regulations exist to outlaw cartels. Currently, in the UK the law allows for very substantial fines to be levied on companies involved in price-fixing arrangements, and the UK Treasury has recently proposed that those found guilty of operating cartels should be subject to the penalty of imprisonment.

In the UK the Competition Commission is the authority that examines cases of alleged anti-competitive practice, which is defined by several different pieces of legislation (for example, the Competition Act 1998). The work of the Commission is described in detail on the website at **www.competition-commission.org.uk**.

Price setters and price takers

The position of an individual business in the market may determine whether or not it has any control over prices. In an intensely competitive market, with many suppliers of goods or services, there may be little scope for an individual supplier to separate from the pack. Sometimes markets are dominated by a few large suppliers, trailed by a large number of smaller providers. In such cases, a small provider of goods or services is unlikely to be able to influence prices; this type of provider is known as a price taker; they have to take the prices determined by the more powerful players in the market. By contrast, a price setter does not have to accept the prices set by other people.

How do producers decide on prices?

As we have just seen, price takers have little scope for making decisions on prices. What about price setters? Theoretically, producers and suppliers of goods and services should have regard to demand and to market conditions. Some producers do examine the market. However, the practice of cost-based pricing is surprisingly common. In this section, we will first examine market-based pricing and then look at cost-based pricing.

Market-based pricing

If market information is available or can be obtained at relatively low cost, businesses should use it. Sometimes pricing is based upon perceptions (and experience) of market demand that have little, if anything, to do with costs.

Example 11.2

Merchandising at rock concerts

How do rock artists make money out of touring? A 2001 newspaper article explains that although ticket prices tend to be high, they are often not the principal source of revenue as far as the band itself is concerned. Costs of running tours and the high prices charged by the venues themselves often eliminate most, if not all, of the revenue from tickets. 'This is borne out by the price of merchandise. Programmes alone at Madonna concerts cost £25 each. At Iron Maiden concerts fans regularly pay £280 for branded jackets which are thought to cost less than one-fifth of that to produce' ('Rocking all the way to the bank', by John Cassy, *The Guardian*, 17 August 2001, page 24).

In each of the cases cited in the article, competition is not really a factor. The goods are unique. The Iron Maiden fan who pays for a branded jacket at the premium price of £280 is not concerned that he or she can buy a similar, unbranded jacket on the market for a great deal less. The brand is what counts.

In some circumstances, however, competition is important and pricing by competitors may be clearly visible. For example, supermarket businesses frequently compete with each other on price. It is, obviously, easy to determine what the competition is charging for a basket of products because prices are visibly displayed. There are relatively few supermarket businesses, and it is not clear that people will always go to the cheapest – other factors such as the range of goods on sale and the general brand identity matter, too. Nevertheless, the level of pricing in such markets is often an important factor in securing sales.

Cost-based pricing

Cost-based pricing, as the term implies, is the fixing of the price for a product or service based upon the cost of providing it. However, cost-based pricing cannot usually be undertaken without any reference at all to the market, especially in the longer term. If a cost-based price results in a product with a very much higher price than similar or identical products in the market, there is likely to be a problem. If the higher costs result from inherent inefficiencies or defects in the manufacturing process the business is likely to fail.

Sometimes international inequalities, very often in the price of labour, result in businesses either being priced out of a particular market, or having to change their source of supply. One of the reasons for the relative decline of manufacturing industry in the UK has been the availability of cheaper labour elsewhere. Firms have often moved their entire manufacturing operation into other countries where labour costs are lower.

Cost-plus pricing

As the name implies, this approach to pricing first establishes the cost and then adds on a 'plus' factor – the required level of profit.

Example 11.3

Binnie Fairweather Limited makes a range of commercial ovens for sale to hotels and restaurants. The company uses a cost-plus approach to pricing. Variable costs of producing an oven are:

	£
Direct materials	49.60
Direct labour	61.30
Other variable costs	21.50
	132.40

The company absorbs production overheads on the basis of machine hours used. Fixed production overheads for the current year are estimated at £695 000 and total machine hours are 25 000 for the year. Each oven uses 1.5 machine hours. Binnie Fairweather requires a profit of 25% on total cost.
The fixed production overhead absorption rate is:

$$\frac{695\ 000}{25\ 000} = £27.80$$

Selling price is calculated as follows:

	£
Variable costs	132.40
Fixed costs: fixed production overheads	
£27.80 × 1.5 machine hours	41.70
Total costs	174.10

	£
Profit mark up: £174.10 × 25%	43.53
Selling price	217.63

Binnie Fairweather may be more or less flexible in relation to this calculated selling price. If the company looks around the other suppliers in the market it may see that selling prices for similar ovens are no more, generally, than £200. The company then has a choice: if it is in a price setting position it may decide to go ahead and market the product at approximately £218 or even higher, based upon factors such as:

- good brand name
- better quality (perceived or actual)
- a carefully targeted marketing campaign.

In fact, the selling price which is arrived at through application of cost-plus pricing may be simply a starting-off point in a long process of determining an appropriate price.

There are several disadvantages of cost-plus pricing:

- Absorption costing may not give a particularly accurate estimate of the fixed costs related to a product. As we have seen in previous chapters, allocation and apportionment of fixed costs can be quite arbitrary and may lead to incorrect decisions.
- The absorption rate is set in advance; it may prove to be quite seriously inaccurate, in which case pricing decisions based on full cost-plus calculations may prove, in retrospect, to be less than optimal.
- The emphasis on costs may result in firms failing to consider market conditions properly. Where the market is highly competitive, even a small price differential could result in a large fluctuation in sales. Fluctuations in volume of sales and production could result in significant misallocation of fixed costs, thus adding to the absorption costing problem already identified.
- In industries where cost-plus pricing is widely accepted as a basis for establishing contractual arrangements, inefficiency may actually be rewarded. Under cost-plus pricing arrangements, the higher the cost the higher the profit margin.

In order to address the problem of the unreliability of absorption costing for this type of decision making, the company could add a higher mark-up to the variable cost only.

Example 11.4

The directors of Binnie Fairweather have concluded that cost-plus pricing on the basis of total cost is simply too unreliable. They have therefore decided to use variable cost as a base, with a mark-up of 55% of the variable cost total.
This approach produces the following selling price:

	£
Variable costs	132.40
Add: profit mark up: £132.40 × 55%	72.82
Selling price	205.22

Whether or not this selling price is more realistic, given current market conditions for the company, would be a matter for the directors to decide. Again, this price might just be a starting point for the decision-making process.

Examples 11.3 and 11.4 illustrate cost-plus pricing in a manufacturing environment. This method is also commonly found in retail and service businesses. For example, a retailer may apply a standard mark-up to products in a particular category. In the case of service businesses a standard hourly charge is often applied to time spent on a particular customer's business. This is likely to be based upon an allocation of total costs of the business over the number of productive service hours available, plus a mark-up. Provided the resulting standard hourly charge is reasonably competitive, the cost-plus approach is likely to work well.

Variable cost-based pricing

We met this approach to pricing in Chapter 10; it is based upon the decision rule that an offer to buy at a given price should be accepted, provided that there is a positive contribution to fixed costs. This can, in practice, lead to the acceptance by businesses of some extremely low prices.

The information capability offered by the internet has allowed for a new type of purchasing and supply to arise in the case of certain goods and services. For example, hotels are businesses that incur high levels of fixed costs and relatively few variable costs. It is important for their continuing commercial viability that occupancy rates are as high as possible. Because of hotels' cost structure it is possible to sell at very low rates and still make a contribution to fixed costs. Late booking discounts, which can be widely advertised through the internet, allow hotels to sell some of their surplus rooms even if the prices obtained are low.

Example 11.5

A hotel in central London has 420 rooms. It regularly obtains occupancy rates of 80%. Recently, however, the hotel management has decided to advertise rooms via a late booking website. Most of the 420 rooms are double bedrooms with bath and shower; the normal price of an overnight stay, including breakfast, for two people is £165 each. Variable costs are £22.50 per person.

Using the basic decision rule, the position is clear: any price over £22.50 per person would theoretically be acceptable as it would result in a contribution to fixed costs. How low a price the hotel would actually accept in practice is, however, a different matter. If it lowers the price by too much it risks attracting the 'wrong' kind of customer, and thus damaging its reputation. Although the position in theory regarding contribution to fixed costs is clear, in practice

▶

the minimum selling price acceptable to the hotel is likely to be substantially in excess of £22.50.

Would the availability of the late rooms service damage the hotel's overall selling price? This would depend on the type of customer the hotel normally attracts. If the rooms are sold well in advance to travel agencies organising tours, for example, the rate offered to the agencies is likely to be very much lower than £165 per room in any case, and the people who occupy the rooms will not usually know how much the agency has paid for them. Business bookings could, however, be damaged; these would often be for only one or two people who would pay something close to the basic £165. If a business person is prepared to take the risk of leaving the booking to the last minute (the risk is that no rooms at all would be available in Central London on the date required) the room could probably be obtained at a substantially lower price.

Special cases

Tendering

Some types of commercial contracts for goods and services are arranged by tender. This is a process that involves several businesses competing for a contract; usually it involves the submission of sealed bids by a certain date and time. The customer opens the tenders on the same occasion, compares prices and conditions, and decides which tender to accept.

The sealed bid system is intended to allow for fair competition, and to give the customer the best opportunity of obtaining a fair price. In this situation, from the supplier's point of view, information about prices in the market is likely to be non-existent or limited (unless the suppliers have banded together in an illegal cartel to artificially adjust prices). Tendering is, therefore, likely to be done on the basis of a cost-plus approach, together with some guesswork about the prices likely to be offered by the competition.

The customer is not obliged to choose the lowest tender price. Sometimes, a supplier will submit a price that is obviously underestimated, perhaps because they wish to obtain the business at very low cost (this may be worth doing, for example, if labour is under-employed at a slack period). Alternatively, they may simply have underestimated what is involved in the contract.

Highly restricted supply of unique products

Some products do not fit particularly easily into either the market-based or cost-based approaches to pricing.

Example 11.6

Pricing original works of art

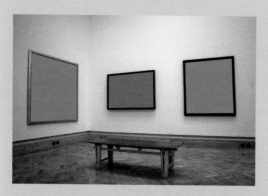

An original work of art is, by definition, unique. In a sense, each work of art creates its own demand because, until it is created, nobody can know with certainty that they want it or need it. However, once a certain class of works of art is established, a market of a sort may be created, and the market price is tied into intangible factors such as reputation and more obvious and quantifiable factors such as scarcity of supply. For example, the works of Vermeer, the 17th century Dutch artist, are so scarce (there are only 36 definitively attributed paintings) that prices become almost irrelevant; there is, effectively, no supply, although the demand would, presumably, be very high were one of his paintings to reach the market. Demand, in economists' terms, is highly inelastic.

The relationship between supply of works of art and prices does follow the classic economic model to some extent. When an artist with a reputation dies, the prices of his or her works will tend to increase because the supply has now definitively ceased.

Art pricing rarely has anything to do with cost, however great or small the reputation of the artist. A painting, for example, is a piece of stretched canvas, board or paper with pigments in some kind of medium applied to it; variable raw materials costs are unlikely in most cases to be very high. The labour required to produce it is rarely costed by the artist; if it were, the hourly rate would, in most cases, be laughably small. Cost-plus pricing in this case is hardly an option – information is lacking and the intrinsic cost of the product is rarely an issue in a decision to purchase in any case.

Target pricing

This approach to pricing turns cost-plus pricing on its head. A target price is established by reference to the market, not cost. Having set this, the firm will then deduct the desired profit margin on selling price. The residual amount then represents the maximum amount of cost that the firm can incur in producing the product or service. If this amount appears to be too small to accommodate all the associated costs, then the firm makes strenuous efforts to reduce those costs so that the target can be met. This may involve:

- Engaging in general cost reduction programmes to reduce fixed costs to a minimum.
- Re-engineering a product.
- Investing to create additional production efficiencies.
- Making compromises on quality of materials.

- Planning for additional volumes of production so as to reduce unit costs (by means of, for example, taking advantage of discounts for large-scale purchases).

Discounting

Many businesses will give discounts on selling price to reward customer loyalty or to ensure early payment for goods or services supplied on credit. Usually, such discounting reduces the supplier's profit margin by a small amount, but the reduction is balanced by a commensurate benefit.

However, sometimes a business may make a rational decision to sell goods or services at less than the cost of producing them. On the face of it this strategy appears foolish; it would clearly lead to the rapid downfall of the business if done too often over too wide a product range. However, it can make sense where:

- There is a large quantity of stock with a short shelf-life to clear.
- The goods or services are being treated as a loss leader.

Some stock is, by its nature, perishable: food and soft drinks, for example. In other cases, the life of stock is limited by fashion considerations. It usually makes sense for retailers to sell fashion items at the end of a season for whatever they can raise, so that room can be made for the new season's stock.

A loss leader product or service is used to attract customer attention to a range of goods or to a particular supplier. Although it does not make long-term sense to provide goods or services at less than cost, a loss leader may help a business to break into a particular market. This occasionally happens on a large scale, as demonstrated by the (fictional) Example 11.7.

| Example 11.7 | Mills Greaves plc is a supermarket group based in one of the English regions. It has turned in a high level of profits relative to other supermarket businesses, and is currently rich in cash. The company's directors are ambitious for the future of the group, and have planned in detail an expansion programme that will in due course mean that its supermarkets are found in all parts of England and Wales. The directors have targeted a series of smaller towns that do not currently have a supermarket. They will open relatively large premises and will provide a huge range of goods at extremely low prices. The company can afford to bear the losses because of its previous profitability, and, because it is mostly still owned by members of the Mills and Greaves families (most of the directors are family members and shareholders), it is not under pressure to pay a dividend. The strategy is fundamentally to drive out the competition by undercutting prices. Once competitors have been forced into closure, Mills Greaves will be able to raise prices in the new areas and return to previous levels of profitability.

The ethics of this type of business decision may cause some concern, especially because of the proposed scale of the operation. However, any new entrant to a market is likely to try a modified version of this approach, especially if price is the principal distinguishing feature in consumer choice. |

Auction

Where prices are established at auction the seller abandons part of his or her control over price setting. For some types of commodity (e.g. art, antiques and certain categories of real estate) selling at auction is the accepted method of contracting; it would not normally apply for new goods. Usually the seller can stipulate a reserve price. For example, a seller sends an antique vase to auction, setting a reserve on it of £1500. This means that if the bidding does not reach that price, the item will not be sold by the auctioneer.

❗ SPOTLIGHT 11.1 Pricing in context

Rather than examining a single case study, this section of the chapter discusses pricing in the context of four very different cases. The cases illustrate some of the approaches to pricing explained earlier in the chapter.

Building contractor

Aziz & Sons Limited is a firm of building contractors. The company has just been invited to submit a tender for constructing a very large office building. Aziz & Sons would like to get the business, if possible. Although the directors do not know the names of the other contractors on the tender list, they are likely to be able to make an educated guess; there are relatively few competitors who have the capacity to take on a job of this size.

How does the company go about establishing a tender price? In practice, tendering for such contracts is an expensive and lengthy process. The cost of submitting the bid is wasted if the company does not obtain the tender; this is an operating cost that has to be accepted by such companies.

Aziz & Sons' management will have to study the architect's drawings in detail in order to understand what is entailed. They will have to cost raw materials, subcontracted elements of the work (such businesses rarely employ directly all the different trades they need), direct labour, managerial time and, probably, an element of fixed overhead recovery. An estimate of the time taken and a programme of works will also be required. Once the costs are established, a tender price can be discussed, based, probably, upon a cost-plus approach where a mark-up is added. At the end of the process an overall contract price is estimated. However, the senior management may feel at this point that the proposed bid price is simply too high: if it seems likely that competitors will bid less, the costs and the mark-up are likely to be re-examined. Sometimes, this may involve an element of target costing; working back from a bid price that seems feasible, management may look for ways of minimising costs.

In this type of case, establishing a price is a lengthy and expensive process. While the basic approach is likely to involve cost-plus calculations, the price that is finally submitted in the tender will usually have been influenced by market-based considerations as well.

▶

Toothpaste manufacturer

Most people clean their teeth pretty regularly; therefore, toothpaste is a product that is sold in large quantities. It is a good example of a product to which people are relatively indifferent, in the sense that they give the purchase little thought. Demand is elastic because purchasers do not place a high value on the product, will accept substitutes relatively easily, and are really not very interested in it. (Contrast the purchase of a tube of toothpaste with the purchase of a new car, for example: which absorbs more of the purchaser's interest?)

Of course, we do not buy toothpaste direct from the suppliers, but almost invariably through the middleman, the retailer. As far as manufacturers are concerned their customers are retailers or wholesalers.

How, then, do manufacturers price their product? If there are many competitors in the market, prices are likely to be kept at a stable level through competition. The manufacturer may not be able to exert very much influence on price. Provided the selling price covers costs and provides some profit, the manufacturer will, presumably, continue to manufacture and sell the product. However, it may not charge the same amount to all customers. Powerful purchasers (like the large supermarket chains) are likely to be in a position to exert influence on the manufacturer's price and to demand discounts for bulk purchases. Smaller purchasers will probably have to pay more.

In the case of a bulk manufacturer of a product for which demand is elastic, price is determined by the market. Some sectors of the market, moreover, are likely to be in a position to demand lower prices; thus, different prices may be paid for the same product depending upon the power and influence of the customer. Although cost is important, in the sense that costs must be covered in the longer term if the manufacturer is to survive, they are less relevant to the pricing decision than in some other types of business.

Writer

Minnie Tanner has just finished her first novel, *Silver Moonlight*, a 'romantic tale of love triumphing over adversity'. Like most writers, Minnie's dream is to have her book published in numerous editions, translated into many languages, with worldwide sales in at least seven figures. Mostly, of course, the dream does not come true. Suppose, for a moment, that Minnie's book is publishable (unlikely) and that she finds someone willing to publish it (highly unlikely). How does Minnie set the price of the book?

The answer, of course, is that, although she is in a sense a producer, she doesn't set the price. In the unlikely event that a publisher accepts the manuscript, the firm will have control over all the details of production and pricing. Minnie's earnings (if any) will be in the form of royalties dependent upon sales, at a royalty rate determined by the publisher. Her only hope of varying this arrangement is if she becomes a really successful author with very high sales. In such cases, which are obviously rare, writers (or more likely, their agents) may be able to command large advances and better royalty deals. Minnie has a long way to go.

How does the publisher set the price of the book? The decision on pricing in this case, is likely to have a lot to do with the market. Romantic novels aren't exactly like toothpaste; there is more differentiation between products, but demand is relatively elastic. It becomes inelastic only once the author has established a faithful following of people who will go into a bookshop for 'the latest Minnie Tanner'; at that point demand for the specific product is assured. However, demand is only relatively inelastic; if the publishers double the price of the book the market probably will not respond by buying it, regardless of price.

Solicitors

Haringay, Fisker and Blott is a firm of solicitors, specialising in matrimonial and property conveyancing work.

How do solicitors establish their prices? Solicitors and other professionals such as accountants, surveyors and business consultants, usually establish charge-out rates, which are used to charge clients on the basis of time spent.

Haringay, Fisker and Blott are all partners in the business; they also employ four full-time solicitors and two legal executives to assist in the conveyancing side of the business – a total of nine fee-earners. Each year, the partners meet to discuss the charge-out rates to be employed in the practice in the coming year. The budget for 20X8 shows total costs of £625 000, which must be covered by income. In addition, of course, the partners wish to make a profit. Their desired mark-up on costs is 25%.

There are three grades of charge-out rate: for partners, staff solicitors and legal executives. During 20X7 the charge-out rates have been £90, £55 and £30, respectively. The partners work on the basis that they and staff are available for 46 weeks per year, 5 days per week, 7.5 hours per day. They aim to be able to charge 80% of available time to clients.

1. By what percentage do the partners need to increase charge-out rates for 20X8 to meet their desired mark-up?
2. What other considerations should the partners take into account in deciding whether or not, and by how much, to increase charge-out rates?

1. Percentage increase

At current rates, provided the estimates of time availability are accurate, accumulated charge-outs could raise the following fee income (based on) time available of 46 weeks × 5 days × 7.5 hours × 80% = 1380 hours per person):

	£
Legal executives: 2 × 1380 × £30	82 800
Solicitors (staff): 4 × 1380 × £55	303 600
Partners: 3 × 1380 × £90	372 600
	759 000

The target total for fees for 20X8 is the budget costs plus a mark-up of 25%:

$$[£625\ 000 \times 25\%] + 625\ 000 = £781\ 250$$

The estimate of available fee income of £759 000 falls short of the target by (£781 250 – 759 000) £22 250. Charge-out rates would have to be raised by:

▶

$$\frac{22\,250}{759\,000} \times 100 = 2.9\%$$

2. Other considerations

The partners would need to take into account the following factors in determining prices:

- *Recovery*. Although charge-out rates are very useful for management accounting purposes within many service businesses, they are sometimes used simply as a basis for establishing the amount of a bill. For various reasons, solicitors may not wish to charge the fees suggested by the bill, or may wish (and be able) to charge more. Usually, a percentage recovery figure will be calculated to indicate the extent to which the fees indicated by the charge-out rate have been recovered. If recovery falls much short of 100% the partners may need to rethink their rates.

- *Competition*. Traditionally, solicitors' fees have been shrouded in mystery. However, with the advent of advertising by solicitors (it used to be prohibited) and a greater willingness on the part of the public to challenge solicitors' bills, competition has become more of an issue. Word of mouth is an important factor for professional practices in gaining new business; if word gets round that Haringay, Fisker and Blott's bills are much higher than average, they could lose business. So, to some extent, price affects demand, and market conditions should be taken into account.

Chapter summary

The chapter began with a brief discussion of the classical economist's model of demand. Several additional factors that complicate the real-world application of the model were described.

The nature of competition was then discussed, and the special cases of monopoly, oligopoly and cartel were described. This was followed by more detailed consideration of market-based and cost-based pricing, including the technique of cost-plus pricing. Despite several disadvantages to the cost-plus approach, cost-plus pricing is widely used.

We considered a range of special cases of pricing:

- tendering
- pricing of unique products
- target pricing
- discounting
- auction.

Finally, a series of four spotlight studies were discussed, as illustrations of the range of pricing techniques and principles that may be adopted in practice. The cases were those of a building contractor, a toothpaste manufacturer, a writer and a firm of solicitors.

Pricing is a difficult area of management decision making. Despite the attractions of the simple demand model, in practice pricing in many industries is more of an art than a science.

 The end-of-chapter exercises that follow are divided into two sections. The first section has answers provided at the end of the book.

The second section, in the white box, has answers on the lecturers' section of the website.

Website summary

The book's website contains the following material in respect of Chapter 11:

Students' section

- Quiz containing five multiple choice questions
- Three additional questions with answers.

Lecturers' section

- Answers to the end-of-chapter exercises 11.7 to 11.9
- Three additional questions with answers.

Exercises: answers at the end of the book

11.1 The demand curve plots the relationship between:

     a)   selling price and cost

     b)   quantity and cost

     c)   quantity and selling price

     d)   selling price and discounts.

11.2 Demand is described as elastic where it:

     a)   is highly sensitive to changes in price

     b)   seldom increases or decreases

     c)   cannot be met

     d)   increases only where there is a substantial change in price.

11.3 An oligopoly exists in cases where:

     a)   one supplier controls the market

     b)   about three to five suppliers control the market

     c)   there are many suppliers of about equal size in the market

     d)   new suppliers enter the market frequently.

11.4 Auger Ambit Limited is a manufacturing company that sets prices based on total costs plus a mark-up. For the year ending 31 December 20X5 the company is forecasting total fixed costs of £788 000. Variable materials costs will be £18.00 per unit and direct labour costs will be £27.56 per unit. The company expects to produce 20 000 units, and normally looks for a profit mark-up of 25%.

     Suggest a suitable cost-based selling price per unit of product for 20X5.

11.5 Belvedere, Bharat & Burgess are in partnership together as accountants. They have recently enlarged their practice and have taken on extra staff. The partners meet to discuss charge-out rates, which currently stand at £110 per hour for each of the three partners, £85 per hour for the five senior staff and tax specialists and £50 per hour for all other grades of qualified accountant (six employees). The partnership operates on the assumption that 75% of hours worked will be chargeable to clients as fees, and that a 43-week year is worked, at 8 hours per working day. Costs are expected to amount to £1 275 000 in the coming year, 20X6.

     1.   If the partners' assumptions are correct, how much in fees could the partnership expect to bill in 20X6?

     2.   If hours are worked exactly as planned, the average recovery rate on billing is actually 94%, and total actual costs are 1% above budget in 20X6, how much profit or loss would the partnership make?

11.6 Discuss the key factors that would arise in determining selling prices for:

a)   a garden centre

b)   a small grocery store that is open for 24 hours.

Exercises: answers available to lecturers

11.7 Ainsley Witt Limited manufactures old-fashioned dolls houses. The manufacturing process is labour intensive and involves a cost of £54 per house. Variable materials costs are £22 per house, and in addition the company pays a royalty per house manufactured of £1 to the designer.

The company's usual level of fixed costs is £125 000 per year. In an average year about 2400 dolls houses will be produced. Ainsley Witt's sales manager has suggested that the company should carry out an exercise to compare the current selling price of £150 for a dolls house with a cost-plus calculation, based upon a target mark-up on cost of 23%.

Calculate the difference between the current selling price and a selling price based upon the cost-plus calculation.

11.8 Burke and Harpur are solicitors who have recently set up in partnership together and are working hard to establish themselves in a town that already has several solicitors. Both have a charge-out rate per hour of £65. They are preparing a bill for Mrs Henrietta Higgs, for whom they have recently drafted a will. The bill contains the following items:

	£
Fees for time: 43 hours @ £65	2 795
Taxation specialist's charges for advice	650
Other sundry charges	240
Total	3 685

The partners disagree about how much to charge. Burke thinks that £3685 is a ridiculously high amount to charge for drafting a will, and that if word gets out that the firm charges that much for the service it will badly damage their chances of increasing business. He says they should charge £1500 and be prepared to take the loss.

Harpur worked the majority of the 43 hours noted on the bill. He defends the high charge on the grounds that it is only so high because Mrs Higgs wasted such a lot of time changing her mind about who should inherit her considerable wealth. Also, because she is so rich, she should be able to afford the charges. He adds that he personally doesn't care if Mrs Higgs doesn't use their services again because she was so difficult to deal with.

Discuss the points of view of the two partners on this pricing problem. Which partner do you think is correct?

11.9 Discuss the key factors that would arise in determining selling prices for:

a)   plumber (sole trader)

b)   biscuit manufacturer.

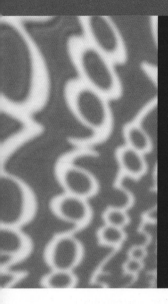

CHAPTER 12

Capital investment decisions

Aim of the chapter

To investigate the techniques used by business managers to make decisions on capital investment.

Learning outcomes

After reading the chapter and completing the related exercises, students should:

- Understand the concept of capital budgeting and the need for control over capital investment decision making.
- Understand and be able to apply two simple methods of capital investment appraisal: payback and accounting rate of return.
- Understand the time value of money.
- Understand and be able to apply more complex methods of capital investment appraisal: net present value and internal rate of return.

What is capital investment?

Over the past few chapters we have examined many aspects of the control of costs, and we have examined short-term decision making involving contribution and pricing. Most businesses, however, are concerned not only with short-term costing decisions, but also with decisions that have an impact over the longer term. As well as expenditure on fixed and variable costs, business managers must make decisions about spending on capital items. Capital expenditure is expenditure on items such as fixed assets and investments in other businesses; its distinguishing feature is that it involves appraisal of profits and cash flows generated over more than one accounting period.

Capital expenditure includes, for example, purchase of land and buildings to be used for the business over several years, and purchase of plant and machinery, fixtures and fittings, computers and equipment that will be of benefit to the business over periods in excess of one year.

It is important to appreciate that the point of this type of expenditure is to generate extra profits for the business. If the expenditure does not contribute to business profitability it should not be made. Sometimes, it is not easy to see the connection; how, for example, does buying an extra filing cabinet for the accounts department contribute to business profitability? The argument for the purchase would probably be along these lines:

> A new filing cabinet will help the accounting department to keep its customer invoices in better order. Therefore, queries from customers can be answered more quickly and efficiently, and proper filing will ensure that copy invoices don't get lost so easily. If our response to customer queries improves, it makes it more likely that good relationships with customers will be maintained. The new filing cabinet therefore makes a positive contribution to the business.

And so on. Try arguing for the income generating potential of a new rubber plant or a coat stand for the reception area. (Be creative . . .)

Capital budgeting

Capital expenditure can be of really significant proportions in a business, and it is important that it should be properly controlled. A decision to invest in a new building, for example, represents a major commitment of resources by the business and such a decision cannot be taken lightly.

The general principles of planning, control and decision making are by now familiar to us. In Chapter 6 we established the need for management to set business objectives and to assess alternatives and make decisions. Capital expenditure must also fit into the general framework of the business's strategy and objectives.

While it is obviously the case that larger investment decisions require more careful thinking and deliberation, many businesses in practice subject capital expenditure at all levels to scrutiny. It is often the case that even quite small amounts of capital expenditure require approval at high level. The reasons for such detailed scrutiny and approval include the following:

- Small items may appear individually insignificant, but taken together, may amount to a significant sum of expenditure;
- Managers at all levels are often quite keen to acquire small status symbols (a new printer, a desk, a comfy chair); unless these items are carefully controlled, the business may waste money.

Capital expenditure should always be geared towards meeting the strategic objectives of the business, and a capital budget should emerge as part of the overall budget procedures which we examined in Chapter 8.

Capital rationing

Businesses need to obtain the finance that is used to make capital investments. Finance may be available from the existing resources of the business. However, if available cash is employed for a capital investment project it cannot be used for anything else; managements need to be sure that the capital investment is the best available use of the resources. If the business has little cash, it may have to borrow in order to invest in capital assets and projects. Borrowing costs money in the form of regular interest payments and, of course, it cannot be infinitely expanded (there is a point, for both businesses and individuals, beyond which it is neither sensible nor practical to borrow more money). Whether finance comes from existing resources or from outside the business, management is likely to have to face difficult decisions about which assets and projects are to be preferred. In conditions of capital rationing it is important that management should have clear criteria, linked to overall strategic objectives, in order to make capital investment decisions.

Capital investment appraisal in practice

Most of the remainder of this chapter will be devoted to an examination of the principal techniques used by managers to make capital investment decisions in practice. We will examine four principal methods, all of which are widely used in practice:

- accounting rate of return (ARR)
- payback
- net present value (NPV)
- internal rate of return (IRR).

All of the methods involve assessing the initial investment required against future returns from the investment. Because investment appraisal looks forward into the future some elements of estimation and imprecision are unavoidable. Also, as in the case of short-term decision making, there are always other, unquantifiable factors to take into account. The calculations can never give a definitive answer; they merely provide input into the decision-making process.

In order to be able to compare the application of the four methods we will use a single, common example. First, the example will be explained in detail so that readers can understand how the figures are derived and estimated.

Example 12.1

Proctor Hedges Limited manufactures a wide range of gardening equipment. It has recently developed a new design of compost bin. A market research project costing £20 000 was undertaken in which the prototype was demonstrated to a large number of gardeners at show gardens around the country. Results of the market research have been very promising. In addition, the company's marketing director has used his contacts to have the new design prominently featured in a prime-time television gardening programme. The programme is due to appear in three months' time, and the company expects to receive a large number of orders very soon afterwards. The directors have decided that they must gear up production to be ready for the anticipated demand for the new product. The principal capital expenditure involved would be the purchase of an advanced plastics moulding machine. The existing factory site has ample spare room for the machine, and no significant additions to fixed costs are anticipated.

The production director has investigated the available machines, and has decided that the choice comes down to two alternatives, which he has imaginatively code-named Machine A and Machine B. Information about the two machines is as follows:

	Machine A	Machine B
	£	£
Capital outlay	450 000	600 000
Residual value at end of 5 years	50 000	100 000
Straight-line depreciation per year	80 000	100 000
Machine hours per year	80 000	120 000

Each compost bin takes two machine hours to manufacture; therefore the maximum capacity available is:

Machine A = 40 000 units per year
Machine B = 60 000 units per year.

The sales director estimates that demand will be greatest in the first couple of years. After that, it is likely that sales will tail off, as other new composting products are introduced to the market by competitors. After five years the product will probably have reached the end of its commercial life and will be discontinued. The machine could then be sold for its residual value, or, possibly, be transferred at net book value into some other line of production.

Demand figures are estimated as follows for the five-year production cycle:

Year	Demand
1	60 000
2	48 000
3	42 000
4	25 000
5	25 000

Machine A could not produce sufficient items to meet demand in the first three years. However, the directors decide that they would, nevertheless, like to consider the purchase of Machine A because it requires only three-quarters of the capital outlay of Machine B.

The costings prepared by the finance director show that compost bins produced by Machine A would be expected to make a profit per unit (before depreciation) of £4.00. Machine B is a more efficient user of raw materials and so would be expected to make a profit per unit (before depreciation) of £4.10.

Establishing relevant information for the appraisal

The basic requirement is that we assist the directors in making their choice between the two machines by use of investment appraisal techniques.

Even in a simple example like this one, there is a great deal of information. For investment appraisal purposes we need to take into account only relevant information. The cost of the market research project (£20 000), for example, is not information that is relevant to the decision. This may seem odd at first sight: why should it not be taken into account? The answer is that the costs have already been incurred and are therefore not relevant to the decision; they are known as **sunk costs**.

The directors must take into account only those costs and future revenues that are relevant to the decision between the machines – i.e. only incremental costs and revenues. Any costs or revenues that would have occurred in any case are irrelevant to the appraisal of the project. For each year of the life of the project the net cash inflow or outflow must be calculated. This involves adding together all the incremental revenues and taking away all the incremental costs.

In real life, taxation is often a significant item of cash inflow or outflow. In this chapter we will ignore the effects of taxation as being beyond the scope of this book. However, students should realise that if they encounter investment appraisal in practice, or go on to study accounting at a higher level, taxation will be an important element of appraisal calculations.

Timing

There are widely accepted conventions in respect of timing for capital investment appraisal.

The first event that would take place after the decision is made would be the outflow of cash to be spent in buying the machine. Capital investment appraisal techniques make the assumption that the cash is spent now, immediately, and 'now' is referred to as Time 0. The capital investment would generate costs and revenues in the future over a five-year (in this example) period. There is a further simplifying assumption that all costs and revenues are incurred on the last day of the year at Time 1, Time 2, Time 3 and so on.

These assumptions about timings are necessary in order to keep the calculations manageable, but it should be recognised that they introduce a further element of imprecision into the appraisal.

Assembling information for the appraisal

First, we will establish an estimated production and sales schedule for each of the two machines:

Year	Demand	Machine A production and sales	Machine B production and sales
1	60 000	40 000	60 000
2	48 000	40 000	48 000
3	42 000	40 000	42 000
4	25 000	25 000	25 000
5	25 000	25 000	25 000

Because Machine A has a maximum production capacity of 40 000 units per year, it cannot meet demand. It will produce up to capacity for the first three years (120 000 units as opposed to demand of 150 000). It is assumed that dissatisfied customers will not wait for a compost bin (people are not likely to put their name down on a waiting list for this type of product) and will simply buy another type.

Once we have established sales and production figures, we can estimate profits before depreciation for each of the five years, as follows:

Year	Machine A	Machine B
1	40 000 × £4.00 = £160 000	60 000 × £4.10 = £246 000
2	40 000 × £4.00 = £160 000	48 000 × £4.10 = £196 800
3	40 000 × £4.00 = £160 000	42 000 × £4.10 = £172 200
4	25 000 × £4.00 = £100 000	25 000 × £4.10 = £102 500
5	25 000 × £4.00 = £100 000	25 000 × £4.10 = £102 500
Total profit	£680 000	£820 000

Having tabulated this basic information we will now examine each of the capital investment appraisal techniques in turn.

Accounting rate of return

The accounting rate of return (ARR) method uses projections of accounting profit to calculate the expected rate of return on capital invested into an asset or project. It is calculated as follows:

$$\frac{\text{Average expected return (accounting profit)}}{\text{Average capital employed}} \times 100 = \text{ARR\%}$$

Calculating average expected return (accounting profit)

Accounting profit takes depreciation into account. Therefore, we must deduct depreciation from each of the annual profit figures calculated earlier, before calculating the average profit over five years:

Year	Machine A £000	Machine B £000
1	160 – 80 = 80	246 – 100 = 146
2	160 – 80 = 80	196.8 – 100 = 96.8
3	160 – 80 = 80	172.2 – 100 = 72.2
4	100 – 80 = 20	102.5 – 100 = 2.5
5	100 – 80 = 20	102.5 – 100 = 2.5
Total profit	280	= 320

The average profit per year generated by Machine A is:

$$\frac{280\ 000}{5} = £56\ 000$$

The average profit per year generated by Machine B is:

$$\frac{320\ 000}{5} = £64\ 000$$

Calculating average capital employed

The capital employed figure to be taken into account is the capital employed by the project or investment (*not* the capital employed by the whole business).

In this particular example, because the straight-line method of depreciation is adopted, the capital investment is assumed to be depleted by the same amount each year (£80 000 for Machine A and £100 000 for Machine B). Therefore, we take initial capital employed (at Time 0) and capital employed by the end of the final year of operation (Time 5) and average the two figures, as follows:

Time	Machine A £000	Machine B £000
0	450	600
5	50	100

	Machine A	Machine B
Average	$\dfrac{450 + 50}{2} = £250$	$\dfrac{600 + 100}{2} = £350$

We now have both elements necessary for the calculation (average accounting profit and average capital employed) of ARR. For Machine A:

$$ARR = \frac{56\ 000}{250\ 000} \times 100 = 22.4\%$$

For Machine B:

$$ARR = \frac{64\ 000}{350\ 000} \times 100 = 18.3\%$$

The ARR calculation shows Machine A as the better of the two options. Although Machine B is estimated to produce more profit, the average investment is considerably higher. If the directors were only to use this one method of investment appraisal they might very well opt for Machine A. Note, however, that the comparison of ARR ignores the fact that Machine B actually produces a higher absolute profit (£64 000) than that produced by Machine A (£56 000). This is a notable weakness of the ARR technique.

Students may well have spotted the similarity between the calculation of ARR and that of return on capital employed (ROCE). When calculating ROCE we looked at figures for the business as a whole. Proctor Hedges Limited will, of course, have a ROCE figure for the business as a whole. If ROCE is substantially in excess of the ARR of 22.4% the directors may wish to think again about the whole project. If a project is undertaken that produces an ARR that is lower than ROCE, the ROCE percentage will be reduced overall.

The Proctor Hedges example requires comparison between two investments. However, sometimes only one possible investment is appraised (because the choice is simply between making the investment and not making the investment). In such cases it is common to find ARR being judged against a yardstick or target return percentage. If the proposed investment's ARR is less than the target then the investment may well be rejected.

Payback

Payback is a simple investment appraisal technique that involves estimating the length of time it will take for cash inflows to cover the initial investment outflow. This can be a useful technique where one of management's principal criteria is the ability of a project to 'pay for itself' quickly, so that proceeds can be reinvested in other projects.

Note that payback appraises investments in terms of cash inflows and outflows. Because depreciation is neither an inflow nor an outflow (remember: depreciation is an accounting adjustment) it is not taken into account.

Payback is relatively simple to calculate:

Time	Machine A £000	Machine B £000
Initial outflow		
0	− 450	− 600
Inflows		
1	+160	+246
2	+160	+196.8
3	+160	+172.2
4	+100	+102.5
5	+100	+102.5
5*	+50	+100

*Note that at the end of year 5 the machine will be sold, or transferred into alternative production at net book value. An inflow of the amount of the net book value is therefore included.

Payback is calculated by taking cumulative cash flows into account, and identifying the point at which the net cumulative cash flow reaches zero. For Machine A:

Time	Cash flow £000	Cumulative cash flow £000
0	− 450	− 450
1	+160	− 290
2	+160	− 130
3	+160	+30
4	+100	+130
5	+100+ 50	+280

Cumulative cash flow reaches the zero position sometime during the third year. We can estimate a figure for payback expressed in years and months as follows:

Payback = 2 years + (130/160 × 12 months) = 2 years and 10 months
(to nearest whole month)

For Machine B:

Time	Cash flow £000	Cumulative cash flow £000
0	− 600	− 600
1	+246	− 354
2	+196.8	− 157.2
3	+172.2	+15
4	+102.5	+117.5
5	+102.5 + 100	+320

Cumulative cash flow reaches the zero position sometime during the third year (as for Machine A). Estimating a figure for payback expressed in years and months:

Payback = 2 years + (157.2/172.2 × 12 months) = 2 years and 11 months
(to nearest whole month)

Comparing the payback measures, we can see that Machine A pays back only slightly more quickly than Machine B. Payback, then, is unlikely to play a major part in this particular investment decision.

Payback is a popular method of appraisal in practice, but it has a major limitation in that it concentrates attention on only one important aspect – the ability of an investment to pay back quickly. As we can see from the Proctor Hedges example, cash flows beyond the point of payback are completely ignored. Surely these later cash flows should be taken into account in investment appraisal?

Net present value, which we examine next, does take into account all of the cash flows associated with an investment.

Net present value

In order to understand the net present value (NPV) technique of investment appraisal, we must first gain an appreciation of the importance of time in examining long-term investments.

The time value of money

The principle of the time value of money rests on the observation that £1 now is not the same as £1 in a month's time or a year's time or 10 years' time. The effect of interest is illustrated in the examples below.

Compounding

A saver puts £100 in the bank on 1 January 20X0. The bank's interest rate is 10% throughout the whole of the year which follows: when the interest is paid on 31 December 20X0 the saver now has £110 in the account. If £110 is kept in the account for the whole of the next year following – 20X1 – and the interest rate remains stable at 10%, by 31 December 20X1 the saver has accumulated:

£110 (at 31 December 20X0) + Interest for 20X1 (10% × £110) = £121

Each year, provided the saver keeps both the original investment and the accumulated interest in the bank, the interest compounds. The amount of interest earned each year gradually increases. The five-year effect, assuming a constant interest rate of 10%, as follows:

Year	Balance at start of year	Interest for year	Balance at end of year
1	100.00	10.00	110.00
2	110.00	11.00	121.00
3	121.00	12.10	133.10
4	133.10	13.31	146.41
5	146.41	14.64	161.05

So, £1 at Time 0 (the beginning of year 1) is the equivalent of £1.61 at the end of year 5.

The compounding effect can be expressed via a formula derived as follows. Using 10% as an example:

$$£1 + (£1 \times 10\%) = £1.10$$

Removing the £ symbols:

$$1 + (1 \times 10\%) = 1.10$$

Simplifying:

$$1 + 0.1 = 1.1$$

So, the initial sum invested × (1 + the rate of interest) = amount at the end of year 1. That is:

$$1 \times (1 + i)$$

where i = the interest rate (expressed as a decimal, e.g. 0.10 rather than 10%).
Test this out by reference to the example of £100 invested at 10% for one year:

$$£100 \times (1 + 0.1) = £110$$

What about a formula for year 2? For the total at the end of year 2 we take the amount at the end of year 1 × (1 + the rate of interest) = amount at the end of year two. That is:

$$1 \times (1 + i) \times (1 + i)$$

Or:

$$1 \times (1 + i)^2$$

Test this out by reference to the example of £100 invested at a rate of 10% per year for two years:

$$£100 \times (1 + 0.10)^2 = £100 \times (1.21) = £1.21$$

The formula for year 3 adds another compounding factor:

$$1 \times (1 + i) \times (1 + i) \times (1 + i)$$

Or:

$$1 \times (1 + i)^3$$

And so on. The formula for the compounding factor is expressed as follows:

$$(1 + i)^n$$

where i = the rate of interest and n = the number of years. For each combination of interest rate and number of years, we can work out a compounding factor. For example, what is the compounding factor for £1 invested at a constant rate of 4% over 3 years? Answer:

$$(1 + 0.04)^3 = (1.04) \times (1.04) \times (1.04) = 1.125$$

So £1 invested at a constant rate of 4% over 3 years will result in a balance at the end of year 3 of £1.125.

? Self-test question 12.1 (answer at the end of the book)

1. Write down the formula for £1 invested at a constant rate of 8% for 4 years and, using a calculator, work out the compounding factor.
2. Write down the formula for £1 invested at a constant rate of 7% for 5 years and, using a calculator, work out the compounding factor.
3. Write down the formula for £1 invested at a constant rate of 6% for 6 years and, using a calculator, work out the compounding factor.

Discounting

In the example and discussion of compounding we noted that, at a constant rate of 10%, £1 invested now (at Time 0) is the equivalent of £1.61 by the end of year 5. Conversely, we could say that £1.61 at the end of year 5 is the equivalent of £1 now. Also, we can say that £1.10 at the end of year 1 is the equivalent of £1 now. How can this be expressed in a formula?

Discounting formulae are the reciprocals of compounding formulae. So, we noted earlier that, at a constant rate of 10% the initial sum invested × (1 + the rate of interest) = amount at the end of year 1. That is:

$$1 \times (1 + i)$$

We can turn this round to discount back from the end of year 1:

$$\text{Amount at the end of year 1} \times \frac{1}{(1 + i)} = \text{amount of the initial sum invested}$$

Similarly, taking the reciprocal of the year 2 compounding formula:

$$\text{Amount at the end of year 2} \times \frac{1}{(1 + i)^2} = \text{amount of the initial sum invested}$$

The formula for the discount factor is:

$$\frac{1}{(1 + i)^n}$$

where i = the rate of interest and n is the number of years.

For each combination of interest rate and number of years, we can work out a discounting factor. For example, what is the discounting factor for £1 at the end of year 3, which has been invested since Time 0 at a constant rate of 4%? Answer:

$$\frac{1}{(1 + 0.04)^3} = \frac{1}{(1.04) \times (1.04) \times (1.04)} = 0.88$$

So, £1 at the end of year 3, which has been invested since Time 0 at a constant rate of 4%, is equivalent to:

$$£1 \times 0.88 = £0.88\text{p at Time 0}$$

So £0.88p is the present value of £1 at the end of year 3 at a discount rate of 4%.

A table showing the value of the discount factors at a range of interest rates and time periods is set out in the appendix at the end of the chapter. Make sure that you can understand how the figures are derived.

? Self-test question 12.2 (answer at the end of the book)

1. Write down the formula to show the present value at Time 0 of £1 at the end of year 3 at a discount rate of 2%. Then, using a calculator, work out the discounting factor.
2. Write down the formula to show the present value at Time 0 of £1 at the end of year 5 at a discount rate of 4%. Then, using a calculator, work out the discounting factor.
3. Write down the formula to show the present value at Time 0 of £1 at the end of year 2 at a discount rate of 9%. Then, using a calculator, work out the discounting factor.

Applying the time value of money in investment appraisal

Using the technique of discounting we can express all future cash flows in the same terms, which allows us to take into account the time value of money and to compare like with like.

Before we can recalculate the cash flows for the Proctor Hedges example, we need to know the discount rate. Assume that the directors use a discount rate of 10% for investment appraisal (later in this section there will be a brief discussion of the factors managers must take into account in determining an appropriate discount rate).

In order to express all the cash flows in the same terms (i.e. in terms of the present value at Time 0 of future £s of cash flow) we take each anticipated cash flow for each of the machines and calculate present value using the appropriate discount factor.

Machine A

The first cash flow is assumed to arise at Time 0, i.e. the original investment of £450 000. Because this is already at Time 0 the effective discount factor is 1.

$$£450\ 000 \times 1 = \text{cash outflow of } £450\ 000 \text{ at Time 0}$$

The next cash flow event is at the end of the first year. From the table in the appendix we can see that the discount factor at 10% for one year is 0.909. Applying the discount factor to the year 1 cash flow (remember that all of the cash inflow is assumed to arise at the end of year 1):

$$£160\ 000 \times 0.909 = £145\ 440$$

We continue to discount the cash flows using discount factors that decrease as the cash flow events recede into the future. Setting the figures out neatly in a table:

Time	Cash flow £	Discount factor (from table)	Discounted cash flow £
0	(450 000)	1	(450 000)
1	160 000	0.909	145 440
2	160 000	0.826	132 160
3	160 000	0.751	120 160
4	100 000	0.683	68 300
5	150 000	0.621	93 150
Total			109 210

The total of £109 210 is known as the net present value (NPV); it is the total of the cash inflows and outflows associated with the investment (hence 'net'), all discounted and expressed in terms of £s at Time 0 (hence 'present value').

Machine B

Time	Cash flow £	Discount factor (from table)	Discounted cash flow £
0	(600 000)	1	(600 000)
1	246 000	0.909	223 614
2	196 800	0.826	162 557
3	172 200	0.751	129 322
4	102 500	0.683	70 008
5	202 500	0.621	125 752
Total			111 253

The net present value of the investment in Machine B is estimated at £111 253. The basic decision rule that is employed in respect of NPV is:

If NPV > 0 accept the project or investment

Or, where there is more than one alternative project or investment:

Accept the project or investment with the larger (largest) NPV

In this case, Machine B produces a slightly larger NPV, and so looks preferable to the investment in Machine A. (Note that both ARR and payback indicate that Machine A is the better investment!)

Ratio of cash inflows to initial investment

In deciding between investment projects it can be helpful to look at the relationship between the discounted cash flows generated by a project against the initial outflow of cash.

Machine A

Total positive discounted cash flows generated = NPV + initial investment:

$$= £109\ 210 + £450\ 000 = £559\ 210$$

(If this step seems complicated, just add up all the positive present values of cash flows from years 1 to 5 inclusive – it will give the same answer.) The ratio of the positive cash flows to the initial investment is:

$$\frac{£559\ 210}{450\ 000} = 1.24$$

Machine B

Total positive discounted cash flows generated = NPV + initial investment:

$$= £111\ 253 + £600\ 000 = £711\ 253$$

The ratio of the positive cash flows to the initial investment is:

$$\frac{£711\ 253}{600\ 000} = 1.19$$

Machine A gives the higher ratio. This means that it produces more positive cash inflow relative to the initial investment. Although the NPV of Machine B is, overall, slightly higher, the calculation of this ratio points towards Machine A as a better investment.

Establishing a discount rate

Proctor Hedges Limited uses a discount rate of 10%. How have the directors arrived at this figure?

A rate of 10% represents an acceptable return for the activities in which the business is engaged. Suppose the general bank interest rate in the economy is 4%: why does Proctor Hedges expect to make more than that? The answer relates to risk. Investing in a business undertaking is a riskier venture than putting money in the bank. Normally, banks can be relied upon to survive and to carry on paying interest at the advertised rate; a normal savings account rate is more or less risk-free (there is always some level of risk; banks do occasionally fail, but this is an unlikely eventuality in most developed economies). A business investor is taking much more of a risk and therefore expects to be rewarded by a greater return in the form of interest or dividends. The 10% rate may be Proctor Hedges' best guess at the risk-free rate plus a premium for the level of risk actually incurred by the company.

Another helpful way of looking at the problem is to consider the alternatives. If Proctor Hedges invests in Machine A, it needs to either borrow £450 000 or to take £450 000 out of existing resources. If there is an alternative use for that money that will yield 10% then the cost of the money is (at least) 10%. The cost of money for a particular business is known as its cost of capital.

Determination of the cost of investment for a particular company is one of the most complex problems in business finance. It is beyond the scope of this book to go into further detail, and in the exercises in the remainder of this chapter we will assume a discount rate without further discussion.

Internal rate of return

The final investment appraisal technique that we will examine is the internal rate of return (IRR). This technique is closely related to the NPV technique that we have just examined. The IRR of an investment or project is the expected yield (expressed as a percentage). IRR is the discount rate, which, applied to expected cash flows, produces an NPV of zero.

This can be quite hard to understand, so we will illustrate the point by means of a graph. Using the example of Machine A, we can see that at a discount rate of 10%, a positive NPV of £109 210 results. What happens if we calculate NPV using, say, 12%, 14%, 16%, 18% and 20%? The following NPVs have been calculated at each of these rates:

Interest rate	NPV £
10%	109 210
12%	82 790
14%	58 410
16%	35 960
18%	14 990
20%	(4 540)

Note: the workings for NPV at 10% are shown in the previous section of the chapter. The workings for the discount rates 12% to 20% are not shown. Use the tables to obtain the discount factors and calculate the NPV at each discount rate. Make sure that you can confirm the NPV results in the table above. (To save time, use a spreadsheet.)

We can see that, as the discount rate used in the calculation increases, the total NPV of the project decreases to the point where it becomes negative. The internal rate of return lies somewhere between 18% and 20%. Plotting these points onto a graph produces the result shown in Figure 12.1. The points plotted show a gentle curve. The point at which the curved line passes through the x axis (discount rate %) is the point of IRR. The graph confirms the observation we have already made from the figures: the IRR of Machine A lies just below 20%.

How can we arrive at a more accurate figure for IRR? There are two principal methods: (a) linear interpolation; and (b) using a computer.

| **Figure 12.1** | Net present value of Machine A cash flows at various discount rates |

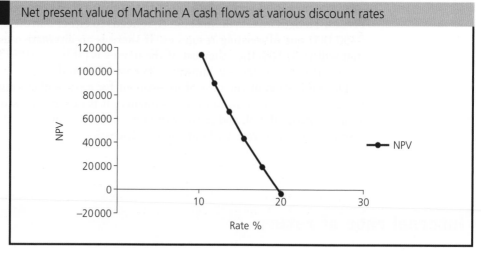

Linear interpolation

We take the two figures from the series that are closest to zero:

Using a discount rate of 18% NPV = £14 990
Using a discount rate of 20% NPV = (£4 540).

The total distance between these two figures is £14 990 + 4 540 = £19 530.

This total of £19 530 represents the whole range possible between 18% and 20%. Expressed diagrammatically:

The distance between 18% and IRR is:

$$\frac{14\,990}{19\,530} \times 2\% = 1.54\%$$

The distance between IRR and 20% is:

$$\frac{4\,540}{19\,530} \times 2\% = 0.46\%$$

IRR is 18% + 1.54% = 19.54% (or alternatively: IRR is 20% − 0.46% = 19.54%: it amounts to the same).

Using a computer

This is so much easier than linear interpolation! IRR can be calculated easily via a spreadsheet program such as Excel.

List the times and cash flows in consecutive descending columns in the spreadsheet and then execute the IRR command. In Excel the command is:

$$= IRR(Range)$$

For the Machine A data, the IRR calculated by the computer is 19.53%. This is slightly different from the result arrived at by linear interpolation; usually there will be a small difference. However, where the estimation of cash flows into the future is so imprecise (and it always is imprecise) there isn't much point in getting too concerned about precision in calculating IRR.

Machine B

We will repeat all of the above steps for Machine B. The following NPVs have been calculated at each of the same discount rates as for Machine A:

Interest rate	NPV £
10%	111 253
12%	79 142
14%	49 093
16%	21 625
18%	(4 083)
20%	(27 989)

We can see that the IRR lies somewhere between 16% and 18%. Plotting these points onto a graph, Figure 12.2 confirms the observation we have already made from the figures: the IRR of Machine B lies about three-quarters of the way between 10% and 20%.

Linear interpolation: Machine B

We take the two figures from the series that are closest to zero:
Using a discount rate of 16% NPV = £21 625
Using a discount rate of 18% NPV = £4 083

The total distance between these two figures is £21 625 + £4 083 = £25 708
This total of £25 708 represents the whole range possible between 16% and 18%. Expressed diagrammatically:

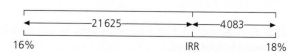

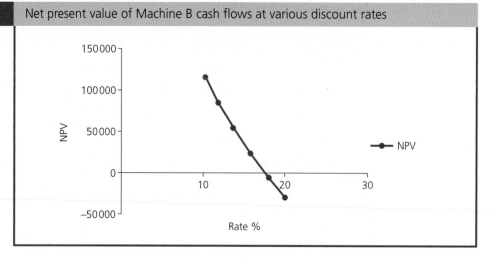

| Figure 12.2 | Net present value of Machine B cash flows at various discount rates |

The distance between 16% and IRR is:

$$\frac{21\ 625}{25\ 708} \times 2\% = 1.68\%$$

The distance between IRR and 20% is:

$$\frac{4\ 083}{25\ 708} \times 2\% = 0.32\%$$

IRR is 16% + 1.68% = 17.68% (or alternatively: IRR is 18% − 0.32% = 17.68%: it amounts to the same).

Using a computer: Machine B

For the Machine B data, the IRR calculated by the computer is 17.68%.

Significance of IRR for decision making

Where IRR is greater than the business's cost of capital the project is acceptable. If, as in the example, a choice has to be made between two possible projects, the one with the higher IRR is preferable.

In the Proctor Hedges example, the Machine A project produces an IRR of 19.53%, whereas the Machine B project produces an IRR of 17.68%. Both are well in excess of the 10% used by the company and so both projects would be acceptable. However, Machine A produces the better IRR rate, and so is preferable.

Choosing between projects

The application of the four methods of investment appraisal to the example of Proctor Hedges produces the following results:

Method	Machine A result	Machine B result	Choice
ARR	22.4%	18.3%	Machine A
Payback	2 years 10 months	2 years 11 months	Machine A
NPV	£109 210	£111 253	Machine B
IRR	19.54%	17.68%	Machine A

Three out of the four sets of results point towards the choice of Machine A (but note that there is little to choose between them in terms of payback). NPV is the exception but in this case the results for the two machines are very similar.

It would seem that Machine A may be the better choice. However, as with all business decisions, the solution indicated by the figures may not be the more sensible once other factors are taken into consideration. A key point for consideration by the directors is that Machine A does not have sufficient capacity to meet demand in the first three years or so of the project. This means that a significant part of customer demand will be unfulfilled. Possible consequences include loss of customer goodwill, bad publicity and a knock-on effect on sales of the company's other products.

On the other hand, if demand for the compost bins proves to have been overestimated, Machine A will emerge, with the benefit of hindsight, as a very much better choice. None of the investment appraisal techniques we have examined in the chapter take account of the relative riskiness of the alternatives. This is a weakness that needs to be recognised by decision makers.

Which of the four techniques provides the most reliable results? The strengths and weaknesses of each of them are examined in the following section.

Strengths and weaknesses of the common investment appraisal techniques

There are some weaknesses common to all of four of the techniques examined. As noted above, the relative risk attached to future cash flows is not taken into account. Also, all of the appraisal techniques are based upon future estimates. As the estimates of cash flow recede into the future they become progressively less reliable. It is possible to accept, for example, that experienced managers are able to make a reliable prediction of the coming year's sales figures, but can they really predict sales figures five years from now with any degree of reliability? The imprecision that inevitably surrounds future figures means that they are open to manipulation by unscrupulous managers (the case study at the end of the chapter expands on this point).

A further problem about attaching apparently precise values to future predictions is that managers may give the figures more credence than they really merit. The figures can only ever provide a guide to decision making.

The principal strength of all of the techniques described is that they are better than nothing. Managers sometimes make decisions based on 'gut feeling' or 'instinct' or 'experience'. These may not be reliable qualities upon which to base decisions; at least by making some effort to formally appraise projects, managers may be able to avoid making really big mistakes.

In addition to these general points, each of the techniques has its own strengths and weaknesses.

Accounting rate of return (ARR)

Strengths

- Calculation of ARR is very straightforward.
- ARR is a widely used measurement (in the form of ROCE); it is easy to compare the ARR of a particular project with the overall ROCE for a business.
- It is a measurement that non-financial managers can readily understand.

Weaknesses

- ARR treats all future cash flows as equal in weight; it takes no account of the time value of money.
- ARR is calculated on the basis of accounting profits rather than cash flow. It includes the effect of depreciation, an accounting adjustment the nature and timing of which is determined by management.
- As noted earlier in the chapter, ARR fails to take into account the relative size of competing projects.

Payback

Strengths

- Calculation of payback is very straightforward.
- It can be useful where rapid recovery of funding is a priority.
- It is a measurement that non-financial managers can readily understand.

Weaknesses

- Payback treats all future cash flows as equal in weight; it takes no account of the time value of money.
- Where rapid recovery of funding is not a major priority, payback provides little useful information.
- All cash flows beyond the payback point are simply ignored.

Net present value (NPV)

Strengths

- NPV builds the time value of money into calculations.
- Unlike payback, NPV takes all of the future projected cash flows into account.
- NPV is very useful for ranking different projects as it deals in absolute values rather than percentages (which, as in the case of ARR, can give unreliable results).

Weaknesses

- It can be difficult to explain NPV to non-financial managers.

Internal rate of return (IRR)

Strengths

- IRR builds the time value of money into calculations.

Weaknesses

- It can be difficult to explain IRR to non-financial managers.
- Because IRR is expressed in percentage terms it ignores absolute values: 15% return on an investment of £100 000 is fine (£15 000), but not as good in absolute terms as a 12% return on £1 000 000 (£120 000).
- It is not always possible to calculate IRR.

The last point perhaps needs explanation. In the Proctor Hedges example, the pattern of cash flow was an initial major outlay of cash, followed by several years of inflows. Where the pattern of cash flows is more irregular (for example, a net inflow in years one and two followed by a net outflow in year three, followed by another inflow in year four) IRR cannot be used.

The best technique?

Of the four techniques examined in the chapter, NPV appears to have the fewest significant weaknesses and the most obvious strengths. All of the techniques described are used fairly extensively in practice, and many firms will routinely use more than one. The widespread availability of computers, and the fact that many business managers are now highly computer literate, means that the calculations of NPV and IRR no longer present any difficulties.

Chapter summary

This chapter has examined decision making for the longer term. It started by looking at capital investment and capital budgeting, and emphasised the need for capital expenditure to be congruent with the business's overall strategy and objectives. Businesses need to have clear criteria upon which to base capital investment decisions, especially in conditions of capital rationing.

Four appraisal techniques were examined within the context of a single detailed example:

- accounting rate of return (ARR)
- payback
- net present value (NPV)
- internal rate of return (IRR).

The concept of the time value of money must be understood if NPV and IRR are to make any sense. Compounding and discounting were explained at some length, including the use of formulae and the table of discount factors.

The basic decision rules for NPV and IRR were explained; however, it is also important to appreciate that the investment appraisal techniques explained in the chapter must be considered alongside other important factors. The formal appraisal techniques have some general drawbacks – notably, that they all involve the estimation of future cash flows and that they do not take risk into account, except in the general risk element incorporated in the cost of capital.

The strengths and weaknesses of each of the four techniques were listed and discussed. The general conclusion was that NPV is likely to be the most useful technique in practice; however, it was noted that all four are widely used.

In conclusion, we should note that non-financial managers will not often be called upon to make capital investment appraisal calculations. However, they are very often involved in decision making that rests, at least in part, on the application of investment appraisal techniques. Therefore, it is important that students should understand the rudiments of these techniques, and not least, the various weaknesses associated with them.

The end-of-chapter exercises that follow are divided into two sections. The first section has answers provided at the back of the book.

The second section, in the white box, has answers on the lecturers' section of the website. Finally, the chapter contains a case study examining capital project evaluation in practice.

Website summary

The book's website contains the following material in respect of Chapter 12:

Students' section

- Quiz containing ten multiple choice questions
- Four additional questions with answers
- Answer to the case study at the end of this chapter.

Lecturers' section

- Answers to the end-of-chapter exercises 12.10 to 12.17
- Five additional questions with answers
- An additional case study Ortega Ruiz plc.

Exercises: answers at the end of the book

12.1 A business is considering whether or not to invest in a new factory building. The managers have incurred expenditure of £15 000 on an initial land survey. For capital investment appraisal purposes this expenditure is:

a)   a fixed cost

b)   a relevant cost

c)   a sunk cost

d)   an estimated cost.

12.2 Mellor & Ribchester Limited, a health drinks company, is considering whether or not to invest in a project to develop and sell a new range of fruit teas. Initial expenditure on a range of development expenses will be £150 000 at Time 0 to get the project up and running. Sales of the products will start in year 2, and it is anticipated that annual net cash inflows will be as follows:

	£
Year 2	68 000
Year 3	71 000
Year 4	54 000
Year 5	28 000
Year 6	10 000

Demand for the product is expected to decline after year 6 to the point where it will not be worth continuing production.

The £150 000 of initial expenditure is treated as a fixed asset, to be depreciated on a straight-line basis over 6 years, with an assumption of nil residual value at the end of 6 years.

i)   Calculate ARR for the project.

ii)   Calculate the payback period for the project.

12.3 The compounding factor for an investment over 4 years at 3% per year is (to 3 decimal places):

a)   0.888

b)   1.093

c)   0.915

d)   1.126.

12.4 At the end of year 4, £312 invested now at an annual rate of 6% interest over 4 years will be worth (to the nearest £):

a)   £394

b)   £387

c)   £372

d)   £418.

12.5 The discounting factor for an investment over 3 years at 10% is (to 3 decimal places):

a) 0.700

b) 0.751

c) 0.100

d) 1.093.

12.6 Assuming a constant discount rate of 12%, the present value of £1300 receivable at the end of year 5 is (to the nearest £):

a) £563

b) £520

c) £2 293

d) £737.

12.7 Naylor Coulthard Limited is considering investing in a major advertising promotion of one of its skincare products. The advertising campaign would cost £250 000, all of which is assumed to be spent at Time 0. The effectiveness of the advertising would be short-lived; it would produce incremental cash inflows only in years 1 and 2. The year 1 net cash inflow is estimated at £196 000. The net cash inflow for year 2 is estimated at £168 000. After the end of year 2 another major advertising campaign would probably be needed to produce further incremental revenues.

The company's cost of capital is 9%. What is the NPV of the advertising promotion project? Does the NPV suggest that the project should be accepted or rejected?

12.8 A company estimates the following net cash inflows and outflows for a capital investment project that is currently under consideration:

Time	£000
0	(680 000)
1	180 000
2	200 000
3	240 000
4	350 000

The company's cost of capital is 12%.

i) Calculate the NPV of the project.

ii) Calculate the IRR of the project.

12.9 Outhwaite Benson Limited runs a chain of hairdressing salons. The company's directors, Linda Outhwaite and David Benson, are considering a proposal to add sunbed facilities to their salons. They have surveyed staff and customers and have found that 55% of their existing customers would consider using the facilities. On the basis of this finding they have constructed a set of costings and revenue projections. The sunbeds would cost £180 000 in total to buy and install; they would have an estimated useful life of 5 years after which they could be sold for

£15 000 in total. Linda and David estimate that the net cash inflow arising each year from the sale of time on the sunbeds would be £46 000.

The £180 000 will be lent to the company by the two directors; it is the proceeds of sale of their second home in Italy. If the money is not put into the sunbed project it would be invested in the opening of a new salon. The average yield from a salon is 14% per year, and the directors decide to use this as the cost of capital in appraising the proposed sunbed investment.

i) Calculate the NPV of the sunbed investment project.

ii) Calculate the IRR of the sunbed investment project.

iii) Advise the directors on whether or not they should make the investment, considering any other relevant factors that might have a bearing on the decision.

Exercises: answers available to lecturers

12.10 Montfort Spelling Limited operates a chain of health clubs. Each year the company opens a club in a new location. For 20X6, the company is examining two possible locations: Broughton Town and Carey City. The directors have collected information about costs and local demographics, and have come up with the following summary of the initial investment required, and cash flows for the subsequent five years. The company's normal policy is to completely refurbish its clubs every five years; it remodels and redecorates the clubs and sells off all the old equipment.

Initial outlay includes the cost of taking out a five-year lease on premises, buying in all the equipment and paying architects and builders to remodel the premises. The net cash inflows from years one to five include estimated takings in annual subscriptions and joining fees, less the costs of employing staff, and various other fixed costs of running the club.

The table below summarises the costs for the two locations:

	Broughton Town £000	Carey City £000
Time 0: initial investment	(630)	(540)
Time 1: net cash inflows	250	242
Time 2: net cash inflows	275	250
Time 3: net cash inflows	280	260
Time 4: net cash inflows	295	270
Time 5: net cash inflows	310	280
Time 5: inflow from sales of equipment	35	30

The initial capital expenditure less the anticipated residual values is to be depreciated on a straight-line basis, in accordance with the company's policy, over five years.

i) Calculate ARR for each project.

ii) Calculate the payback period for each project.

iii) Advise the directors as to which location should be preferred.

12.11 The compounding factor for an investment over 6 years at 8% per year is (to 3 decimal places):

a)   1.587

b)   0.627

c)   1.595

d)   0.630.

12.12 At the end of year 6, £1900 invested now at an annual rate of 17% interest over 6 years will be worth (to the nearest £):

a)   £3 838

b)   £741

c)   £4 874

d)   £2 223.

12.13 The discounting factor for an investment over 5 years at 19% is:

a)   0.419

b)   0.190

c)   0.950

d)   0.810.

12.14 Assuming a constant discount rate of 14%, the present value of £85 000 receivable at the end of year 4 is (to the nearest £):

a)   £50 320

b)   £47 600

c)   £49 045

d)   £73 100.

12.15 Nuria Nailsworth Products Limited is a fashion clothing company. Nuria, the chief executive, regularly attends major fashion events in order to spot trends in the market. She has recently returned from a show that featured fake fur waistcoats and she thinks these could be next season's big fashion story. Unfortunately, fake fur tends to clog up the production machinery used in the company's factory, and it will be necessary to make an additional investment of £28 000 in new cutting and sewing machinery. Nuria thinks it quite likely that sales of 6000 waistcoats are achievable in the first year, and possibly up to 2000 in the second year. Her knowledge of fashion trends tells her that after that point the waistcoats will probably be unsaleable except at very heavy discounts. The first 5000 waistcoats will almost certainly sell at full price, and should produce a net cash flow of £4 each. The final 3000 of production may have to be sold at a discount and it is safest to assume that net cash flow will be only £3 per waistcoat. The machinery will be saleable at the end of the second year for around £10 000.

i)   Assuming that the company's cost of capital is 13%, what is the NPV of the project?

ii)   If Nuria's initial projections were wrong, and only 5000 of the waistcoats could be sold, all in the first year and producing net cash flow of £4 each, what would be the NPV of the project? Assume in this case that the machinery is saleable at the end of the first year for £13 000.

12.16   A company estimates the following net cash inflows and outflows for a capital investment project that is currently under consideration:

Time	£000
0	(1 650 000)
1	480 000
2	450 000
3	390 000
4	360 000
5	450 000

The company's cost of capital is 8%.

i)   Calculate the NPV of the project.

ii)   Calculate the IRR of the project.

12.17   Oppenheim Orgreave Limited sells sofas, armchairs and other furniture items from its premises in a retail park. Customers often ask for home delivery to be arranged, and the company has contracted out the service to a series of small delivery firms. The delivery services are of inconsistent quality; customers often ring Oppenheim's to complain that the delivery was late, or that the goods were damaged in transit. Oppenheim's directors have decided that the delivery problem must be properly addressed because the company is losing sales and acquiring a reputation for unreliability. The company's finance director has examined three options:

- *Option 1*. Buy three new delivery vehicles and employ full-time drivers. The initial outlay for the vehicles would be £76 000, and the annual incremental costs of employment, fuel and other motor expenses would be £82 000. At the end of their five-year useful life the vehicles could be sold for £9000.

- *Option 2*. Contract the service out to a single, high quality provider who would take on full responsibility for van purchase, maintenance and other costs, including the employment of drivers. Quotations for the service have been obtained; a good quality service can be purchased under a five-year contract for £105 000 per year.

- *Option 3*. Lease the three vehicles required for the service at a cost of £10 000 per year per vehicle for a term of five years. Fuel and other running costs, and the costs of employing three drivers, would be incurred direct under this option at a total cost of £77 000 per year.

The finance director estimates that an improved service would boost sales. Incremental sales of £113 000 per year would be made under all three options. Oppenheim's cost of capital is 12%.

i) Calculate the NPV for each option.

ii) Advise the directors on the most appropriate course of action, taking into account any other relevant factors.

! CASE STUDY 12.1 A competition for investment funding

The case study for this chapter examines the way in which investment appraisal techniques and estimates of future cash flows can be manipulated by managers in practice.

Lawson Pollard Packaging plc manufactures and sells a large range of packaging and office supplies. The company operates on a decentralised basis; its operations are split into three major divisions: cardboard, plastics and office stationery, each of which is responsible for most of its own administration and decision making. A small head office building houses the principal directors and some general administrative functions.

Although each division makes its own day-to-day operating decisions, responsibility for major capital investment decisions is in the hands of the directors at head office (all expenditure over £1000 must be approved by head office). As part of the budgeting process, each divisional management team must decide on how much capital investment they need to request for the coming year. The senior divisional manager prepares a detailed presentation for the directors that explains the purpose of the investment and justifies the amounts requested. On the basis of the presentation and the detailed working papers submitted with it, the directors decide upon whether or not they are going to fund the investment requested. The chief executive, Ernie Lawson, is very much in favour of competitive bidding for the available capital funds; if one of the divisions makes a better case than the other two it will get the lion's share of the capital funding. Ernie believes that the divisions should really have to fight for their funding; he thinks this will stop the management teams getting complacent and lazy and will ensure that funds are used in the most effective way possible.

Doug is the senior manager in charge of the cardboard division. It is now October 20X1 and he is working on the 20X2 budget with his management team. Doug and the cardboard division are having a hard time. Profitability has slipped over the last three years or so; almost half of the machinery used in the factory is fully depreciated, and is performing inefficiently. Production costs are therefore higher than they need to be; raw materials are used less efficiently, and expenditure on repairs and maintenance has shot up. The division is desperately in need of new investment.

Until a couple of years ago, Doug and the senior managers of the other two divisions had a useful informal arrangement that helped to get round Ernie's competitive approach to capital spending. The managers would get together once a year in secret to discuss their capital spending priorities, and would decide between them which bids were most important. The important bids would be polished up carefully and the others ranked as less important would be made to appear less attractive. This arrangement meant that sometimes Doug and the cardboard division got less in capital funding in one year, but Doug was happy enough because he knew that the other managers would let his bids take priority in the next year or two.

All this changed two years ago. Kamal, who had headed up plastics for years, retired and was replaced by a new appointment, Donna. Donna is not yet 30 and has an MBA from a leading business school. Doug has heard Ernie say that Donna's on the fast track for rapid promotion to the board, and that she could end up heading the whole company when he, Ernie, retires. Doug has never been on the fast track for anything in his entire life. He's in his late 40s and, until recently, has been quite happy at Lawson's. He knows that he's unlikely to get another job now if he leaves the company and he intends to stay put until he can retire.

In each of the previous two years Donna has made brilliant bids for new capital funding for the plastics division; she succeeded in convincing the directors that practically all of the capital spending should be devoted to plastics. Sales of plastics have grown by nearly 30% in each of the two years that she has been in charge and all the financial indicators show that the plastics side of the business is extremely strong.

Doug tentatively suggested to Donna recently that she might hold back on the capital bidding this year to let cardboard and office supplies get a share. Donna won't hear of it; she tells Doug that plastics is the future of the business and she, frankly, couldn't care less about the tribulations of the cardboard division. She is planning another major bid that will soak up practically all of the available funding for 20X2.

Doug is depressed; he can see that unless the cardboard division can make a really persuasive bid this year, a further year of declining sales and profitability will follow, and his personal reputation in the company will sink to an all-time low. He knows that he has to put together a great bid that will be more persuasive than Donna's. He decides to go for something really bold – nothing less than the replacement of the major part of the production line. This will involve purchasing the most up-to-date machinery and completely overhauling the organisation of production. Fewer production line workers would be required, raw materials would be used more efficiently and consequently contribution would increase. While there would be some increase in fixed costs, because of improved quality inspection and general supervision, some categories of cost (like maintenance and repairs) would be substantially reduced. Doug finds himself getting really quite enthusiastic about the plan; he suddenly realises that he's not been putting a lot of effort into the job recently, and that the division could actually perform a lot better if he could get the money to invest.

Doug and his team do some careful work on all aspects of the bid. Doug's assistant, Ron, summarises the work and prepares scenarios based upon two alternatives. The first supposes a modest rate of sales growth and improved efficiency in the factory. The second was specially requested by Doug; it assumes a high rate of sales growth between 20X1 and 20X2 (matching the 30% achieved by the plastics division), with regular increases in the following years, and a very substantial increase in efficiency. Doug examines the cash flows and tells Ron that he should concentrate from now on only on the optimistic scenario.

Ron: But the second one is really wildly optimistic – it assumes that our competitors will make no attempt to prevent us taking market share off them, and that everything will run perfectly in the factory at all times. I mean, how likely is that?

Doug: We've got to pull all the stops out with this one or we'll not get a penny. That pushy Donna wants all the money again this year and we've got to make sure she doesn't get it.

▶

Ron: So, this time it's personal, eh? . . . But Ernie and the others are going to see through this if it looks too unrealistic.

Doug: Not if we do a really thorough job on the back-up. We want detailed sales projections, plans for seeing off the competition, lots and lots of impressive looking supporting graphs and charts and so on. You can manage that, can't you, Ron? I mean, it could make the difference between keeping the division going and us all losing our jobs. It's that serious.

Ron makes no further objections, and gets on with the work. The two sets of figures Ron has prepared are set out in the following table.

Year	Realistic £000	Optimistic £000
0	(7 800)	(7 800)
1	1 380	1 680
2	1 470	1 770
3	1 530	1 860
4	1 590	1 950
5	1 650	2 040
6	1 710	2 130
7	1 770	2 220
8	1 830	2 310
9	1 890	2 400
10	1 950	2 490
10 (sale of plant)	180	300

The company uses the NPV investment appraisal technique. The company's cost of capital is 12%.

The following is required:

i) Calculate the NPVs for the realistic and optimistic sets of figures, and comment on the results.

ii) Discuss the company's approach to appraising capital projects, identifying any particular strengths or weaknesses.

iii) Discuss Doug's plan for handling this year's bid for capital funds for the cardboard division.

Appendix: Discount factors

The table gives the present value of a single payment received *n* years in the future discounted at *x*% per year. For example, with a discount rate of 7% a single payment of £1 in six years' time has a present value of £0.6663 or 66.63p.

Years	1%	2%	3%	4%	5%	6%	7%	8%	9%	10%
1	0.9901	0.9804	0.9709	0.9615	0.9524	0.9434	0.9346	0.9259	0.9174	0.9091
2	0.9803	0.9612	0.9426	0.9426	0.9070	0.8900	0.8734	0.8573	0.8417	0.8264
3	0.9706	0.9423	0.9151	0.8890	0.8638	0.8396	0.8163	0.7938	0.7722	0.7513
4	0.9610	0.9238	0.8885	0.8548	0.8227	0.7921	0.7629	0.7350	0.7084	0.6830
5	0.9515	0.9057	0.8626	0.8219	0.7835	0.7473	0.7130	0.6806	0.6499	0.6209
6	0.9420	0.8880	0.8375	0.7903	0.7462	0.7050	0.6663	0.6302	0.5963	0.5645
7	0.9327	0.8706	0.8131	0.7599	0.7107	0.6651	0.6227	0.5835	0.5470	0.5132
8	0.9235	0.8535	0.7894	0.7307	0.6768	0.6274	0.5820	0.5403	0.5019	0.4665
9	0.9143	0.8368	0.7664	0.7026	0.6446	0.5919	0.5439	0.5002	0.4604	0.4241
10	0.9053	0.8203	0.7441	0.6756	0.6139	0.5584	0.5083	0.4632	0.4224	0.3855
11	0.8963	0.8043	0.7224	0.6496	0.5847	0.5268	0.4751	0.4289	0.3875	0.3505
12	0.8874	0.7885	0.7014	0.6246	0.5568	0.4970	0.4440	0.3971	0.3555	0.3186
13	0.8787	0.7730	0.6810	0.6006	0.5303	0.4688	0.4150	0.3677	0.3262	0.2897
14	0.8700	0.7579	0.6611	0.5775	0.5051	0.4423	0.3878	0.3405	0.2992	0.2633
15	0.8613	0.7430	0.6419	0.5553	0.4810	0.4173	0.3624	0.3152	0.2745	0.2394
16	0.8528	0.7284	0.6232	0.5339	0.4581	0.3936	0.3387	0.2919	0.2519	0.2176
17	0.8444	0.7142	0.6050	0.5134	0.4363	0.3714	0.3166	0.2703	0.2311	0.1978
18	0.8360	0.7002	0.5874	0.4936	0.4155	0.3503	0.2959	0.2502	0.2120	0.1799
19	0.8277	0.6864	0.5703	0.4746	0.3957	0.3305	0.2765	0.2317	0.1945	0.1635
20	0.8195	0.6730	0.5537	0.4564	0.3769	0.3118	0.2584	0.2145	0.1784	0.1486
21	0.8114	0.6598	0.5375	0.4388	0.3589	0.2942	0.2415	0.1987	0.1637	0.1351
22	0.8034	0.6468	0.5219	0.4220	0.3418	0.2775	0.2257	0.1839	0.1502	0.1228
23	0.7954	0.6342	0.5067	0.4057	0.3256	0.2618	0.2109	0.1703	0.1378	0.1117
24	0.7876	0.6217	0.4919	0.3901	0.3101	0.2470	0.1971	0.1577	0.1264	0.1015
25	0.7798	0.6095	0.4776	0.3751	0.2953	0.2330	0.1842	0.1460	0.1160	0.0923
26	0.7720	0.5976	0.4637	0.3607	0.2812	0.2198	0.1722	0.1352	0.1064	0.0839
27	0.7644	0.5859	0.4502	0.3468	0.2678	0.2074	0.1609	0.1252	0.0976	0.0763
28	0.7568	0.5744	0.4371	0.3335	0.2551	0.1956	0.1504	0.1159	0.0895	0.0693
29	0.7493	0.5631	0.4243	0.3207	0.2429	0.1846	0.1406	0.1073	0.0822	0.0630
30	0.7419	0.5521	0.4120	0.3083	0.2314	0.1741	0.1314	0.0994	0.0754	0.0573
35	0.7059	0.5000	0.3554	0.2534	0.1813	0.1301	0.0937	0.0676	0.0490	0.0356
40	0.6717	0.4529	0.3066	0.2083	0.1420	0.0972	0.0668	0.0460	0.0318	0.0221
45	0.6391	0.4102	0.2644	0.1712	0.1113	0.0727	0.0476	0.0313	0.0207	0.0137
50	0.6080	0.3715	0.2281	0.1407	0.0872	0.0543	0.0339	0.0213	0.0134	0.0085

11%	12%	13%	14%	15%	16%	17%	18%	19%	20%	Years
0.9009	0.8929	0.8850	0.8772	0.8696	0.8621	0.8547	0.8475	0.8403	0.8333	1
0.8116	0.7972	0.7831	0.7695	0.7561	0.7432	0.7305	0.7182	0.7062	0.6944	2
0.7312	0.7118	0.6931	0.6750	0.6575	0.6407	0.6244	0.6086	0.5934	0.5787	3
0.6587	0.6355	0.6133	0.5921	0.5718	0.5523	0.5337	0.5158	0.4987	0.4823	4
0.5935	0.5674	0.5428	0.5194	0.4972	0.4761	0.4561	0.4371	0.4190	0.4019	5
0.5346	0.5066	0.4803	0.4556	0.4323	0.4104	0.3898	0.3704	0.3521	0.3349	6
0.4817	0.4523	0.4251	0.3996	0.3759	0.3538	0.3332	0.3139	0.2959	0.2791	7
0.4339	0.4039	0.3762	0.3506	0.3269	0.3050	0.2848	0.2660	0.2487	0.2326	8
0.3909	0.3606	0.3329	0.3075	0.2843	0.2630	0.2434	0.2255	0.2090	0.1938	9
0.3522	0.3220	0.2946	0.2697	0.2472	0.2267	0.2080	0.1911	0.1756	0.1615	10
0.3173	0.2875	0.2607	0.2366	0.2149	0.1954	0.1778	0.1619	0.1476	0.1346	11
0.2858	0.2567	0.2307	0.2076	0.1869	0.1685	0.1520	0.1372	0.1240	0.1122	12
0.2575	0.2292	0.2042	0.1821	0.1625	0.1452	0.1299	0.1163	0.1042	0.0935	13
0.2320	0.2046	0.1807	0.1597	0.1413	0.1252	0.1110	0.0985	0.0876	0.0779	14
0.2090	0.1827	0.1599	0.1401	0.1229	0.1079	0.0949	0.0835	0.0736	0.0649	15
0.1883	0.1631	0.1415	0.1229	0.1069	0.0930	0.0811	0.0708	0.0618	0.0541	16
0.1696	0.1456	0.1252	0.1078	0.0929	0.0802	0.0693	0.0600	0.0520	0.0451	17
0.1528	0.1300	0.1108	0.0946	0.0808	0.0691	0.0592	0.0508	0.0437	0.0376	18
0.1377	0.1161	0.0981	0.0829	0.0703	0.0596	0.0506	0.0431	0.0367	0.0313	19
0.1240	0.1037	0.0868	0.0728	0.0611	0.0514	0.0433	0.0365	0.0308	0.0261	20
0.1117	0.0926	0.0768	0.0638	0.0531	0.0443	0.0370	0.0309	0.0259	0.0217	21
0.1007	0.0826	0.0680	0.0560	0.0462	0.0382	0.0316	0.0262	0.0218	0.0181	22
0.0907	0.0738	0.0601	0.0491	0.0402	0.0329	0.0270	0.0222	0.0183	0.0151	23
0.0817	0.0659	0.0532	0.0431	0.0349	0.0284	0.0231	0.0188	0.0154	0.0126	24
0.0736	0.0588	0.0471	0.0378	0.0304	0.0245	0.0197	0.0160	0.0129	0.0105	25
0.0663	0.0525	0.0417	0.0331	0.0264	0.0211	0.0169	0.0135	0.0109	0.0087	26
0.0597	0.0469	0.0369	0.0291	0.0230	0.0182	0.0144	0.0115	0.0091	0.0073	27
0.0538	0.0419	0.0326	0.0255	0.0200	0.0157	0.0123	0.0097	0.0077	0.0061	28
0.0485	0.0374	0.0289	0.0224	0.0174	0.0135	0.0105	0.0082	0.0064	0.0051	29
0.0437	0.0334	0.0256	0.0196	0.0151	0.0116	0.0090	0.0070	0.0054	0.0042	30
0.0259	0.0189	0.0139	0.0102	0.0075	0.0055	0.0041	0.0030	0.0023	0.0017	35
0.0154	0.0107	0.0075	0.0053	0.0037	0.0026	0.0019	0.0013	0.0010	0.0007	40
0.0091	0.0061	0.0041	0.0027	0.0019	0.0013	0.0009	0.0006	0.0004	0.0003	45
0.0054	0.0035	0.0022	0.0014	0.0009	0.0006	0.0004	0.0003	0.0002	0.0001	50

Source: Drury, C. (2001) *Management Accounting for Business Decisions*, Second Edition, London: Thomson Learning.

CHAPTER 13

Performance measurement and reporting

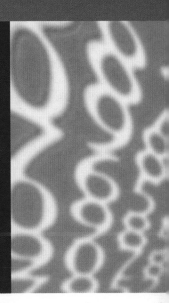

Aim of the chapter

To develop understanding of ways in which performance is measured and reported within the firm.

Learning outcomes

After reading the chapter and completing the related exercises students should:

- Understand the reasons for, and nature of, performance reporting within organisations.
- Understand why larger organisations often divide their activities into divisions.
- Be able to argue the advantages and drawbacks of divisionalisation.
- Understand the nature of financial performance measurement in divisions.
- Appreciate the importance of non-financial measures within organisations.
- Understand the 'Balanced Scorecard' approach to financial and non-financial performance measurement.

Performance reporting within organisations

As we noted in Chapter 5, financial reports are the means of providing a range of users external to the business with the information that they need. However, financial reporting by a business to outsiders is normally done only at relatively lengthy intervals, and the range of information included in financial reports is limited.

For most business organisations, reporting performance within the organisation is of at least equal or – more likely – greater importance than the periodic reporting to shareholders, lenders and so on. Internal reporting allows business managers to:

- assess the impact of their decision making
- monitor the performance of parts of the business
- make better informed decisions about future courses of action
- control the activities of the business
- plan for the future.

In Section Two of this book, on management accounting, we have already examined some aspects of the internal reporting of performance. Chapter 6, the introductory chapter, examined some of the features of cost and management accounting information. Chapter 8 looked at the processes involved in budgeting, one of which is the monitoring of actual outcomes compared to budgets. Chapter 9 examined the reporting of variances in standard costing systems. In this chapter we will develop an understanding of the some of the principal processes and practices involved in performance measurement and reporting.

Forms of business organisation

Chapter 1 described the differences between three different forms of business organisation: sole traders, partnerships and limited companies, and these different organisational forms have been referred to frequently throughout the book. This chapter does not introduce any new forms of business organisation but it does expressly recognise that the nature of performance measurement and reporting vary depending upon the size of the business. Where a business remains relatively small, a single manager or small team of managers can retain day-to-day control over all of its activities. This type of control becomes progressively more difficult to organise as the organisation increases in size. Large business organisations, which are usually constituted as companies but which may occasionally be partnerships, need to evolve effective managerial control structures. The nature, extent and frequency of performance reporting depend very much on the size and complexity of the business.

Later in this chapter we will examine in some detail a common way of organising activities within very large businesses. This involves splitting up business activities into divisions that can operate with a substantial degree of autonomy. A head office or central body of senior management can require uniform divisional reports in order to retain control over all of the organisation's activities. They can use a set of measurements to assess individual divisional performance and to compare the performance of one division with another.

Measuring and reporting performance in different sizes of business

A small business such as a sole trader or a partnership of two or three individuals probably require only rudimentary performance measurement and reporting mechanisms. For example, a sole trader might examine his or her cash position once a fortnight against budget to ensure that sufficient cash is going to be available to meet short-term needs. Few measurement techniques would be involved in such a comparison; it is simply a question of comparing one figure with another, and perhaps drawing up a summary of expected cash inflows and outflows for a brief period. Performance measurement might also involve collating figures, both financial and non-financial, into a simple monthly report, as demonstrated in the example below:

Example 13.1

Padma is a hairdresser who operates as a sole trader. Her salon employs two stylists and two apprentices. Until recently, Padma gauged the success of her business simply by the amount of takings she banked each week. Since the beginning of her new financial year, however, she has been using a monthly revenue performance report which her accountant helped her to draw up. This is a single-sheet form which Padma can fill in every month using her record of daily takings and the appointments book:

MONTH _____ YEAR _____ No of working days _____

Activity

	Padma	Stylist 1	Stylist 2
Week 1 appointments booked			
Week 2 appointments booked			
Week 3 appointments booked			
Week 4 appointments booked	_____	_____	_____
TOTAL	_____	_____	_____

Value of work done

	Padma	Stylist 1	Stylist 2
Week 1			
Week 2			
Week 3			
Week 4			
TOTAL	_____	_____	_____
BUDGET FOR MONTH	_____	_____	_____
SAME MONTH LAST YEAR			

Value of sundry sales (conditioner, shampoo etc.) £_____

This form allows Padma to assess the monthly performance of her business, and to monitor the activity level of her two stylists. Gradually over time, she will be able to build up a record of business revenue performance which could help her to make more effective decisions on questions such as:

- Whether or not to close the salon for two weeks for summer holidays
- What targets should be used when introducing a performance-related pay system for the stylists
- Employment of an additional part-time stylist.

Padma will also be able to use the accumulated information to track longer-term business performance, and to identify particular weeks in the year where business activity is consistently at a low level. Because Padma is a sole trader, she does not need complicated reporting systems. The form shown above can be collated with a little bit of extra work from information that she already has available and without the involvement of anyone else.

A slightly larger business may evolve more complex measurement and reporting techniques. For example, a legal practice with three partners might meet once a month to consider a report showing such indicators as hours billed, bad debts, work-in-progress hours, and expenditure for the month just ended. Each partner may take responsibility for collating a section of the information, and for then taking any necessary remedial action. As well as contributing to an assessment of overall firm performance, some of this data might form part of the performance evaluations of individuals. In legal and accounting practices, for example, it is usual for professional staff (that is solicitors and accountants but not secretarial and other support staff) to record fairly precisely the time spent on different clients' work. This is so that the time spent can be charged to the client. Most practices have a target level of chargeable time per day: for example, solicitors may be expected to be able to charge 75% of their daily time at work to clients. The remainder would be absorbed by general administrative tasks. The partners are likely to examine the time charge summaries of their staff to identify those who are performing well or badly against target.

The larger a business becomes, the greater the complexity of its management accounting processes. Very large businesses are likely to employ many full-time staff in a management accounting department with a responsibility to produce reports that will be useful to management at various levels. Example 13.2 indicates some of the reports that might be useful in one particular type of business.

Example 13.2

Wisharts plc is a national firm of estate agents, with 180 branches around the country. The market for estate agency services is highly competitive in most locations, with several national and local firms competing for business. The company runs its head office operations in Birmingham where a small team of management accountants collates information submitted via the firm's intranet in a standard form. Each time a new instruction is received, or a property is sold, details are logged onto the computer system.

Senior managers at head office require weekly updates on the following key indicators:

- number of new instructions
- number of houses/ flats sold, in total, and by each agent
- value of sales made
- average turnover of instructions in days (i.e. the average length of time a house remains on the books of the agency).

Each Saturday, at close of business, the branch manager enters the information into standard formats that are submitted to head office via the intranet. Senior managers at head office meet on the following Monday afternoon to discuss the results for the week, which are presented on hard-copy report forms, summarised into fourteen regions. The management accounting team also updates a set of graphs showing the movement over a rolling 12-month period of indicators such as average house price in each region and number of sales made per region. Where a region appears to be under-performing, managers are able to drill down into the regional data to identify individual office performance. The performance of individual agents is accumulated and a national ranking is produced at the end of each month. The top five agents in the country receive a substantial financial bonus and an allocation of points towards Wisharts annual agents' awards. Where branch or individual performance gives cause for concern, a member of the senior management team calls or visits the branch to determine the reasons and to take remedial action.

At the end of each four-week period, senior managers are presented with monthly management accounts showing total revenue and expenditure for the month, together with the totals for the key regional indicators of new instructions, number of houses/flats sold and average selling price. The Wishart management accounting system is designed to be flexible and responsive so that managers are able to request special purpose reports, which they normally receive within 24 hours. Recently, for example, the chief executive requested a special report listing the details of all individual house sales in excess of £300 000 for region 12.

Example 13.2 demonstrates a system that is apparently flexible and responsive to the information requirements of senior managers. It should be noted that hardly any of the information reported internally to senior managers to help them in running the business would be reported in the organisation's annual report. Important indicators such as new instructions received are for internal use only; this type of information is not reported in the annual financial statements.

Internal performance reports can take any form: they might be a one page monthly summary (as in Example 13.1 earlier in the chapter), or, at the other extreme, could comprise many pages of detail. The key point is that they should provide information that is useful to managers in their planning, controlling, monitoring and decision-making functions. Management information should ideally have the following characteristics:

- It should be produced quickly so that managers can respond rapidly to it.
- It should be easily comprehensible, useful, accurate and reliable.
- The cost of producing it should not outweigh its benefits.

Also, the lines of responsibility within an organisation should be clearly set out and understood by all concerned, and they should be oriented towards achieving the objectives of the business. For example, in the Wishart organisation described in Example 13.2, senior managers are likely to be concerned with growing their market share in a highly competitive market. Having determined that growth in market share is a key objective, they must communicate the objective effectively to all the business's employees so that every individual understands their role in achieving it. So, for example, promoting the organisation, marketing its services and establishing an effective system of rewards are all functions that are likely to be the responsibility of head office managers. Branch managers will be responsible for organising their operations so as to achieve the maximum number of high quality instructions. The reporting of new instructions received each week would thus clearly link into the organisation's lines of responsibility.

Divisional responsibility in large business organisations

In some cases the sheer size and complexity of a business organisation may make it difficult for a single management team to control all of the operations of the business. Where this is the case, part of the control can be devolved to divisional managers, leaving the most senior level of management free to deal with issues of major strategic importance (for example, a decision to launch a takeover bid). Divisions may be established, for example, by reference to the nature of their function or their geographical location, or both. A business that produces four major product groups might organise their activities into four divisions: one for each group. A major multinational car maker – say Nissan or Volkswagen – might organise its activities into geographical groups such as North American, Asia-Pacific and Europe. Example 13.3 shows how a manufacturing business might organise its operations into divisions.

Example 13.3	Popps is a manufacturer and bottler of soft-drinks operating in France and Spain. The French operations comprise the bottling of naturally sourced mineral water, and, at a separate location, the manufacturing and bottling of fizzy cola drinks. The Spanish operation is based at one location, manufacturing and bottling a similar range of cola drinks to those produced in France.

It would be possible to create two simple geographical divisions – one based in France and one in Spain. However, the two French operations differ somewhat from each other; they operate at different locations and are probably selling in slightly different markets. Therefore, Popps might find it advantageous to split operations into three divisions: Spain, France (cola) and France (water).

Divisions operate with varying degrees of autonomy. Highly decentralised organisations devolve a great deal of control to divisions, whereas, by contrast, in centralised organisations control is retained at the centre. There are advantages and disadvantages to both approaches.

Centralisation and decentralisation

The advantages of decentralisation include the following:

- Managers of decentralised parts of a business are likely to be given a high level of autonomy in decision-making. This is likely to lead to a more flexible and rapid response to problems.
- Managers in decentralised businesses may be highly motivated if they are given sufficient responsibility in the running of their divisions.
- The comparisons made by senior management between the performances of different divisions in a decentralised business can help to generate a healthy level of competition between divisional managers.

However, there are some drawbacks, too. Healthy competition, if left unchecked, can result in a short-termist approach to decision making. Managers may take decisions that are not in the best overall interests of the organisation for the sake of gaining some short-term advantage for their own division. Also, decentralised organisations can be more expensive to run where, for example, a separate sales department is required for each division. It would probably be cheaper and might be more efficient to run a single centralised sales department.

The advantages of a centralised approach to organisational management are:

- The operations of the business remain under close scrutiny and control by senior managers.
- There are none of the inter-divisional rivalries that can lead to sub-optimal decision making.
- By centralising functions such as accounting, marketing and selling, cost savings can be made.

However, highly centralised operations are very demanding of senior management time, and may operate relatively inefficiently as a result. The opportunity of motivating staff by assigning divisional responsibilities to them is lost.

? Self-test question 13.1 (answer at the end of the book)

Identify each of the following statements about centralisation and decentralisation as TRUE or FALSE:

1. Inter-divisional rivalries can lead to sub-optimal decision making.
2. Decentralisation means that divisional managers are always motivated to make decisions that are in the best interests of the organisation as a whole.
3. By decentralising, senior managers may be able to concentrate more on the overall strategy of the organisation.
4. Decentralisation is likely to result in a more flexible and rapid response to problems in specific parts of the business.

Assessing divisional performance

The nature of divisional performance assessment varies depending upon the degree of autonomy assigned to the division. A key principle is that divisional managers should be assessed only in respect of elements of performance that are under their control. A highly autonomous division will be responsible for virtually all aspects of its operations within a general framework of overall business strategy. Such responsibilities would include, for example, determining the level of investment in assets, the nature and direction of marketing strategies and fixing selling prices. By contrast, divisional control might be limited to minor issues.

Broadly, three levels of autonomy can be recognised under the following descriptions:

1. Cost centre: divisional managers are responsible for controlling costs, but not revenue or investment. Decisions on matters such as fixing selling prices, determining sales mix targets and making capital investments would be made by more senior managers at a higher level in the organisation.

2. Profit centre: divisional managers have more autonomy than in a cost centre; they decide on selling strategies and fix their own prices. Also they are responsible for managing assets assigned to them by head office in the most cost effective way. They are not, however, responsible for determining capital investments.

3. Investment centre: this describes the highest level of autonomy where divisional managers are responsible for costs, revenue and capital investment decisions.

? **Self-test question 13.2** (answer at the end of the book)

> Division Beta is part of the Glenpool organisation. Beta division manufactures kit radios for export. The divisional management team is able to set prices for its products. An allocation of capital expenditure funds is made from head office each year, and the divisional managers are able to spend this as they choose.
> Is Beta a profit centre, a cost centre or an investment centre?

The method of assessment of divisional performance varies, depending upon whether the division is a cost, profit or investment centre.

Cost centre

Divisional performance should be assessed only in respect of costs, because revenue is beyond the control of managers at a divisional level. Reporting in such divisions would therefore focus principally upon analyses of costs that can be controlled by divisional managers. This would exclude any depreciation charges (because depreciation is controlled at head office level) and probably any sales related costs because the division has no autonomous control over sales strategies.

Figure 13.1	Scope of divisional control

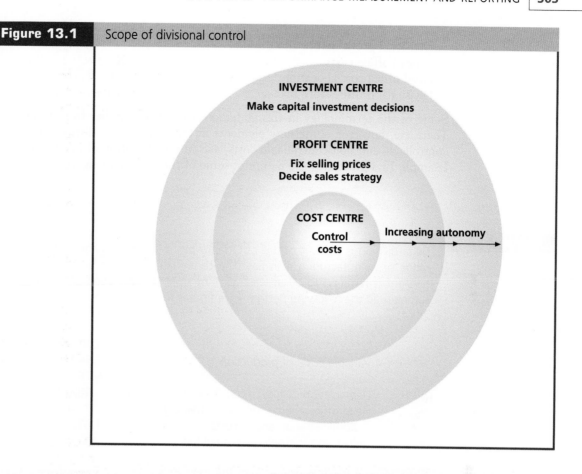

Profit centre

Divisional performance in a profit centre is likely to be reported using some form of profit and loss account statement. There is no definitive form for such a statement; remember that management accounting statements are purely for internal use, and so they can take whatever form is most useful to managers.

A divisional performance statement should distinguish clearly between the categories of costs controllable at divisional level and those that are controllable at head office level. The example below includes headings that would typically be found in a profit centre performance statement.

Divisional performance statement for a profit centre

	£000
Sales	X
Less: variable costs	(X)
Contribution	X
Less: Controllable fixed costs	(X)
Controllable profit	X
Less: Non-controllable fixed costs	(X)

	£000
Divisional profit before allocation of head office costs	X
Head office cost allocation	(X)
Divisional profit before tax	X

Some of the terminology in this statement should be familiar from Chapter 10. There are, however, some new elements in the form of the distinction between controllable and non-controllable costs, and in the allocation of head office costs. Example 13.4 illustrates the nature of some of the important figures.

Example 13.4

Delta division is a profit centre of Otranto plc, a listed company with a diverse range of manufacturing activities. The controllable profit of all the company's divisions is required to be at least 35% of sales. The division's accountant has summarised the following performance figures for the year ended 31 December 20X4:

	£000
Variable costs of production	3 588
Sales	6 782
Depreciation of fixed assets	982
Head office charge for central training, administration and IT costs	1 033
Delta's administration costs (all fixed)	433

If we arrange this information into the form of a divisional performance statement we will be able to assess Delta's performance, and to see whether or not it has achieved the required performance criteria for the year.

Delta: divisional performance statement for a profit centre

	£000
Sales	6 782
Less: variable costs	(3 588)
Contribution	3 194
Less: Controllable fixed costs	(433)
Controllable profit	2 761
Less: Non-controllable fixed costs	(982)
Divisional profit before allocation of head office costs	1 779
Head office cost allocation	(1 033)
Divisional profit before tax	746

Note that the depreciation charge for the year has been treated as a non-controllable fixed cost. Delta is a profit centre, not an investment centre, and its managers have no authority over investment decisions. It would therefore be unfair to treat depreciation as a controllable item.

Has Delta met the group criterion for controllable profit? Controllable profit (£2 761 000) as a percentage of sales (£6 782 000) is 40.7%. So we can see that the division has returned a controllable profit well in excess of the target. This result is beneficial to the division, its managers (whose reputations within the business are likely to be enhanced) and to the business as a whole.

This example is very straightforward in order to illustrate the principles involved in preparing a divisional performance statement. In practice, however, the distinction between controllable and uncontrollable costs may be difficult to determine. Taking training costs as an example: suppose that the head office of Otranto plc is responsible for organising and running training courses. Divisions can choose whether or not to participate in training activities: if divisional staff wish to attend training courses, they must ask their manager if the division is prepared to bear the cost. The courses are not charged at full cost; the element of cost that is not covered by fees paid is treated as part of the head office cost allocation. In this case, some element of training cost is controllable at a divisional level, but some of it is not. The amount of head office allocation depends upon the popularity of the training courses, and the willingness of divisional management to fund attendance by staff. If a division's managers decide that their staff will not participate in centrally organised training activities, an element of controllable cost is saved, the overall amount of head office training cost allocation increases and other divisions are penalised (even if only marginally).

Depreciation may be another grey area. In practice, divisional managers may be able to influence head office allocations and decisions on investments. Where this is the case, depreciation expense cannot truly be said to be non-controllable at divisional level.

The allocation of costs may be highly significant to managers, where their own performance appraisal is based upon divisional results. Where, for example, managerial bonuses are paid on the basis of controllable profit, senior managers at head office should carefully scrutinise the divisional performance statements to ensure that costs have been fairly allocated under the different headings in accordance with group policy.

Investment centre

The managers of an investment centre control both costs and the level and nature of capital investment. Therefore, it is possible to assess divisional performance in this case on the basis of **Return on Investment (ROI)**. This is a commonly used form of divisional performance measurement in cases where the divisions operate as investment centres. ROI is calculated as follows:

$$\frac{\text{Divisional net profit}}{\text{Investment in net assets}} \times 100$$

The advantages of using this type of simple measure are that it:

- relates net profit to the resources used to produce it
- is easy for managers to understand
- provides a benchmark for comparison across corporate divisions.

However, as with most measurements based on the relationship between accounting numbers, there are problems in ensuring that ROI provides a valid and consistent measure of divisional performance.

Determining divisional net profit

Often, divisions within a company sell to each other, and these inter-divisional sales and purchases have an impact on the profits of the divisions involved. A suitable selling price for such transactions has to be agreed between the divisions, and this can have a significant impact on the level of profits in the divisions involved.

Example 13.5

Bartolemi plc divides its operations into various divisions. Division P produces components that are used in the production process of Division Q – these components are sold by P and by other companies for £20.00 per unit, and are readily available at all times. Up till now, R has purchased these components from other companies, but Paul, the divisional manager of P has suggested that the profit from the sale of these components might as well stay within Bartolemi, so as to boost overall corporate profit, rather than being earned elsewhere. R's manager, Rosie, agrees, but argues that a discount on the market price would be appropriate given that P will have a captive market and will not have to expend any effort on marketing the components to R. She suggests that a price of £18 per unit is more appropriate. Variable costs per unit are £10, and fixed costs would not be affected by the extra production in division P. The number of units purchased annually by R is 16 000. What will be the effect on the profit of the two divisions if P sells at

a) £20 per unit
b) £18 per unit?

Because fixed costs would not change, the additional profit made by division P would be the contribution from the sales of 16 000 extra units. Depending on which selling price is used, the additional profit could be either:

$$16\ 000 \times (20 - 10 \text{ variable costs}) = £160\ 000$$

$$16\ 000 \times (18 - 10 \text{ variable costs}) = £128\ 000$$

There is a difference of £32 000 between these profit figures. If P sells to R, an additional profit of £160 000 is made for the company, Bartolemi, as a whole, and a profit of at least £128 000 for division P. But the key question to be resolved is which division obtains the benefit of the £32 000 profit figure. Clearly, Paul would prefer to sell at £20 so that the additional £32 000 remains in his division. Equally, Rosie wants to buy at £18, thus saving £2 per unit on the market price, and therefore adding £32 000 to her division's profit. The discussion between the two managers would have added importance for them if their personal bonuses depended upon divisional performance.

The danger for Bartolemi plc is that Paul and Rosie fail to reach an agreement, and that Rosie continues to source the component from outside. From Rosie's point of view as a divisional manager, if she sources the component at a price of £20, it doesn't actually matter whether the supplier is division P or an outsider. If Paul and Rosie fall out over this issue, she may decide to continue to source from outside, in order to deny Paul's division the opportunity to make profits (and perhaps to deny him the opportunity for personal gain in the form of bonus).

The scenario outlined in Example 13.5 illustrates what is usually known as the transfer pricing problem. More detailed consideration of transfer pricing is outside the scope of this book, but students should be aware of the nature of the problem because it is often an important issue in practice. The example also illustrates a problem of divisionalisation: divisional managers may identify closely with their divisions to the detriment of the company as a whole. Senior management at head office level need to be aware of this type of problem, and should take all possible steps to minimise inter-divisional rivalries. The company should aim for goal congruence, which means that all divisions should be working together to maximise returns for the company as a whole.

A further problem in determining divisional profit relates to the allocation of head office expenses. Example 13.4, earlier in the chapter, highlighted some of the important issues relating to cost allocation between divisions.

Determining investment in net assets

The other component of the ROI calculation is investment in net assets. Where ROI is used for comparison purposes, it is important to ensure that investment in net assets is calculated on a consistent basis across divisions. Also, the investment in net assets should represent those resources involved in generating divisional profit that are controllable by divisional management. Investment in net assets may not always provide a useful basis for measurement: in service businesses, the principal 'asset' often comprises the members of staff who provide the service and their value does not appear in the balance sheet of the business.

Another problem is that the working of the ROI calculation contains, potentially, an incentive to divisional management to delay investment, as Example 13.6 illustrates.

Example 13.6

Scala Main plc conducts most of its business activities via five operational divisions. Division Gamma manufactures a well-established range of laboratory benches and other equipment. Investment strategy is determined at divisional level. The three principal managers of Gamma division are rewarded partly in salary and partly in bonuses that are dependent upon year-on-year improvements in ROI. The three managers have met to discuss the potential replacement of a significant piece of machinery. The proposed investment will cost £1.3 million, to be depreciated on a straight-line basis over ten years, with an assumed residual value of nil. The existing machinery is ten years old and has reached the end of its originally estimated useful life. In the year ended 31 December 20X4, the depreciation charge relating to the existing machine was £80 000, and its net book value at that date was £0. Normally, machinery is replaced when it reaches the end of its useful life. However, one of the managers suggests that the division should defer the investment. He points out that the machine is still working fairly well. Repair costs of £20 000 were incurred in the year ended 31 December 20X4, and it is reasonable to suppose that repair costs in 20X5 probably wouldn't be any higher. A new machine would not incur repair costs during the first three years of ownership because it would be covered by a repair warranty.

Divisional profits were £1 600 000 for 20X4 (before taking into account depreciation and repair costs relating to the machine), and are likely to be at the same level in 20X5. Investments in net assets at 31 December 20X4 totalled £12 000 000. If the new machinery is purchased, investment in net assets at 31 December 20X5 is forecast to be £13 470 000. If the purchase is deferred, investment in net assets is forecast to be £12 580 000. ROI in the division is calculated as follows:

$$\frac{\text{Divisional net profit}}{\text{Investment in net assets at year end}} \times 100$$

Assess the effects on ROI, and upon the business, of

a) replacing the machine
b) deferring its replacement.

We can compare the effects of the alternative strategies as follows:

	2004 Actual	2005 (replacing machine)	2005 (deferring replacement)
Profits before depreciation and repair of the machine	1 600 000	1 600 000	1 600 000
Depreciation	(80 000)	(130 000)	0
Repairs	(20 000)	0	(20 000)
Divisional profits	1 500 000	1 470 000	1 580 000
Investment in net assets	12 000 000	13 470 000	12 580 000
ROI	12.5%	10.9%	12.6%

Deferring the replacement of the machine is forecast to produce a significantly higher level of divisional profits, and a small increase in ROI over the 20X4 figure. If the investment is made, however, the ROI decreases. The divisional managers are likely to be tempted to defer investment so as to earn additional rewards in the form of bonuses. In 20X5, the strategy is likely to work reasonably well, provided that the machine continues to function at the required level of reliability. However, in one year's time the managers are likely to be tempted to adopt the same strategy in respect of this machine, and possibly other assets. If this approach is taken consistently, the efficiency of the asset base is likely to decline. All other things being equal, ROI is likely to increase, and managers will be rewarded for failing to keep the fixed assets up to date.

ROI can be a useful measure, but it needs to be treated with some caution, especially where divisional managers' rewards are based on achieving a specified ROI performance. Divisionalisation can lead to a lack of goal congruence in the organisation, where divisions compete against each other, divisional managers spend too much time and effort on internal politics, and less than optimal decisions are made. Also, there is a danger that divisional managers will focus upon short-term gains and will neglect longer-term strategic considerations. Senior managers in the organisation need to be sensitive to the factors that affect divisional performance, and should be aware of the problems that may arise because of divisionalisation.

Non-financial performance measures

Some of the drawbacks of financial performance measures such as ROI can be addressed by assessing performance using a set of non-financial measures. These do not have to be an absolute alternative; the best way of assessing the performance of a division, of a whole organisation or of management is likely to be via a combination of financial and non-financial performance indicators. Some examples of non-financial performance indicators at a divisional level are given in Example 13.7.

Example 13.7	

Tony has recently been appointed to head the Light Aircraft division of a major aeronautical manufacturer, Lipp & Smeeton plc. Lipp & Smeeton's other principal divisions manufacture passenger aircraft and corporate jets, and build engines for the defence industry. The company's stated aims are to grow market share, and to maintain outstanding levels of quality and service to customers. The activities of the Light Aircraft division comprise the manufacture of small aircraft for sale to private owners and clubs, and of powered gliders and hang-gliders. Whereas the other divisions have been consistently good performers, Light Aircraft has turned in losses for the last three years under poor quality divisional management, despite buoyant market conditions. Although the basic engine quality of the products has remained high, there have been complaints from customers about the long lead-time for delivery, high prices, and poor quality interior finish. Tony's task is to turn the division around, returning it to profit within 18 months.

What performance measures are likely to be appropriate in assessing both divisional performance and Tony's own performance?

Financial performance measures will be of importance in assessing how quickly the division can be returned to profit. Measures such as ROI, gross profit margin and sales revenue growth will be useful. The measures should correspond, as far as possible, with the aims of the company as a whole. Its first stated aim is to grow market share, and so it is important to ensure that the Light Aircraft division, and Tony, as its head, are assessed on market share measurement.

The division has maintained reasonable quality standards, but has failed on several aspects of customer satisfaction. The second stated aim of Lipp &

Smeeton is to maintain 'outstanding levels of quality and service to customers'. Tony needs to ensure that the division first achieves those levels, before he need worry about maintaining them. The measurement of quality and service standards is likely to involve the following:

Customer service

Post-sales questionnaires to elicit customer satisfaction levels in respect of:

- competence of sales staff
- availability of sales staff
- effectiveness of staff in dealing with complaints (if any)
- delivery schedules
- product finish and quality
- product pricing compared to competitors.

Quality

Similarly, post-sales questionnaires can provide information:

- number of defects detected during quality inspection
- number of defects detected post-delivery
- customer satisfaction levels in respect of quality
- number of customer complaints per month/year.

The most appropriate non-financial measures to use naturally vary from one organisation to another. In the aircraft business, the safety and quality characteristics of the product are of surpassing importance, and measures of performance are likely to focus heavily on quality issues. In another context, for example, on-line travel booking, performance measures are likely to focus upon ease of use and accessibility of the service, efficiency and speed of information processing, and the appearance and design of the website. Where customers are being provided with a face-to-face service, for example, travel booking using a high street travel agent, other factors come into play. Customers are likely to value not only efficiency, but also the friendliness and helpfulness of the staff and their competence in making bookings. Performance measures are likely to reflect these factors.

? **Self-test question 13.3** (answer at the end of the book)

HB is the handbag division of a luxury goods manufacturer, BYPH. HB's business objective is to lead the market in the sales of very high quality, exclusive leather handbags. Each season HB changes most of its designs, apart from a small number of classic items.

Discuss whether or not the following performance indicators are likely to be appropriate non-financial measures of success:

1. Market share
2. Number of defective products
3. Volume of sales by product line
4. Customer perceptions of exclusivity
5. Competitiveness of product pricing.

The balanced scorecard

As noted in the previous section of the chapter, the best way of assessing the performance of an organisation or division is likely to be via a combination of financial and non-financial measures. In this section, we examine a popular method of performance measurement and reporting using financial and non-financial measurements that can be tailored to individual organisations.

The balanced scorecard is an idea developed by two US academic researchers, Robert Kaplan and David Norton. The term describes an easily understood set of performance measures that can be used to provide managers with a relevant and thorough summary of complex information about the business. In a 1992 paper (the reference is given in full at the end of the chapter) Kaplan and Norton likened the scorecard to the dials and indicators in an aeroplane cockpit:

For the complex task of navigating and flying an aeroplane, pilots need detailed information about many aspects of the flight. They need information on fuel, air speed, altitude, bearing, destination, and other indicators that summarize the current and predicted environment. Reliance on one instrument can be fatal. Similarly, the complexity of managing an organisation today requires that managers be able to view performance in several areas simultaneously.

The balanced scorecard uses both financial and non-financial measures to examine the performance of the business. Kaplan and Norton identify four fundamental perspectives that can be applied to any business, in the form of questions:

- How do customers see us? (Customer perspective)
- What must we excel at? (Internal perspective)
- Can we continue to improve and create value? (Innovation and learning perspective)
- How do we look to shareholders? (Financial perspective).

These four perspectives are represented on the balanced scorecard as set out in Figure 13.2.

In order to use the balanced scorecard, managers must be able to identify the key performance measures under each of the four perspectives. It is important that these should be linked in to the overall business strategy. Certain advantages are claimed for the balanced scorecard:

- It minimises information overload by limiting the number of performance measures used, ensuring that only really important measurements are reported.
- It brings key aspects of a business's performance together into a single management report.
- It ensures that managers are obliged to consider all of the really important measurements together, so that if good performance in one area has been achieved at the expense of diminishing performance in another area, the trade-off should be obvious.

Figure 13.2	The balanced scorecard

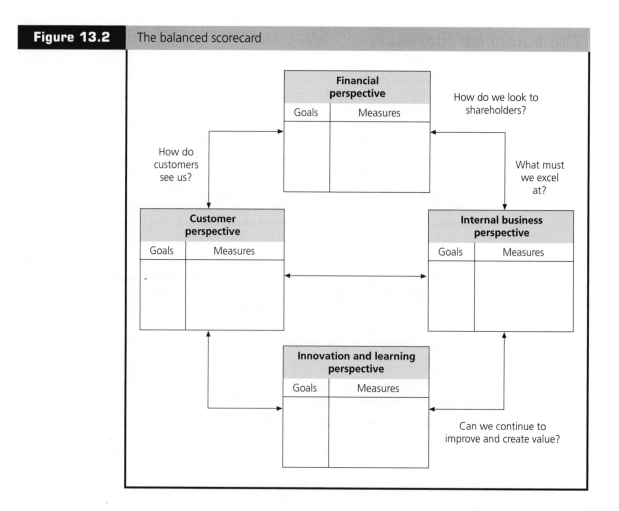

The four key perspectives of the balanced scorecard

Customer perspective

Customer satisfaction is a critical area for all businesses. Kaplan and Norton observe in their paper that customers' concerns tend to relate to time (for example, time taken to fulfil orders), quality, performance and service, and cost. In putting the balanced scorecard into operation, a business might, for example, identify two key goals: increasing market share and improving the delivery schedule. In this case, relevant performance measures are likely to include:

- number of new customers gained
- percentage of sales from new customers
- percentage of total market share
- average time lapse between order and delivery.

Internal business perspective

In order to achieve the goal of customer satisfaction, a business's managers must be able to identify the key internal processes that contribute to success or failure. Taking the same example as above, increased market share might hinge upon the business's relative success in introducing new products into a competitive market. If this is the case, business goals might include meeting a schedule of planned product innovations. The relevant performance measurement might be performance against this schedule.

Innovation and learning perspective

As Kaplan and Norton point out, the intense nature of global competition means that businesses must continually innovate in order to survive and to create value for customers and shareholders. If a business is to grow, it needs to invest in its infrastructure to create the right conditions. This could involve investment in people (in the form of recruitment and training), organisation of the business in order to maximise creativity and motivation amongst staff and investment in systems (such as computer systems) that will help to achieve the business's strategic objectives. A specific business goal could be, for example, to create the conditions necessary for first-class product innovation and development. Relevant performance measures might include:

- retention rate of employees in key areas
- number of new appointments in relevant departments
- satisfaction levels amongst key employees.

(Note that the 'innovation and learning' perspective identified by Kaplan and Norton is referred to in some subsequent writings as the 'learning and growth' perspective.)

Financial perspective

The way in which shareholders see the business from a financial perspective is heavily influenced by the contents of the important financial statements such as the balance sheet, cash flow statement and profit and loss account. Such statements provide a summary of the financial effects of decisions made by managers in pursuing the goals they have identified for the business. The financial statements can be viewed as the acid test of success or failure. It may take time for the effects of innovative strategies to filter through and to be evidenced in the financial statements presented to shareholders. However, the success or failure of the strategies must eventually be judged by financial measurements. As Kaplan and Norton put it:

> A failure to convert improved operational performance, as measured in the scorecard, into improved financial performance should send executives back to their drawing boards to rethink the company's strategy or its implementation plans.

The balanced scorecard in practice

The balanced scorecard idea has proved to be very pervasive and influential. Kaplan and Norton published their first paper in 1992, but have followed it with several others and a couple of books. Around the world, many organisations, in both the private and public sector, use the balanced scorecard as an essential management tool. A recent estimate is that half of the top 1000 companies in the USA use it, and 35–45% of companies in Europe and in Australia. In the USA it is used by several government departments and by large corporations such as IBM and DaimlerChrysler.

Chapter summary

This chapter has explained a range of approaches to measuring and reporting performance within the firm. The early part of the chapter stressed the importance of linking performance measurement to the strategic objectives of the business. The topic of divisional responsibility was introduced in order to explain how larger organisations might monitor performance across a range of different activities. Students should by now understand the advantages and drawbacks of decentralisation.

Three levels of divisional autonomy were identified and discussed: cost centre, profit centre and investment centre. Appropriate methods of performance assessment were identified in respect of each level of autonomy. Problems in determining the performance of individual divisions were also discussed.

Non-financial performance measures should not be overlooked; these can play a very important role in performance assessment. The chapter explained some of the non-financial measures that might be appropriate in the context of a particular firm.

Finally, the chapter briefly outlined the key features of one of the most important recent developments in performance measurement: the balanced scorecard. The ideas of Kaplan and Norton were explained, by reference to their original 1992 paper on the topic.

The end-of-chapter exercises are divided into two sections. The first section has answers provided at the end of the book. The second section, in the white box, has answers on the lecturers' section of the website.

 Finally, the chapter contains a case study that examines some features of performance measurement at divisional level. Answers to the case study requirements can be found on the students' section of the website.

@ Website summary

The book's website contains the following material in respect of Chapter 13:

Students' section

- Quiz containing ten multiple choice questions
- Three additional questions with answers
- Answer to case study.

Lecturers' section

- Answers to exercises 13.8 to 13.13
- Three additional questions with answers.

Internet and other resources

A great deal has been written about the Balanced Scorecard. The original paper, from which much of the final section of the chapter was drawn, was published in the *Harvard Business Review* in 1992. It is readable and interesting: if students would like to expand their study of this very important aspect of performance appraisal they are encouraged to read this paper. The full reference is:

Kaplan, Robert S. and Norton, David P. (1992) 'The balanced scorecard: measures that drive performance', *Harvard Business Review*, Jan–Feb.

A useful website on the same subject is:

www.balancedscorecard.org – this contains a lot of up-to-date information about the balanced scorecard and the experiences of some of the various organisations that have adopted it.

Exercises: answers at the end of the book

13.1 Identify three key characteristics of management information.

13.2 Golfstore Retail plc was established five years ago by a small team of golf enthusiasts in Scotland. The company retails a range of quality golfers' clothing and equipment from stores around Scotland. Last year it expanded its stores into the north of England and into Wales. The management team has ambitions to open stores throughout the United Kingdom and Ireland, with the ultimate aim of expanding into western Europe within the next eight years. The board has met to discuss the best way of managing the expansion, and to consider a proposal to establish relatively autonomous divisions based on geographical areas so that eventually, for example, there will be a Golfstore France with its own divisional management team.

Explain to the directors the principal advantages of divisionalisation within the context of their business.

13.3 The managers of division Alpha of Burntwood and Down Holdings plc determine selling prices for the division, and control costs. Decisions on fixed assets purchases are made at head office level. Is Alpha

a)   a profit centre

b)   a cost centre

c)   an investment centre?

13.4 Perkora Bains plc manufactures household fittings. The company uses a system of divisional management, with divisions split by product type. All divisions are treated as profit centres. The accountant in the bathroom division (BD) has gathered the following data for production of the quarterly performance statement which is due for submission to head office:

	£000
Direct materials cost	280
Direct labour cost	311
Sales	1 671
Depreciation of fixed assets	112
Fixed costs excluding depreciation	580
Head office cost allocation	337

Of the fixed costs, £37 000 is non-controllable at divisional level. The head office cost allocation relates to research and development and marketing expenditure.

a)   prepare a divisional performance statement for BD

b)   identify the amount of profit that should be used as an indicator of divisional performance.

13.5 Identify and explain two reasons why Return on Investment (ROI) may be an unreliable measurement of divisional performance.

13.6 Tripp and Hopp Limited is a booking agency that specialises in selling London theatre tickets. During the late 1990s and early 2000s the business ran four central London booking offices and a website. But in late 2003, the company decided to transfer all its operations to the website. The company's objective is 'to provide a competitive, efficient and secure service to London's theatregoers'.

Draw up a list of six appropriate non-financial performance indicators that will help Tripp and Hopp's management to assess the extent to which the company is meeting its objectives. For each indicator, suggest a way of measuring it.

13.7 Your company is considering the introduction of a balanced scorecard system. Your head of department has attended a briefing session on the new system and has circulated the following memo:

To: Marketing department staff

From: Head of department

BALANCED SCORECARD

You may have heard by now that our chief executive wants to introduce a so-called 'Balanced Scorecard' system for performance measurement. Frankly, even after attending the briefing I'm still a bit clueless on the subject. I don't think it involves any figures, which would be good news, but we would have to measure things like customer satisfaction. Brian, the accountant, said that lots of companies have tried this system and it's well known. I think he also said it's like flying an aeroplane but perhaps I'd dozed off at that point. Have any of you heard of it? I'd like to hear from anyone who can provide me with a brief, comprehensible account of the Balanced Scorecard.

Reply to the memo, explaining the Balanced Scorecard as concisely as possible.

Exercises: answers available to lecturers

13.8 Identify and briefly discuss the principal drawbacks to divisional organisation within large businesses.

13.9 The management team of Florian Space Products plc are meeting to discuss a proposal to divide the company's operations into three divisions. Each division will deal with one of the business's three principal products. The finance director proposes that the divisions should be given cost centre status. The marketing director, however, argues that if divisionalisation is to be effective, the divisions should operate on a fully decentralised basis as investment centres.

Identify and explain two arguments supporting each of the directors' views.

13.10 Identify one from each list of words given below to fill in the missing words in the following sentence:

A divisional performance statement for (1) _____ centre identifies contribution, (2)_____ profit, divisional profit before allocation of (3)_____ costs and divisional profit before tax.

List 1	List 2	List 3
a profit	non-controllable	interest
a cost	operating	divisional
an investment	controllable	head office

13.11 Spall Spelling plc operates several manufacturing divisions, with each division treated as a profit centre. Division D's accountant has drawn up the following list of data prior to preparing the monthly performance statement for submission to head office.

	£
Sales	272 600
Fixed costs	72 400
Depreciation	36 000
Variable materials	47 000
Variable labour	63 700

Of the depreciation charge for the month, 25% relates to fixed assets over which the division has complete control; 15% of the fixed costs are non-controllable.

The accountant has been notified that the head office cost allocation for the month is £43 200.

Prepare a divisional performance statement for Division Delta.

13.12 Answer TRUE or FALSE to the following statements about the balanced scorecard method of performance measurement:

1. The balanced scorecard is helpful to managers who are not accountants because it uses only non-financial measurements of performance.

2. The balanced scorecard can help managers by cutting down information overload.

3. A problem with the balanced scorecard is that it uses the same performance measurements across all companies, and sometimes these are not appropriate.

4. In order to use the balanced scorecard effectively, managers must be able to link performance measurement to the overall business strategy.

13.13 As part of its implementation of the balanced scorecard method of performance appraisal, the directors of Bretton Tallis plc have met to discuss the key question: 'Can we continue to improve and create value?' The company, which is engaged in the manufacture and sale of replacement windows and doors, faces tough competition: recent entrants to the market have introduced a range of innovative product improvements, with the result that Bretton Tallis's product range is starting to look old-fashioned. The directors conclude that the company can continue to improve and create value only if it takes urgent steps to improve the quality and design of its product ranges. Two specific goals are identified: to promote the rapid development of new plastics (in order to produce better and more distinctive products), and to create conditions in which innovative design can flourish.

For each of these goals suggest four performance measurements that could assist the company's directors in assessing progress towards the goals.

CASE STUDY 13.1   Rewarding divisional performance

Smallheath Carraldo Instruments plc (SCI) is a successful company engaged in the manufacture and sale of precision equipment to the pharmaceutical and chemical research industries. The company is run by a small head office management team, and its activities are split amongst three decentralised divisions, Pharma, Chem and Components. Pharma and Chem are both engaged in the manufacture and sale of precision instruments to their respective industry areas. The Components division produces complex electronic components, some of which are sold to the other two divisions. Intra-company sales of this type account for about 40% of the output of Components. The remaining 60% of its output is sold to customers outside SCI plc.

It is now four months since Khaleb took up an appointment as senior manager of Components division. Prior to his appointment he had worked as a technical manager in a highly centralised company, and so he has experienced a steep learning curve in getting accustomed to a divisional management system. The senior managers who appointed him made no secret of the fact that the performance of Components has been disappointing over the last three or four years, and that Khaleb would be expected to use his management skills to return the division to the point where it would make a healthy return on investment. Lara, Khaleb's predecessor at Components, was widely regarded in the company as a poor manager with a tendency to overspend.

The senior manager of each division is rewarded by a mixture of salary and bonuses. The annual bonus is based on the division's Return on Investment performance. For each percentage point achieved in excess of the company's annual ROI target, the manager concerned receives a bonus of several thousand pounds. The divisional managers of Chem and Pharma have usually received bonuses in the past, but Lara never succeeded in doing so. The targets and actual ROI figures for the last three years are shown below:

	20X5	20X6	20X7
Target ROI	18.7%	19.0%	19.3%
Actual ROI			
Components	3.4%	1.4%	(0.4%)
Pharma	21.2%	20.1%	19.1%
Chem	23.4%	21.6%	19.4%

Competitive pressures in the industry have grown in the last few years, and margins have been squeezed, which helps to explain the small drops in the ROI performance of Pharma and Chem divisions. SCI's senior managers have chosen, until this year, to ignore external pressures by insisting on an increase in the ROI target. However, in the current year, 20X8, they have succumbed to pressure from the divisional managers and have set the ROI target at 18.9%. The managers of Pharma and Chem appear likely to exceed the target by at least one percentage point, and so they will qualify to receive bonuses. As is clear from the table, the Components division is a very long way indeed from the point where Khaleb would qualify for a bonus. Three-quarters of the way through the 20X8

▶

financial year, Components ROI stands at 3.8%, and any improvement before the year end is likely to be marginal.

Since Khaleb joined the company, he has conducted a detailed review of his division's operations. The significant points arising from the review include the following:

1. The selling price of components to Pharma and Chem produce a contribution margin of 5% for Components. If the other divisions had to buy similar components outside SCI, the component cost to them would rise by between 7% and 10% (depending upon the particular component).

2. Components' contribution margin on products sold outside SCI averages 16.2%.

3. Khaleb's predecessor, Lara, had spent the last two years of her tenure conducting a review of fixed assets. Many of the major productive fixed assets had been replaced, with the aim of improving efficiency and profitability. Most of the machines that were replaced in this exercise had reached the end of their expected useful lives many years previously. Khaleb has found that productive efficiency has, indeed, improved in the current year, and further improvements are likely to feed through over the next couple of years.

4. The asset replacement programme means that there is spare productive capacity. Khaleb has had lengthy discussions with the sales manager, Ester, about the potential for increasing sales. Ester points out that she has difficulty motivating her staff because they have fixed salaries (i.e. no commission), which are low relative to the rest of the industry. The division tends to employ new graduates in sales, but the most effective of them leave after a couple of years for more highly paid jobs. Ester herself receives no bonus if she produces a better sales performance.

Having conducted his review, Khaleb can see that it will be very difficult to raise ROI by a significant amount in the short- to medium-term. From a personal point of view, his chances of receiving a profit-related bonus in the near future are vanishingly small. He knows that he can make improvements at divisional level, but feels that there are some problems that can be addressed only by senior management at head office.

Required:

a) Identify the business issues and problems arising from Khaleb's review that he is unable to address at a divisional level. (This should include an identification of any problems inherent in the current system of managerial bonuses).

b) Suggest strategies that the senior management of SCI could adopt in order to address the problems identified in part a).

Answers to self-test questions

CHAPTER 7

7.1

Cost	Classification
Canvas material	Direct materials
Metal spokes for wheels	Direct materials
Spare parts for sewing machine repairs	Indirect production overheads
Advertising expenditure	Other indirect overheads
Machine oil	Indirect production overheads
Electricity bill for factory	Indirect production overheads
Wages of assembly line workers	Direct labour
Wages of factory canteen staff	Indirect production overheads
Wages of assembly line supervisor	Indirect production overheads
Secretary's salary	Other indirect overheads
Delivery vehicle depreciation	Other indirect overheads

7.2 *a) FIFO*

	Deliveries into stock			Transfers to production			Balance	
Date	Units	£	£	Units	£	£	Units	£
1 Mar							55	165.00
10 Mar	160	3.20	512.00				215	677.00
12 Mar				35	3.00	105.00	180	572.00
25 Mar				20	3.00	60.00	160	512.00
				50	3.20	160.00	110	352.00

Tutorial note: the 110 items remaining in stock after the transfer to production on 25 March are all assumed to belong to the batch of items delivered on 10 March, and so are valued at £3.20 each (110 × £3.20 = £352.00).

b) LIFO

	Deliveries into stock			Transfers to production			Balance	
Date	Units	£	£	Units	£	£	Units	£
1 Mar							55	165.00
10 Mar	160	3.20	512.00				215	677.00
12 Mar				35	3.20	112.00	180	565.00
25 Mar				70	3.20	224.00	110	341.00

Tutorial note: the 110 items remaining in stock are assumed to have been in stock the longest. Therefore closing stock comprises 55 units @ £3.00 each + 55 units (110 − 55) @ £3.20 each:

55 × £3	=	165.00
55 × £3.20	=	176.00
		341.00

c) AVCO

Date	Deliveries into stock Units	£	£	Transfers to production Units	£	£	Balance Units	AVCO £	£
1 Mar							55	3.00	165.00
10 Mar	160	3.20	512.00				215	3.149	677.00
12 Mar				35	3.149	110.21	180	3.149	566.79
25 Mar				70	3.149	220.42	110	3.149	346.37

7.3 Batch No: 30453A

	£	£
Direct materials		
Metal: 100kg @ 4.50 per kilo	450.00	
Paint: 2 litres @ £6.80 per litre	13.60	
Glass: 500 pieces @ 30p per piece	150.00	
		613.60
Direct labour		
Grade A: 22 hours @ £4.80	105.60	
Grade B: 19 hours @ £6.00	114.00	
		219.60
Prime cost		833.20

Cost per picture frame equals:

$$\frac{£833.20}{500} = £1.67 \text{ (to two decimal places)}$$

7.4 Swift Metals Limited: Apportionment of production overheads, year ending

31 December 20X4

| | | Total | Cost centre | | |
	Basis	£	Preparation £	Tooling £	Finishing £
Factory costs	Floor area	700 000	245 000	315 000	140 000
Canteen costs	Employees	18 496	8 704	6 528	3 264
Machinery depreciation	Net book value	17 650	2 600	11 200	3 850
Machinery maintenance and repair	Call-outs	2 961	658	1 974	329
Supervisory salaries	Employees	23 358	10 992	8 244	4 122
Totals		762 465	267 954	342 946	151 565

Tutorial note: by contrast with the Choremaster example, note that supervisory salaries for Swift Metals are apportioned on the basis of the number of employees supervised. Remember, there are no fixed rules about the way in which costs are apportioned – the basis of apportionment is whatever is most appropriate for the business.

CHAPTER 9

9.1 *i) Flexed budget for 900 units*

	£
Sales: 900 units @ £35	31 500
Costs	
Direct materials: 900 units × (2kg ×£6)	(10 800)
Direct labour: 900 units × (1 hour × £7.50)	(6 750)
Production overheads	(4 000)
	9 950
Selling and administrative overheads	(2 300)
Net profit	7 650

ii) Calculation of variances

Summary of budget, flexed budget and actual statements:

	Original budget £	Flexed budget £	Actual £
Sales	28 000	31 500	32 400
Direct materials	(9 600)	(10 800)	(9 405)
Direct labour	(6 000)	(6 750)	(7 560)

	Original budget £	Flexed budget £	Actual £
Production overhead	(4 000)	(4 000)	(4 400)
	8 400	9 950	11 035
Selling and administrative overhead	(2 300)	(2 300)	(2 450)
Net profit	6 100	7 650	8 585

The overall variance is:

	£
Original budget net profit	6 100
Actual net profit	8 585
	2 485 (F)

Sales profit volume variance

This variance is the difference between the original budget profit and the flexed budget profit: £6100 – £7650 = £1550. The flexed budget profit is greater than the original budget profit, so this is a favourable variance.

Sales price variance

	£
Actual volume of sales at actual selling price:	
900 × £36	32 400
Less: actual volume of sales at budget selling price:	
900 × £35	31 500
Sales price variance	900 (F)

Direct materials variances

Comparing the figure for direct materials in the flexed budget statement with the figure in the actual statement:

	£
Flexed budget for direct materials	10 800
Actual direct materials	9 405
	1 395 (F)

Direct materials price variance. We compare:

■ The actual quantity of materials used at the price actually paid (actual price).

■ The actual quantity of materials used at the price budgeted (standard price).

	£
Actual quantity at actual price	
1.9kg was used for each of 900 casings	
Actual quantity used is 1.9kg × 900 = 1 710kg	
1 710kg × price actually paid (£5.50)	9 405

Actual quantity at standard price
1 710kg × standard price (£6.00)   10 260

Direct materials price variance   855 (F)

Direct materials quantity variance. We compare:

- The actual quantity of materials used at standard price.

- The standard quantity of materials used at standard price.

	£
Actual quantity at standard price Actual quantity used (already worked out): 1 710kg Standard price per kg: £6 Actual quantity at standard price = 1 710 × £6	10 260
Standard quantity at standard price Standard quantity: 2kg × 900 casings = 1 800kg Standard price per kg: £6 Standard quantity at standard price = 1 800 × £6	10 800
Direct materials quantity variance	540 (F)

In summary, the direct materials variances are:

	£	
Direct materials price variance	855	(F)
Direct materials quantity variance	540	(F)
Direct materials variance	1 395	(F)

Direct labour variances

Comparing the figure for direct labour in the flexed budget statement with the figure in the actual statement:

	£	
Flexed budget for direct labour	6 750	
Actual direct labour	7 560	
	810	(A)

Direct labour rate variance. We compare:

- The actual hours of direct labour used at the wage rate actually paid (actual rate).

- The actual hours of direct labour used at the wage rate budgeted (standard rate).

	£
Actual hours at actual rate Actual hours was 1.2 hours for each of 900 casings 1.2 × 900 = 1 080 hours 1 080 hours × rate actually paid (£7.00)	7 560

	£
Actual hours at standard rate	
1 080 hours × standard rate (£7.50)	8 100
Direct labour rate variance	540 (F)

Direct labour efficiency variance. We compare:

- The actual hours of direct labour used at standard rate.
- The standard hours of direct labour used at standard rate.

	£
Actual hours at standard rate	
Actual hours used (already worked out): 1 080 hours	
Standard rate per hour: £7.50	
Actual hours at standard rate = 1 080 × £7.50	8 100
Standard hours at standard rate	
Standard hours: 1 hour × 900 = 900	
Standard rate per hour: £7.50	
Standard hours at standard rate = 900 × £7.50	6 750
Direct labour efficiency variance	1 350 (A)

In summary, the direct labour variances are:

	£
Direct labour rate variance	540 (F)
Direct labour efficiency variance	1 350 (A)
Direct labour variance	810 (A)

Production overhead variance

	£
Budget figure for production overhead	4 000
Actual figure for production overhead	4 400
Production overhead variance	(400) (A)

Selling and administrative overhead variance

	£
Budget figure for selling and administrative overhead	2 300
Actual figure for selling and administrative overhead	2 450
Production overhead variance	(150) (A)

iii) Standard cost operating statement

Bridge and Blige Limited: Standard cost operating statement for February 20X6

	Total £
Original budgeted net profit	6 100
Sales profit volume variance	1 550
Flexed budget net profit	7 650

Other variances	Favourable £	(Adverse) £
Sales price variance	900	
Direct materials price variance	855	
Direct materials quantity variance	540	
Direct labour rate variance	540	
Direct labour efficiency variance		(1 350)
Production overhead variance		(400)
Selling and administrative overhead variance		(150)
Total	**2 835**	**(1 900)**
		935
Actual net profit		8 585

9.2 *a) Flexed budget for 2000 units*

	£
Sales: 2 000 × £45	90 000
Costs	
Direct materials: 2 000 × (16 metres × £1)	(32 000)
Direct labour: 2 000 × (2 hours × £5.00)	(20 000)
Variable production overheads: 2 000 units × (2 machine hours per unit × £1)	(4 000)
Fixed production overheads: 2 000 units × (2 machine hours per unit × £6)	(24 000)
Profit before other overheads	10 000

b) Variance calculations

First of all, we will set the original budget, flexed budget and actual side by side:

	Original budget £	Flexed budget £	Actual £
Sales	81 000	90 000	90 000
Direct materials	(28 800)	(32 000)	(32 000)
Direct labour	(18 000)	(20 000)	(20 000)
Variable production overhead	(3 600)	(4 000)	(3 800)
Fixed production overhead	(21 600)	(24 000)	(23 400)
	9 000	10 000	10 800

The overall variance is:

	£
Original budget net profit	9 000
Actual net profit	10 800
	1 800 (F)

Sales profit volume variance

This variance is the difference between the original budget profit and the flexed budget profit: £9000 − 10 000 = £1000 (F). The variance is favourable because the flexed budget profit is higher than the original budget profit.

There are no variances for sales price, direct material, direct labour and selling and administrative overheads. Once the budget is flexed, it becomes clear that sales prices, direct material and direct labour costs are exactly as would have been predicted if 2000 units had been budgeted for.

Variable production overhead variance

The overall variance can be calculated in the same way as, say, the total direct materials variance – by comparing the totals in the flexed budget statement with the actual statement:

	£
Flexed budget for variable overhead	4 000
Actual variable overhead	3 800
	200 (F)

Fixed production overhead variance

The overall variance is calculated in the same way by comparing the totals in the flexed budget statement with the actual statement:

	£
Flexed budget for fixed overhead	24 000
Actual fixed overhead	23 400
	600 (F)

c) Standard cost operating statement

Singh and Waterhouse Limited: Standard cost operating statement

for April 20X8

	Favourable £	(Adverse) £	Total £
Original budgeted net profit			9 000
Sales profit volume variance			1 000
Flexed budget net profit			10 000
Other variances			
Sales price variance	—	—	
Direct materials price variance	—	—	
Direct materials quantity variance	—	—	
Direct labour rate variance	—	—	
Direct labour efficiency variance	—	—	
Variable overhead variance	200	—	
Fixed overhead variance	600		
Selling and administrative overhead variance	—	—	
Total	800	—	800
Actual net profit			10 800

CHAPTER 10   **10.1** Brinn Bartholomew Limited: Budget for June 20X9

	£
Sales: 1400 bins × £250 each	350 000
Variable costs	
Direct materials: 1400 bins × £97	(135 800)
Direct labour: 1400 bins × £36	(50 400)
Contribution	163 800
Fixed costs	(120 400)
Net profit	43 400

10.2 The following points can be plotted onto the graph:

Level of production	Fixed costs £	Total costs £
0	50 000	50 000
10 000	50 000	100 000

We do not need to plot any other points in order to draw the graph, because variable costs increase at a steady rate in line with the level of production. The data produces the graph shown in Figure 1.

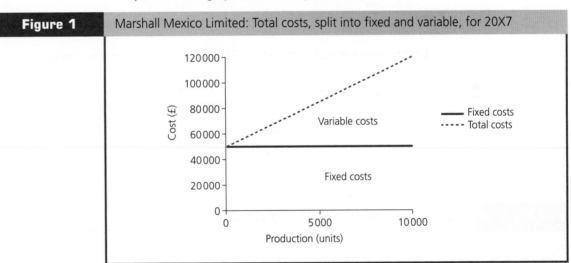

| **Figure 1** | Marshall Mexico Limited: Total costs, split into fixed and variable, for 20X7 |

10.3 From Figure 2 we can see that the break-even point is 5000 units. In terms of sales value this is between £60 000 and £80 000 on the vertical axis – probably at approximately £75 000.

We can check this answer by working out a profit statement at a production and sales level of 5000 units:

	£
Sales (5000 × £15)	75 000
Variable costs (5000 × £5)	(25 000)
Contribution	50 000
Fixed costs	(50 000)
	0

| Figure 2 | Marshall Mexico Limited: Break-even chart for 20X7 |

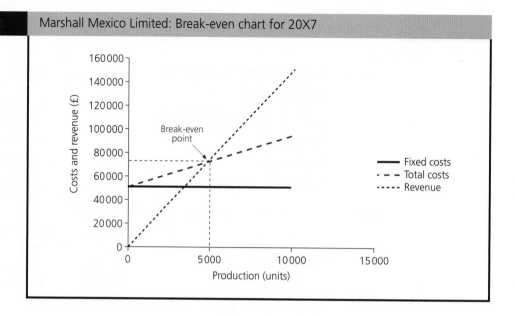

10.4 Calculating Neasden Northwich Limited's break-even point (in units):

Sales revenue per unit = £20.00
Variable costs per unit = £6.00

Contribution per unit is, therefore, £14.00 (sales minus variable costs).

$$\frac{\text{Break-even point}}{\text{(in units)}} = \frac{\text{Fixed costs}}{\text{Contribution per unit}}$$

$$= \frac{70\,000}{£14} = 5000 \text{ units}$$

CHAPTER 12

12.1 *1. Formula for £1 invested at 8% over 4 years*

$$£1 \times (1.08)^4$$

Compounding factor = $(1.08) \times (1.08) \times (1.08) \times (1.08) = 1.360$

2. Formula for £1 invested at 7% over 5 years

$$£1 \times (1.07)^5$$

Compounding factor = $(1.07) \times (1.07) \times (1.07) \times (1.07) \times (1.07) = 1.403$

3. Formula for £1 invested at 6% over 6 years

$$£1 \times (1.06)^6$$

Compounding factor = $(1.06) \times (1.06) \times (1.06) \times$
$(1.06) \times (1.06) \times (1.06) = 1.419$

12.2 *1. Present value (PV) at Time 0 of £1 at the end of year 3 at a discount rate of 2%*

$$PV = £1 \times \frac{1}{(1.02)^3}$$

$$\text{Discounting factor} = \frac{1}{(1.02)} \times \frac{1}{(1.02)} \times \frac{1}{(1.02)} = 0.942$$

2. Present value (PV) at Time 0 of £1 at the end of year 5 at a discount rate of 4%

$$PV = £1 \times \frac{1}{(1.04)^5}$$

$$\text{Discounting factor} = \frac{1}{(1.04)} \times \frac{1}{(1.04)} \times \frac{1}{(1.04)} \times \frac{1}{(1.04)} \times \frac{1}{(1.04)} = 0.822$$

3. Present value (PV) at Time 0 of £1 at the end of year 2 at a discount rate of 9%

$$PV = £1 \times \frac{1}{(1.09)^2}$$

$$\text{Discounting factor} = \frac{1}{(1.09)} \times \frac{1}{(1.09)} = 0.842$$

CHAPTER 13

13.1 Statements 1, 3 and 4 are TRUE

Statement 2 is FALSE

13.2 The divisional management of Beta appears to have considerable autonomy over its operations, including control over investment strategy. This indicates that Beta is an investment centre.

13.3 In any business, appropriate non-financial measures of success are those that relate to the overall business strategy. There is a contradiction hidden in HB's business objective: it wants to lead the market, which implies a greater market share than its competitors. On the other hand, it also aims to provide exclusive products, that is luxury products that people can own, safe in the knowledge that they belong to an elite. This contradiction epitomises the luxury goods business. Of the five performance indicators listed, all except the fifth are likely to be appropriate.

Market share (1) and sales volume (3) relate directly to the strategic objective of leading the market. Defective product items (2) relates to the objective of supplying high quality items. Customer perceptions of exclusivity (4) again links directly to the business strategy. However, competitive pricing (5) is not really an issue. In the luxury goods business, the perception of exclusivity is assisted by high prices. The higher the price, the greater is the customer's perception of exclusivity.

Answers to exercises

CHAPTER 1

1.1   The only correct statement is c): the sole trader is entirely responsible for the management of the business.

1.2   The only correct statement is d): partners are personally liable for the debts of the business.

1.3   The only correct statement is a): a limited company is a separate person in law.

1.4   Out of those listed the most appropriate form of finance for purchasing a new office building is a ten-year mortgage loan. The correct answer, therefore, is a).

1.5   Out of those listed, the most appropriate form of finance for the new office photocopier is a lease. The correct answer, therefore, is c).

1.6   *Advice to Arnold Tapwood:* It is not difficult to set up in partnership. By contrast with the establishment of a limited company, there is no requirement to submit information to the authorities. However, the partners would be well advised to consider drawing up a partnership agreement, for which they would require legal advice. Although the provisions of the Partnership Act 1890 apply where there is no partnership agreement, in most circumstances it is preferable to have a formal agreement. This would cover areas such as profit-sharing and arrangements in the event of a dispute between the partners.

1.7   Geoffrey will probably find it difficult to finance this business start-up because of its risky nature. He appears to be quite sure that lots of people will want to pay a subscription to his website, but he appears to have nothing but optimism to support this view. It is highly unlikely that a bank would be at all interested in making a loan in the circumstances.

   Geoffrey has no existing resources to draw upon and his family have refused to put money into the business. It is remotely possible that grant finance might be available from a specialist organisation, and Geoffrey should explore this avenue. A further possibility is to join forces in partnership with another dangerous sports enthusiast who does have some resources to draw upon.

   This appears to be a business proposition that will be very difficult to finance. If Geoffrey cannot find a business partner who is prepared to put some money into the venture, he may have to shelve the idea for the time being. If he gets a job, pays off his debts and saves some cash he might be able to finance the start-up himself at some point in the future.

CHAPTER 2   **2.1**   Erika: The main points for the business plan, and the related questions, are as follows:

Description of the service to be offered
Is the service highly specialised, or is it a more general design service? For example, the design services offered may be principally focused on, say, company identity and logo designs, or alternatively upon graphic input into advertising material. Or, Erika may be planning to cover a broad range of services, depending upon her talents and interests.

Market for the service
- Who will be the principal customers for the services offered?
- Has Erika investigated the market by carrying out any market research?
- Who are the principal competitors? Are they well established?
- How difficult will it be to break into the market for design services?

Profile of Erika
This will include training and education, relevant experience, age, an analysis of personal strengths and weaknesses, and a current portfolio of her best work.
- Does Erika have the appropriate profile of experience for the work she is planning to do?
- Is her portfolio up to date and does it contain examples of the type of work she will be undertaking to provide as a self-employed designer?

Initial investment required
This will be a particularly important section if Erika is planning to borrow money. Has she prepared a plan of her expenditure and income in the first year to 18 months following her business start-up? Relevant expenditure will probably include the following:
- office rental and business rates
- utilities bills (water, electricity, phone)
- advertising and marketing
- office equipment and computer
- insurance.

Also, how will Erika support herself in the early months of her new business? In this type of business, Erika will need to find the work, do it, submit it and then invoice the client. Under normal commercial arrangements payment will follow about a month later. So, there is a time lag of up to several months between initially being commissioned for the work and finally receiving payment. In the meantime, Erika needs to live off something, and this element must be built into her initial plans.

Detailed financial projections
If Erika is looking for business start-up finance she will need to prepare detailed financial projections in the form of a budget, showing the projected profit and loss and cash flow in the business. Once the business starts she will need to keep

business accounting records and submit tax returns. She may need to register for VAT.

- Does Erika have financial management or accountancy skills?
- Will she need an accountant to provide accountancy and tax advice?

Other issues

Will any other professional services be required in the first year or so of the business? For example, Erika may need legal advice in negotiating a lease on her office. Is Erika planning to employ any staff?

2.2 There are several risks attached to Ben's business start up plan:

Risk of not obtaining work

Although Ben has a good contact list, they have all been made through Amis & Lovett, his employers. Much will depend on whether or not any of Amis & Lovett's existing clients will give their work to Ben's agency. If their relationship with Amis & Lovett is good, and they are satisfied with the work, they may be quite happy to stay with the larger agency. However, if they want to stay with Ben, they may be prepared to move their work to his new agency. Ben is taking a big risk.

Risk of running out of money

Even if the work does follow Ben, the nature of the type of service he offers means that he will not start receiving payment for his work for quite some time. He has £45 000 which sounds like a lot, but this may not keep him going for very long. If he has not already done so, he needs to make a realistic plan so that he can budget for the first year or so of his new business.

Risk of employing people

Ben is taking a risk by employing people straight away. He may not have enough work to justify employing anybody in the early months of the business. His employees will expect to be paid at the end of month, whether or not Ben has much work. He would probably be well advised to get the work first, and then employ staff.

CHAPTER 3

3.1 *Nancy*: As regards costs, because there is sufficient space for another person to work on the premises, there will be no significant additional premises costs involved. There will be a small additional cost in consumables such as hair products and electricity, but the main cost will be in paying the salary of the new stylist, plus any additional administrative costs. Nancy already employs one person, so presumably she or her accountant already operates a payroll system that makes sure that the employee and the Inland Revenue are paid the correct amount.

There are two main risks:

1. That there will not be sufficient extra business to keep the new stylist busy. Employing another person does not make financial sense unless the new employee can generate enough additional business to cover the costs of employing him or her;

2.   That the new stylist will prove to be unsatisfactory in some way. Perhaps there will be personality clashes with Nancy or with the customers, or perhaps he or she will not produce work of sufficient competence. An employee who turns up late, or not at all, or who is unpleasant to clients will create problems.

As regards benefits, if the appointment of a new stylist turns out well, there could be two main benefits for Nancy and her business:

1.   Additional profits could be generated that would increase Nancy's wealth. She could either draw down more money from the business or could invest the profits in further expansion, perhaps by moving to larger premises and employing more staff.

2.   The range of services offered could be expanded and improved.

3.2   Oleander Enterprises Limited

Buying into another business
Buying into another company may be advantageous because Libby and Lisa will be buying up an established business with employees who have knowledge of holiday operations in Turkey. They will not need to start from scratch in finding out about a new country. However, Oxus Orlando is, essentially, a service business which is very dependent upon the quality of its employees. Loretta, the main director, plans to retire, so her expertise will be lost. If the key employees also choose to leave, there may not be much value left in the company, and Libby and Lisa may find out that they have paid too much for the investment.

Information needed
Libby and Lisa need to know:

■ The price of the investment in Oxus Orlando, which Loretta wishes to sell. (Note that Libby and Lisa would almost certainly need to have the investment independently valued.)

■ What they would get in exchange for the investment (for example, does the business own its own premises?).

■ How profitable Oxus Orlando is (they will be able to ascertain this information from the business's annual accounts).

■ Details about the employees of the business. How much are they paid, how long have they been in their current jobs and how likely is it that they will stay if the company changes ownership?

CHAPTER 4   **4.1**   Ashton Longton plc: The company has 8 000 000 shares in issue, each valued at £3.85. Market capitalisation is 8 000 000 × £3.85 = £30 800 000.

4.2   The Alternative Investment Market is a market for companies that do not currently wish to proceed to full listing. The correct answer, therefore, is a).

4.3   The rights issue gives the holder of 50 000 shares the right to buy 50 000/5 shares = 10 000 shares. Each new share costs £5.42, so the total amount payable to take up the rights is: 10 000 × £5.42 = £54 200. The correct answer, therefore, is c). (Note that if the issued share capital is £3 000 000 denominated in 50p shares, the total number of shares in issue is 6 000 000. The shareholder in this question holds 50 000 shares of 50p each.)

4.4 Brighton Bestwines plc: Potential drawbacks of quotation on the Alternative Investment Market include:

1. Additional regulation applies to quoted companies; for example, they have to produce additional published financial reports. The additional compliance costs often involve employing more staff to deal with the extra requirements.

2. Although the company could raise the capital it needs, there will be legal and other professional fees involved. These are likely to be around 10% of the amount raised. This means that, for every share sold at the target price of £2.50, approximately 25p will be spent on fees. The percentage could be even higher.

3. Many directors are uncomfortable with the additional attention paid to quoted companies by the media. They may have to start meeting journalists, and there may be additional costs involved if professional public relations advice is required. (Tutorial note: AIM quoted companies are generally subject to rather less attention than companies with a full listing, but financial journalists will obviously take some interest when things go wrong.)

4. The company's share price may fluctuate for reasons that are difficult to explain (because they are related to general market sentiment, or the unpopularity of the industry sector to which the company belongs, for example).

5. There is a potential drawback in allowing other parties to buy shares in that the company may lay itself open to takeover bids. However, in this case the shares issued for sale will amount to only one-third of the total share capital, so the company will be safe from takeover unless and until it issues more shares for sale.

CHAPTER 5

5.1 The only correct statement is d): a sole trader must submit a tax return annually.

5.2 The only correct statement is b): a limited company must send annual accounts to all of its shareholders.

5.3 Podgorny & Weaver Limited

List of amounts owed by retail businesses
The directors would be able to see if any of the retailers owed very large amounts. If, in addition, the list contained details of the length of time the amounts had been outstanding, the directors would also be able to see if the amounts owing were significantly overdue for payment.

Summary of the value of goods held in stock
It is important for a fashion goods business not to carry excessive stocks of goods that may be about to go out of fashion. The business will lose money if the stock cannot be sold. The directors need this statement to assess the risk of having excess stocks.

Summary of the value of orders received in the last month
The directors need to assess whether the orders received meet their expectations. If the value of orders received is less than expected, the directors need to take action to address the problem.

Profit and loss account for the last month
The directors will be able to assess the performance of the business compared to their expectations, and perhaps, compared to the same month in the previous financial year.

5.4 Burnip Chemicals plc: the activist group would probably be looking for the following types of information:

- Details about the amounts of emissions.
- Details of the sums the company has paid in fines.
- Details of plans for improvements to the factory that will minimise the emission of toxic waste.

A company's financial statements contain principally information about the financial performance and condition of the business. Details about the amounts of emissions during the year are not financial items, and it is quite possible that the company would make no reference to the matter.

The amount of fines paid might be evident from the financial statements. However, the expenses listed in the profit and loss account are summarised information (it would not be feasible to list each individual payment), and the amount paid in fines might well not be evident. Details of planned improvements, similarly, may not be evident from the financial statements. Although annual financial statements can be of interest to activist groups, they do not necessarily provide a full picture. (Tutorial note: some companies voluntarily publish information about their environmental policies and performance in addition to their financial statements, but they are not obliged by law to do this.)

Note: the answers to the Chapter 6 questions are guidelines only. There are many relevant points that could be made in respect of each of the questions, and they may not all be included in the answers given below.

CHAPTER 6 **6.1** Cueline Limited's directors are looking at two options: renewal of the lease and purchase of freehold premises. They need to examine projected financial information for both options in order to ensure that they reach the right decision.

Renewal of the lease
The following items of information would be useful:

- The estimated cost of any lease premium (a lease premium is a capital sum payable at the outset of a lease).

- The regular annual rental and any service charges that will have to be paid over the lease term.

- If a large sum has to be paid at the outset of the lease, the directors need to examine financing options. Does Cueline Limited have the cash available? Will it need to borrow? If it does have the cash available are there better uses to which the cash can be put?

- If a loan has to be taken out, how much will the regular charge for interest be?

Purchase of freehold premises

The directors need to identify a range of possible properties for purchase by contacting local commercial agents. By doing this they will be able to estimate an approximate capital outlay for the purchase. They need to plan any necessary financing for the purchase, taking into consideration the following points:

- Will a mortgage loan be available for this type of property?

- What effect will a loan have on the company's gearing?

- How much will the regular charge for interest be?

- What are the implications of the loan and interest repayments for the company's cash flow?

6.2 Putt plc's directors need to make a thorough assessment of the consequences of a change in strategy. They should obtain information on the following:

- The state of the market for golf-related items and the outlook for sales over the next few years. This may involve commissioning specific market research.

- An estimate of the impact of the change on the future performance of the company. How profitable is the company likely to be in the future? Will future performance be an improvement on past performance? How big a difference will the change in strategy make?

- An assessment of the competition. How successful have competitor businesses been in obtaining market share? Are there any new entrants to the market who are likely to pose a threat to Putt plc?

- The likely effects of the proposed change on the need for selling space. Would the existing shops expand their range of golf-related items if more space were to be made available? Would shops need to move (for example, nearer to golf courses)? Are there any implications for staffing (for example, would some staff need to be made redundant)?

- Disposal of existing non-golf stock items. Would these items need to be sold quickly, and would they have to be sold at a loss? If so, what is the projected effect on the company's profit and loss account?

6.3 Bulstrode, Barker and Bennett

a) Employing a new solicitor in the conveyancing department
The obvious financial impact of employing another member of staff is the cost of the salary, plus other costs such as employer's national insurance, employer's contributions to the pension scheme (if any) and any other incidental costs of employment such as health benefits. It would appear to make sense to employ another person if the department's income would, in consequence, increase by enough to cover the additional costs, and the partners would require information about the effect on both income and costs.

However, there are other relevant considerations. If the conveyancing department is genuinely short-staffed, either or both of the following effects could occur:

- Existing staff will be overworked and may become disgruntled. If sufficiently dissatisfied they may seek to change employment.

- There might be an adverse effect on quality. If a serious mistake is made in conveyancing, the firm could lay itself open to legal action, or to criticism from regulators. If it acts inefficiently in dealing with clients' business, the consequence could be a loss of reputation. Prospective clients may take their business elsewhere.

b) Employing a specialist divorce solicitor
This involves a significant strategic decision. The existing partners will seek information on:

- The likely cost of bringing in another partner. The new partner would be entitled to a share of the profits of the business, although this could be made dependent upon performance to some extent. She would also expect the same range of benefits (health benefits, pension scheme and so on) as the existing partners. There would, presumably, also be other knock-on effects on staffing (for example, she would almost certainly need some secretarial assistance).

- The expected benefits in terms of increased fees. How much extra business could a divorce specialist be expected to generate? Would she be able to contribute any capital to the business?

- How many solicitors experienced in divorce law actually operate in the area? Is there really a gap in the market for another one? Are there any cross-selling opportunities (for example, people who are getting a divorce often sell joint property, and there may be new opportunities for generating extra conveyancing work)?

- It is important that partners (as joint proprietors of a business) are able to agree among themselves. Would the proposed new partner be an easy person to work with?

CHAPTER 7   **7.1**   Paige Peverell plc

Expense	Classification
Plastic moulding machine depreciation	Indirect production overheads
Sales office fixtures and fittings depreciation	Other indirect overheads
Plastic materials	Direct materials
Advertising expenditure	Other indirect overheads
Depreciation of factory building	Indirect production overheads
Electricity bill for factory	Indirect production overheads
Wages of assembly line workers	Direct labour
Wages of factory canteen staff	Indirect production overheads
Wages of assembly line supervisor	Indirect production overheads
Secretary's salary	Other indirect overheads
Delivery vehicle depreciation	Other indirect overheads
Factory consumables	Indirect production overheads
Royalty payable per item produced to telephone designer	Direct expenses
Mobile phone bill – sales director	Other indirect overheads

7.2

ArtKit Supplies Limited: Cost statement for the year ending
31 August 20X3

	£	£
Direct materials		
Metal	18 006	
Lacquer paint	1 600	
Hinge fittings	960	
		20 566
Direct labour		
Machine operators' wages	18 250	
Finishing operative's wages	10 270	
		28 520
Prime cost		49 086
Production overheads		
Rental of factory	6 409	
Machine repair	176	
Depreciation – machinery	1 080	
Electricity – factory	1 760	
Factory cleaning	980	
Sundry factory costs	2 117	
		12 522
Production cost		61 608
Other overheads		
Secretarial and administration salaries	12 460	
Salesman's salary	18 740	

	£	£
Office supplies	2 411	
Office telephone	1 630	
Sundry office costs	904	
Delivery costs	1 920	
		38 065
Total costs		99 673

7.3 Because Porter Farrington adopts a FIFO policy for stock valuation, the 40 items left in stock at the end of May 20X4 are deemed to be those most recently delivered. The most recent delivery before the end of the month was the 50 items delivered on 2 May at a cost of £3.30 per unit. The correct valuation is, therefore:

$$40 \text{ units @ } £3.30 = £132.00$$

The correct answer, therefore, is d).

7.4 Clement
Total prime cost:

Job No: 3223; 12 dining chairs	£	£
Direct materials		
Mahogany: 18 @ £36	648.00	
Seat padding: 12 @ £3.50	42.00	
Leather cloth: 6 metres @ £42.00 per m.	252.00	
		942.00
Direct labour		
Grade 1: 115 hours @ £8.50	977.50	
Grade 2: 86 hours @ £9.25	795.50	
		1 773.00
Prime cost		2 715.00

The prime cost total for 12 dining chairs is £2715. The prime cost per chair is:

$$\frac{£2\ 715}{12} = £226.25$$

7.5 Jersey Brookfield & Co. Limited: Apportionment of production overheads for the year ending 31 December 20X2

	Basis	Total £	Bulk production £	Packaging £
			Cost Centre	
Factory building depreciation	Floor area	5 670	3 240	2 430
Factory rates	Floor area	11 970	6 840	5 130
Factory insurance	Floor area	7 980	4 560	3 420
Canteen costs	No. employees	18 876	8 580	10 296
Supervisory salaries	No. employees	29 480	13 400	16 080
Other indirect labour	Machinery NBV	18 275	12 410	5 865
Machinery depreciation	Machinery NBV	21 500	14 600	6 900
Cleaning	Floor area	17 850	10 200	7 650
Electricity	Actual	30 290	18 790	11 500
Building maintenance	Floor area	5 040	2 880	2 160
		166 931	95 500	71 431

7.6 *i) Overhead absorption rate based on direct labour hours*

Each unit uses one hour of direct labour; production of 60 000 units is planned, therefore 60 000 direct labour hours will be used.

$$\text{Overhead absorption rate} = \frac{218\ 000}{60\ 000} = \text{£3.63}$$

ii) Overhead absorption rate based on machine hours

Each unit uses 0.5 hours of machine time. Anticipated total machine time is, therefore, $60\ 000 \times 0.5 = 30\ 000$.

$$\text{Overhead absorption rate} = \frac{218\ 000}{30\ 000} = \text{£7.27}$$

iii) Overhead absorption rate based on units of production

$$\text{Overhead absorption rate} = \frac{218\ 000}{60\ 000} = \text{£3.63}$$

(i.e. the same rate as calculated on the basis of direct labour hours).

7.7   Washington and Middlewich Limited

Totals for direct materials based on production of 6 000 of each product

	£
Metal machining department	
Domestic shelves: £18.00 × 6 000	108 000
Commercial shelves: £27.00 × 6 000	162 000
	270 000
Painting and finishing department	
Domestic shelves: £3.30 × 6 000	19 800
Commercial shelves: £4.60 × 6 000	27 600
	47 400

Totals for direct labour based on production of 6 000 of each product

	£
Metal machining department	
Domestic shelves: 0.75 × £6 × 6 000	27 000
Commercial shelves: 1 × £6 × 6 000	36 000
	63 000
Painting and finishing dept	
Domestic shelves: 1 × £6 × 6 000	36 000
Commercial shelves: 1.5 × £6 × 6 000	54 000
	90 000

i) Overhead absorption rates based on % of direct materials

$$\text{Metal machining department} = \frac{172\ 490}{270\ 000} = 63.9\%$$

$$\text{Painting and finishing department} = \frac{116\ 270}{47\ 400} = 245.3\%$$

ii) Overhead absorption rates based on % of direct labour

$$\text{Metal machining department} = \frac{172\ 490}{63\ 000} = 273.8\%$$

$$\text{Painting and finishing department} = \frac{116\ 270}{90\ 000} = 129.2\%$$

Materials are relatively much more significant than labour hours in the machining department. Therefore, it would probably make sense to use an overhead absorption rate based on the % of direct materials consumed.

By contrast, in the painting and finishing department, direct labour is relatively more important than the input of materials. Therefore, it would probably make sense to use an overhead absorption rate based on the % of direct materials consumed.

Because the machining department probably involves use of a relatively high level of machine hours, it may be worth considering the calculation of an overhead absorption rate based on machine hours.

CHAPTER 8

8.1 Subject: Summary of the benefits of effective budgeting
To: the directors of Brewster Fitzpayne Limited
From: Management accountant

A budgeting system assists senior management in its tasks of planning and controlling business activity by ensuring that a detailed plan is laid out and quantified for a specified period (usually one year). The budget should help the company to attain its longer-term objectives, and it is important to ensure that there is a clear relationship between the budget and the longer-term business strategy determined by the directors.

Budgets allow for coordinated efforts on the part of all personnel and departments. Once the key elements of the budget have been determined (usually starting with the sales budget) budget guidelines can be issued to all departments and managerial staff. They will then be required to submit draft budgets for their own areas. Senior management must then ensure that these drafts are amended where necessary to ensure proper coordination of plans. Senior staff have an overview of the business objectives and should be able to ensure that individual budgets mesh together to achieve optimal outcomes.

If properly used, budgets can inspire and motivate staff to greater efforts. It is important that staff lower down the hierarchy feel a sense of 'ownership' of the budget so that they will be more inclined to make the extra effort to achieve targets.

It is important to ensure that actual business performance is monitored carefully against budget. If this is done properly and on a timely basis, senior managers are able to control operations much more effectively than is possible without a budget. Timely and effective control allows for higher quality decision making.

Finally, it is possible to use budgets as a basis for individual and group performance evaluation. For example, sales staff could be rewarded by means of bonuses or extra commission for exceeding budget targets. This use of budgets must be handled carefully, however. If targets for achievement are set too high then dissatisfaction and demotivation may well result.

8.2 Buckle Purslane Limited. The forecast for opening stock at 1 March 20X7 is 75% of forecast sales in March:

$$75\% \times 12\,000 \text{ units} = 9000 \text{ units}$$

The forecast for closing stock at 31 March 20X7 is 75% of forecast sales in April:

$$75\% \times 14\,800 \text{ units} = 11\,100 \text{ units}.$$

Transfers out of finished goods stock will be 12 000 units in March (i.e. the quantity sold), so production required is:

	£
Opening stock	9 000
Production (bal. fig)	14 100
Transfers out of stock	(12 000)
Closing stock	11 100

The correct answer, therefore, is b).

8.3 Luminant Productions Limited

a) Production budget July–September 20X6

	Opening stock: units	Production: units	Transfers out of production (for sales): units	Closing stock: units
July	6 000	8 100	(8 600)	5 500
August	5 500	7 700	(8 200)	5 000
September	5 000	8 500	(9 000)	4 500

b) Raw materials purchases budget: July–September 20X6

Closing stock + Raw materials used in production – Opening stock
= Raw materials purchases

	Opening stock of raw material £	Purchases of raw materials £ (bal. fig.)	Raw materials used in production £	Closing stock of raw material £
July	2 800	16 400	£2 × 8 100 = (£16 200)	3 000
August	3 000	15 500	£2 × 7 700 = (£15 400)	3 100
September	3 100	17 100	£2 × 8 500 = (£17 000)	3 200

8.4 Barfield Primrose Limited
Budget overhead recovery rate, based on machine hours:

$$\frac{\text{Budget production overheads}}{\text{Machine hours}} = \frac{312\ 390}{17\ 355} = £18.00 \text{ per machine hour}$$

The total production cost of one ice cream maker is, therefore:

	£
Prime cost	61.00
1.5 machine hours × £18.00 per hour	27.00
Production cost	88.00

Barfield Primrose Limited: Budgeted profit and loss account for three months ending 31 March 20X2

	Jan £	Feb £	Mar £
Sales	620 × £145 = 89 900	610 × £145 = 88 450	640 × £145 = 92 800
Cost of sales (= production cost)	620 × £88 = (54 560)	610 × £88 = (53 680)	640 × £88 = (56 320)
Gross profit	35 340	34 770	36 480
Admin and selling expenses	(18 400)	(19 250)	(18 900)
Net profit	16 940	15 520	17 580

8.5 In February Reinhart's budget sales receipts will be estimated as follows:

	£
In respect of sales made in January: 75% × £21 000	15 750
In respect of sales made in December: 25% × £26 800	6 700
Total	22 450

The correct answer, therefore, is c).

8.6 Skippy's tour operating business

i) Budget cash flow

Skippy: Budget cash flow statement for January–March 20X4

	January £	February £	March £	Total £
Receipts				
Trip 1	25 440	—	—	25 440
Trip 2	—	25 440	—	25 440
Total receipts	25 440	25 440	—	50 880
Payments				
Hotel: Trip 1	7 140	7 140	—	14 280
Trip 2	—	7 140	7 140	14 280
Coach	2 600	2 600	—	5 200
Insurance bond: 2 × £1 500	3 000	—	—	3 000
Phone bill	—	—	360	360
Office expenses	200	200	200	600
Total payments	12 940	17 080	7 700	37 720
Opening balance	0	12 500	20 860	
Add: receipts	25 440	25 440	—	
Less: payments	(12 940)	(17 080)	(7 700)	
Closing balance	12 500	20 860	13 160	

ii) Budget profit and loss

Skippy: Budget profit and loss account for the three months ending 31 March 20X4

	£
Sales	50 880
Expenses	
Hotel costs (£14 280 × 2)	28 560
Coach	5 200
Insurance bonds	3 000
Phone	360
Office costs	600
Advertising	3 000
Computer depreciation: £2 000 × 20%	
= 400 – for 3 months = £100	100
	40 820
Net profit	10 060

iii) Budget balance sheet

Skippy: Budget balance sheet at 31 March 20X4

	£
Computer at cost	2 000
Less: accumulated depreciation	(100)
Net book value	1 900
Cash at bank	13 160
	15 060
Capital introduced	5 000
Profit	10 060
	15 060

Note that capital introduced by Skippy consists of the advertising expenditure paid for before January 20X4 (£3000) and the computer (£2000).

8.7 Skippy's tour operating business

Working 1: Actual sales

	£
Trip 1: 42 × £530	22 260
Trip 2: 50 × £530	26 500
	48 760

Working 2: Hotel costs

	£
Trip 1: 42 × 7 nights × £42.50 per person	12 495
Trip 2: 50 × 7 nights × £42.50 per person	14 875
	27 370

Skippy: Actual and budgeted profit and loss account for the three months ending 31 March 20X4

	Actual £	Budget £	Variance* £
Sales (working 1)	48 760	50 880	(2 120)
Expenses			
Hotel costs (working 2)	27 370	28 560	1 190
Coach	5 200	5 200	—
Insurance bonds	3 000	3 000	—
Phone	455	360	(95)
Office costs (£230 + £350 + £270)	850	600	(250)
Advertising	3 000	3 000	—
Computer depreciation: £2000 × 20% = 400 – for 3 months = £100	100	100	—
	39 975	40 820	845
Net profit	8 785	10 060	(1 275)

* Variance is the term used in costing for differences between actual and budget figures. Adverse variances are shown in brackets in the comparison and favourable variances are shown without brackets. Variances are examined in more detail in Chapter 10.

Skippy: Actual and budgeted balance sheet at 31 March 20X4

	Actual £	Budget £
Computer at cost	2 000	2 000
Less: accumulated depreciation	(100)	(100)
Net book value	1 900	1 900
Cash at bank (see working 3)	11 885	13 160
	13 785	15 060
Capital introduced	5 000	5 000
Profit	8 785	10 060
	13 785	15 060

Working 3: Actual cash at bank

	£	£
Receipts (same as sales revenue)		48 760
Payments	39 975	
Less: depreciation (non-cash item)	(100)	
Less: advertising paid for by Skippy	(3 000)	
		(36 875)
		11 885

Overall, Skippy's business has performed slightly worse than budget: actual sales are 95.8% of budget, but there has been a related saving on hotel costs which helps to offset the variance. Office and telephone costs are higher than budgeted. However, overall, the differences are fairly minor and Skippy is likely to be quite pleased with his first three months in business.

CHAPTER 9   **9.1**   Denholm Pargeter Limited

March 20X1: Budget for XP04/H flexed for 1300 units

	£
Sales: 1 300 unit × £30 per unit	39 000
Costs	
Direct materials: 1 300 units × (3kg × £1.20)	4 680
Direct labour: 1 300 units × (2 hours × £8.50)	22 100
Prime cost	26 780

9.2   Darblay Harriett Limited

November 20X9: Budget flexed for 2600 units

	£
Sales: 2 600 units × £19.50	50 700
Costs	
Direct materials: 2 600 × (2 metres × £2.00)	(10 400)
Direct labour: 2 600 × (1 hour × £6.00)	(15 600)
Production overhead	(10 000)
	14 700
Selling and administrative overhead	(3 000)
Net profit	11 700

The correct answer, therefore, is c).

Edwards and Sheerness Limited: General information for the answers to questions 9.3 to 9.8

The flexed budget for 2650 units is as follows:

	£
Sales: 2 650 units × £29.00	76 850
Costs	
Direct materials: 2 650 × (3 kg × £3.00)	(23 850)
Direct labour: 2 650 × (1.5 hours × £4.40)	(17 490)
Production overhead	(17 000)
	18 510
Other overheads	(3 500)
Net profit	15 010

Comparison of original budget, flexed budget and actual:

	Original budget £	Flexed budget £	Actual £
Sales	72 500	76 850	74 200
Costs			
Direct materials	(22 500)	(23 850)	(24 486)
Direct labour	(16 500)	(17 490)	(18 921)
Production overhead	(17 000)	(17 000)	(16 900)
	16 500	18 510	13 893
Other overheads	(3 500)	(3 500)	(3 600)
Net profit	13 000	15 010	10 293

9.3 Sales profit volume variance

	£
Flexed budget net profit	15 010
Original budget net profit	13 000
	2 010 (F)

The correct answer, therefore, is d).

9.4 Sales price variance

	£
Actual volume of sales at actual selling price: 2 650 × £28	74 200
Actual volume of sales at standard selling price: 2 650 × £29	76 850
	2 650 (A)

The correct answer, therefore, is d).

9.5 Direct materials price variance

	£
Actual quantity of materials used at actual price: 2 650 × 2.8kg = 7 420 × £3.30	24 486
Actual quantity of materials used at standard price: 7 420 × £3.00	22 260
	2 226 (A)

The correct answer, therefore, is b).

9.6 Direct materials quantity variance

	£
Actual quantity of materials used at standard price: 7 420 × £3.00	22 260
Standard quantity of materials used at standard price: 2 650 × 3.0kg = 7 950 × £3.00	23 850
	1 590 (F)

The correct answer, therefore, is c).

9.7   Direct labour rate variance

	£
Actual hours at actual wage rate: 2 650 × 1.7 hours	
= 4 505 × £4.20	18 921
Actual hours at standard wage rate: 4 505 × £4.40	19 822
	901 (F)

The correct answer, therefore, is d).

9.8   Direct labour efficiency variance

	£
Actual hours at standard wage rate: 4 505 × £4.40	19 822
Standard hours at standard wage rate: 2 650 × 1.5 hours	
= 3 975 × £4.40	17 490
	2 332 (A)

The correct answer, therefore, is b).

9.9   Ferguson Farrar Limited

a) Variable production overhead variance

	£
Actual variable production overhead	26 250
Flexed budget variable production overhead	25 200
	1 050 (A)

b) Fixed production overhead variance

	£
Actual fixed production overhead	48 750
Flexed budget fixed production overhead	50 400
	1 650 (F)

9.10   Grindleton Gears Limited

i) Significant variances
The variances that are regarded as significant according to the company's 5% criterion are:

■ Direct materials price variance (£1650 (A): 5.8% of flexed budget).

■ Variable production overhead variance (£1400 (F): 16.2% of flexed budget).

ii) Possible reasons for the variances

■ Direct materials price variance
  - successful negotiation for lower prices
  - obtaining quantity discounts for large orders
  - variation in material quality
  - volatile market for material, leading to unexpected increases or decreases in price.
■ Variable production overhead variance

- price changes because of events in the wider economy
- improved management control over costs.

It is also possible in this case (the variance being so large) that some items of expense have simply gone unrecorded.

iii) Actual figures

Actual costs can be derived from the information given by adding the flexible budget amount to the variances, as follows:

	£
Sales: £123 470 + £1 030	124 500
Direct materials: £28 250 + £1 650 + £106	(30 006)
Direct labour: £29 900 – £200	(29 700)
Variable production overheads: £8 640 – £1 400	(7 240)
Fixed production overheads: £19 780 – £339	(19 441)
Actual profit	38 113

CHAPTER 10   **10.1** Billericay Ashworth Limited

i) Cost classification
The cost of raw materials is a variable cost; the cost of factory insurance is a fixed cost; telephone charges are a semi-variable cost.

ii) Graphs
For the graph of raw materials cost, two points are plotted:

- cost of raw materials at zero production: £0

- cost of raw materials at 3000 production level: 3000 × £13 = £39 000.

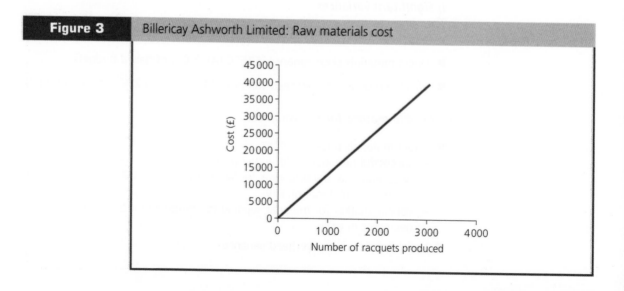

| **Figure 3** | Billericay Ashworth Limited: Raw materials cost |

For the graph of factory insurance, two points are plotted:

- cost of factory insurance at zero production level: £800
- cost of factory insurance at 3000 production level: £800.

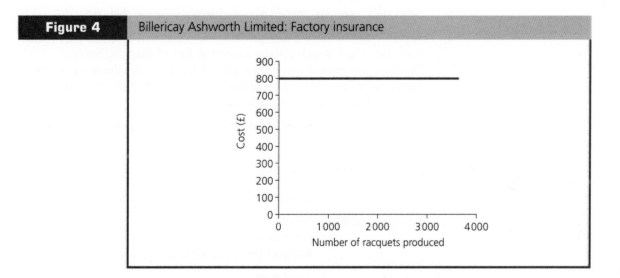

Figure 4 Billericay Ashworth Limited: Factory insurance

For the graph of telephone charges, three points are plotted:

- Telephone charges where no calls made: £1000 (i.e. basic rental charge).

- Telephone charges where 500 calls are made: £1250 (i.e. basic rental charge of £1000 + £250 in call charges).

- Telephone charges where 1000 calls are made: £1500 (i.e. basic rental charge of £1000 + £500 in call charges).

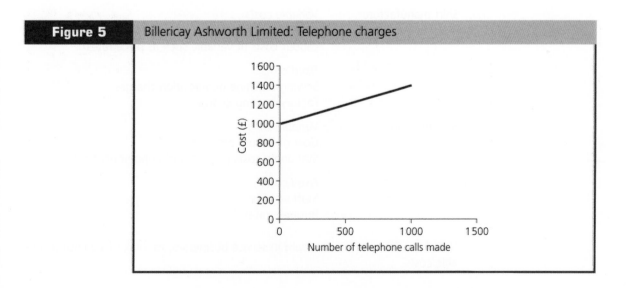

Figure 5 Billericay Ashworth Limited: Telephone charges

Note that the activity level in this case is the number of calls made: we have no information that links call charges with the level of production or any other measurement of activity.

10.2 Cost classification

i)   Sales staff members' mobile phone charges: semi-variable cost.

ii) Factory machine oil: it depends! This would probably be a relatively minor cost and would, in practice, be treated as part of fixed factory costs. However, the more the machines are used, presumably the more oil they consume, so it could be argued that this cost is variable with production. It would depend upon the particular circumstances.

iii) Metered water charges: this is a variable cost based upon the number of units consumed.

10.3 Examples of fixed and variable costs

Type of business	Examples of fixed and variable costs
Self-employed taxi driver	*Variable costs* Petrol or diesel Replacement parts for cab *Fixed costs* Accountancy and tax advisory charges Cab licence
Solicitor	*Variable costs* Stationery costs (e.g. files for holding documents) Overtime payments to staff called out to attend clients in police custody *Fixed costs* Rental of office premises Employment costs of secretarial staff
Shirt manufacturer	*Variable costs* Cost of shirt material Labour costs (if variable such as piece rates) *Fixed costs* Sewing machine depreciation charges Factory heating charges
Beauty salon	*Variable costs* Cost of beauty products Stationery costs (e.g. cost of appointment cards) *Fixed costs* Staff salaries Business rates

Note how difficult it is, especially in service businesses, to think of significant variable costs.

10.4 Porton Fitzgerald Limited

Porton Fitzgerald Limited: Budget statement for April 20X4

	£
Sales: 450 wardrobes × £210 each	94 500
Variable costs	
Direct materials: 450 wardrobes × £52	(23 400)
Direct labour: 450 wardrobes × £34	(15 300)
Contribution	55 800
Fixed costs	(43 200)
Net profit	12 600

10.5 Fullbright Bognor Limited

i) Break-even chart
For the break-even chart for the year ending 31 December 20X1 the points plotted are:

Production level	Fixed costs £	Total costs £	Total revenue £
0	62 000	62 000	0
3 000	62 000	185 000	255 000
		(£62 000 in fixed costs)	(3 000 × £85)
		+ [3 000 × £41]	

ii) Break-even point estimates
Reading from the chart, the break-even point in units lies somewhere between 1000 and 2000 units, at around 1400 to 1500 units. The sales value appears to be around £120 000. (Note: the larger the scale chosen for the graph, the more accurate the estimate of break-even is likely to be.)

iii) Break-even points at end-December 20X1

	£
Selling price per unit	85.00
Variable costs per unit	41.00
Contribution per unit	44.00

$$\text{Break-even point (in units)} = \frac{\text{Fixed costs}}{\text{Contribution per unit}}$$

$$= \frac{62\ 000}{44.00} = 1409 \text{ units (to nearest whole unit)}$$

The break-even point in sales value = 1409 units × £85 = £119 765.

Figure 6	Fullbright Bognor Limited: Break-even chart

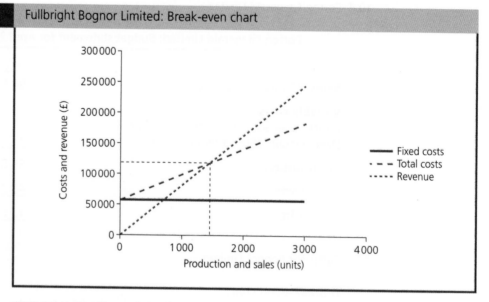

10.6 Foster Beniform Limited

a) Where fixed costs are £40 000

i) Break-even chart
For the break-even chart for 20X8 (fixed costs at £40 000) the points plotted are:

Production level	Fixed costs £	Total costs £	Total revenue £
0	40 000	40 000	0
2 000	40 000	90 000	110 000
		(£40 000 + [2 000 × £25])	(2 000 × £55)

ii) Break-even point estimates
Reading from the chart, the break-even point in units appears to be around 1300 units; the break-even point in sales value appears to be around £73 000.

iii) Formula calculations

	£
Selling price per unit	55.00
Variable costs per unit	25.00
Contribution per unit	30.00

$$\text{Break-even point (in units)} = \frac{\text{Fixed costs}}{\text{Contribution per unit}}$$

$$= \frac{40\ 000}{30.00} = 1333 \text{ units (to nearest whole unit)}$$

Break-even point in sales value = 1333 units × £55 = £73 315.

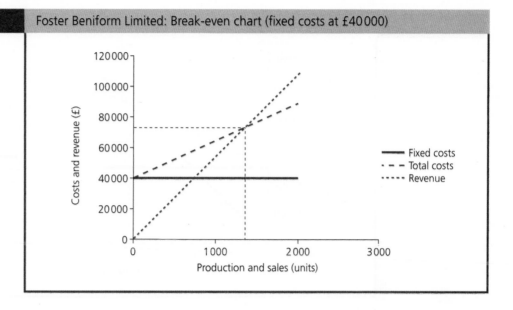

Figure 7   Foster Beniform Limited: Break-even chart (fixed costs at £40 000)

b) Where fixed costs are £50 000

i) Break-even chart
For the break-even chart for 20X8 (fixed costs at £50 000) the points plotted are:

Production level	Fixed costs £	Total costs £	Total revenue £
0	50 000	50 000	0
2 000	50 000	100 000	110 000
		(£50 000 + [2 000 × £25])	(2 000 × £55)

ii) Break-even point estimates
Reading from the chart, the break-even point in units appears to be around 1700 units; the break-even point in sales value appears to be around £90 000.

iii) Formula calculations

	£
Selling price per unit	55.00
Variable costs per unit	25.00
Contribution per unit	30.00

$$\text{Break-even point (in units)} = \frac{\text{Fixed costs}}{\text{Contribution per unit}}$$

$$= \frac{50\ 000}{30.00} = 1667 \text{ units (to nearest whole unit)}$$

Break-even point in sales value = 1667 units × £55 = £91 685.

| **Figure 8** | Foster Beniform Limited: Break-even chart (fixed costs at £50 000) |

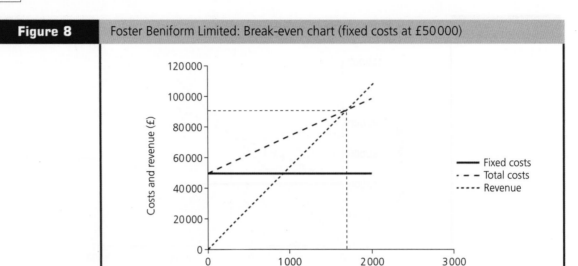

10.7 Gropius Maplewood Limited

	£
Selling price per unit	150
Variable costs per unit	(63)
Contribution per unit	87

$$\text{Break-even point (in units)} = \frac{\text{Fixed costs}}{\text{Contribution per unit}}$$

$$= \frac{90\ 000}{87} = 1034 \text{ units}$$

The correct answer, therefore, is d).

10.8 Gimball Grace Limited

Target net profit for 20X3: £36 500 × 110% = £40 150.

Contribution per unit = £21.00 (selling price) − £7.50 (variable costs) = £13.50.

$$\text{Target sales in units} = \frac{\text{Fixed costs} + \text{Target profit}}{\text{Contribution per unit}}$$

$$= \frac{54\ 000 + 40\ 150}{13.50} = 6\ 974 \text{ units}$$

The correct answer, therefore, is a).

10.9 Garbage Solutions Limited

Contribution calculation:

	£
Selling price per unit	25.00
Less: variable labour costs	(3.20)
Variable raw materials costs	(4.20)
Contribution per unit	17.60

$$\text{Break-even point} = \frac{\text{Fixed costs}}{\text{Contribution per unit}}$$

$$= \frac{178\ 900}{17.60} = 10\ 165 \text{ units}$$

$$\text{Target sales in units} = \frac{\text{Fixed costs} + \text{Target profit}}{\text{Contribution per unit}}$$

$$= \frac{178\ 900 + 83\ 150}{17.60} = 14\ 889$$

The margin of safety is the difference between target sales and break-even sales:

$$14\ 889 - 10\ 165 = 4724$$

The correct answer, therefore, is d).

10.10 Harrison Haworth Limited

The contribution per unit from the rucksack designed for the Moroccan market would be:

	£
Selling price per unit	50.00
Variable costs per unit	(26.30)
Contribution per unit	23.70

The contribution per unit is a positive figure, therefore the advice to management, based solely upon the accounting figures, would be to accept Raoul's order. This advice would be appropriate provided that spare production capacity was available and provided the level of fixed costs would not increase. What non-financial factors should be taken into consideration?

The sales of this special order are all to Morocco; therefore it is quite likely that UK and Scandinavian buyers would not find out that similar rucksacks were available at a substantially lower price. The fact that the specification is lower also helps; if UK or Scandinavian buyers were to ask why the rucksacks were priced so much lower in Morocco, it would be quite reasonable to point out that the product was of a different quality (although the difference in variable costs is only £2.70 between the two grades of product, suggesting that the quality difference is not very great).

Would the company suffer if it became known that it was offering a product of lesser quality? This is a factor that needs to be borne in mind by producers of high quality goods. However, as noted above, the quality differential is not likely to be very noticeable.

In the circumstances, the company should consider seriously accepting Raoul's order, although the sales director might like to investigate Raoul's assertions regarding the Moroccan market. Is it really true that there would be few buyers in Morocco at the company's normal prices? Or is Raoul just saying this to beat the company down on price?

10.11 Inez & Pilar Fashions Limited

Because fixed costs increase with the increase in production capacity, it is necessary to look at the level of incremental profits that could be made. We can examine these at two levels:

Optimistic incremental sales forecast

	£
Sales (£345 000 − 310 000)	35 000
Incremental variable costs: £35 000 × 30%	(10 500)
Incremental fixed costs	(15 000)
Incremental net profit	9 500

Pessimistic incremental sales forecast

	£
Sales	20 000
Incremental variable costs: £20 000 × 30%	(6 000)
Incremental fixed costs	(15 000)
Incremental net loss	(1 000)

Clearly, if the pessimistic forecast is accurate, a net loss will be incurred by expanding the production facilities. However, at most levels of incremental sales some profit would be made. Unless the directors are very averse to taking risks, and/or they feel that the pessimistic forecast is the most likely outcome, it is probably worth expanding production facilities.

Other factors to take into account would be:

■ Could the additional capacity be used to produce new product lines?

■ Is the current constraint on production capacity causing problems with customers? (If customers are becoming impatient because of delays in production there may be a loss of goodwill; this could be an argument in favour of expanding the facilities even if there is a small risk of an incremental loss.)

10.12 Juniper Jefferson Limited

i) Contribution per unit of limiting factor

	De Luxe £	Super De Luxe £
Selling price	150	165
Variable cost of raw materials		
Aluminium (at £8.50 per kg)	(38.25)	(42.50)
Other raw materials	(12.50)	(15.00)
Variable cost of labour	(13.65)	(15.60)
Contribution per unit	85.60	91.90
Kilos of material used		
De Luxe: £38.25/8.50	4.5	
Super De Luxe: £42.50/8.50		5
Contribution per unit of limiting factor	85.60/4.5 = £19.02	91.90/5 = £18.38

ii) Production plan

The directors should follow a production plan that produces the De Luxe model in preference to the Super De Luxe, where possible.

The availability of the raw material in the next three months is:

	kg
Already in stock	350
3 month's purchases	3 000
	3 350

If all of this material were to be used in the production of De Luxe buggies, it would be possible to make 3350/4.5 = 744 De Luxe buggies (rounded down to the nearest whole number).

a)   If demand for the De Luxe is 800 units, then it makes sense to turn production over completely to the production of the De Luxe (800 > 744).

b)   If demand for the De Luxe is 600 units, then the maximum 600 should be produced. This would mean using 600 × 4.5kg = 2700kg of the scarce raw material, leaving 3350 − 2700 = 650kg for producing Super De Luxe buggies.

So 650kg would produce 650/5 = 130 Super De Luxe buggies at a rate of usage of 5kg per buggy. The production plan would thus be:

De Luxe = 600
Super De Luxe = 130.

11.1 The demand curve plots the relationship between quantity and selling price. The correct answer, therefore, is c).

11.2 Demand is described as elastic where it is highly sensitive to changes in price. The correct answer, therefore, is a).

11.3 An oligopoly exists in cases where about three to five suppliers control the market. The correct answer, therefore, is b).

11.4 Auger Ambit Limited

$$\text{Fixed costs per unit} = \frac{788\ 000}{20\ 000} = £39.40$$

Cost-plus calculation:

	£
Variable materials cost per unit	18.00
Variable labour costs per unit	27.56
Fixed costs per unit	39.40
Total costs per unit	84.96
Profit mark-up: £84.96 × 25%	21.24
Selling price	106.20

11.5 Belvedere, Bharat and Burgess

1. Fees billed
The partnership could expect to bill fees (based on time available: 43 weeks × 5 days × 8 hours × 75% = 1290 hours per person) as follows:

	£
Accountants: 6 × 1 290 × £50	387 000
Senior staff and tax specialists: 5 × 1 290 × £85	548 250
Partners: 3 × 1 290 × £110	425 700
	1 360 950

2. Recovery rate of 94%
If the average recovery rate on billing is 94% this means that the partnership has not been able to recover all of the hours charged by its staff and partners.

	£
Billed: £1 360 950 × 94%	1 279 293
Costs: £1 275 000 × 101%	1 287 750
Loss for 20X6	(8 457)

11.6 Selling prices

A garden centre
The managers of a garden centre will have regard to local competition in setting selling prices. If there is little competition it may be possible to charge higher

prices. In the long run, of course, the business must be able to cover all of its costs. It would be normal practice for the management of such a business to apply a standard mark-up on cost.

Probably, cost-based pricing will be the principal price-setting strategy, but management will also keep an eye on the competition. Even if competitors are charging lower prices, management may feel justified in charging more if, for example, it offers complementary services such as garden design, a coffee shop and a bookshop.

A small grocery store, open for 24 hours

Generally, convenience stores are able to charge relatively high prices, simply because of the additional convenience they offer. Much depends upon the competition, of course. Now that many large supermarkets are offering 24 hour service, a small grocery store may find that it has to bring down prices in order to be able to compete.

There is a cost element to take into account in setting pricing; in a 24-hour business, labour must be employed at highly unsocial hours, and there may be a wage premium to pay (although the extent of this depends upon the local employment market, availability of hard-up students to work through the night and so on). Additional costs have to be met either by increasing selling prices or reducing profit margins.

CHAPTER 12

12.1 The £15 000 spent on the initial land survey is irrelevant to the business decision because the expenditure has already been made. This is an example of a sunk cost; the correct answer, therefore, is c).

12.2 Mellor & Ribchester Limited

i) ARR calculations

$$\frac{\text{Average expected return (accounting profit)}}{\text{Average capital employed}} \times 100 = \text{ARR\%}$$

£150 000 of fixed asset expenditure, depreciated over 6 years on a straight-line basis, results in an annual depreciation charge of £150 000/6 = £25 000. This must be taken into account in calculating accounting profit.

Year	£000
1	0 – 25 = (25)
2	68 – 25 = 43
3	71 – 25 = 46
4	54 – 25 = 29
5	28 – 25 = 3
6	10 – 25 = (15)
Total profit	81

The average profit per year generated is:

$$\frac{81\ 000}{6} = \text{£13 500}$$

Time	£000
0	150
6	0
Average	150/2 = 75

$$ARR = \frac{13\,500}{75\,000} \times 100 = 18\%$$

ii) Payback period

	Cash flow	Cumulative cash flow
Time	£000	£000
0	(150)	(150)
1	0	(150)
2	68	(82)
3	71	(11)
4	54	43
5	28	71
6	10	81

Cumulative cash flow reaches the zero position sometime during the fourth year. Payback to the nearest whole month is:

3 years + (11/54 × 12 months) = 3 years and 2 months

Note that the cash inflows in this example do not start until the second year. This does not change the methods of working out ARR or payback.

12.3 The compounding factor for an investment over 4 years at 3% per year is:

$$(1.03)^4 = (1.03) \times (1.03) \times (1.03) \times (1.03) = 1.126.$$

The correct answer, therefore, is d).

12.4 The compounding factor is: $(1.06)^4 = 1.263$. To the nearest £:

$$1.263 \times £312 = £394$$

The correct answer, therefore, is a).

12.5 The discounting factor is:

$$\frac{1}{(1.1)^3} = 0.751$$

The correct answer, therefore, is b).

12.6 The correct discount factor (from tables) is 0.567. The PV of £1300 receivable at the end of year 5, assuming a constant discount rate of 12% is:

$$£1300 \times 0.567 = £737 \text{ (to nearest £)}$$

The correct answer, therefore, is d).

12.7 Naylor Coulthard Limited

Calculation of NPV of the advertising promotion project:

Time	Cash flow £	Discount factor (from table)	Discounted cash flow £
0	(250 000)	1	(250 000)
1	196 000	0.917	179 732
2	168 000	0.842	141 456
Total			71 188

The NPV is positive, which suggests that the project should be accepted.

12.8 NPV and IRR calculations

i) NPV at 12% cost of capital

Time	Cash flow £	Discount factor (from table)	Discounted cash flow £
0	(680 000)	1	(680 000)
1	180 000	0.893	160 740
2	200 000	0.797	159 400
3	240 000	0.712	170 880
4	350 000	0.636	222 600
Total			33 620

ii) IRR
12% cost of capital produces a positive NPV. The IRR (the point at which NPV = 0) must therefore be higher than this. Calculating NPV at 16%

Time	Cash flow £	Discount factor (from table)	Discounted cash flow £
0	(680 000)	1	(680 000)
1	180 000	0.862	155 160
2	200 000	0.743	148 600
3	240 000	0.641	153 840
4	350 000	0.552	193 200
Total			(29 200)

IRR must, therefore, lie somewhere between 12% and 16%.

Using a discount rate of 12% NPV = £33 620
Using a discount rate of 16% NPV = (£29 200)

The total distance between these two figures is £33 620 + £29 200 = £62 820.
Expressed diagrammatically:

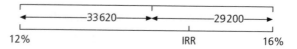

The distance between 12% and IRR is:

$$\frac{33\ 620}{62\ 820} \times 4\% = 2.14\%$$

IRR is 12% + 2.14% = 14.14%

(Note that the IRR according to computer calculation is 14.07%.)

12.9 Sunbed investment project

i) NPV at 14% cost of capital

Time	Cash flow £	Discount factor (from table)	Discounted cash flow £
0	(180 000)	1	(180 000)
1	46 000	0.877	40 342
2	46 000	0.769	35 374
3	46 000	0.675	31 050
4	46 000	0.592	27 232
5	46 000 + 15 000	0.519	31 659
Total			(14 343)

ii) IRR

14% cost of capital produces a negative NPV. The IRR (the point at which NPV = 0) must therefore be lower than this. Calculating NPV at 10%:

Time	Cash flow £	Discount factor (from table)	Discounted cash flow £
0	(180 000)	1	(180 000)
1	46 000	0.909	41 814
2	46 000	0.826	37 996
3	46 000	0.751	34 546
4	46 000	0.683	31 418
5	46 000 + 15 000	0.621	37 881
Total			3 655

IRR must, therefore, lie somewhere between 10% and 14% (but much nearer to 10% than to 14%).

Using a discount rate of 10% NPV = £3 655.

Using a discount rate of 14% NPV = (£14 343).

The total distance between these two figures is £3 655 + 14 343 = £17 998. The distance between 10% and IRR is:

$$\frac{3\ 655}{17\ 998} \times 4\% = 0.81\%$$

$$\text{IRR is } 10\% + 0.81\% = 10.81\%$$

Note that the IRR according to computer calculation is 10.77%.

iii) Advice
On the basis of the results of the NPV and IRR calculations it appears that the directors should not make the investment in the sunbeds. The company's cost of capital is 14% and this investment falls well short of that target. However, the directors may consider other factors in making their decision. For example:

- How important is it to the future of the business that it diversifies its range of services? Will the hairdressing business continue to produce strong returns? If there is some uncertainty, it may make sense to diversify.

- Are competitors offering sunbeds? If they are, the existing hairdressing business could be damaged if Outhwaite Benson Limited does not do the same.

- Is it possible that the provision of the sunbed service will attract new customers who may also use the hairdressing services? If so, has this potential for additional sales been taken into account in the projected cash flow figures?

Finally, how reliable are the estimates? If the projected cash flows are put into a spreadsheet the directors can perform a series of 'what if' calculations to test out various levels of projection (optimistic, pessimistic, average).

CHAPTER 13   **13.1** Three key characteristics of management information:

1. It should be produced quickly so that managers can respond rapidly to it.
2. It should be useful, and easily comprehensible.
3. The cost of producing the information should not outweigh its benefits.

13.2 Golfstore Retail plc
The advantages of divisionalisation for this company include the following:

1. Divisions based on regions or (eventually) countries in western Europe will ensure that management can exploit local opportunities that might not come to the attention of head office management. For example, a regional management team should be better aware of the trading conditions in their area, and if, say, a new golf course is planned for a particular town, they could ensure that a new store is opened in the area.

2. Divisionalisation can result in better motivated managers. This can be enhanced if senior divisional managers are rewarded at least partly on the

basis of results achieved. A degree of competition between divisions can be healthy and productive.

3. In this particular case, the company is beginning to expand. If divisionalisation is instituted now along a geographical split within the UK, a pattern is established which could make the addition of future divisions within Europe relatively straightforward.

13.3 Division Alpha is a profit centre.

13.4 a) Quarterly divisional performance statement for BD

	£000
Sales	1 671
Less: variable costs (280 + 311)	(591)
Contribution	1 080
Less: Controllable fixed costs (580 – 37)	(543)
Controllable profit	537
Less: Non-controllable fixed costs (37 + 112)	(149)
Divisional profit before allocation of head office costs	388
Head office cost allocation	(337)
Divisional profit before tax	51

b) The division's performance should be judged on the basis of the amount of profit over which it has control. Controllable profit is £537 000.

13.5 1. Transfer pricing can have an impact on divisional performance. Where divisions sell goods to each other, it is necessary to identify an appropriate price for the goods. The level of price affects the allocation of profit between divisions and so may affect profit-related remuneration. Where it is difficult to agree realistic transfer prices, divisions have an incentive to source goods from outside the company and in this case the profit goes outside the company. If divisional performance is affected by transfer pricing agreements, there is a knock-on effect on the Return on Investment measurement.

2. The calculation of Return on Investment can also be affected by the valuation of net assets. Higher asset valuation results in a lower ROI. For this reason, managers may be reluctant to replace worn out fixed assets.

13.6 Both financial and non-financial performance indicators should relate to the company's strategic plans. The company's objective relates to the provision of a service, so its performance indicators should be service-oriented.

There are many possible ways of measuring the company's progress in meeting its objectives. The table below suggests some possible performance indicators, and ways of measuring them.

Aspect of service	Performance indicator	Measurement
Competitive	Price of service	Comparison with competitors' commission arrangements.

Competitive	Customer satisfaction	Could be measured using a questionnaire on the website, or a follow up survey.
Efficient	Number of complaints	Website link to a complaints form. Monitoring number of complaints and outcomes.
Efficient	Speed of transaction	Measure speed of each transaction on the website, and compare.
Efficient	Ease of use by customer	Could be measured using a questionnaire on the website, or a follow-up survey.
Secure	Number of security breaches over a given period	Could be measured by analysing customer complaints.

13.7 Memo
To: Head of Department

Balanced scorecard

The Balanced Scorecard (BS) is a summary of management information that is used by managers to examine the performance of the business. The BS contains four dimensions relating to the fundamentals of a particular business. Any business that uses it has to ask the following questions:

■ How do customers see us? (The customer perspective)

■ What must we excel at? (The internal perspective)

■ Can we continue to improve and create value? (The innovation and learning perspective)

■ How do we look to shareholders? (The financial perspective).

The business needs to establish goals in respect of each of the four perspectives, and related performance measures that will help management in judging progress towards the goals. This may all seem fairly complicated, and it would certainly involve quite a lot of work up-front, but it results in a way of reporting useful and relevant performance measures in a concise way. Incidentally, some of the performance measures (although not necessarily all of them) would involve the use of figures.

Brian is quite right – the BS system has been adopted by very large numbers of US, European and Australian companies. The aeroplane analogy comes from the originators of the BS (two American academics: Robert Kaplan and David Norton). They compared running a business to flying an aeroplane: both pilots and managers need information about all sorts of measurements to be clearly set out in front of them.

I hope this explanation helps. There are several detailed sources of information on the subject of the BS – books, articles and websites. Let me know if you'd like any references.

Glossary

Absorption costing The costing of products and services to include both direct and indirect costs of production.

Accounting standards Regulations containing detailed guidance and rules on the preparation of financial accounts. In the UK accounting standards are issued in the form of Financial Reporting Standards (FRSs) by the Accounting Standards Board (ASB).

Adverse variance An unfavourable difference between a budget figure and an actual figure. (In terms of sales, an actual figure that is lower than budget; in terms of costs an actual figure that is higher than budget.)

Audit An independent examination by a properly qualified professional auditor of the records and financial statements of a business. (Note that in the context of this book the entity is a business enterprise, but audit of charities, local government and central government, for example, also takes place.)

Audit report The report by an independent auditor on the financial statements of a business.

Balance sheet A statement of the resources owned and controlled by a business at a single point in time. Most businesses prepare balance sheets at least annually.

Balanced scorecard Developed by Kaplan and Norton, the balanced scorecard provides an easily understood set of key performance measures for an organisation.

Batch costing The accumulation of costs relating to a batch of identical products.

Break-even chart A graph showing lines for costs and revenues, from which the break-even point can be estimated.

Break-even point The point at which neither a profit nor a loss is made – i.e. where total costs equal total revenues.

Budget A statement, prepared in advance, usually for a specific period (e.g. for one year), of a business's planned activities and financial outcomes.

Budgetary slack An adverse effect observable in some businesses where managers deliberately set themselves easily achievable targets.

Business entity concept The business is regarded as separate from its owner(s).

Business plan A detailed document produced to support an application for business finance.

Capital introduced The resources in the form of money and other goods put into a business by its owner(s) when it starts up.

Capital rationing Where a shortage of capital available for investment requires prioritisation of investment projects.

Cartel A price-fixing arrangement where a few major suppliers in a market agree between themselves to keep prices high.

Cash flow The movement of cash in and out of a business.

Chairman's statement A written statement by a company chairman that accompanies the annual financial statements of all companies in the UK listed on the London Stock Exchange.

Charge A legal arrangement for security for a loan. A lender puts in place a charge over specified property of the borrower. If the borrower fails to repay the loan, the proceeds of sale of the property are used to reimburse the lender.

Cost accounting The process of identifying and summarising the costs associated with business operations.

Cost and management accounting Accounting oriented towards the provision of information resources that managers can use to run the business.

Cost centres Functions or areas into which costs can be organised.

Cost of capital The interest rate that is applicable to a particular business.

Cost unit An item of production or a group of products or a service for which it is useful to have product cost information.

Debentures Company bonds that entitle their holder to eventual repayment of the value of the stock plus a regular annual rate of interest (debentures are sometimes referred to as 'loan stock').

Demand curve An economic model of the relationship between price and quantity demanded.

Direct costs Those costs directly associated with the manufacturing process.

Direct expenses – Direct costs other than direct materials and direct labour costs.

Directors The senior managers of a limited company. Directors have special responsibilities in law.

Dividend A payment periodically made by a limited company to its shareholders.

Drawings The taking of cash (or other resources) out of an unincorporated business by its owner(s).

Equity shares The share capital in a company that entitles its owner(s) to a share of the business's profits (in the form of dividend) and to voting rights.

Factoring An arrangement to obtain cash from a factoring company in exchange for debtors of the business.

Favourable variance An advantageous difference between a budget figure and an actual figure. (In terms of sales, an actual figure that is higher than budget; in terms of costs an actual figure that is lower than budget.)

Financial accountants Specialists in the provision of financial information oriented towards interested parties external to the business.

Financial accounting The processes and practices involved in providing interested parties external to the business with the financial information that they need.

Financial reporting Reporting financial information to interested parties external to the business.

Fixed cost A cost that remains the same, regardless of variations in the level of business activity.

Fixed overheads Those costs that do not tend to vary directly with increases and decreases in activity in a business.

Goal congruence Ensures that all divisions within an organisation work together to maximise returns for the organisation as a whole.

Goodwill The intangible factors that add value to a business, such as brand names and customer loyalty.

Hostile bid A takeover bid which is not welcomed by the target company.

Incorporation The process of setting up a limited company.

Incremental budgets Budgets that are set by taking a previous period's budget total and adding a standard percentage increase.

Indirect costs Those costs that are not directly identifiable with a unit of production.

Interim financial statements Financial accounts issued half-yearly (or in rare cases in the UK, quarterly) by companies listed on the London Stock Exchange.

Investment centre A method of divisional organisation where managers are able to control costs, pricing strategy and investment strategy.

Job costing An accumulation of costs relating to one identifiable job or task.

Leasing A financing arrangement for obtaining the use of business assets without having to purchase them.

Lessee A person or business that obtains the use of an asset under a leasing arrangement.

Lessor A person or (usually) business that makes assets available to businesses under leasing arrangements.

Limited company A legal arrangement for regulating the ownership of business.

Limited liability The liability of the shareholders of a limited company is limited to the amount of their original investment.

Limiting factors Constraints on the level of business activity.

Loan stock Company bonds that entitle their holder to eventual repayment of the value of the stock plus a regular annual rate of interest (loan stock is sometimes referred to as 'debentures').

Loss leader A product or service that is used to attract customer attention to a range of goods or to a particular supplier.

Management accountants Specialists in the provision of financial information for use within the business.

Management accounting Accounting carried out within a business for its own internal uses, to assist management in controlling the business and in making business decisions.

Margin of safety The excess of planned or actual sales above the break-even point.

Marginal cost The cost of one additional unit.

Marginal costing An approach to costing that excludes fixed costs.

Market capitalisation The total value obtained by multiplying the number of shares a listed company has in issue by the market value of one share.

Market value [of a share] The price at which the share can be traded on the stock market.

Monopoly A market condition where only one supplier supplies the market with a particular good or service.

Mortgage A loan secured on real estate.

Net present value The aggregate of a set of cash inflows and outflows forecast to take place at future dates, discounted to present values.

Nominal value The basic denomination of a share – for example, 50p or 25p.

Offer for sale A general invitation to both the public and financial institutions to buy shares in a company.

Oligopoly A market condition where there are few suppliers (about three to five) of a particular good or service. Typically, the market shares between the suppliers are fairly evenly spread.

Overhead absorption A method of allocating an appropriate portion of production overheads to cost units.

Overhead absorption rate A rate used to estimate the amount of production overhead incurred in manufacturing.

Partnership A business that is run by two or more people with a view to making a profit.

Period costs Costs incurred during the accounting period.

Placing Offering a limited group of prospective buyers the opportunity to buy new shares in a company.

Present value The discounted value at the present time (i.e. now) of a cash flow expected to arise in the future.

Price setter An influential supplier in a market with the power to influence the level of prices for a product or service.

Price taker A supplier in a market with little or no influence over the level of prices charged for a product or service.

Prime cost The total of all direct costs associated with manufacture.

Product costing The accumulation of costs relating to the production of a large number of identical units.

Product costs Those costs relating to the production of goods or services for sale by a business.

Profit The surplus that remains after deducting business costs from business income.

Profit and loss account A statement prepared by businesses of all sizes, at least annually, which shows the total business revenue less expenses. The net total is the profit or loss of the business.

Profit centre A method of divisional organisation where managers are able to determine pricing strategy and control costs, but do not determine investment strategy.

Prospectus A document produced in accordance with (in the UK) Financial Services Authority regulation. It is prepared by a company which offers its shares for sale to the general public, and contains a large amount of information about the history and prospects of the company.

Registered auditors Professionally qualified auditors who are authorised to conduct the audits of businesses and other organisations.

Responsibility accounting Accounting within the business that identifies the person or department responsible for particular outcomes.

Retained profits The amount of profit left in a business (i.e. profit not distributed to the owners of the business).

Return on Investment (ROI) A commonly used method of assessing divisional performance; it expresses divisional net profit as a percentage of the investment in divisional net assets.

Rights issue An offer of shares made to existing shareholders in a company, in proportion to the number of shares already held (e.g. a one for seven rights issue involves offering one new share for every seven already held).

Rolling budget A budget that is updated on a regular basis as each period of time (usually one month) elapses.

Security An arrangement between a lender and a borrower where specified items of property can be used to meet the loan if the borrower defaults (i.e. does not repay the loan).

Semi-variable cost A cost that varies to some extent with the level of business activity; it has both fixed and variable elements.

Shareholders The investors in a limited company; each investor owns a share or shares in the company.

Sole trader A person who operates a business himself or herself, keeping any profits that are made.

Standard costing A system of costing that attributes consistent costs to elements of production.

Stewardship Taking responsibility for the management of resources on behalf of somebody else. (The principal example in this book is that of company directors managing a company on behalf of its shareholders.)

Sunk costs Costs that are irrelevant to a capital expenditure decision, because they have already been incurred.

Takeover bid A move to take over a majority of shares in a target company so as to gain control of it.

Transfer pricing The method of pricing sales of goods or services between divisions in an organisation.

Variable cost A cost that varies in proportion to the level of business activity.

Work-in-progress Items of part-completed stock.

Working capital The elements of financing required for investment in items that move rapidly in and out of the business, for example, stock.

Index